THE MISSISSIPPI COOKBOOK

THE
MISSISSIPPI
COOKBOOK

Compiled and Edited by the
HOME ECONOMICS DIVISION
of the
MISSISSIPPI COOPERATIVE
EXTENSION SERVICE

PUBLISHED BY THE

UNIVERSITY PRESS OF MISSISSIPPI

JACKSON

Book Design by J. Barney McKee

Illustrations by Lucille Parker

ACKNOWLEDGMENTS

Grateful appreciation is expressed to Dr. W. M. Bost, Director of the Mississippi Cooperative Extension Service, for authorizing the book and for his administrative support and cooperation during its development; to Dr. Marilynn Purdie, State Leader, Home Economics Programs; to Mrs. Ina G. Kimbrough, Extension Specialist in Foods and Nutrition, who compiled the book; to the Extension Home Economists in each of the counties who gathered the recipes; and to the many other persons who contributed and assisted in the preparation of this book, particularly Miss Lucille Parker for the illustrations on the heading of each chapter.

Appreciation is also due the United States Department of Agriculture for the reproduction of materials and to the American Home Economics Association for permission to reproduce information from *The Handbook of Food Preparation, 1971.*

INTRODUCTION

The Mississippi Cookbook was prepared in an attempt to collect, make available, and, in the process, preserve the favorite recipes of fine cooks throughout Mississippi. Over 7,000 recipes were collected from all areas of the state, each a time-proven favorite. From this total, the home economists of the state Cooperative Extension Service had the painfully difficult task of screening the total down to the 1,200 limit that was required for publication.

The name of the individual who submitted the recipe follows each recipe. In some cases, historical data about the recipe is included. In a special section, favorite recipes of the wives of former Governors are presented. In the appendix section are tables and charts that provide such valuable technical information as substitutions and equivalents, measuring ingredients, time and temperature guide, definitions, and servings.

This comprehensive collection of the most popular recipes of Mississippi records the state's culinary heritage. It was a massive effort to compile, edit and produce but if it contributes to the preservation and further development of the Mississippi tradition of deliciously prepared foods, *The Mississippi Cookbook* will have been a successful effort.

—THE PUBLISHER

CONTENTS

THE MISSISSIPPI COOKBOOK

⸙[Appetizers]⸙

It may be an elaborate tray of hors d'oeuvres or a simple glass of tomato juice, but the creative hostess uses an appetizer to add that special flair to her meal.

Fruits, juices, vegetables and sea foods make good appetite teasers when served at the beginning of a meal. Breakfast is a good time to serve melon wedges, fresh berries or canned fruits and juices. Seafood cocktails from oysters, shrimp and crab are used mainly for the dinner meal. There is nothing more colorful than a tray of cauliflower, carrots, radishes and other vegetables arranged around a spicy curry dip.

Canapes and hors d'oeuvres are appetizers that are usually offered with drinks and are served away from the table before guests are seated.

The canape has a built-in bread or pastry. The hors d'oeuvre is served alone and may be accompanied by, but not served on, a pastry or bread base. Cheese balls, marinated mushrooms and shrimp, dips and assorted crackers all make excellent appetizers.

[3]

GARLIC CHEESE ROLL

1 pound grated New York or
  aged cheddar cheese
1 teaspoon salt
2 (6-ounce) packages cream
  cheese
1 mashed clove garlic
3 dashes Tabasco

1 tablespoon Worcestershire
  sauce
2 tablespoons mayonnaise
¼ teaspoon dry mustard
1 tablespoon onion juice
1 ounce chili powder
¾ ounce paprika

Blend all ingredients except chili powder and paprika. Work until smooth
paste is formed. Divide into two rolls about the size of a dollar. Roll in
chili powder and paprika mixture, completely coating outside. Wrap in
waxed paper and refrigerate for 24 hours to ripen. Serve with assorted
crackers.

Mrs. Felder Dickey, Brookhaven

PARTY CHEESE BALLS

8 ounces cream cheese
milk to soften

¼ cup chopped dates
½ cup chopped nuts

Soften cream cheese with milk gradually so it will mold easily in balls.
Take care not to add too much milk. Add chopped dates and ¼ cup
chopped nuts. Roll into 8 balls and roll in remaining nuts.

Mrs. Nell Dennis, Fayette

CHEESE BALL

1 (8-ounce) package cream
  cheese
1½ ounces Roquefort or blue
  cheese
5 ounces smoked or sharp
  cheese spread
1 tablespoon minced onion or
  onion juice

1 tablespoon finely chopped
  stuffed green olives
(garlic juice may be added if
  desired)
½ cup chopped nuts
chopped parsley

Mix thoroughly all ingredients except nuts and parsley. Chill in refrigerator overnight. Form into a ball and then roll in finely chopped
parsley (about 2 tablespoons) and ½ cup finely chopped nuts.

Mrs. C. S. Anderson, Jr., Monticello

PARTY CHEESE BALL

2 (8-ounce) packages cream cheese
2 cups (8-ounces) shredded sharp Cheddar cheese
1 tablespoon chopped pimiento
1 tablespoon chopped green pepper
1 tablespoon finely chopped onion
2 teaspoons Worcestershire sauce
2 teaspoons lemon juice
dash of cayenne
dash of salt

Combine softened cream cheese and Cheddar cheese, mixing until well blended. Add other ingredients, mixing well. Chill. Shape into a ball and roll in chopped pecans. Will keep, wrapped in foil, for several days in the refrigerator. This recipe is a generous one, great for a large party. For variation roll in finely chopped parsley, dried beef or chopped toasted almonds.

Mrs. E. G. Branch, Brookhaven

CHEESE BALL

1 pound mild cheese, grated
1 large (8-ounce) package cream cheese
2 tablespoons grated onion
1 minced clove garlic
½ cup finely chopped cocktail peanuts or pecans
2 tablespoons minced parsley

Mix first four ingredients and place in refrigerator until chilled enough to form into a ball. Roll ball in chopped nuts and minced parsley. Add sprig of holly to top at Christmas time or sprig of parsley at other times. Good for a party. Serves at least 25.

Mrs. N. W. Fulton, Louisville

CHEESE PUFFS

¼ pound sharp Cheddar cheese
1 (3-ounce) package cream cheese
1 stick butter or margarine
2 stiffly beaten egg whites
1 (16-ounce) loaf unsliced bread, cut into 1-inch cubes

Mix cheeses and butter or margarine on top of stove until of slightly thick sauce consistency (do not overcook). Remove from heat and fold in egg whites. Dip bread cubes into cheese mix. Coat well. Place on cookie sheet and refrigerate overnight. Bake in 400 degree oven for 12

[5]

to 15 minutes, or until puffy or golden brown. Makes 4 dozen. NOTE: These can be frozen before baking. When ready to bake, remove from freezer and let stand at room temperature until thawed; then bake.

Mrs. J. H. Burt, Wayside

DEVILED HAM PUFFS

1 (8-ounce) package cream
  cheese
1 teaspoon onion juice
½ teaspoon baking powder
1 egg yolk, beaten

salt to taste
24 small bread rounds (1½ inch
  diameter)
2 (2½-ounce) cans deviled ham

Blend together the cheese, onion juice, baking powder, egg yolk and salt. Toast the bread round on one side. Spread the untoasted side with deviled ham and cover each with a mound of the cheese mixture. Place on ungreased cookie sheet and bake in a moderate oven, 350 degrees for 10 to 12 minutes or until puffed and brown. Serve hot. Makes 24 deviled ham puffs.

Mrs. W. B. White, Booneville

CHICKEN PUFFS AMANDINE

½ cup chicken broth
¼ cup butter
⅛ teaspoon salt
½ cup flour
2 eggs

1 (4¾-ounce) can deviled
  chicken
3 tablespoons diced and toasted
  almonds
¼ teaspoon almond extract

Heat oven to 450 degrees. Put broth in boiler and let come to boil. Add salt and butter; stir until butter melts. Put flour in and stir over low heat until mixture leaves sides of pan, about 1 minute or until mixture forms ball in pan. Remove from heat and beat in eggs one at a time. Beat until shiny and smooth. Stir in chicken and almonds and almond flavoring. Drop by small teaspoon on greased cookie sheets. Bake 10 to 12 minutes or until golden brown. If desired, puffs may be cooked ahead and reheated on a cookie sheet in 350 degree oven for 5 to 7 minutes. Serve warm. Makes about 2 dozen.

Mrs. Vernon Seals, Madison

CHEESE PUFFS

2 cups grated sharp cheese
½ cup soft butter or margarine
1 cup sifted all-purpose flour
½ teaspoon salt

1 teaspoon paprika
dash cayenne pepper
50 small stuffed green olives

Blend cheese with soft butter. Stir in flour and seasonings which have been sifted together. Mix well. Press 1 teaspoon of this mixture around each olive, covering it completely. Arrange on an ungreased baking sheet and chill until firm. Bake in a 400 degree oven for 15 minutes. Serve hot. Makes 50 puffs. These are so good and can be frozen.

Mrs. Anthony Garst, Clarksdale

CHEESE STRAWS

1 (5-ounce) jar sharp old
  English cheese spread
1 stick margarine, softened
1½ cups flour

¼ teaspoon red pepper (or to
  taste)
½ teaspoon salt

Blend cheese spread and margarine. Work flour into this. Add red pepper and salt. Put through a cookie press onto a cookie sheet. Bake at 375 degrees for 12 minutes.

Mrs. Sidney Henley, Lexington

PARTY CHEESE STRIPS

1 package pie crust mix
1 cup grated sharp Cheddar
  cheese
¼ teaspoon dry mustard

¼ teaspoon salt
⅛ teaspoon cayenne pepper
5 tablespoons cold water
1 teaspoon celery seed

Preheat oven to 350 degrees F. Combine pie crust mix, ½ cup cheese, mustard, salt and cayenne. Add water and mix with fork until mixture forms a ball. On lightly floured board, roll dough into 12-inch square, cutting rectangle into 4 x 1 inch strips with pastry wheel. Sprinkle with remaining cheese and celery seed. Bake on greased cookie sheet until golden brown, 15 to 20 minutes. Serve warm or cold. Serves 12.

Mrs. Bill Purcell, Indianola

CHEESE STRAWS

½ pound sharp Cheddar cheese
2 sticks butter or oleo
1¾ cups flour, all-purpose
1 teaspoon salt

½ teaspoon red pepper
1 teaspoon Tabasco
garlic salt

Grate cheese, blend with soft butter and add Tabasco. Sift flour and add salt and pepper. Mix thoroughly. Roll on floured board. Cut in narrow strips. Use potato slicer to cut, if you like. Bake at 375 degrees until a golden brown. While still warm, sprinkle garlic salt over straws. These freeze nicely. Yield: About 4 dozen.

Mrs. C. H. Compton, Poplarville

SAUSAGE PINWHEELS

4 teaspoons baking powder
2 cups plain flour
½ teaspoon salt
3 tablespoons shortening

1 cup milk
1 pound highly seasoned
sausage

Sift dry ingredients together; cut in shortening. Make a well in center of flour mixture; pour in milk. Mix lightly with spoon, keeping dough as soft as can be handled. Turn out on board and knead about 1 minute. Roll dough to thickness of cookies; spread with sausage. Roll up as for jelly roll. Wrap in waxed paper and chill for several hours. Remove wrap, slice in ¼ inch (or less) slices and bake on shallow sheet 25 to 30 minutes at 325 degrees. Yield: 40 pinwheels.

Mrs. J. T. Kerr, Rolling Fork

CHEESE WAFERS

8 ounces of sharp cheese, grated
1 stick butter or oleomargarine
1 cup self-rising flour

¼ teaspoon cayenne pepper
1¾ cups Special K cereal

Cream butter and cheese. Add flour, cayenne pepper and Special K cereal. Make small balls and flatten with fork in criss-cross pattern. Bake on ungreased cookie sheet at 400 degrees for about 12 minutes. Let cool on cookie sheet. Makes about 75 wafers.

Mrs. Sherman P. Noble, Jackson

CHEESE TEA BISCUITS

½ pound sharp cheese, grated, at room temperature
½ pound butter (or oleo) at room temperature

2¼ cups sifted flour, plain
1/16 teaspoon red pepper
1/16 teaspoon salt

Preheat oven 450 degrees. Mix all ingredients in order given. Roll on lightly floured board and cut. Place in oven for 12 to 15 minutes. Will make 24 tea biscuits.

Dough can be kept in refrigerator a week. Dough may be rolled in waxed paper, and sliced like ice box cookies.

Mrs. Mary Geoghegan, Fayette

CHEESE WAFERS

2 sticks margarine
2 cups grated sharp cheese
2½ cups all-purpose flour

¾ teaspoon salt
1 teaspoon red pepper

Mix cheese, margarine, flour, salt and pepper. Mix well. Divide in three parts. Roll each into a roll 1-inch thick. Wrap in waxed paper. Chill. Slice thin, place pecan half on each slice. Bake on ungreased cookie sheet at 350 degrees for 10-15 minutes. Yield: Approximately 6 dozen.

Mrs. A. J. Clark, Woodville

PEANUT BUTTER STICKS

2 loaves whole wheat bread
2½ cups peanut butter

1 cup cooking oil

Cut crusts off bread. Cut each slice into 5 or 6 strips. Put crust and strips in separate pans and bake at 250 degrees for 1 hour. Turn oven off and let stand for 15 minutes or longer. Roll crust edges into crumbs. (Make fine with rolling pin.) Mix peanut butter and oil. Blend to creamy consistency. Dip strips in this mixture, scraping off surplus. Roll in crumbs. Let dry.

(If two people make these together, it is easier—one to dip and one to roll. Keep dip free of crumbs and they are prettier.)

Mrs. J. D. Barron, Crystal Springs

[9]

LOVELIGHT CANAPE

¼ pound aged Cheddar cheese
4 ounces cream cheese
2 tablespoons sherry wine

5 tablespoons coffee cream
10 slices raisin bread
20 pecan halves

Soften aged Cheddar and cream cheese with sherry wine and cream until easy to spread. Use a base of raisin bread, cut in attractive shapes and garnish with a pecan half.

Mrs. Mary B. Marks, Magnolia

RUM BALLS

½ pound vanilla wafers (about
  1½ cups)
1 cup nuts, chopped
2 tablespoons cocoa

½ cup light corn syrup
¼ cup rum
Confectioner's sugar

Crush vanilla wafers fine. With hands, mix crumbs with nuts, cocoa, corn syrup and rum until a firm paste is formed. Dust palms of hands with sugar and shape little balls (about 1 inch). Allow to dry for 1 hour. Roll in more sugar. Store in air-tight container several hours. Roll in sugar again just before serving. Makes 30 balls.

Mrs. Ethel A. Richardson, West Point

CHEESE KRISPES

1 pound sharp cheese, grated
  (such as New York or Coon)
2 sticks oleo
2 cups flour, all-purpose

1 teaspoon red pepper
½ teaspoon salt
2 cups rice cereal, such as Rice
  Krispies

Cream oleo well; add grated cheese and blend thoroughly. Add seasonings and mix with hand. Make tiny balls and press out with fork. Bake at 350 degrees 15 or 20 minutes or less. Yield: 4-5 dozen.

Mrs. D. C. Beevers, Cleveland

CHEESE RICE CRISPY

2 cups grated cheese
2 sticks butter or margarine

2 cups flour, all-purpose
2 cups Rice Krispies

Mix cheese and butter. Add flour and mix well. Add Rice Krispies and mix well. Shape into small balls, flatten with fork. Bake on ungreased cookie sheet at 375 degrees for 10 minutes. Yield: About 60.

Miss Addie Hester, Amory

CHEESE NIBBLERS

1 cup self-rising cornmeal
1 cup self-rising flour
¼ teaspoon garlic powder
¼ cup shortening
1 cup shredded Cheddar cheese
½-¾ cup sweet milk

Preheat oven 425 degrees. Stir together cornmeal, flour and garlic powder. Cut in shortening until resembles coarse crumbs. Stir in cheese. Blend in enough milk to make a soft dough. Turn onto lightly floured board. Knead gently 30 seconds. Roll out to 8 x 16-inch rectangle. Cut lengthwise in half, then crosswise in ½-inch strips. Place on baking sheet. Bake 10-12 minutes or until lightly browned. Serve warm or cool. Store in tightly covered container.

Jacqueline H. Mikell, Port Gibson

OLIVE CHEESE NUGGETS

¼ pound shredded Cheddar
  cheese
¼ cup butter or margarine,
  softened
¾ cup sifted all-purpose flour
½ teaspoon paprika
24 small stuffed olives

Blend shredded cheese with butter. Sift flour and paprika into cheese and butter mixture. Mix to firm dough. Take one teaspoon of dough and roll into a ball. Flatten in palm of hand; place one olive in center. Shape dough around olive, rolling back into a ball. Bake on ungreased cookie sheet at 400 degrees, 12-15 minutes. Serve hot. Yield: 24 servings.

Jacqueline H. Mikell, Port Gibson

CHEESE NUT APPETIZERS

½ pound sharp aged cheese,
  grated
½ pound, butter, softened
½ cup sifted powdered sugar
3 cups sifted all-purpose flour
¼ teaspoon salt
1 cup peanuts, with skins

Combine and cream together cheese, butter and sugar. Combine flour and salt. Add gradually to creamed mixture. Shape dough into small balls approximately ½ inch in diameter. Place on ungreased cookie sheet. Press a peanut into each ball and flatten slightly. Bake in a moderate oven (350 degrees) for 12 to 15 minutes or until wafer is light brown. Yield: 125 appetizers.

Mrs. N. S. Pearson, West Point

[11]

SWEDISH MEAT BALLS

6 slices stale bread	4 eggs
1 cup milk	½ cup parsley, finely chopped
½ cup green onion tops, finely chopped	4 stalks celery, finely chopped
2 medium white onions, finely chopped	garlic salt
	black pepper
3 pounds ground beef	salt
1 pound ground veal	¾ teaspoon nutmeg
¼ pound ground pork	2 cans consomme
	1 pint sour cream

Soak 6 slices of stale bread in milk. Add onions, meat, eggs and seasoning; mix thoroughly. Shape into small balls and fry in margarine. Remove meat balls and place on paper toweling to absorb grease, then to cookie sheet and place into warm oven for a few minutes to dry.

Mix consomme and sour cream and pour over meat balls before serving. (Makes 250 small meat balls.)

Mrs. Edward LeVasseur
Mrs. K. T. Breland, Waveland

MEAT BALL (COCKTAIL) IN WINE SAUCE

5 slices bread soaked in milk	½ teaspoon black pepper
1½ pounds ground beef	3 eggs
1 onion grated	1 cup catsup
2½ teaspoons salt	1 cup burgundy or sherry
2 teaspoons mace	½ teaspoon oregano
2 teaspoons paprika	1 tablespoon Worcestershire
1 teaspoon dried herbs	sauce
1 teaspoon mustard	salt and pepper to taste

Squeeze bread dry, discard milk. Add bread to meat, onions, dry seasonings and eggs and mix thoroughly. Chill. Make into bite size balls. Brown in oil and drain on brown paper until cold.

Combine catsup, burgundy or sherry, oregano, Worcestershire sauce, salt and pepper and simmer the meat balls in this sauce for 20 minutes. Serve hot from chafing dish.

Mrs. R. B. Harris, Midnight

HOT CRAB MEAT DIP

3 (8-ounce) packages cream
    cheese
2 (6½-ounce) cans crab meat
½ cup mayonnaise
2 teaspoons prepared mustard

1 teaspoon confectioner's sugar
1 button garlic
¼ cup sherry or white wine
taste of seasoning salt

Melt cheese in double boiler. Add remaining ingredients. Serve in chafing dish surrounded by potato chips, corn chips, etc. to use in dipping. Yield: About 3 cups.

Mrs. Stewart Vail, Booneville

SAUCY SHRIMP-EGGPLANT APPETIZER

1 pound raw shrimp, cleaned
    and deveined
2 medium sized eggplants
1 cup minced green onions
2 tablespoons minced celery
½ cup minced green pepper
3 teaspoons peanut oil
2 cups frozen shrimp soup,
    thawed
2 cloves of garlic, minced
2 eggs, slightly beaten
1 cup seasoned packaged bread
    crumbs
½ cup milk

2 bay leaves, crumbled
½ tablespoon thyme
1 teaspoon powdered seafood
    seasoning
1½ teaspoons monosodium
    glutamate
1 teaspoon Tabasco
salt to taste
bread crumbs for topping
½ cup Parmesan cheese
2 tablespoons butter
24 oyster shells, scrubbed and
    bleached
1 pound rock salt

Clean shrimp and set aside. Peel eggplant, cut into pieces and par-boil for 20 minutes, until tender. Drain. Sautè onions, celery and green pepper in peanut oil. Add eggplant, then thawed shrimp soup. Add garlic, slightly beaten eggs, seasoned bread crumbs, milk, crumbled bay leaves and other seasonings. Add prepared raw shrimp. Stir all together. Spoon into oyster shells, not filling too full. Sprinkle with crumbs and Parmesan cheese, and dot with butter. Place filled shells in a pan that has first been covered with rock salt. Bake in a 350 degree oven for 25 minutes. Best to serve it immediately after removing from oven. May be kept in a warm oven covered with foil. This is a rich, tasty appetizer. Will serve about 12 people. May be served on a large round tray with cocktail forks. This is a very colorful appetizer and a grand conversation piece.

Mrs. E. O. Newmon, Gulfport

SHRIMP SAUCE

1 chopped garlic button
1 small grated onion
¼ cup ketchup
¼ cup chili sauce
½ teaspoon paprika
dash Tabasco
½ teaspoon mustard
¼ cup liquid cooking oil
½ teaspoon Worcestershire sauce
½ teaspoon pepper
juice of ½ lemon
salt to taste

Mix all the above ingredients and let set for 30 minutes before using. Will keep in refrigerator for several weeks. Makes 1 pint. To be served with boiled shrimp.

Mrs. R. L. Agnew, Macon

HAM DIP

1 (6-ounce) jar pimiento and cheese spread
½ cup mayonnaise
1 (2½-ounce) can deviled ham
1 teaspoon grated onion

Mix all together very well. Chill. Take out of refrigerator about 30 minutes before serving. Good with corn chips. Makes about 1½ cups.

Mrs. Marteal Alexander, Kosciusko

CALIFORNIA AVOCADO DIP

1 (8-ounce) package cream cheese
1 mashed avocado
3 tablespoons lemon juice
1 teaspoon finely cut onion
1 teaspoon salt
dash of Worcestershire sauce

Allow cream cheese to soften at room temperature. Add avocado a little at a time, blending until smooth. Stir in lemon juice, onion, salt and Worcestershire sauce. Mix well. Makes 2 cups.

Mrs. Abe Davis, Clarksdale

SHRIMP DIP

1 cup cooked deveined shrimp
2 (3-ounce) packages cream
   cheese
1 tablespoon Worcestershire
   sauce
1 tablespoon grated onion
1 teaspoon horseradish

1 teaspoon dry mustard
½ teaspoon salt
½ teaspoon pepper
dash of hot sauce
dash of garlic salt
mayonnaise—to consistency
   desired

Cream together and serve. Serve with small crackers such as wheat thins. Serves 25.

Mrs. C. D. Chapman, Louisville

SHRIMP DIP

1 (8-ounce) package of cream
   cheese
pinch of salt
1/3 cup sour cream
1 tablespoon mayonnaise

½ teaspoon onion juice
2 teaspoons lemon juice
½ teaspoon Worcestershire
   sauce
¾ cup chopped cooked shrimp

Soften cream cheese and add pinch of salt. Add other ingredients except shrimp. Blend well. Add shrimp and mix.

Mrs. James Willoughby, Mendenhall

BAC-O'S DILL DIP

2/3 cup mayonnaise or salad
   dressing
2/3 cup dairy sour cream
1 teaspoon parsley flakes

1 teaspoon dill seed
1 teaspon seasoned salt
dash garlic salt
¼ cup Bac-Os

Blend all ingredients except Bac-Os. Refrigerate. Just before serving, stir in Bac-Os and, if desired, sprinkle with additional Bac-Os. Makes 1½ cups.

Mrs. Eugene Holcombe, Macon

BACON-WRAPPED CHICKEN LIVERS

1 pound chicken livers
salt to taste

10 pieces bacon or as many as
   needed
toothpicks

[15]

Preheat oven to broil. Cut chicken livers into halves, and cut bacon slices into halves. Salt chicken livers to taste. Wrap each piece of liver with a piece of bacon, and place on a baking sheet so that the bacon cannot come unwrapped. Broil for 20 minutes or until liver and bacon are done. Skewer securely each piece with a party toothpick, place on a serving dish, and serve hot.

Mrs. J. D. Landin, Jr., Utica

PARTY ROLL UPS

12 thin slices white bread
8 slices cooked bacon

2 (3-ounce) packages
softened cream cheese
12 cooked asparagus spears

Trim crust from bread, roll with rolling pin to flatten slightly. Crumble bacon and blend with cream cheese. Spread mixture on bread slices. Lay cold asparagus spear on each slice of bread and roll up. Place on baking sheet, seam side down, cover and refrigerate until serving time. Then brush with melted butter and toast under broiler until lightly browned. Serves 12. May be made day before serving.

Mrs. J. C. Leech, Tupelo

CORNED BEEF CHEESE LOGS

1 (8-ounce) package cream
cheese, softened
2 tablespoons milk
2 cloves garlic crushed or finely
minced
1 tablespoon Worcestershire
sauce

⅛ teaspoon hot pepper sauce
1 (12-ounce) can corned beef,
unchilled
¾ cup minced parsley
sesame crackers or unflavored
melba style crackers

Blend softened cream cheese with milk until mixture is smooth. Blend in garlic, Worcestershire sauce and pepper sauce. Flake unchilled corned beef with a fork. Blend into cheese mixture. Refrigerate 1 to 2 hours. Remove from refrigerator and divide mixture in half. Shape each portion into a log about 1½ inches in diameter and about 7 inches long. Sprinkle parsley on waxed paper. Roll logs in parsley to coat evenly. Wrap well in plastic wrap and chill thoroughly before serving. When ready to serve, remove plastic wrap, place on serving tray and surround with desired crackers. Makes 2 logs.

Mrs. LaVerne Y. Lindsey, Lexington

SAUSAGE CRISP

3 cups Bisquick
2 cups grated Cheddar cheese

1 pound hot sausage

Mix the dry Bisquick, cheese and then sausage. Roll into balls 1-inch in diameter and then mash in center with finger. Bake at 350 degrees for 12 to 15 minutes. Serves 36.

Mrs. C. W. King, Inverness

HAM NIBBLES

2 cups ground cooked ham
1 (12-ounce) can vacuum-pack
   golden whole kernel corn,
   drained

¼ cup mayonnaise or salad
   dressing
2 cups cheese cracker crumbs
2 eggs, well beaten

Combine ham, drained canned corn, mayonnaise or salad dressing, eggs and 1 cup cracker crumbs in medium bowl. Shape mixture in small balls about 1½ inches in diameter. Roll in remaining cracker crumbs. Fry in deep hot fat (365-375 degrees) 2 to 3 minutes or until golden brown. Drain on absorbent paper. Yield: About 2½ dozen.

Mrs. Charles Everett, West Point

CRABMEAT CANAPE

6 (½-ounce) can crabmeat
¼ cup mayonnaise
½ cup finely chopped celery
1½ teaspoons lemon juice
2 chopped hard boiled eggs

dash of Worcestershire sauce
salt and pepper to taste
thin slices of pimiento peppers
   for garnish
bread fingers

Combine first 7 ingredients in mixing bowl. Mix thoroughly. Spread on bread fingers and garnish with pimiento strips.

Mrs. Mary S. Parkman, Monticello

PIZZA MIX

1 cup coarsely grated white
   pepper cheese
1 cup coarsely grated Cheddar
   cheese
1 teaspoon oregano

3 green onions, chopped fine
garlic salt to taste
½ teaspoon salt
1 (8-ounce) can tomato paste
2/3 cup mayonnaise

Mix lightly. Spread on rounds of toast and broil. Serve hot.

Mrs. Owen Roberts, Brookhaven

SHRIMP SPREAD

1 (3-ounce) package cream
cheese
dash of Worcestershire sauce
scant teaspoon prepared
mustard
dash of red pepper
scant teaspoon curry powder

juice of 1 button of garlic
2 tablespoons salad dressing
1 (4½-ounce) can shrimp
(or 1 cup fresh cooked
shrimp)
1 tablespoon pickle relish
2 tablespoons chili sauce

Cream cheese and season with Worcestershire, mustard, red pepper, curry powder, garlic juice and salad dressing. Add can or cup of shrimp which has been deveined and cut up finely. After blending well, add pickle relish and chili sauce. Mix. If too sharp to taste, add a pinch of sugar. (For dip, use 8-ounce package cream cheese and more salad dressing.)

Mrs. R. B. Harris, Midnight

SHRIMP-OLIVE SNACKS

1½ cups prepared pie pastry
½ cup chopped ripe olives
¾ cup chopped, cleaned,
cooked shrimp

½ teaspoon curry powder
mayonnaise

Roll out prepared pie pastry thin and cut into 2 inch rounds. Combine ½ cup chopped ripe olives with ¾ cup finely chopped, cleaned, cooked shrimp, ½ teaspoon curry powder and enough mayonnaise to hold together. Place a teaspoon of this filling on one half of each pastry round. Moisten edges and fold other half of pastry over filling. Pinch edges to seal. Bake in very hot oven (375 degrees) about 10 to 12 minutes. Serve hot. Makes 40 snacks.

Mrs. Luzon Truly, Fayette

OYSTER PASTRIES CHABLIS

24 medium or 30 small oysters
1 stick butter
2 teaspoons minced parsley
1 tablespoon minced onion

salt and pepper to taste
1 teaspoon Worcestershire sauce
1 teaspoon lemon juice
¼ cup Chablis wine

Sautè parsley and onion in butter; add oysters. Cook slowly. Add salt, pepper, Worcestershire and lemon juice. Place on low heat and let bubble gently until oysters are small and liquid gummy. Cool to lukewarm. Add wine and mix well with liquid. Refrigerate until liquid becomes cold and thick. On one side of 3-inch pastry square, put one oyster and one spoon of wine sauce. Fold and seal. Refrigerate if desired until ready to use, or freeze, but do not freeze for more than 3 weeks. When ready to use, bake in 425 degree oven until brown. Serve sizzling on sprigs of parsley. (I serve with silver sugar tongs onto individual napkins.)

Mrs. John B. Howell, Canton

SURPRISE PIES

¼ cup boiling water	1 cup grated Cheddar cheese
½ cup vegetable shortening	½ cup minced pimiento
½ teaspoon salt	⅛ teaspoon garlic salt
1½ cups flour	1/3 cup mayonnaise

Pour hot water over shortening and salt and beat until creamy. Add flour and mix to a soft dough. Wrap pastry in waxed paper and chill.

Blend remaining ingredients. Roll pastry thin, cut with biscuit cutter. Put 1 rounded teaspoonful of filling mixture on each round. Fold over, seal with fork tines, and fry in deep fat. Drain on paper towels.

Mary S. Palmer, Corinth

CARROT FRITTERS

1 cup flour	¼ teaspoon salt
1 egg	½ cup milk
1/3 cup sugar	1 cup cooked carrots (mashed)
1 teaspoon baking powder	juice of 1 lemon

Mix above ingredients together and drop by teaspoonful into hot fat, brown, remove from skillet and roll in powdered sugar. Serve with coffee or spiced tea.

Mrs. Tom Hurst, Corinth

DEVILED EGGS

3 hard cooked eggs	2 tablespoons pickles
1 tablespoon green onion blades	2 tablespoons mayonnaise
1 tablespoon celery leaves	1 teaspoon salt

Mash egg yolk. Chop onions, celery leaves and pickles very fine. Mix all ingredients well and serve on crackers or spoon back into egg whites to serve on lettuce leaves. This can also be used as a dip by adding 2 tablespoons of sour cream or pickle juice. Serves 6.

Mrs. S. F. O'Neal, Wiggins

STUFFED CELERY

1 stalk celery
2 cups grated Cheddar cheese
¼ cup pickle juice
¼ cup mayonnaise

Wash, clean and cut celery in pieces about 3 inches long. Place in a plastic bag with ice water and refrigerate for several hours until crisp. Remove and blot dry with cloth or paper towel.

Mix together grated cheese with enough mayonnaise and pickle juice until it is spreading consistency. Spoon mixture into cavity of celery. Place in refrigerator until serving time.

Mrs. Ollie J. Lane, Yazoo City

TOASTED PECANS

4 cups pecans
1 stick margarine
salt to taste

Place pecans on cookie sheet and pour melted margarine over pecans, coating each pecan with margarine. Preheat oven to 350 degrees. Toast until brown. Salt to taste.

Mrs. E. F. Buckner, Louisville

COATED PECANS

1 cup white sugar
¼ teaspoon salt
¼ teaspoon cinnamon
6 tablespoons milk (cream preferably)
2 cups pecan halves
¼ teaspoon vanilla

Mix sugar, salt, cinnamon, milk. Cook and stir until sugar is dissolved. Add pecans. Cook until soft boil. Take off heat and add vanilla. Stir until creamy and thick. Pour on buttered dish and, with two forks, separate nuts.

Martha Swann, Macon

NUTS AND BOLTS

¾ (9-ounce) box Kix
1 (10½-ounce) box Cheerios
1 (12-ounce) box Wheat Chex
1 (6-ounce) box Rice Chex
1 (5½-ounce) box Slim Jim pretzels
6½ ounces Pretzel Bits or 2 or 3 packages of cheese nugget pretzels
2 pounds mixed nuts
2 cups Wesson or peanut oil
2 tablespoons Worcestershire sauce
1 tablespoon garlic salt (heap the spoon)
1 heaping tablespoon Lowrey's (or Lawry's) seasoned salt

Mix thoroughly and toast in large pan in 250 degree oven for 2 hours; stir every 15 minutes. Keep in a tin box with a tight closing lid. Three weeks is about the limit for freshness of taste.

Mrs. M. E. Brooks, Newton

❖⟧Beverages⟦❖

"Come over for a cup of coffee."

That invitation may include tea, soft drinks or other beverages, but in the Deep South it's a way of extending hospitality.

A morning coffee or an afternoon tea may be a simple affair with a neighbor as the only guest, or it may be planned to entertain a large number of people. Today our pattern of living is less formal so the tea or coffee often replaces the more formal reception of yesterday, and with it comes a more relaxed atmosphere and an air of ease and friendliness.

Mississippi social life provides many opportunities for this type of entertainment. There are debutante teas, coffees to welcome guests to the annual art festival, and at least one such party for each bride-to-be.

Beverages may consist of milk, water, milk drinks, coffee, tea and fruit punches. The most important beverage is water. It has no food value but is just as necessary to life as food.

Milk has been called nature's most perfect food because it contains so many food elements. Children need to get at least three to four cups of milk each day in their diet while adults need approximately two cups. This amount of milk may be served in hot or cold drink, soups, puddings, sauces and ice cream or used in other cooked foods.

[23]

HOT EGGNOG

1 quart milk
3 egg yolks
1/3 cup sugar
¼ teaspoon salt

3 egg whites
3 tablespoons sugar
½ cup bourbon, brandy or rum
freshly grated nutmeg

Scald milk. Beat egg yolks with sugar until thoroughly blended. Add salt and milk and stir well. Return mixture to medium heat and cook, stirring constantly, until thickens. Do not boil. Beat egg whites until stiff; add three tablespoons sugar and beat until sugar is well dissolved. Fold beaten whites into hot milk mixture. Blend in the bourbon, brandy or rum. Serve hot, sprinkled with freshly grated nutmeg. Serves 6 to 10.

Mrs. Henry Stiller, Bay St. Louis

HOT PINEAPPLE EGGNOG

8 eggs
1 cup sugar
6 cups pineapple juice

1 pint whipping cream
grated orange peel

Separate egg yolks and whites. Gradually add ½ cup sugar to egg yolks as you beat thoroughly. Bring pineapple juice to boil. Add cream. Pour over egg yolks and heat, stirring constantly. Beat egg whites gradually adding ½ cup sugar and fold into hot mixture. Serve with grated orange peel. Serves 10 to 12. Delicious chilled, too.

Mrs. V. E. Cartledge, Dublin

PARISIAN CHOCOLATE

2½ (1-ounce) squares
   unsweetened chocolate
½ cup water
2/3 cup sugar

½ teaspoon salt
½ cup heavy cream, whipped
1 quart hot milk

Heat chocolate and water over low heat; stir until melted. Add sugar and salt. Bring to boil, lower heat; simmer 4 minutes. Cool to room temperature. Fold whipped cream into chocolate mixture. To serve, place 1 heaping tablespoon in each cup, fill with hot milk, stir well. Keep chocolate-cream mixture in refrigerator several days, use small amounts as needed. Serves 8 to 10.

Mrs. Jacqueline Mikell, Port Gibson

COCOA

3 tablespoons cocoa
3 tablespoons sugar
⅛ teaspoon salt

½ cup water
1 quart milk

Stir cocoa, sugar, salt and either hot or cold water together. Boil for three minutes. Scald the milk in a double boiler. Add cocoa mixture after boiling for three minutes and let stand over hot water in double boiler until hot and well blended. Beat with an egg beater to make foamy before serving. Makes 4 cups cocoa.

For parties, add 1 teaspoon vanilla and put whipping cream or marshmallows on top.

Mrs. D. T. Moody, Columbia

PARTY PUNCH

1 (46-ounce) can pineapple
   juice

1 quart ginger ale
1 quart apple cider

Mix pineapple juice, ginger ale, and apple cider well. Refrigerate several hours before serving. Serve over ice cubes. Serves about 30.

Mrs. Margaret Nichols, Tupelo

PUNCH

1 (0.15-ounce) package
   strawberry soft drink
   powdered mix
1 (0.14-ounce) package
   cherry soft drink powdered
   mix

2 (0.15-ounce) packages lemon
   soft drink powdered mix
3 cups sugar
1 quart pineapple juice
2 (10-ounce) 7-Up soft drinks
1 gallon water

Mix soft drink powdered mixes and sugar. Add one quart of water and stir until well-mixed. Add 3 quarts water, pineapple juice, carbonated beverage. Chill in refrigerator or freezer. Makes approximately 1½ gallons.

Mrs. Vera Bogan, Tishomingo

CAROL'S PUNCH

1 (46-ounce) can pineapple
   juice
1 (46-ounce) can yellow
   Hawaiian Punch

1 (28-ounce) bottle ginger
   ale
2 (6-ounce) cans frozen
   lemonade

[25]

Chill all ingredients thoroughly. When ready to use, mix all ingredients thoroughly and pour into punch bowl. Serves 25.

Mrs. Bill Gafford, Water Valley

PATIO PUNCH

1 (46-ounce) can of red
  Hawaiian Fruit punch,
  chilled

¾ cup lemon juice
1 quart vanilla ice cream
1 quart of ginger ale, chilled

Combine punch and lemon juice. Spoon about half the ice cream into 10 tall glasses. Add half the punch mixture with the ice cream. Add remaining punch with ginger ale and pour into glasses. Top each one with a scoop of ice cream. Trim with lemon peel. Serves 10.

Mrs. Angus Adams, Macon

MINT PUNCH

1 (8-ounce) glass mint jelly
2 cups orange juice
2 cups pineapple juice
1 cup lemon juice

8 (6-ounce) bottles 7-Up soft
  drink
2 cups boiling water

Dissolve the mint jelly in 2 cups boiling water. Add orange juice, pineapple juice and lemon juice. Before serving add 7-Up. Serves 16.

Mrs. Charles Everett, West Point

CHERRY PUNCH

2 (3-ounce) boxes cherry
  gelatin
4 cups boiling water
1 cup sugar

1 quart chilled pineapple
  juice
1 quart orange juice
1 quart ginger ale

Dissolve gelatin in boiling water, add sugar and stir until dissolved. Cool to room temperature (do not cool in refrigerator). Add fruit juices. Just before serving, add ginger ale. Makes 25 to 30 servings.

Lime gelatin may be used for *green punch*. Lime punch is good poured over pineapple sherbet.

Orange-pineapple gelatin may be used for *orange colored punch*. Use orange juice to make ice ring for orange punch.

Thelma Day, Rolling Fork

LIME PUNCH

½ pint lime syrup
3 quarts water
2 cups sugar

1 (6-ounce) can frozen orange juice, thawed
1 (12-ounce) can frozen pineapple juice, thawed

Mix all ingredients and chill. When ready to serve, add 1 quart lime sherbet and 2 or 3 10-ounce plain carbonated beverages. Serves 25 to 30.

Mrs. Marteal Alexander, Kosciusko

BRIDE'S PINK PUNCH

1 (3-ounce) package strawberry gelatin
1 cup boiling water
1 (0.15 ounce) package strawberry powdered drink mix
2 quarts cold water

2½ cups sugar
1 (46-ounce) can pineapple juice
1 (10-ounce) bottle 7-Up soft drink
2 pints pineapple sherbet

Dissolve gelatin in boiling water. Dissolve drink mix in cold water; add sugar and stir well. Add pineapple juice and dissolved gelatin. Refrigerate. Add carbonated beverage and sherbet just before serving. Serves about 30.

Mrs. V. L. Sandifer, Hollandale

PARTY PUNCH

9 (0.14 to 0.16 ounce) packages powdered soft drink mix
5 pounds sugar
2 (46-ounce) cans pineapple juice
2 (6-ounce) cans frozen orange juice

4 (6-ounce) cans frozen lemonade
1 no. 2 can crushed pineapple or fruit cocktail or cherries (optional)
1½ quarts chilled ginger ale

Mix soft drink mix according to package directions. Add other ingredients except the ginger ale. Just before serving, add chilled ginger ale. For green punch use lemon-lime soft drink mix, for red use strawberry or cherry flavored soft drink mix. Makes about 5 gallons. Will serve 20 to 25 punch cups per gallon of punch.

Mrs. Roy Naron, Cleveland

CHILDREN'S PARTY PUNCH

2 (6-ounce) cans pink
    lemonade concentrate, thawed
2 pints vanilla ice cream,
    softened
1 quart milk
red food coloring

Combine lemonade and 1 pint ice cream; beat until smooth. Add milk, colored to tint desired. Chill; put in bowl. Top with scoops of additional pint of ice cream. Serves 14.

Mrs. H. B. Camp, Chunky

INDIAN PUNCH

1 pint sugar
1 quart water
juice of 4 lemons
1 cup strong tea
1 tablespoon vanilla extract
1 tablespoon almond extract
1 quart ginger ale, chilled

Boil sugar, water and lemon juice for three minutes. Cool. Combine with tea, vanilla and almond extract. Immediately before serving, add ginger ale and pour over chipped ice. Yield: 1 gallon.

Mrs. Cora Goggins, Pontotoc

CHRISTMAS PUNCH

1 (6-ounce) can frozen limeade
    concentrate
1 (6-ounce) can frozen
    lemonade concentrate
1 (1 pound 4-ounce) can
    unsweetened grapefruit juice
1 (1 pound 4-ounce) can
    pineapple juice
2 (1 quart) bottles ginger ale,
    chilled
1½ quarts cracked ice
17 red maraschino cherries
17 green maraschino cherries
boiling water

In punch bowl blend undiluted fruit juices and add water in accordance with instructions on concentrate cans. Just before serving, stir in ginger ale and ice. On top float a Christmas wreath made as follows:

Wash excess color from cherries. Arrange cherries in a 1½ quart ring mold. Pour enough boiling water to cover cherries. Freeze solid. Unmold when ready to float on Christmas punch. Yield: 2 gallons.

Mrs. Fred D. Ferguson, Ovett

CHRISTMAS PUNCH FOR 75

2 (0.15-ounce) packages lime
    soft beverage drink mix
2 cups sugar

2 quarts water
46 ounces pineapple juice
2 quarts ginger ale

Combine lime drink mix, sugar, water and pineapple juice. Just before serving add to ginger ale. Pour the entire mixture over ice cubes. A sprig of mint or bits of cherries may be added. Serves 75.

Mrs. Doc Taylor, Brooksville

WEDDING PUNCH

4 lemons or 1 (6-ounce) can
    frozen lemonade
8 limes or 2 (6-ounce) cans
    frozen limeade
2 teaspoons salt
4 (46-ounce) cans
    pineapple juice

12 (6-ounce) cans frozen
    orange juice
6 quarts ginger ale
sugar to taste

Squeeze lemons and limes if fresh fruit is used. Mix all ingredients. Add ginger ale as needed. Make frozen ice ring in salad mold or angel cake pan to use in punch bowl. Serves approximately 80.

Mrs. C. E. Holland, Long Beach

PUNCH FOR 150

12 cups sugar
3 pints water
6 (3-ounce) packages lime
    gelatin
12 cups hot water

3 cups frozen orange juice
3 cups frozen lemon juice
3 quarts pineapple juice
1 (2-ounce) bottle almond
    extract

Boil sugar and 3 pints water together for a few minutes, long enough to mix thoroughly. Dissolve gelatin in 12 cups hot water, add to first solution. When ready to serve add orange juice, lemon juice, pineapple juice and almond extract. Serves 150.

Mrs. Doc Taylor, Brooksville

PUNCH FOR 300

3 gallons water
10 pounds sugar
3 (46-ounce) cans orange juice
3 (46-ounce) cans pineapple
juice

3 (6-ounce) cans frozen
lemonade
3 quarts ginger ale
dash of salt
green food coloring, to desired
color

Boil water and dissolve sugar. Add all other liquids, mix well. Use any food coloring you like. Put in open containers and freeze; use big pickle or candy jars. Leave headspace in jars. It freezes in about 12 hours. Set out to thaw. Do not add ice, just stir. Serves 300.

Mrs. C. H. Compton, Poplarville

PUNCH

½ gallon water
1 (2-ounce) jar citric acid
(from drug store)
3 or 4 pounds sugar—3 pounds
first and taste (add more if
desired)

3 (12-ounce) cans frozen
orange juice OR 6 (6-ounce)
cans frozen orange juice
3 dozen fresh lemons
2 (46-ounce) cans pineapple
juice

Mix ½ gallon water, citric acid and sugar. Heat until dissolved. Cool. Add juices and water to make 4 gallons of punch. Different colors may be obtained as follows: Blue cake color makes green punch, Yellow cake color makes yellow and orange, Red cake color makes pink or red according to amount coloring used.

Freeze ice ring in salad mold the day before using. Let ice mold float in punch bowl.

Mrs. Edgar Barnhill, Louisville

HOT SPICED PERCOLATOR PUNCH

3 cups water
3 cups pineapple juice
1 tablespoon whole cloves
½ tablespoon whole allspice

3 sticks cinnamon
¼ teaspoon salt
½ cup brown sugar

Place water and pineapple juice in the lower part of an 8-cup percolator, and put the rest of the ingredients in the basket of the percolator. Perk for 10 minutes until spices are well blended. Will serve 8 or 10 cups in mugs, cups or punch cups.

Mrs. Virginia Smith, Brookhaven

RUSSIAN TEA

12 small tea bags
1 cup sugar
1 (12-ounce) can frozen orange
  juice
juice from 2 to 3 lemons

1 (12-ounce) can frozen
  lemonade
1 cup cinnamon red hots
2 cups water

Brew tea in ½ gallon water. Add the sugar, orange juice, lemon juice and lemonade to tea mixture. Boil red hots in 2 cups water until thoroughly dissolved. Add to tea mixture. Now add enough hot water to make 1 gallon. Serve piping hot. This can be kept in refrigerator and heated when needed.

Lucianne Hawkins, Amory

HOT SPICED TEA

1½ cups sugar
1½ cups water
3 (2 inch) cinnamon sticks
3 teaspoons grated lemon rind
4½ teaspoons grated orange
  rind
¾ cup orange juice

¾ cup pineapple juice
9 cups boiling water
6 tablespoons lemon juice
½ cup apricot nectar
9 tablespoons tea

Place sugar, water, cinnamon sticks, grated lemon and orange rind in a saucepan. Boil for 5 minutes. Pour this sweetened syrup through a strainer into a large saucepan, add the juices and continue heating. Pour boiling water over tea and steep 5 minutes. Strain and add to juices. Serve hot. Yield: 12 cups.

Georgia L. Williams, Hazlehurst

SPICED TEA

1 cup tea leaves
4 quarts water
16 sticks cinnamon
24 whole cloves
2 cups sugar
4 cups lemon juice

4 cups orange juice
4 quarts pineapple juice
8 cups cranberry juice
8 quarts apple cider
8 quarts ginger ale

Brew tea in 4 quarts water. Strain leaves from tea. Add other ingredients to tea. Simmer and remove cloves and cinnamon sticks before serving. Makes 50 servings or more.

Mrs. C. L. Dickerson, Madison

[31]

APRICOT-ORANGE TEA

2½ cups apricot nectar
1 cup orange juice
1 cup water
1 tablespoon sugar

1 teaspoon ground cinnamon
12 whole cloves
4 lemon slices
2 teaspoons instant tea

Combine apricot nectar, orange juice, water, sugar and cinnamon in a medium size saucepan. Insert 3 cloves into each lemon slice; add to saucepan.

Heat just to boiling; reduce heat, cover. Simmer 5 minutes. Stir in tea. Serve hot. Serves 4 to 6.

Mrs. C. E. Orr, Corinth

HOT SPICED TEA MIX

2 cups Tang
1 cup instant tea
1 (3-ounce) package lemonade
   mix

2½ cups sugar
½ teaspoon ground cloves
½ teaspoon ground cinnamon

Mix all dry ingredients and store in a tightly covered jar. When ready to use, put one heaping tablespoon in cup and fill with boiling water and stir. Makes one quart. Needs no refrigeration.

Mrs. Rosalyn B. Ferguson, Canton

MINT TEA

8 cups boiling water
5 small tea bags
5 sprigs mint

rinds of 2 lemons
½ cup lemon juice
1½ cup sugar

Steep tea, mint and lemon rinds in boiling water for 5 minutes. Remove from water, add juice and sugar and strain. Chill and serve over ice. Serves 8.

Mrs. C. R. Crowder, West Point

HOT MULLED CIDER

1 teaspoon whole cloves
1 teaspoon whole allspice
dash nutmeg
2 quarts apple cider

½ cup brown sugar
¼ teaspoon salt
1 orange, sliced thin crosswise
3 sticks cinnamon

Tie cloves, allspice and nutmeg in a small piece of cheese cloth, add to cider. Stir in sugar and salt. Slowly bring to a boil, cover and simmer 20 minutes. Remove spices. Serve hot with orange slice floaters (oranges sliced very thin). Use "cinnamon stick muddlers". Serves 10.

Mrs. E. B. (Grace) Tinsley, Scooba

WASSAIL CIDER

1 (6-ounce) can frozen
   lemonade
4 quarts apple cider
½ cup sugar, or sweeten to
   taste

1 tablespoon whole cloves
4 sticks cinnamon
½ teaspoon ground allspice

Combine all ingredients and heat to boiling but do not let boil hard. Simmer 5 to 10 minutes. Remove spices and serve hot. Will serve approximately 40 people.

Mrs. J. C. Rainey, Hattiesburg

ORANGEADE

3 cups cold water
¾ cup sugar
1½ cups orange juice

2 to 3 tablespoons lemon juice
sprig of mint

Make a syrup of the sugar and 1/3 of the water. Cool and add remaining water and fruit juice. Serve with generous quantities of ice. Garnish with mint sprig.

Mary Nell Magee, Poplarville

MUSCADINE OR BLACKBERRY WINE

1 gallon of berries (muscadine
   or blackberry)
1 quart of boiling water

3 pounds sugar for each 1
   gallon of juice

To 1 gallon of berries add 1 quart of boiling water. Let stand 24 hours. Crush berries to extract juice and strain. To 1 gallon of juice add 3 pounds of sugar. Let stand until it quits fermenting. Then store in bottles.

Mrs. M. M. Cox, Yazoo City

[33]

BLACKBERRY ACID

2 quarts water

5 ounces tartaric acid
(obtained at the drugstore)

12 pounds mashed blackberries

sugar

Dissolve acid in water. Pour over the berries and let stand 48 hours. Strain. To each pint of clear juice add 1 cup sugar. Bring to a rolling boil for one minute. Place in bottles, seal tightly. Makes a nice summer drink, served either cold or over crushed ice.

Mrs. John D. McCraine, Woodville

COFFEE ICE CREAM FLOAT

1 gallon coffee

1 pound can chocolate syrup

½ gallon vanilla ice cream

1 (12-ounce) bottle sparkling
water

Make one gallon strong coffee. Cool and mix with the syrup. Mash and add ½ of ice cream. Stir until melted. Just before serving add sparkling water. Pour into chilled punch bowl, containing about a 6-inch cube of ice. Top with spoonsful of ice cream. Will serve 50 persons.

Mrs. Jim Justice, Clarksdale

CHILLED COFFEE

1 (2-ounce) jar instant coffee

1 cup hot milk

2 quarts chocolate ice cream

2 quarts vanilla ice cream

1 pint cream, whipped

1 pint soft vanilla ice cream

Dissolve coffee in hot milk. Let cool. Blend coffee with quarts of chocolate and vanilla ice cream and whipped cream until custard consistency. Place in punch bowl, chill in deep freeze, if possible. Before serving, add soft vanilla ice cream in center. Float whipped cream on top and sprinkle with nutmeg. Serves 50.

Mrs. Ernest Moody, Arcola

⁙[Soups]⁙

When the weather is cold or rainy, there's nothing better than a bowl of steaming hot, hearty soup. When it's hot outside, a cold consomme or jellied soup is refreshing.

When soups contain substantial amounts of fish, meat, milk, dry beans or peas, they are filling enough to be the main part of a meal. Or they can be served with a salad or sandwich. A less nourishing soup or clear broth is a good way to start any meal.

Soups are usually divided into those made with meat or meat stock and those made without. White sauce or vegetable broths to which milk is added are used as bases for soups without meat stock.

Homemade soups are a favorite of Mississippians. The ones in this chapter are favorites of "good" cooks throughout the state. Try them!

OYSTER STEW

¼ stick butter or margarine
1 tablespoon finely chopped
onion
8 to 10 small oysters—more,
if desired

½ teaspoon salt
¼ teaspoon seasoned pepper
1 pint sweet milk
Worcestershire sauce

Melt butter in skillet or saucepan. Sautè onion and oysters in melted butter until onions are tender and oysters curl; salt and pepper. Heat milk in saucepan, add onion, oysters and butter. Put in dash of Worcestershire sauce. Heat to serve; do not boil. Add crackers to thicken, if desired. Serves 2.

Mrs. Jacqueline Mikell, Port Gibson

OYSTER MILK STEW

3 pints milk
½ cup evaporated milk
½ stick butter or margarine
1 medium onion, chopped very
fine
5 or 6 green onions, chopped
very fine

salt and pepper to taste
dash of garlic powder, optional
1 pint drained oysters
(small size are better)
parsley

Combine all ingredients except oysters and parsley in top of double boiler or in heavy teflon-lined pan. Cook over low heat for 45 minutes stirring often from bottom of pan.

Add oysters into mixture and cook for 20 additional minutes. Serve sprinkled with parsley. Serves 4 or 5.

Mrs. W. D. Andrews, Jr., Biloxi

CHICKEN SOUP

6 cups chicken broth
1 tablespoon finely chopped
raw ham
1 carrot, cut in cubes
2 stalks celery

1 small bay leaf
1 sliced onion
1/3 cup hot boiled rice
1 cup chicken, chopped fine

Add all ingredients except rice and chicken to broth. Heat to boiling point and boil 30 minutes; add rice and chicken and serve. May be served without chicken meat. Serves 6.

Mrs. J. L. Alexander, West Point

HUNGARIAN CHICKEN SOUP WITH NOODLES

2 pounds bony parts of chicken
   (with liver and gizzard
   chopped)
2 tablespoons cooking oil
½ cup chopped onion
flour
8 cups (2 quarts) water

2 carrots, diced
1 cup diced celery
2 tablespoons parsley flakes
1 tablespoon salt
1 teaspoon black pepper
1 tablespoon paprika

Sear chicken in cooking oil, add onion. Sprinkle flour over chicken, stir well. Add water, vegetables and seasonings. Bring to a boil, reduce heat to simmer, and cook for 45 minutes. Then add noodles made of: 1 cup of all-purpose flour, 1 egg, ¼ cup cold water, ¼ teaspoon salt.

Mix flour, egg, water and salt thoroughly in a mixing bowl. Then take a small spoon and chip off noodle dough by spoonfuls into soup. Cook over medium heat for 12 to 15 minutes. Serve hot.

Mrs. Sadie Teck, Purvis

ONION SOUP

3 tablespoons margarine
2 large onions, sliced
2 egg yolks
6 cups milk

2 teaspoons salt
¼ teaspoon pepper
croutons for garnish

Melt margarine in large skillet and cook onions until tender. Beat egg yolks in large bowl; stir in milk, salt and pepper. Add this mixture to onions and cook, stirring constantly, until soup begins to thicken. Sprinkle with croutons when serving. Serves 6.

Mrs. Lamar Scott, Fayette

ASPARAGUS SOUP

1 quart chicken or meat stock
1 cup asparagus pieces
2 cups milk
4 tablespoons butter

4 tablespoons flour
2 teaspoons salt
¼ teaspoon pepper

Boil asparagus slowly in stock. Make white cream sauce with milk, butter, flour and salt in large kettle with cover. Add asparagus, stock and pepper slowly to cream sauce and let simmer for 15 minutes. Serve hot. Serves 4 to 6.

Mrs. June Truly, Fayette

[37]

POTATO SOUP

4 large potatoes, cut in
quarters
1 medium onion
1 quart water
salt and pepper to taste

1 tablespoon flour
1 quart milk
1 egg
2 tablespoons butter

Boil potatoes and onion in water until done. Remove onion. Mash potatoes fine. Add salt and pepper, mix flour with small amount of the milk. Add to remaining milk and bring to a boil. Add potatoes to hot milk and reheat. Put lightly beaten egg in tureen. Add butter, strain hot soup over this. Stir well and serve. Serves 4.

Mrs. E. L. Robbins, Woodville

TOMATO SOUP

6 cups tomatoes
1 onion chopped
1 stalk celery
1 sprig parsley

1 bay leaf
1 teaspoon salt
dash of Tabasco
minced parsley

Place all ingredients, except minced parsley, in large saucepan. Bring to a full boil; reduce heat and simmer 20 minutes. Serve very hot with a sprinkling of minced parsley in each serving. Serves 6.

Mrs. Curtis Orman, West Point

FRESH CORN SOUP

2 cups fresh cream cut corn
1 quart chicken broth
½ cup okra
1 clove garlic

½ cup celery
1 cup diced chicken
2 teaspoons butter
2 cups hot milk

Cook corn in chicken broth until tender; add okra, garlic, celery and diced chicken and simmer for about 15 or 20 minutes. Add butter, salt and pepper to taste. Gradually stir in hot milk and serve. Serves 8.

Mrs. Ethel Mitchell, Picayune

SPLIT PEA SOUP

1 large onion
3 ribs of celery
3 pods of garlic
1 large bell pepper

½ stick oleo
1 pound split peas
1 ham hock
3 quarts of water

Sautè onion, celery, garlic and bell pepper in oleo in heavy pan. In separate container put split peas in enough water to cover and cook for about 15 minutes. Put ham hock and 3 quarts water in heavy container, along with sautèd mixture. After peas have cooked add them to the water with the ham hock and the remainder of the vegetables. Let this cook down until thick; then put through a sieve. Season to taste, using a good bit of black pepper for flavor. Soup will be nice and thick.

Mrs. Bernice Myers, Canton

VEGETABLE SOUP

1 beef soup bone	1 cup diced celery (optional)
3 quarts water	1 cup chopped onions
1 tablespoon salt	(optional)
1½ cups corn	salt to taste
1 quart tomatoes	2 cups green lima beans
3 cups okra	

Cook soup bone in three quarts of water and 1 tablespoon of salt. When meat is tender, pull off bone and chop in small pieces. Return to broth and add remaining ingredients. Cook slowly 1½ hours. Serve while hot with crackers.

Gloria Rayburn, Wiggins

VEGETABLE SOUP

2 pound soup bone	1 (8-ounce) can tomato sauce
2 quarts water	½ cup chopped celery
2 teaspoons salt	1 cup diced potatoes
1 chopped onion	½ cup diced carrots
1 (16-ounce) can okra,	pepper to taste
tomatoes and corn	spaghetti

Place soup bone, water, salt and onion in a four-quart covered pot, and boil slowly for one hour. Add canned vegetables, tomato sauce, and fresh vegetables and simmer slowly for another hour. Add pepper to taste. Remove soup bone and cut meat from bone in bite-size pieces. Then return to soup. Add small amount of spaghetti during the last twenty minutes of cooking. Serves 8.

Mrs. W. H. Hay, Port Gibson

VEGETABLE SOUP

3 pounds lean beef
2 pounds marrow bone
2 quarts cold water
1 large can tomatoes
1 teaspoon peppercorns
1 tablespoon salt
1 bay leaf

2 tablespoons butter
½ cup chopped carrots
½ cup chopped turnip or
½ cup chopped parsnip
1 cup chopped onion
½ cup chopped celery
1 sprig parsley

Cut lean meat in small pieces. Place half in kettle with marrow bone, water and tomatoes. Brown the rest of meat in butter and add vegetables and seasoning now or later, as the cooking time is 5 hours at just below boiling point. May be served with vegetables and rice, or strained and cleared. Serves 8.

Mrs. Ethel A. Richardson, West Point

CANADIAN CHEESE SOUP

1 stick butter
6 tablespoons flour
1 quart milk
1 teaspoon salt
2 teaspoons Worcestershire
    sauce
2 cups cubed cheese

2 tablespoons butter
½ cup chopped celery
½ cup chopped onion
½ cup chopped carrots
½ cup bell pepper
1 pint chicken stock

Make rich cream sauce by melting 1 stick of butter in 4-quart saucepan, stirring in flour until well blended. Add milk slowly, stirring constantly, then add salt, Worcestershire sauce and cubed cheese.

Sauté in 2 tablespoons of butter, the celery, onion, carrots and bell pepper. Add chicken stock and cook very little as vegetables must be crunchy. Combine with the cream sauce. Make day before. Serves 4.

Mrs. Stovall Milam, Leland

BEEF STEW

¼ cup flour
1 teaspoon salt
¼ teaspoon pepper
1½ pounds boneless beef
3 teaspoons shortening
water

4 to 6 medium potatoes
6 carrots, cut crosswise
4 to 6 small onions
1 quart green beans, cut
flour

Combine flour, salt and pepper. Dredge meat with seasoned flour. Brown slowly in fat. Pour off fat. Add enough water to cover. Cook slowly for 1½ hours. Add potatoes, carrots, onions and fresh beans. Continue cooking 45 minutes. If canned green beans are used, drain and add 15 minutes before stew is done. Arrange meat and vegetables on warm platter. Thicken cooking liquid with flour for gravy. Serves 4 to 6.

Mrs. Stennis Clardy, West Point

CAMP STEW

1 (2½ pound) hen
4 large onions
2½ cups okra, diced
1 lemon, diced
2½ pounds potatoes, peeled
  and diced
2 (no. 2½) cans whole
  tomatoes

1 (15-ounce) can corn
1 tablespoon black pepper
1 tablespoon garlic
1 teaspoon Accent
1 (8-ounce) bottle catsup
2 tablespoons salt
1/3 cup Worcestershire sauce

Boil hen until tender; take meat off bone. Dice all vegetables and cook in chicken broth until tender. Mix all ingredients together and simmer for 5 hours on low heat. Serves approximately 15. May be frozen for later use.

Mrs. Rachel Hunt, Ackerman

CORN CHOWDER

6 (no. 2) cans cream style corn
3 cups hot milk
1 (13-ounce) can of evaporated
  milk

1 (6-ounce) can crab meat
  (optional)

Heat corn, add hot milk and the large can of evaporated milk. Add the crab meat, if desired. Serves 5 to 6.

Mrs. Marian H. Quinn, Canton

POTATO CHOWDER

2 cups cubed, uncooked
  potatoes
1 tablespoon chopped onion
1 clove garlic, minced
2 tablespoons fat
1 cup canned tomatoes

1 (10½ to 11-ounce) can
  condensed chicken soup
1 teaspoon salt
⅛ teaspoon pepper
1 cup light cream

[41]

Cook potatoes, onion, and garlic in hot fat until potatoes are transparent (not tender), stirring occasionally. Add tomatoes, chicken soup, and seasonings. Cover. Simmer until potatoes are tender, about 25 minutes. Add cream. Serve at once. Serves 4.

Mrs. LaVerne Y. Lindsey, Lexington

NAVY BEAN SOUP

4 slices bacon, chopped
½ cup chopped onion
1 (16-ounce) package navy
  beans (soak overnight in cold
  water)

1 large potato, cubed
6 cups water
2 teaspoons salt
½ teaspoon black pepper

Sautè onion and bacon in pressure cooker. Add soaked beans (drained), potatoes, water, salt and black pepper. Process at 15 pounds pressure for 25 minutes. Serves 6 to 8.

Mrs. Arthur H. Moss, Bruce

CREAMY BEAN SOUP

1 pound pea beans
1½ cups boiling water
1¼ pounds smoked ham hock
  or meaty ham bone
1 teaspoon salt
½ teaspoon seasoned pepper

3 tablespoons butter
¾ cup minced onion
1 (1-pound 3-ounce) can
  tomatoes, with juice
3 cups milk

Wash and clean beans; cover with cold water, soak overnight. Drain. Place in dutch oven with boiling water, ham bone, salt and pepper. Heat to boiling; reduce heat, cover, simmer 2½ hours. Remove from heat. Melt butter in small saucepan; add onion, sautè until tender. Take ham bone from broth and cut off meat. Add meat, onions and tomatoes to broth; mix. Cover and simmer 1 hour. Stir in milk; heat a few minutes. Serve immediately. Serves 6.

Mrs. Jacqueline Mikell, Port Gibson

CHILI

½ pound pinto beans
5 cups cooked tomatoes
1 pound green peppers, chopped
1 pound onions, chopped
1½ tablespoons salad oil
1 clove crushed garlic
½ cup chopped parsley
½ cup butter

2½ pounds ground beef
1 pound lean ground pork
1/3 cup chili powder
2 tablespoons salt
1½ teaspoons pepper
1½ teaspoons cumin seed
1½ teaspoons monosodium
glutamate

Wash beans, soak overnight in water 2 inches above beans. Simmer, covered, in same water until tender. Add tomatoes and simmer 5 minutes. Sautè green peppers in salad oil 5 minutes. Add onion. Cook until tender, stirring often. Add garlic and parsley. Melt butter in large skillet and sautè meat for 15 minutes; add to onion mixture. Stir in chili powder and cook 15 minutes. Add this to beans, and add spices. Simmer, covered for one hour. Cook uncovered for 30 minutes. Skim fat from top. Makes four quarts and freezes well.

Mrs. Ruel Ewing, Brooksville

CHILI CON CARNE

2 pounds ground beef
2 tablespoons cooking oil
1 large onion, chopped
1 bell pepper, chopped
2 packages chili seasoning mix
2 (no. 300) cans tomatoes

2 (no. 300) cans red kidney
beans
2 to 3 cups water or tomato
juice
salt

Brown ground beef in oil in 4-quart dutch oven or heavy, deep iron pot, over medium heat. When the meat has lightly browned, add the chopped onion and pepper and the 2 packets of chili seasoning mix. Continue cooking meat and vegetables in the mix, stirring often. When onions and peppers have become soft, add the tomatoes and kidney beans, plus the water or tomato juice. The water or juice should completely cover the ingredients. Simmer at low temperature for 1½ hours, stirring occasionally and adding liquid if needed. Season with salt to taste. Serve over rice. Serves 8.

Mrs. Doris Wise, Starkville

[43]

CHILI (QUICK)

1½ pounds ground beef
1 medium onion
1 clove garlic
2 cups hot water

1 tablespoon chili powder
1 or 2 (no. 300) cans
   kidney beans, with juice

Brown ground beef with onion and garlic. Sprinkle with flour. Add hot water to make soupy. Add chili powder and the kidney beans with the juice. Cook 30 minutes. Serve with crackers and fruit salad. Serves 6.

Mrs. Betty Baldwin, Canton

·⟦Salads⟧·

What better way to serve a variety of fruits, vegetables and even meats than in a colorful salad? As an appetizer, side dish, dessert or the main course of a meal, a salad brings lots of goodness to your table.

A salad should appear on the menu at least once a day—not only does it give color and texture, but it is rich in vitamins, minerals and bulk—all necessary for good health.

Select top-quality fruits and vegetables for your salads. Give these foods the best care to avoid damage and to keep them fresh. If you prepare salad ingredients ahead of time, store them, without dressing, in the refrigerator. A vegetable salad will be crisper if you place it in the freezer for a few minutes just before serving. If you plan to use unpeeled fruits or vegetables in a salad, choose those with smooth, tender and colorful skins.

Always thoroughly drain the greens used in salads and tear them into fairly large pieces to give more body. Some salad fruits are likely to turn dark on standing and should be dipped in a little citrus juice.

Some salad combinations are traditional—like lettuce and sliced tomatoes, canned peaches and cottage cheese. No family reunion dinner in Mississippi would be complete without a large bowl of potato salad, and a fish fry would be unsuccessful without a creamy, homemade cole slaw. Don't be afraid to try a new salad recipe on your family and friends.

CRANBERRY SALAD

1 3-ounce package cherry
  flavored gelatin
1 cup hot water
1 cup sugar
1 tablespoon lemon juice
1 cup pineapple syrup
1 cup raw cranberries

1 ground orange, rind
  included
1 cup drained, crushed
  pineapple
1 cup chopped celery
½ cup chopped walnuts

Dissolve gelatin in hot water. Add sugar, lemon juice and pineapple syrup. Chill in a 6½ x 10-inch dish until partially set. Add remaining ingredients. Chill. Yield: 15 2" x 2" servings.

Dr. Frances McGuffee, Clinton

ICE CREAM CRANBERRY SALAD

1 (no. 1) can whole cranberry
  sauce
1 (8-ounce) can mandarin
  orange slices

1 tablespoon lemon juice
1 (3-ounce) box orange
  gelatin
1 pint vanilla ice cream

Drain the fruit, add lemon juice and add water to make 1 cup of liquid. Bring to boil, add gelatin. Cool—while still warm add ice cream; stir well, then add fruit. Pour into mold to jell.

Mrs. Steve Frank, Egypt

CONGEALED CRANBERRY SALAD

2 (3-ounce) packages
  raspberry or cherry flavored
  gelatin dessert
2¼ cups boiling water
1¾ cups sugar

1 pound fresh cranberries
1 large California navel orange
1 large apple
1 small can crushed pineapple
½ cup or more chopped pecans

Dissolve gelatin dessert and sugar in boiling water; set aside to cool and thicken. Wash and stem cranberries; quarter and core apple and orange (select orange with thick skin), but do not remove peel. Put all fruit through food chopper or blender. Add chopped fruit, juices, crushed pineapple and pecans to gelatin. Pour into 8 x 8-inch square cake pan and allow to congeal 24 hours, or overnight, before cutting into squares. Serve with turkey, chicken or ham. Yield: 16 generous servings.

Mrs. Sherrill Nash, Starkville

CRANBERRY WALDORF SALAD

2 cups ground cranberries
3 cups miniature marshmallows
¾ cup sugar
2 cups diced apples

½ cup seedless green grapes
½ cup broken walnuts
¼ teaspoon salt
1 cup cream, whipped

Combine cranberries with marshmallows and sugar. Cover; chill overnight. Add apples, grapes, walnuts and salt. Fold in whipped cream; chill. Serves 8 to 10.

Mrs. Eugene Holcombe, Macon
Mrs. Shirley Mooney, Collins

AVOCADO SALAD

1 head lettuce, washed and
  chilled
1 small red onion, thinly
  sliced

3 ripe medium avocados
½ (8-ounce) bottle oil and
  vinegar dressing

Break lettuce into bite-size pieces into a medium salad bowl. Separate onion slices into rings and mix with lettuce. Just before serving, peel and quarter avocados and place on top of lettuce and onions. After shaking dressing well, pour it on salad and toss gently. Serves 8 to 10.

Mrs. June Truly, Fayette

AVOCADO ORANGE SALAD

1 (3-ounce) package lemon
  gelatin
1 teaspoon vinegar
1 teaspoon each, grated
  lemon and orange peel
2 teaspoons lemon juice

2 tablespoons sugar
1 (11-ounce) can mandarin
  oranges, diced
1 diced avocado
2 tablespoons pimiento,
  for color

Prepare gelatin according to package directions. Add vinegar, fruit peel, lemon juice and sugar. Let cool to consistency of egg whites. Add diced oranges, avocado and chopped pimiento. Pour into a 9 x 9-inch dish and chill. Serves 9.

Mrs. Annie Kate Thompson, Clarksdale

[47]

24-HOUR SALAD

3 egg yolks, beaten
2 tablespoons sugar
2 tablespoons vinegar
2 tablespoons pineapple syrup
1 tablespoon margarine
dash of salt

2 cups canned pitted white
    cherries, drained
2 cups pineapple tidbits,
    drained
2 pared oranges, cut in pieces
1 cup heavy cream, whipped
2 cups tiny marshmallows

Combine egg yolks, sugar, vinegar, pineapple syrup, margarine and salt in top of double boiler. Cook over hot (not boiling) water till thick, stirring constantly. Cool. Stir in cherries, pineapple, oranges and marshmallows. Fold in whipped cream. Spoon gently into serving bowl. Chill 24 hours in refrigerator.

Mary Nell Magee, Poplarville

CINNAMON APPLE SALAD

1 cup red cinnamon candies
2 cups water
6 tart apples

6 lettuce leaves
1 package cottage cheese

Boil cinnamon candies in water over high heat until candies dissolve. Pare apples, core and cut into halves. Reduce heat to low; place apples in boiling syrup and cook until tender, basting occasionally to color apples evenly. Chill mixture; drain when apples are thoroughly colored. Arrange two apple halves on each lettuce leaf and fill with cottage cheese. Serves 6.

Mrs. Fred D. Ferguson, Ovett

CREME DE MENTHE SALAD

1 (3-ounce) package lemon
    gelatin
1 (3-ounce) package lime
    gelatin
2 cups boiling water
1 pound cottage cheese,
    drained
1 (20-ounce) can crushed
    pineapple, drained

4 tablespoons creme de menthe
1 (5 1/3-ounce) can
    evaporated milk
½ cup sour cream
3 tablespoons salad dressing
1 to 3 tablespoons creme de
    menthe
1 tablespoon sugar
1 teaspoon poppy seeds

Mix gelatin in boiling water. Let cool. Stir together cottage cheese, pineapple, 4 tablespoons creme de menthe and milk. Add to cooled gelatin and pour into a 12 x 8-inch pan and congeal.

Mix sour cream, salad dressing, 1 to 3 tablespoons creme de menthe, sugar and poppy seeds together for a dressing and serve over salad. Serves 8.

Mrs. Carl H. Gerrard, Clarksdale

ANGEL SALAD

1 can crushed pineapple, drained
1 package miniature marsh-mallows
1 small jar maraschino cherries, chopped
1 (3-ounce) package cream cheese
2 tablespoons sugar
2 tablespoons mayonnaise
½ pint cream, whipped
½ cup halved pecans

Combine the pineapple and marshmallows. Mix cherries, cream cheese, sugar and mayonnaise together. Add to pineapple mixture. Whip cream and fold in pineapple mixture. Add pecans. Chill until firm.

Mrs. Harry Williams, Holly Springs

DREAM SALAD

1 cup cream, whipped
¼ cup confectioner's sugar
3 cups diced, unpeeled red apples
2 cups orange sections
1½ cups green grapes
2 cups banana slices
½ cup maraschino cherries
½ cup coarsely chopped pecans
½ cup raisins
1 cup tiny marshmallows
1 cup grated coconut
¼ cup confectioner's sugar
4 tablespoons lemon juice

In 1-quart mixing bowl, whip cream until stiff and add ¼ cup confectioner's sugar. Chill until ready to use.

In a 3-quart salad bowl, mix together the apples, orange sections, grapes, banana slices, cherries, pecans, raisins, coconut and marsh-mallows. Sprinkle lemon juice on top and toss lightly to prevent discoloration. Add ¼ cup confectioner's sugar and the whipped cream. Mix thoroughly and chill until ready to serve. Serves 12 (1 cup servings).

Mrs. Ike C. Presley, Rolling Fork

FRUIT SALAD

2 (3-ounce) packages cream
  cheese
½ cup mayonnaise
1 tablespoon grated lemon peel
1 (no. 2½) can fruit cocktail

1 (11-ounce) can mandarin
  oranges
1 (no. 2½) can sliced peaches
2 cups miniature marshmallows
1 cup heavy cream, whipped
2 tablespoons powdered sugar

Soften cream cheese and blend in mayonnaise and lemon peel. Drain fruit and then stir the fruit and marshmallows into creamed mixture. Whip cream, then add the powdered sugar and continue whipping until stiff. Fold into fruit mixture. Pour into a 2-quart loaf pan lined with waxed paper and chill until firm (about 4 hours). This salad may be frozen and will keep well for 3 to 4 weeks. Seal in foil to freeze. Serves 12.

Mrs. Lloyd Owen, Senatobia

APRICOT SALAD

2 packages apricot
  gelatin
2 cups boiling water
2 cups cold water
1 (no. 2) can crushed pineapple
2 large bananas, sliced
½ cup of white sugar

½ cup pineapple juice
1 egg, well beaten
2 tablespoons flour
2 tablespoons butter
1 (8-ounce) package cream
  cheese
1 box Dream Whip

Mix gelatin and water and let the mixture begin to congeal. Add pineapple and bananas. Set aside while you cook the sugar, pineapple juice, egg, flour and butter until the mixture is thick. While the mixture is still hot, add cream cheese and melt. Cool. Put the mixture in the refrigerator and let it get cold. Whip Dream Whip as directed on box and fold into the cooked sauce. Spread on the top of gelatin and chill well before serving.

Mrs. Lois Herring, Leakesville

APRICOT CONGEALED SALAD

1 package orange gelatin
1 package lemon gelatin
2½ cups boiling water
1 (8-ounce) package cream
  cheese

1 (1-pound) can apricots,
  pitted
1 cup chopped nuts

Mix hot water with gelatin and dissolve well. Add cream cheese to hot mixture. Cool. Then add mashed apricots and juice and chopped nuts. Pour into a shallow dish and chill for several hours. Serves 8 (1 cup servings).

Mrs. Ethel Loyd, Pattison

CONGEALED FRUIT SALAD

1 cup mashed canned pears
2 (3-ounce) packages cream
   cheese
1 tablespoon mayonnaise

1 (3-ounce) package lime
   gelatin
1 cup boiling pear juice
½ pint cream, whipped

Mash pears, then mix with softened cream cheese and mayonnaise. Dissolve gelatin in boiling pear juice; let cool until it starts to set. Add fruit and cream cheese to gelatin, then fold in whipped cream. Pour into 1½ quart mold or individual molds. Refrigerate. Top with dab of mayonnaise to serve. Serves 9 or 10.

For variation, use crushed pineapple and orange gelatin.

Mrs. Emmons Turner, Jr., Booneville

FROZEN FRUIT SALAD

2 (3-ounce) packages of cream
   cheese
1 cup mayonnaise
1 cup heavy cream, whipped
½ cup quartered red
   maraschino cherries

½ cup quartered green
   maraschino cherries
2½ cups drained, crushed
   pineapple
2½ cups diced marshmallows

Combine cheese and mayonnaise, blend until smooth. Fold in whipped cream, fruit and marshmallows. Pour into 1-quart refrigerator tray. Freeze firm. Can be used as a salad or dessert. Serves 8.

Mrs. W. A. Vaiden, Hernando

FROZEN FRUIT SALAD

2 cups sour cream
2 tablespoons lemon juice
½ cup sugar
⅛ teaspoon salt
1 (8-ounce) can crushed pineapple, drained

1 diced banana
4 drops red food coloring
¼ cup chopped pecans
1 (1-pound 1-ounce) can fruit
   cocktail, drained
12 paper muffin cups

[51]

Combine sour cream, lemon juice, sugar, salt, pineapple, banana and enough red food coloring to give a pink tint. Lightly fold in nuts and fruit cocktail. Spoon into paper muffin cups which have been placed in 3-inch muffin cup pans. Freeze. Cover with plastic and store in freezer. Remove from freezer 15 minutes before time to serve. Serves 12.

For variation, bing cherries may be substituted for fruit cocktail.

Mrs. Ray Reynolds, Meadville
Mrs. Manley Abel, Duck Hill

FROZEN FRUIT SALAD

1 (no. 2½) can apricots, cut fine
1 (8-ounce) jar maraschino cherries, cut
1 (8-ounce) package cream cheese

1 (no. 1 flat) can crushed pineapple
8 tablespoons powdered sugar
¾ cup mayonnaise
1 cup cream, whipped

Put fruit in colander to drain. Sprinkle with sugar. While fruit drains, mix mayonnaise and cream cheese in large bowl. Add fruit and whipped cream. Pour into refrigerator trays and freeze. Serves 8.

Mrs. G. H. Hariston, Sr., Silver City

FROZEN FRUIT SALAD

2 (3-ounce) packages cream cheese
¼ cup maple syrup
1 cup drained crushed pineapple

1 cup chopped dates
1 cup chopped pecans
½ pint cream, whipped

Mix and freeze. Serves 8 to 10.

Mrs. Lenora Beatus, Belzoni

HOLIDAY SALAD

1 (3-ounce) package lemon gelatin
2 cups cranberry juice
pinch of salt

1 cup diced apples
1 cup diced celery
½ cup chopped nuts

Dissolve gelatin in ½ cup cranberry juice; add salt. Heat remaining juice to boiling, pour over gelatin. Let thicken slightly and fold in apples, celery and nuts. Mold and chill. Serves 8 to 10.

Mrs. C. E. Orr, Corinth

CHRISTMAS SALAD

2 (3-ounce) packages lime
    gelatin
2 (3-ounce) packages cream
    cheese

small bottle maraschino
    cherries

Drain cherries. Use the juice with water to dissolve gelatin according to directions on package. Put cherries in bottom of mold (use a round mold). Pour just enough gelatin over cherries to cover and hold in place. Break cream cheese in small pieces and put into remaining hot gelatin. Beat with beater until well mixed. Chill until it begins to thicken and pour over cherries and finish chilling. Serves 10.

Mrs. John Mixon, Hattiesburg

LIME MARSHMALLOW SALAD

16 large marshmallows, cut up
1 cup sweet milk
1 (3-ounce) package lime
    gelatin
1 (3-ounce) package cream
    cheese

1 (4½-ounce) can crushed
    pineapple, drained
1 cup cream, whipped
½ cup chopped pecans

Place marshmallows and milk in top of double boiler, heat until marshmallows are melted. Add gelatin, stir until dissolved and cool slightly. Beat cheese until fluffy, mix with pineapple and stir into first mixture. Fold in whipped cream and nuts. Turn into a 7 x 11-inch pan and chill until firm. Keeps well several days in refrigerator. Serves 10 to 12.

Mrs. Stanley Henderson, Hickory

FROSTED LIME SALAD

1 (3-ounce) package lime-
    flavored gelatin
1 cup boiling water
1 (no. 2) can crushed
    pineapple
½ cup finely sliced celery
1 cup chopped pecans

1 cup small curd cottage cheese
1 tablespoon chopped
    pimiento
1 (3-ounce) package cream
    cheese
1 tablespoon mayonnaise
1 teaspoon lemon juice

Dissolve gelatin in boiling water; cool until syrupy. Stir in crushed pineapple, celery, pecans, cottage cheese and pimiento. Turn into an 8 x 4 x 4-inch loaf pan rinsed in cold water; chill. When firm, unmold or leave in pan. Blend and beat until smooth the cream cheese, mayonnaise and lemon juice and frost top of the molded salad. Serves 12.

Mrs. L. H. Stutts, Booneville

BLACK CHERRY SALAD

1 can pineapple chunks
1 (16-ounce) can dark sweet
   pitted cherries
¼ cup fruit syrup
2 tablespoons sugar

2 tablespoons lemon juice
dash of salt
1 cup miniature marshmallows
½ cup of pecans, chopped
½ cup dairy sour cream
1 fresh egg, beaten

Drain cherries and pineapple. Reserve ¼ cup of the mixed fruit juice. Combine beaten egg, lemon juice, fruit syrup, sugar and salt. Cook over medium heat in thick saucepan until thickened. Stir frequently. Remove from heat, cool slightly, fold in sour cream and finish cooling.

In mixing bowl combine cherries, pineapple, pecans and marsh-mallows. Add sauce and fold lightly to blend. Chill in refrigerator for 1 hour or more. Serve in lettuce lined salad bowl. Serves 5 to 6.

Mrs. Mary S. Parkman, Monticello

COKE SALAD

2 (3-ounce) packages cherry
   gelatin
1 large can chunk or
   crushed pineapple
1 medium jar maraschino
   cherries

2 small colas
1 (8-ounce) package cream
   cheese
1 cup pecans

Drain pineapple and cherry juice, heat to boiling and pour over gelatin to dissolve. Cool and add colas. Let thicken slightly and add other ingredients. Serves 10 to 12.

Mrs. Bruce Aultman, Sumrall

COKE SALAD

1 (no. 2) can crushed
   pineapple
1 (no. 2) can dark, sweet
   cherries
1 (3-ounce) package cherry
   gelatin

1 (3-ounce) package
   strawberry gelatin
1 (8-ounce) package cream
   cheese, softened
1 (12-ounce) cola beverage
¼ cup chopped pecans
salad oil

Drain fruit and heat juices to boiling. Combine gelatins. Pour boiling juices over gelatins, stir until dissolved and cool slightly. Cream softened cheese with a small portion of the cola. Add remaining cola, fruit and nuts. Stir this mixture into gelatin mixture. Lightly grease with salad oil a 1½-quart mold. Pour all ingredients into the mold and chill until firm. Remove from mold and place onto crisp lettuce. Serves 8.

Mrs. Webster Cleveland, Jr., Booneville

BLUEBERRY SALAD

2 (3-ounce) packages mixed fruit gelatin
2 cups boiling water
1 (15-ounce) can blueberries
1 (8¼-ounce) can crushed pineapple
1 (8-ounce) package cream cheese
½ cup sugar
½ pint sour cream
1 teaspoon vanilla
½ cup chopped pecans

Dissolve gelatin in boiling water. Drain blueberries and pineapple and measure liquid; add enough water to make 1 cup and add to gelatin mixture. Stir in drained blueberries and pineapple. Pour into a 2-quart flat pan, cover and put in refrigerator until firm. Combine cream cheese, sugar, sour cream and vanilla and spread over congealed salad. Sprinkle with chopped pecans. Serves 10 to 12.

Mrs. Polly Lowry, Verona

CONGEALED FRUIT SALAD

1 (16-ounce) can peaches
1 (16-ounce) can pears
1 (16-ounce) can apricots
½ medium size cantaloupe
1 medium size banana
1 package lemon gelatin
1 package orange gelatin
½ tablespoon gelatin
⅛ cup cold water
½ cup sugar
1 teaspoon dry mustard
1 teaspoon salt
½ tablespoon onion juice
1/3 cup salad vinegar
1 cup salad oil
1 tablespoon celery seed

Cut fruits in large pieces in 9 x 13-inch glass dish. Mix lemon and orange gelatins with hot juice from canned fruits. Soften ½ tablespoon gelatin in ⅛ cup cold water and mix well. Pour into hot juice; stir to dissolve. Let cool a few minutes and pour over fruit; put in refrigerator.

Mix sugar, mustard, salt and onion juice. Beating with electric mixer, gradually add half of vinegar and half of oil and beat. Then add other half of vinegar and oil. Add celery seed. Cut salad in squares and serve with the celery seed dressing. Refrigerate remaining dressing in closed jar. Serves 12.

Mrs. Carl W. Blomquist, Port Gibson

STRAWBERRY SWEETHEART

2 (3-ounce) packages cream cheese
1 cup cream, whipped
1 cup mayonnaise
1 (8¼-ounce) can crushed pineapple, drained
1 cup chopped pecans
16 marshmallows, cut fine
1 (12-ounce) package strawberries, thawed

Soften and fluff the cream cheese. Fold in small amount of whipped cream, then fold in remainder of whipped cream. Next, gently blend in remaining ingredients. Freeze in oiled molds or 2½-quart oblong pyrex dish. Serves 8 to 10.

Mrs. C. S. Woodruff, Boyle

STRAWBERRY SALAD

2 (3-ounce) packages strawberry gelatin
2½ cups boiling water
2 (10-ounce) packages frozen strawberries
1 (no. 2) can crushed pineapple
1 cup sour cream

Dissolve gelatin in boiling water. Add frozen strawberries and crushed pineapple with juice. Mix and chill until mixture has the consistency of egg whites. Fold in sour cream and pour in mold. Serves 12.

Mrs. M. A. Rowzee, State College

RING-AROUND-THE-FRUIT

1 (6-ounce) package strawberry gelatin
2 cups boiling water
1 (1-pound 1-ounce) can fruit cocktail
1 (8¾-ounce) can pineapple tidbits
½ cup maraschino cherry halves
1/3 cup coarsely chopped nuts
½ cup miniature marshmallows
1 cup cream, whipped and sweetened
8 individual ring molds

Dissolve gelatin in boiling water. Drain fruit cocktail and pineapple tidbits. Measure syrup; add water to make 2 cups. Add to gelatin. Pour into individual ring molds. Chill until firm. Combine fruits, nuts and marshmallows. Fold in the whipped cream. Chill. Then unmold gelatin onto large serving plate. Spoon the fruit mixture into center of ring. Serves 8.

Mrs. Ray Reynolds, Meadville

FROZEN STRAWBERRY SALAD

15 large marshmallows
2 teaspoons strawberry juice
1 (3-ounce) package cream
  cheese, softened
1 cup frozen strawberries,
  drained

1 cup crushed pineapple,
  drained
½ cup mayonnaise
1 cup heavy cream, whipped

Stir marshmallows in juice over low heat until melted. Remove from heat and blend in cream cheese until smooth. Stir in fruits and mayonnaise. Fold in whipped cream. Pour in 8-inch square pan. Freeze until firm. Serves 10 to 12.

Mrs. Myrtle Baker, Wiggins

CONGEALED TUNA SALAD

1 (3-ounce) package lemon
  gelatin
1½ cups boiling water
3 tablespoons vinegar
½ teaspoon salt
2 tablespoons chopped
  pimiento

1 teaspoon onion juice
½ cup mayonnaise
½ cup chopped nuts
½ cup chopped sweet cucumber
  pickles
1 (6½-ounce) can tuna

Combine gelatin and boiling water, stirring until dissolved; let stand. Mix other ingredients and add to gelatin. Pour into salad mold or individual molds and chill. Serves 6.

Mrs. Alner McNeil, Louin

TUNA SALAD

1 can tomato soup
1 envelope unflavored gelatin
¼ cup cold water
1 can grated tuna
1 (3-ounce) package cream
  cheese, softened

1 cup salad dressing
1 small bottle stuffed olives
1 cup chopped celery
3 hard-boiled eggs, cut up

[57]

Soften gelatin in the cold water. Bring soup to boiling point and add gelatin, stirring to dissolve thoroughly. Add other ingredients and mix well, but lightly. Refrigerate, using ring mold, or serve on lettuce leaf and top with mayonnaise and stuffed olive. Serves 10 to 12.

Mrs. Eliza Green, Leakesville

CRABMEAT TOMATO ASPIC

2 tablespoons unflavored gelatin
½ cup cold water
½ cup tomato soup
3 (3-ounce) packages cream cheese
1 cup finely chopped celery
½ cup finely chopped green pepper
½ cup finely chopped stuffed olives

2 cups lump crab (or 2 cups shrimp may be used)
1 tablespoon (heaping) grated onion
2 tablespoons lemon juice
1 cup mayonnaise
1 tablespoon Worcestershire sauce
½ teaspoon Tabasco
salt to taste

Soften gelatin in cold water. Heat soup in a double boiler. Then add cream cheese. Whip with rotary egg beater and add gelatin. Stir until dissolved, cool and add other ingredients. Pour into oiled mold or pan. Chill until firm. Serves 8 to 10.

Mrs. Oscar Parsons, Water Valley

JAPANESE SALAD

2 cups cooked rice
1½ tablespoons minced onion
1 cup French dressing
1 can sardines, drained
1 cup shrimp
¼ cup vinegar
lettuce

2 hard-cooked eggs
3 gherkins, chopped
2 tablespoons chili sauce
1 tablespoon capers
1 teaspoon minced parsley

Combine rice, onion and ½ cup French dressing; chill. Marinate sardines and shrimp in vinegar 10 minutes. Drain. Heap rice in mounds on lettuce leaves; arrange sardines and shrimp alternately around mounds. Grate egg yolks and whites separately and sprinkle over salad; garnish with gherkins and serve with dressing made by combining remaining French dressing with chili sauce, capers and parsley. Serves 4 to 6.

Mrs. Jaola Buckley, Quitman

REFRESHING SHRIMP SALAD

¾ pound cooked, peeled
  shrimp, OR 3 (4½ or 5-
  ounce) cans shrimp
1 quart shredded cabbage
  (fine)
½ cup finely sliced green pepper
1 cup sour cream

1 tablespoon lemon juice
1 teaspoon Worcestershire
  sauce
¼ teaspoon dill seed
dash nutmeg
½ cup almonds

If canned shrimp are used, drain and rinse in cold water. Cut large ones in half. Combine cabbage, green pepper and shrimp. Chill. Combine sour cream, lemon juice, Worcestershire sauce and seasonings. Salt to taste. Chill. Add slivered almonds and dressing to shrimp mixture. Toss lightly. Serve on crisp lettuce cup.

Mrs. J. D. Barron, Crystal Springs

SHRIMP SALAD

1 pound boiled and deveined
  shrimp, chopped fine
1½ cups finely chopped
  lettuce
¾ cup chopped celery
½ cup minced onion
¼ cup chopped green peppers

¼ cup chopped green onions
½ cup sweet pickle relish
2 tablespoons catsup
2 teaspoons prepared mustard
1 tablespoon soy sauce
1 cup mayonnaise

Combine all ingredients. Mix well. Chill several hours. Serve alone or with party sandwiches. Serves 6 to 8.

Mrs. W. D. Andrews, Jr., Biloxi

CORNED BEEF SALAD

1 (12-ounce) can corned beef
2 envelopes unflavored gelatin
1 cup beef bouillon, hot
1 cup cold water
½ cup chopped celery

1 medium chopped bell pepper
1 small can pimiento
3 hard-boiled eggs
1 cup salad dressing

Soften gelatin in hot bouillon. Add cold water and set aside. Break corned beef into small pieces with a fork. Add all ingredients in order given, adding gelatin mixture last. Pour into a greased mold and refrigerate until firm. Serves 8 to 10.

Mrs. T. E. Collins, Jr., Utica

LUNCHEON SHRIMP SALAD

2 packages lemon gelatin
2 cups hot water
1 cup mayonnaise
1 cup small English peas
1 small onion, grated
½ cup bell pepper, finely chopped

1 cup celery, finely chopped
1 small can pimiento
1 cup nuts
2 (6½-ounce) cans shrimp
salt to taste

Dissolve gelatin in hot water. When cool, add all ingredients and turn into molds to set. Serve on lettuce leaf with mayonnaise. Serves 12 to 14.

Mrs. Si Parkman, Brookhaven

AVOCADO-SHRIMP SALAD

1 pound shrimp
1 onion
1 small button garlic
2 or 3 avocados
1 tomato, firm ripe
1 tablespoon Worcestershire sauce

1 teaspoon salt
1 teaspoon pepper
2/3 cup celery
1 small sweet onion
mayonnaise

Cook cleaned and deveined shrimp with onion, garlic, Worcestershire sauce, salt and freshly ground pepper for 10 or 15 minutes. Put shrimp into refrigerator to cool, while cutting up celery, tomato and sweet onion. Mix with shrimp and enough mayonnaise or French dressing to moisten thoroughly. Peel and halve 2 or 3 ripe but firm avocados. Sprinkle the outside lightly with salt and fill the inside with the shrimp mixture. Serve very cold on crisp lettuce. Serves 6.

Mrs. Clara Jean Pittman, Montrose

MOLDED CHICKEN SALAD

2 envelopes unflavored gelatin
½ cup cold water
1 cup hot chicken broth or boullion cubes
¼ cup lemon juice
2 tablespoons sugar

1 cup salad dressing or mayonnaise
salt to taste
1 cup cooked chicken, finely cut
1 cup celery, diced
½ cup stuffed olives, sliced

Soften gelatin in cold water; dissolve in hot stock. Add lemon juice, sugar, salad dressing or mayonnaise and salt; beat until well blended.

Chill. When slightly set, fold in chicken, celery and olives. Pour into a loaf pan and chill until firm. Serves 6.

Mrs. Martee B. Rayburn, Pontotoc

HOT SEAFOOD OR CHICKEN SALAD

2 cups cut up crab, shrimp or chicken
2 cups celery, thinly sliced
½ cup cashew nuts
½ teaspoon salt
1 small onion, grated

1 cup mayonnaise (not salad dressing)
2 tablespoons lemon juice
½ cup grated sharp cheese
1 cup crushed potato chips

Combine all ingredients except cheese and chips. Pile lightly in a 2-quart casserole or individual baking dishes. Sprinkle with cheese and chips. Bake in preheated oven at 400 degrees about 20 minutes, or until mixture is heated and cheese is melted. Serves 8 to 10.

Mrs. Carolyn Ellard, Kosciusko

FLYING CHICKEN SALAD

5 cups cooked chicken, cut in chunks
2 tablespoons salad oil
2 tablespoons orange juice
2 tablespoons vinegar
1 teaspoon salt
1 (11-ounce) can mandarin oranges

3 cups cooked rice
1½ cups small green grapes
1½ cups mayonnaise
1½ cups diced celery
1 (13½-ounce) can pineapple chunks, drained
1 cup toasted slivered almonds

Combine chicken, salad oil, orange juice, vinegar and salt; let stand while preparing remaining salad ingredients (or refrigerate mixture overnight). Gently toss together all ingredients. Serves 12.

Mrs. J. E. Bourne, Grace

ENGLISH PEA SALAD

1 can tender small peas, drained
2 boiled eggs, chopped
¼ cup chopped pickles
¼ cup finely chopped celery

¼ cup chopped bell pepper
¼ cup fine grated carrot
¼ cup grated cheese, optional
mayonnaise

Mix all together and just before serving, add enough mayonnaise to blend the ingredients to preferred consistency. Serves 4 to 6.

Mrs. Robert R. Covington, Columbus

FOUR BEAN SALAD

1 (16-ounce) can cut green
  beans
1 (16-ounce) can cut yellow
  wax beans
1 (16-ounce) can lima beans
1(16-ounce) can English peas
1 medium onion, chopped
1 medium pepper, chopped

1 (4-ounce) jar pimiento,
  chopped
1 cup vinegar
1 cup salad oil
1 cup sugar
1 teaspoon dry mustard
1 teaspoon celery seed
1 teaspoon salt

Drain the canned vegetables. Place beans and peas, prepared onions, pepper and pimiento in a large bowl. Mix remaining ingredients well and pour over the vegetables. Stir well and let marinate several hours or overnight. The longer it stands, the better the salad. Stir several times while marinating. Pour off the marinade to serve the salad. Serves 8 to 10.

Mrs. Fred Smith, Louin

BEAN SALAD, MARINATED

½ cup salad oil
2/3 cup wine vinegar
¾ cup sugar
1 teaspoon salt
1 teaspoon herb seasoning
1 (16-ounce) can whole green
  beans

1 (16-ounce) can white beans
1 (16-ounce) can red kidney
  beans
1 big onion, sliced in rings
1 large bell pepper, sliced in
  rings

Mix the first 5 ingredients. Slice onion in thin rings and separate. Slice pepper in thin rings and cut in half. Drain beans. Add sauce mixture to pepper, onion rings and beans; toss lightly. Marinate for 24 hours. Will keep up to a week in refrigerator. Drain off marinade before serving in individual bowls or as vegetable dish. Serves 6 to 8.

Mrs. C. T. Myers, Magee

MACARONI SALAD

¼ pound elbow macaroni,
    cooked
½ cup diced cheese
2/3 cup chopped onion
2 red and 2 green peppers,
    chopped
½ cup chopped celery
2 teaspoons celery seed

3 boiled eggs, chopped
1 sweet or dill pickle,
    chopped
1 medium clove garlic, chopped
    or grated (optional)
salt to taste
½ cup salad dressing

Mix in order given. Let set in refrigerator 30 minutes or longer to blend seasonings. Serves approximately 10.

Mrs. W. V. Lester, Batesville

MACARONI SALAD

3 tablespoons celery seed
salt to taste
1 large cucumber, chopped
1 green pepper, chopped
4 tomatoes, chopped

red hot sauce to taste
1 pint mayonnaise
1 large onion, chopped
1 (8-ounce) box elbow
    macaroni, cooked

Mix mayonnaise, celery seed, salt and hot sauce; chill. Mix remaining ingredients; toss lightly with mayonnaise mixture. Serves 8.

Mrs. Lloyd P. Chatham, Holly Springs

SAUERKRAUT SALAD

1/3 cup water
2/3 cup vinegar
2/3 cup salad oil
1¼ cups sugar
2 (no. 303) cans sauerkraut,
    drained

1 cup diced celery
2 green peppers, diced
1 large onion, chopped
1 small jar pimiento, diced
1 small can water chestnuts,
    diced

Combine water, vinegar, oil and sugar. Heat and stir until sugar is dissolved. Mix other ingredients in a large bowl and pour hot mixture over these. Refrigerate at least 24 hours before serving. Keep well. Serves 12.

Miss Doris Parkinson, Kosciusko

14-DAY SLAW

1 head cabbage, shredded
1 medium onion, sliced
¾ cup sugar
1 cup vinegar
¾ cup salad oil

2 tablespoons sugar
1 teaspoon celery seed
1 teaspoon dry mustard
1 teaspoon salt

Layer cabbage and onion into a bowl and spread sugar over each layer. Bring other ingredients to a boil, cool and pour over slaw. Refrigerate until ready for use. Keeps well.

Mrs. Ruth Dawson, Tishomingo

STAY-CRISP SLAW

8 cups hand-shredded cabbage
2 medium carrots, shredded
1 medium green pepper, thinly
  sliced
½ cup chopped onion
¾ cup cold water
1 envelope unflavored gelatin

¼ cup cold water
2/3 cup sugar
2/3 cup vinegar
2 teaspoons celery seed
1½ teaspoons salt
¼ teaspoon black pepper
2/3 cup salad oil

Mix shredded cabbage, carrots, green pepper and onion; sprinkle with ½ cup cold water; chill. Soften gelatin in ¼ cup cold water. Mix sugar, vinegar, celery seeds, salt and pepper in saucepan; bring to boil. Stir in softened gelatin. Cool until slightly thickened; beat well. Gradually beat in salad oil.

Drain vegetables; pour dressing over top; mix lightly until all vegetables are coated with dressing. May be served immediately, or stored in refrigerator. Stir just before serving to separate vegetables. Serves 8 to 10.

Mrs. J. H. Burt, Wayside

CUCUMBER SALAD

1 (3-ounce) package lime
  gelatin
2 cups boiling water
1 envelope plain gelatin
1/3 cup cold water

¼ cup mayonnaise
½ cup sour cream
½ medium size onion, grated,
  OR ¼ cup chopped green
  onion or chives

1 tablespoon sugar
2 tablespoons lime juice
(fresh or bottled)
1 tablespoon sweet cucumber
pickle juice
1½ ounces (½ of a 3-ounce
pack) cream cheese

2 or 3 medium size cucumbers,
coarsely grated or shredded
¼ teaspoon salt
2 teaspoons horseradish

Mix lime gelatin with boiling water. Add plain gelatin that has been softened in cold water. Add sugar, lime and pickle juices. Soften cream cheese by adding a little warm gelatin. Beat until smooth. Add mayonnaise and sour cream to this. Cool gelatin in refrigerator. When it is cool add cream cheese mixture, grated onion, cucumber, salt and horseradish. Chill until mixture is the consistency of egg whites. Stir and pour into mold or molds. Serves 6 to 8.

Mrs. M. A. Rowzee, State College

CUCUMBER MOLD

1½ packages plain gelatin
½ cup cold water
1 teaspoon salt
3 large cucumbers
1 (8-ounce) carton cream
cottage cheese
1 (8-ounce) package cream
cheese, softened
1 (8-ounce) carton sour cream

½ cup, or more, salad
mayonnaise
green food color
2 tablespoons lemon juice
2 tablespoons Worcestershire
sauce
½ teaspoon paprika
4 green onions, finely chopped
2/3 cup very finely chopped
celery

Peel and remove seeds from cucumbers; grate or chop to pulp stage; drain. Soften gelatin in water. Add salt. Heat and stir over low heat until gelatin dissolves. Beat cheeses, sour cream and mayonnaise together until well blended. Add a few drops of green food color (careful!), lemon juice, paprika and Worcestershire. Fold in gelatin, cucumber pulp, chopped onion and celery. Pour into ring mold and chill several hours, or overnight, until firm. When ready to serve, unmold on bed of lettuce and surround with bright red tomato wedges. Fill center with shrimp or chicken salad topped with ripe or stuffed olive.

Mrs. Kate Woods, Starkville

THE MISSISSIPPI COOKBOOK

SOUR CREAM POTATO SALAD

7 medium potatoes, cooked in jacket
1/3 cup French or Italian dressing
¾ cup sliced celery
1/3 cup sliced green onions and tops

4 hard-boiled eggs
1 cup mayonnaise
½ cup sour cream
1½ teaspoons horseradish mustard
salt and pepper to taste
1/3 cup diced cucumber

Peel and slice potatoes. While potatoes are warm, pour dressing over them and chill for 2 hours. Add celery and onion. Chop egg whites; sieve yolks and save some for garnish. Combine sieved yolk with mayonnaise, sour cream and horseradish mustard. Fold into salad. Add salt and pepper to taste. Chill for 2 hours; add cucumber. To garnish, sprinkle reserved sieved yolk and sliced onion tops over salad. Serves 10 to 12.

Mrs. Angus Adams, Macon

POTATO SALAD

6 cups diced, salted, cooked potatoes
6 boiled eggs, diced
½ cup chopped sweet pickle
½ cup chopped celery

1 cup salad dressing
¼ cup prepared mustard
1/3 cup sugar
½ teaspoon salt

Place diced potatoes in a 4-quart bowl. In a separate bowl, mix together remaining ingredients. Pour this mixture over potatoes and mix well. Yield: About 2 quarts.

Mrs. Maynard Borntrager, Macon

RICH POTATO SALAD

¼ cup salad oil
2 tablespoons vinegar
1½ teaspoons salt
⅛ teaspoon pepper
4 cups diced, cooked potatoes
1 cup ripe olives

2 eggs, hard-cooked and diced
1 cup chopped celery
¼ cup dill pickles, chopped
¼ cup pimiento, chopped
½ cup mayonnaise

Blend first 4 ingredients together; pour over hot potatoes and toss. Set aside to cool. Cut olives from pits and add with rest of ingredients to potatoes; toss. Chill. Serves 6.

Mrs. Clifton Reed, Magee

TOMATO BLOSSOM SALAD

1 (3-ounce) package cream
    cheese
2 tablespoons prepared yellow
    mustard
¼ teaspoon salt

4 hard-cooked eggs, chopped
½ cup cucumber, chopped
¼ cup green onions, chopped
4 to 6 tomatoes

Mix cream cheese, mustard and salt together. Stir in egg, cucumber and onions. Peel and cut each tomato into 8 sections, cutting almost through the bottom. Spread sections out and fill with egg salad. Serves 4 to 6.

Mrs. Virginia Hicks, Fayette

CARROT SALAD

1 (6-ounce) package lemon
    gelatin
2 cups boiling water
1 (8-ounce) package cream
    cheese

1 (16-ounce) can crushed
    pineapple
1 cup pecans
1 large carrot, shredded or
    grated

Dissolve gelatin in hot water; when cool, mix thoroughly with softened cream cheese. Add pineapple, pecans and carrots. Mix well. Pour into 5 or 6-cup mold. Chill until stiff. Serves 6 to 8.

Mrs. W. E. Martin, Kosciusko

BEET SALAD

1 cup grated beets
1 cup hot dog relish
1 cup celery
1 package lemon gelatin

1 package plain gelatin
2 cups liquid
1 cup chopped nuts
small amount grated onion

Dissolve plain gelatin in ¼ cup cold water. Dissolve lemon gelatin in hot liquid from beets and water to make 2 cups. Cool. Combine with rest of ingredients, pour in oblong dish to jell. Cut in squares to serve or may be molded. Serves 8 to 10.

Mrs. George Cain, Jr., Jackson

RICE SALAD

4½ cups hot, cooked rice	2 hard-cooked eggs, diced
¼ cup salad oil	1½ cups sliced celery
2 tablespoons vinegar	¼ cup pimiento, chopped
2 tablespoons prepared mustard	1 small onion, minced
1½ teaspoons salt	½ cup mayonnaise
⅛ teaspoon pepper	¼ cup dill pickles, chopped
1 cup ripe olives, cut in large pieces	

Cook 1½ cups rice in 3 cups chicken broth. Blend together salad oil, vinegar, mustard, salt and pepper; pour over hot rice; toss and set aside to cool. Add remaining ingredients; toss. Chill thoroughly. Serve on lettuce leaf and garnish with extra sliced eggs. Serves 6 to 8.

Mrs. Rex Kimbriel, Greenville

·⟦Salad Dressings⟧·

A salad can be only as good as its dressing. However some dressings seem designed to turn a salad into a costume piece. Good salad dressings should complement, never repeat the salad ingredients they grace.

Main-dish salads made with meat, fish, poultry, eggs, beans, cheese or potatoes usually call for a mayonnaise-type dressing. Some are good with French or Italian dressing.

On vegetable salads and vegetable-fruit combinations, try French, Italian, Thousand Island, Roquefort or blue cheese dressings. Fruit salads taste best with sweet dressings such as sweet French, orange-honey, or celery seed dressings.

Prevent sogginess and wilting by using just enough dressing to moisten the salad ingredients. Add the dressing to raw vegetable salads at the last minute unless your recipe calls for marinated vegetables.

MAYONNAISE

1 egg	dash black pepper
1 teaspoon salt	dash paprika
¾ teaspoon sugar	1 tablespoon vinegar
¼ teaspoon dry mustard	1½ cups salad oil
dash cayenne pepper	1 tablespoon lemon juice

Place egg, salt, sugar, mustard, cayenne pepper, black pepper, paprika and vinegar in mixing bowl. Slowly add ½ cup salad oil, a tablespoon at a time, while beating at high speed. Gradually add remaining oil, then lemon juice, continue to beat at high speed for about 3 minutes or until thick. Yield: 2 cups.

Mrs. Clara Bartley, Liberty

MAYONNAISE

2 egg yolks	1 teaspoon salt
1 pint Wesson oil	dash red pepper
juice of 1 lemon	¼ teaspoon paprika
1 teaspoon vinegar	1 teaspoon boiling water

Have eggs and Wesson oil cold. In summer time, chill bowl and beater. Beat eggs until thick. Slowly add a small amount of oil until dressing becomes thick. Add lemon juice a few drops at a time, then more oil. Repeat until half the oil and all lemon juice and vinegar are used. Add salt, red pepper and paprika. Mix well, then add remainder of oil slowly. After all oil is used, add teaspoon boiling water. This will keep the mayonnaise from separating. Store in covered jar in refrigerator. Yield: 1 pint.

Mrs. W. A. McDonald, Hazlehurst

GARLIC MAYONNAISE

3 cloves garlic	1½ teaspoons Lea and Perrin
2 egg yolks	1 teaspoon French mustard
1 teaspoon salt	1 teaspoon horseradish
juice from 2 lemons	1 teaspoon celery seed
1 quart salad oil	½ teaspoon paprika
½ teaspoon sugar	

Dice the garlic very fine or put through garlic press. Beat the yolks a few minutes. Add a rounding teaspoon of salt, a little at a time. Beat well. Add the juice of ½ lemon. Beat well. (Beat until salt dissolves.) Add a few drops of oil at a time until you have added about 1 cup. Then alternate lemon juice and oil. When you have added about 1/3, add Lea and Perrin, mustard, horseradish, garlic, beating all the time. As soon as the last oil is added, add the celery seed and paprika. Taste may call for addition of most seasonings, depending on individual preferences. Yield: 4 to 5 cups.

Mrs. Edwina Belding, Mendenhall

LEMON MAYONNAISE

1 cup mayonnaise
1 tablespoon chopped bottled
    capers
¼ cup lemon juice

1 teaspoon prepared mustard
1 teaspoon salt
½ teaspoon white pepper

Combine all ingredients, mix well. Refrigerate until ready to serve. Delicious with seafood salad. Yield: 1 cup of dressing.

Mrs. Webster Meredith, Clarksdale

SANTE FE SALAD DRESSING

1 pint mayonnaise
½ cup buttermilk
3 tablespoons wine vinegar

2 tablespoons catsup
5 cloves of garlic (put
    through garlic press)

Blend all ingredients together well and store in refrigerator in covered jar. Will keep 2 weeks. Yield: 3 cups.

Mrs. C. T. Myers, Magee

SALAD DRESSING

1 cup mayonnaise
½ cup catsup
½ cup salad oil
½ cup chili sauce
2 cloves garlic, mashed
juice of ½ medium onion, grated

1 tablespoon black pepper
1 tablespoon Worcestershire
    sauce
2 teaspoons water
1 teaspoon mustard
dash of paprika

Put all ingredients in a bowl and mix well by hand. Store in refrigerator. Yield: 2 pints.

Mrs. Joyce W. Clark, Greenville

TANGY SALAD DRESSING

2 cloves garlic, grated or
  chopped fine
¼ cup onion, grated or
  chopped fine
¼ cup catsup
¼ cup chili sauce
1 teaspoon prepared mustard
1 teaspoon Worcestershire
  sauce

1 teaspoon paprika
½ cup salad oil
2 teaspoons lemon juice, OR
  1 teaspoon vinegar
1/16 teaspoon of Tabasco sauce
½ to 1 teaspoon salt
1 tablespoon water, for a thinner
  sauce
1 cup of mayonnaise

To grated garlic and onion, add other ingredients and blend well after each addition. Very good for mixed green salad and shrimp salad. Also good to serve with fried fish. Yield: 1½ cups.

Mrs. J. D. Mann, Fayette

ARGYLE DRESSING

4 egg yolks
1 teaspoon salt
1 cup sugar
dash red pepper
1 teaspoon mustard
4 tablespoons vinegar

1 teaspoon butter
1 cup cream, whipped
½ cup nuts, chopped
1½ cups miniature marsh-
  mallows

Beat egg yolks, add dry ingredients, mustard, vinegar and butter. Mix well. Cook in double boiler until thickened. Cool, fold in whipped cream, nuts and marshmallows. Store in refrigerator.

Mrs. Gene Norton, Guntown

GRAPEFRUIT DRESSING

3 egg yolks
2 tablespoons sugar
3 tablespoons butter
juice of 1 lemon

salt
paprika
1 cup cream, whipped

Cook and stir until thick, using low heat. Remove from heat and add juice of lemon, salt and paprika and again put back in double boiler and cook until thick. Remove and beat until cool. Add whipped cream. Pour over grapefruit sections. Delicious.

Mrs. Fred A. Tyson, Holly Springs

POPPY SEED DRESSING

¾ cup sugar
1 teaspoon salt
1 teaspoon dry mustard
1/3 cup vinegar

2 teaspoons onion juice
1 cup salad oil
1 tablespoon poppy seed

Combine sugar, salt and mustard. Add the other ingredients and blend all together in a pint jar until very smooth. Serve over fresh or canned fruits on lettuce leaves. This keeps well for a long time in refrigerator.

Mrs. S. G. Thigpen, Picayune

POPPY SEED DRESSING

½ cup salad oil
juice of 2 lemons
½ teaspoon grated lemon rind
1 teaspoon salt

3 tablespoons honey
1 tablespoon poppy seed
1½ teaspoons onion juice

Combine all ingredients and mix with blender or mixer at high speed. Bottled onion juice is all right to use, but flavor is best from a sliced onion. Serve over your favorite choice of fruit sections.

Mrs. Lute Ellison, Lexington

CELERY SEED DRESSING

1¼ cups sugar
2 teaspoons mustard
2 teaspoons salt
1 tablespoon onion juice

2/3 cup vinegar
2 cups salad oil
2 tablespoons celery seed

Combine sugar, mustard, salt, onion juice and ½ of the vinegar. Then gradually add the oil alternately with the remaining vinegar, and beat until a stable emulsion has been formed. Add the celery seed. Good on fruit salad. Keeps well.

Mrs. Jim Best, Yazoo City

FRUIT DRESSING

1 tablespoon cornstarch
4 tablespoons sugar
¼ teaspoon salt
juice of 1 lemon

juice of 1 orange
2 eggs, beaten
1 cup cream, whipped
1 cup pineapple juice

[73]

Thoroughly mix cornstarch, sugar and salt. Add fruit juices. Cook in double boiler until thick. Add eggs and cook 5 minutes, stirring constantly. Cool. Add whipped cream just before serving.

Mrs. Cecil Underwood, Picayune

LEMONADE DRESSING

1/3 cup undiluted frozen
   lemonade concentrate
1/3 cup honey

1/3 cup salad oil
1 teaspoon celery seed

Combine ingredients. Beat with rotary beater till smooth. Serve over fruit salad. May triple recipe. Keeps well in a jar in the refrigerator. Yield: 6 servings.

Mrs. J. E. Bourne, Grace

GOLDEN SALAD DRESSING

¼ cup pineapple juice
¼ cup orange juice
2 tablespoons lemon juice
⅛ teaspoon salt

1/3 cup sugar
2 well beaten egg yolks
2 stiffly beaten egg whites

Heat fruit juices to simmering stage. Add salt, beaten egg yolks and half of sugar. Beat egg whites stiff and add the rest of sugar. Just before removing from the range add the egg whites. Serve over fresh fruit salad. Yield: 1 cup.

Mary Jane Hall, Jackson

SALAD DRESSING

1 cup mayonnaise
1 cup catsup
¼ teaspoon garlic salt
¼ teaspoon black pepper
1 teaspoon Tabasco sauce
1 teaspoon white vinegar

¼ cup Worcestershire sauce
2 hard-boiled eggs,
   finely chopped
4 ounces American cheese,
   shredded

Blend in a blender or beat by hand until smooth. This is good for a green salad or boiled shrimp.

Mrs. O. W. Idom, Raleigh

COCKTAIL SAUCE

6 tablespoons tomato catsup
2 tablespoons horseradish
4 tablespoons lemon juice

celery salt
Tabasco sauce

Shake the ingredients in a jar or wide-mouthed bottle until well mixed. Use seasonings according to taste. Yield: 4 servings of 3 tablespoons each.

Mrs. Dolly G. Hill, Macon

REMOULADE SAUCE FOR SHRIMP SALAD

2½ cups mayonnaise
1 cup Zatarainis Creole
  mustard

1¼ tablespoons prepared
  horseradish

This is delicious over a salad made of salad greens, boiled egg slices, tomato wedges, boiled shrimp. Top with some anchovy filets, and then the sauce. Serve with crisp crackers.

Mrs. Ray Leeper, Pontotoc

ITALIAN SALAD DRESSING

½ cup mayonnaise
½ cup brown sugar
½ cup salad oil

½ cup catsup
1 tablespoon Italian seasoning

Combine all ingredients and pour into a 1-pint jar. Shake to a good emulsion and it is ready to use on green salads.

Mrs. Carl P. Holt, Raleigh

FRENCH DRESSING

1 (10¾-ounce) can
  condensed tomato soup
1 cup oil
½ to 1 cup vinegar
¾ cup sugar

1 teaspoon paprika
1 teaspoon garlic powder
1 teaspoon salt
1 teaspoon onion powder

Mix in quart jar and serve with green salad. Store in the refrigerator.

Mrs. R. A. Ward, West Point

[75]

FRENCH DRESSING

1 cup salad oil	3 tablespoons lemon juice
1 cup sugar	1 small onion, grated
2/3 cup catsup	1 teaspoon salt
½ cup vinegar	1 teaspoon paprika

Put ingredients in quart jar; shake well. Cover tightly. This dressing should be allowed to blend at least overnight. Shake well each time before using. Yield: Approximately 1½ pints.

Mrs. C. L. Ryan, Booneville

BEAN SALAD DRESSING

¾ cup granulated sugar	½ cup cider vinegar
½ cup onion, cut fine	1 teaspoon salt
½ cup green pepper, cut fine	1 teaspoon pepper
½ cup salad oil	

Blend together, cover, and chill several hours. Will keep a week refrigerated. Yield: 8 servings.

Mrs. C. C. Richardson, West Point

ROQUEFORT DRESSING

1 cup mayonnaise	½ pound Roquefort or
1 tablespoon lemon juice	blue cheese
1 cup coffee cream	

Combine mayonnaise, lemon juice and cream. Crumble the cheese into the mixture. Mix well. Store in refrigerator.

Mrs. V. L. Sandifer, Hollandale

ROQUEFORT DRESSING

1 pint sour cream	1 tablespoon lemon juice
1 pint mayonnaise	1 tablespoon sugar
½ pint salad dressing	½ teaspoon salt
2 tablespoons wine vinegar	6 ounces Roquefort cheese,
¼ teaspoon paprika	crumbled

Blend together all ingredients, except cheese. Add well crumbled cheese and stir slightly. Store in refrigerator overnight before serving. Yield: 6 cups.

Mrs. Dianne Walker, Wiggins

BLUE CHEESE DRESSING

6 ounces good blue cheese
1 cup buttermilk
2 tablespoons mayonnaise

¼ teaspoon garlic powder
½ teaspoon salt
dash of cracked black pepper

Mash cheese, add other ingredients. Delicious and not too "calorie laden."

Mrs. W. F. Brown, Port Gibson

CREAMY THOUSAND ISLAND DRESSING

½ cup mayonnaise or
  salad dressing
½ cup chili sauce
1 teaspoon Worcestershire
  sauce
dash of Tabasco
½ teaspoon salt
¼ teaspoon paprika

2 tablespoons chopped celery
2 tablespoons pickle relish
2 tablespoons chopped stuffed
  olives
1 teaspoon minced onion
1 hard-cooked egg, grated
½ cup sour cream

Combine mayonnaise, chili sauce, Worcestershire sauce, Tabasco, salt and paprika in quart bowl. Stir in celery, relish, olives, onion and egg. Mix well. Fold in sour cream. Chill. Sour cream is the secret to this creamy dressing. Yield: 1 pint.

Mrs. Johnnie Baker, Port Gibson

THOUSAND ISLAND DRESSING

1 onion, chopped
3 cloves garlic, chopped
¼ cup catsup
¼ cup chili sauce
½ cup oil
3 tablespoons water

1 cup mayonnaise
1 tablespoon Worcestershire sauce
1 teaspoon mustard
4 drops Tabasco
dash black pepper

Mix all ingredients in jar and shake well. Yield: 3 cups.

Mrs. A. G. Parkison, Sledge

SOUR CREAM DRESSING

1 cup sour cream
1 tablespoon grated onion
¼ cup tarragon vinegar
2 tablespoons sugar

½ teaspoon celery seed
⅛ teaspoon white pepper
1½ teaspoons salt
½ cup whipping cream

Mix ingredients in order given. Whip the cream and add last. This dressing is especially good on green salad, cold thick slices of tomatoes, cucumbers, potato salad, Waldorf salad, or mixed fresh fruit salad. Yield: 1½ cups.

Mrs. Georgia Mason, Clarksdale

CREAM CHEESE DRESSING

3 tablespoons chopped green onions
1 tablespoon chopped parsley
1 (2-ounce) can chopped anchovy filets
3 tablespoons tarragon vinegar
juice of 1 lemon
1 (3-ounce) package cream cheese
milk
1 cup mayonnaise

Put onions, parsley and anchovy filets in the vinegar and lemon juice. Cream the cheese to the consistency of mayonnaise by adding milk. Combine all the ingredients and mix well. Paprika or pimiento may be added for color. Yield: 2 cups.

Mrs. V. E. Cartledge, Dublin

COTTAGE CHEESE DRESSING

1 cup cottage cheese
¼ cup catsup
6 tablespoons vinegar
6 tablespoons oil
¼ teaspoon salt
¼ teaspoon pepper
¼ teaspoon paprika

Blend cheese with catsup, then add other ingredients gradually. Serve with green or tart fruit salads, or sliced tomatoes. Yield: 2 cups.

Mrs. Robert Carter, Clarksdale

TARTAR SAUCE

¾ cup mayonnaise
4½ teaspoons chopped onion
1 teaspoon chopped pickle relish, sour or sweet
1 teaspoon olives
1 tablespoon chopped parsley
2 teaspoons minced capers
2 tablespoons vinegar
2 tablespoons lemon juice

Combine all ingredients and mix. Yield: 1½ cups.

Mrs. Carter Dobbs, Calhoun City

DIETER'S DELIGHT DRESSING

1 (8-ounce) can tomato sauce
2 tablespoons vinegar
1 teaspoon onion juice
¼ teaspoon powdered basil

1 teaspoon Worcestershire
    sauce
½ teaspoon salt
½ teaspoon dill seed

Combine all ingredients in a bottle and shake. Chill and serve over salad greens. Yield: ½ pint.

Mrs. J. R. Westbrook, Egypt

WEIGHT WATCHER'S DRESSING

1 cup vinegar
½ cup salad oil
¾ cup catsup
2 tablespoons lemon juice

3 tablespoons brown sugar
dash of salt
1 onion, grated
½ teaspoon paprika

Mix together. Pour into bottle and shake well. Store in refrigerator. Thirty calories per tablespoon. Yield: 1 pint.

Mrs. David B. Phillips, Iuka

COME-BACK SALAD DRESSING

3 buttons garlic, grated
1 cup mayonnaise
¼ cup chili sauce
¼ cup tomato catsup
½ cup salad oil
1 teaspoon black pepper
juice of 1 lemon

salt to taste
1 teaspoon prepared mustard
1 teaspoon Worcestershire
    sauce
1 teaspoon paprika
dash of Tabasco
1 onion, grated

Mix all ingredients. Shake well in jar and chill. Serve over lettuce or combination salad. Yield: 1 pint.

Mrs. H. A. McCarley, Port Gibson

⁖[Meats]⁖

Most meals are planned around meat. It is a relatively expensive item in the food budget but occupies a central place in the meal since it contains many of the nutrients essential to health and is enjoyed by most people.

Certain cuts of beef, pork and lamb are delicious cooked alone. Others, especially ground beef and pork, are best combined with other ingredients to make tasty main dishes. Cuts differ in tenderness according to the part of the animal from which they are taken, and to the age and fatness of the animal. They also differ in the amount of bone and gristle they contain and in the direction the muscles run. The best quality meat has well-marbleized lean (intermingling of fat with lean), fine grained texture, and a color typical of the particular meat.

Fresh meat should be stored, uncovered or loosely covered, in the coldest part of the refrigerator. Closely cover cooked meat and wrap cured meat before storing in the refrigerator. Meat should be closely wrapped for freezing and stored at 0 degrees Fahrenheit.

Meat cooked at low to moderate temperatures is more tender, juicy, and flavorful than meat cooked at high temperatures. This also keeps shrinkage at a minimum.

Beef may be cooked rare, medium or well done. Lamb can be enjoyed either medium or well done. However pork should always be cooked well done. Broiling, pan-frying, and roasting are recommended for tender meats only. Less tender cuts are most satisfactorily prepared if braised, pot-roasted or simmered.

[81]

BAKED WHOLE HAM

1 ham	2 cups bread crumbs
water	2 tablespoons brown sugar
¼ cup sugar per quart of water	2 tablespoons molasses
	2 teaspoons prepared mustard
2 tablespoons vinegar per quart of water	2 tablespoons melted butter or butter substitute
cloves	

Wash ham. Place in large kettle. Cover with water. To each quart of water add ¼ cup sugar and 2 tablespoons vinegar. Place over slow heat. Heat slowly to boiling. Simmer until tender. Remove from heat. Let ham remain in broth until cold. Skin ham. Stick cloves in the fat at 1-inch intervals. Combine crumbs, brown sugar, molasses, mustard and butter or substitute. Spread on ham. Bake in slow oven, 325 degrees, until brown (about 3 hours). Baste with ham broth.

Norah B. Hales, Mendenhall

HAM AND SCALLOPED POTATOES

4 medium-sized potatoes, sliced	½ pound thinly sliced uncooked ham, cut in serving pieces
1 tablespoon grated onion	
2 tablespoons flour	salt and pepper
2 cups hot milk	

Put half of the potatoes into a greased baking dish. Sprinkle with half the onion, half the flour, and a little salt and pepper. Use salt sparingly. Add ham and cover with rest of potatoes, seasonings, flour and onion. Add milk until it barely shows between the potato slices on top. Save rest of milk to add during cooking if needed. Cover dish and bake at 350 degrees about 1 hour. Remove cover last 15 or 20 minutes to allow potatoes to brown on top. Serves 4.

Mrs. Leonia Suggs, Derma

HAM-POTATO PATTIES

1 cup mashed potatoes	1 tablespoon milk
1 tablespoon chopped onion	1 egg, beaten
¼ teaspoon dry mustard	½ cup fine dry bread crumbs
¼ teaspoon salt	shortening
2 cups ground cooked ham	

Combine potatoes, onion, mustard and salt. Add ham and chill about 1 hour. Shape mixture into 18 patties. Blend milk into egg. Dip patties in egg mixture and then in crumbs. Fry patties in deep hot fat until golden brown. Serve plain or with your favorite sauce. Serves 6.

Georgia L. Williams, Hazlehurst

HAM PIE

1 onion, chopped	3 tablespoons lemon juice
½ cup chopped bell pepper	2 cups chopped ham
½ stick oleo	1 can pimiento, chopped
6 tablespoons all-purpose flour	1 cup all-purpose flour
1 (10½-ounce) can condensed	½ cup grated cheese
cream of chicken soup	½ cup sweet milk
3 cups sweet milk	3 tablespoons lard

Sautè onion and pepper in oleo. Turn off heat. Add flour, chicken soup, milk, lemon juice, ham and pimiento. Cook until thickened. Pour into shallow casserole. Combine all other ingredients according to procedure for biscuits. Roll out, cut, and place cheese biscuits on top of pie. Bake in 375 degree oven until biscuits are lightly browned. Serves 6.

Miss Myrtie Mae Horton, Port Gibson

HAM TETRAZZINI

2 tablespoons chopped onion	1 cup diced cooked ham
1 tablespoon butter or	2½ or 3 cups cooked
margarine	spaghetti
1 (10½-ounce) can cream of	2 tablespoons chopped parsley
chicken soup	2 tablespoons chopped
½ cup water	pimiento
½ cup grated sharp cheddar	
cheese	

In saucepan, cook onion in butter until tender. Blend in soup, water and cheese. Heat until cheese melts. Stir often. Add remaining ingredients. Heat. Stir now and then. Serves 4.

Mrs. M. A. Randle, Canton

[83]

HAM HOCK WITH CORNMEAL DUMPLINGS

2 pounds ham hock
3 cups plain cornmeal
1 teaspoon salt

½ teaspoon black pepper
5 or 6 green onions

Boil ham hock 1½ hours or until tender. Sift and measure meal. Combine with dry ingredients. Sprinkle chopped green onions over and add enough ham hock broth to make a moderately stiff dough. Shape into small balls. Drop into remaining boiling broth with ham hock. Cook 20 to 25 minutes. The dumplings will remain whole and are delicious.

This recipe has been passed down for 5 generations in the Edwards family. It is said to be a favorite of the Confederate soldiers. It comes from the kitchen of Mrs. Ginny Shropshire Edwards, a noted Mississippi cook.

Mrs. Bill Johnston, Carthage

HAM LOAF

1¼ pounds smoked ham, ground
¾ pound pork shoulder, ground
2 eggs, beaten
1 cup milk
1 cup dry bread crumbs

½ teaspoon pepper
1 teaspoon salt
1 cup peach juice
½ teaspoon dry mustard
1 cup brown sugar
¼ cup vinegar

Mix first seven ingredients and shape into loaf. Bake in slow oven (325 degrees) for 1½ hours. Baste every 20 minutes with the rest of the ingredients which have been blended. Broil peaches from the juice and serve with loaf.

Rosalyn B. Ferguson, Canton

HAM LOAF

2 pounds ground fresh pork
1 pound ground cured ham
1 egg, beaten
1 cup bread crumbs
½ cup milk
3 tablespoons canned tomato soup
½ teaspoon paprika

½ teaspoon salt
1 medium onion
½ cup vinegar
½ cup tomato soup
½ cup prepared mustard
½ cup sugar
½ cup butter or margarine
3 egg yolks, beaten

[84]

Mix first 8 ingredients together and shape into a loaf. Place in pan and slice one medium onion over top. Bake in moderate oven (350 degrees) for 1½ hours, basting with a few tablespoons of hot water. Combine last of the ingredients and cook in double boiler until thick. Serve with the ham loaf. This sauce may be kept indefinitely in refrigerator.

Mrs. Lucille M. Green, Lorman

PORK STEAKS WITH RAISIN SAUCE

6 pork steaks, ½-inch thick
2 tablespoons shortening
½ teaspoon salt
3 tart red apples
3 cups toasted bread cubes
1½ cups chopped, unpared apples
½ cup seedless raisins

½ cup chopped celery
½ cup chopped onion
1 teaspoon salt
1 teaspoon poultry seasoning
¼ teaspoon pepper
1 beef bouillon cube dissolved in ½ cup hot water

Brown pork steaks on both sides in the shortening. Season with salt. While steaks are browning, core and halve the apples and make the raisin stuffing by tossing together the bread cubes, chopped apple, raisins, celery, onion, salt, poultry seasonings, pepper and beef bouillon broth. Place browned steaks in baking dish. Cover each with a layer of raisin stuffing and top with an apple half. Sprinkle with sugar. Cover dish tightly with foil. Bake in moderate (350 degrees) oven for 1 hour. Serves 6.

Mrs. Walter Dilworth, Rienzi

HAM STEAKS IN SKILLET

1-inch thick ham slice
½ cup brown sugar
1 tablespoon prepared mustard
1 teaspoon dry mustard

⅛ teaspoon powdered cloves
¼ cup pineapple juice
3 tablespoons vinegar

Slash fat edge of ham to prevent curling. Place ham in hot skillet and brown to a light brown. Turn and brown on other side. Reduce heat and cook about 15 minutes. Mix and add other ingredients. Cook 15 minutes more. Allow ½ pound per serving.

Mrs. Taylor Eaves, Louisville

QUICK BARBECUED SPARERIBS

1 cup chili sauce
½ cup chopped onion
2 tablespoons vinegar
1 tablespoon Worcestershire
  sauce
dash Tabasco sauce

½ cup flour
¾ teaspoon salt
¼ teaspoon paprika
dash of pepper
2 pounds lean spareribs or
  loin back ribs

Cut ribs into 6 serving pieces. Mix chili sauce, onion, vinegar, and Worcestershire and Tabasco sauces in pressure pan. Mix flour, salt, paprika and pepper. Dredge ribs in mixture. Place in sauce in pressure pan. Spoon sauce over ribs. Close pan and cook at 10 pounds pressure for 15 minutes. Allow pressure to go down normally. Remove meat to warm platter. Skim fat from sauce. Serve the sauce over the meat. Serves 6.

Mrs. Walter Dilworth, Rienzi

BARBECUED SPARERIBS

3 or 4 pounds ribs, cut in pieces
1 cup catsup
½ cup chopped onion
1/3 cup Worcestershire
  sauce

1 teaspoon chili powder
1 teaspoon salt
¼ to ½ teaspoon hot sauce
2 cups water

Place ribs in shallow roasting pan. Bake in 450 degree oven for 30 minutes. Combine all other ingredients and bring to a boil. Pour over ribs and cover pan with aluminum foil. Reduce oven to 350 degrees and continue cooking 1 hour or until tender. Baste ribs with sauce several times during cooking. If sauce becomes too thick, add more hot water.

Mrs. Mary Worsham, Iuka

BARBECUED RIBS

5 pounds of ribs
1 bottle barbecue sauce
1 cup mustard
2 cups tomato paste

1½ tablespoons salt
dash of black pepper
1 onion, chopped

Boil ribs until tender. Add salt and place in baking pan. Mix barbecue sauce well with mustard, tomato paste, chopped onions, and pepper and put over ribs. Place in oven and cook on 250 degrees for 40 minutes.

Mrs. Willie M. Dukes, Pachuta

APPLE STUFFED PORK ROAST

4 to 4½ pounds pork rib roast
¾ cup chopped celery
½ cup chopped onion
6 tablespoons butter or
  margarine
3 cups herb-seasoned stuffing
  mix

1½ cups chopped pared apple
¾ cup water
½ teaspoon salt
½ teaspoon dried rosemary,
  crushed

Have butcher loosen backbone and cut 8 pockets in rib roast. Cook celery and onion in butter or margarine until tender but not brown. In mixing bowl, toss together stuffing mix, apple, water, salt, rosemary, and celery mixture. Stuff about 1/3 cup of the mixture into each pocket of roast. Place roast, fat side up, in open roasting pan. Roast in moderate oven (325 degrees) about 2½ hours, or until meat thermometer registers 170 degrees. Bake remaining stuffing in small casserole last 30 minutes of roasting time. Remove backbone from roast before serving. Serves 8.

Mrs. Eugene Holcombe, Macon

FRENCH ONION PORK CHOPS

1 egg, slightly beaten
1 tablespoon evaporated milk
4 pork chops
½ teaspoon salt

¼ teaspoon pepper
¼ cup flour
2 tablespoons fat
1 can onion soup

Mix egg and milk. Season pork chops with the salt and pepper. Dip chops in milk and egg mixture. Dredge in flour. Brown chops in shortening until golden brown. Place in 1-quart baking dish. Cover with undiluted onion soup. Bake in slow oven (250 degrees) for 1½ hours. Serves 2.

Mrs. Larry Alexander, Carthage

PORK CHOPS WITH BROWNED RICE

6 pork chops
1 cup uncooked rice
2 cups canned tomatoes
1¼ cups water

2/3 cup chopped green pepper
½ cup chopped onion
1 teaspoon Worcestershire sauce
salt and pepper to taste

Brown pork chops in dutch oven or deep skillet with lid. Take pork chops from skillet and drain off excess fat. Brown rice in drippings stirring often until brown. Add remaining ingredients and mix well. Place pork chops on top. Cover and cook on low heat about 25 minutes. Turn off heat and let set on stove about 20 minutes longer. Serves 6.

Mrs. J. D. Mann, Fayette

PORK CHOPS AND RICE

1 small pork chop per serving
onions, sliced
bell pepper (optional)
1 tablespoon rice per serving

2 cups canned tomatoes and
juice
salt and pepper to taste

Brown pork chops on medium heat until brown. Place 1 slice onion on each chop and a ring of pepper, if used, on onion. Place 1 tablespoon rice in each pepper ring. The tomatoes and juice are then placed around pork chops. Salt and pepper to taste. Turn to high heat until steaming; then cook on lowest heat to maintain simmering. Cook covered until chops and rice are tender, about 45 minutes to 1 hour. Add water only if tomato juice is evaporated and absorbed.

Mrs. Vela M. Hunter, Greenville

STUFFED PORK CHOPS

2 thick pork chops
½ cup bread crumbs
¼ teaspoon salt
⅛ teaspoon pepper

1 teaspoon minced parsley
⅛ teaspoon grated onion
¼ cup diced apple
3 tablespoons milk

Have butcher cut a pocket on the bone side of each chop. Combine remaining ingredients and mix well. Stuff each chop with this mixture. Place in greased shallow pan and bake at 350 degrees about 1 hour, or until pork chops are tender. Serves 2.

Georgia L. Williams, Hazlehurst

PORK SKILLET MEAL

6 small potatoes, peeled
6 medium carrots
6 pork chops, ½ to ¾-inch
    thick

1 tablespoon salt
¼ cup chopped green pepper
¼ teaspoon black pepper
1 (8-ounce) can tomato sauce

Slice potatoes ½-inch thick and cut carrots in half lengthwise. Preheat large skillet on medium heat, lightly brown pork chops, turning once to brown evenly. Remove chops from skillet and pour off excess fat. Return chops to skillet arranging on the bottom. Sprinkle with salt. Layer potatoes and carrots on top of chops, sprinkling each layer with salt. Top with green pepper, sprinkle with black pepper, and pour tomato sauce over all. Cover and heat on medium until cover is hot. Reduce heat to low and cook 1¼ hours. Uncover and cook 15 minutes longer. Serves 6.

Mrs. C. E. McMillan, Enterprise

PORK CHOPS WITH MUSHROOM SOUP

6 thick pork chops
salt and pepper to taste
½ cup flour
3 tablespoons bacon grease

2 cups cold water
1 (10½-ounce) can mushroom
  soup
1 teaspoon Worcestershire sauce

Salt and pepper each side of pork chops then dredge in flour. Brown on each side in hot bacon grease. Place in casserole. Brown 3 tablespoons flour mixture in drippings. Add water, mushroom soup and Worcestershire sauce. Stir well and pour over pork chops. Bake 30 minutes at 350 degrees. Serves 6.

Mrs. Larry McClellan, Winona

BARBECUED BRISKET

6 or 7 pounds beef brisket
celery salt
onion salt
garlic salt

meat tenderizer
liquid smoke
barbecue sauce

Rub both sides of meat with each type of salt and the meat tenderizer. Then place in a roaster and pour the liquid smoke over the meat and let stand overnight. Pour off liquid smoke and cover beef with your favorite barbecue sauce. Bake in a 275 degrees oven for 6 hours. Chill before slicing. Slice very thin against the grain of the meat. Meat can be reheated in a moderate oven with barbecue sauce over the top. It can also be prepared ahead of time, frozen, then reheated without hurting the flavor. Serves 12.

Mrs. M. P. Moore, Senatobia

BEEF ROAST

4 pounds beef rump roast
1 bunch carrots
4 Irish potatoes, cut up
1 large onion
salt and pepper

1 (10½-ounce) can cream
  of mushroom soup
1 (10½-ounce) can cream of
  chicken soup (optional)

Place roast on heavy aluminum foil in shallow pan. Slice vegetables around. Add seasoning and soups. Wrap securely and bake at 450 degrees for 15 minutes, then 250 degrees for 3½ hours. Serves 8.

Mrs. R. C. Guthrie, Pontotoc

LEMON BAKED CHUCK ROAST

3 to 4 pounds chuck roast
2 tablespoons soft butter
1 teaspoon salt
¼ teaspoon pepper
1 large lemon, sliced
1 medium onion, sliced

¼ cup water
¾ cup catsup
1 tablespoon horseradish
  (optional)
2 tablespoons Worcestershire
  sauce

Rub roast with softened butter and place in large baking dish. Season and cover with lemon and onion slices. Combine catsup, Worcestershire sauce, and water, and pour over roast. Cover tightly so meat will steam tender. Bake in 350 degree oven 2 hours, or until tender. Serves 6 to 8.

Mrs. C. Bascom Hunter, Greenville

POT ROAST AND VEGETABLES

1 tablespoon fat
1 (3 to 4 pound) beef, chuck,
  or rump roast
salt and pepper

½ cup water
4 to 6 small potatoes
4 to 6 small onions
4 to 6 small carrots

Brown roast on all sides in hot fat in pressure pan. Season and add water. Cover and cook roast at 15 pounds pressure for 30 to 35 minutes. Let pressure return to normal. Open cooker, place vegetables on top of roast, and season. Cover and cook at 15 pounds pressure for 10 minutes longer. Serves 4 to 6.

Mrs. J. T. Kerr, Rolling Fork

PIZZA SWISS STEAK

¼ cup all-purpose flour
2 teaspoons salt
¼ teaspoon pepper
2 pounds round steak, 1 inch thick
3 tablespoons fat
1 (8-ounce) can (1 cup)
  seasoned tomato sauce

1 (5-ounce) can pizza sauce
½ cup water
½ teaspoon sugar
1 bay leaf
1 medium onion, sliced

Combine flour, salt and pepper. Pound into steak. Brown slowly on both sides in fat. Combine remaining ingredients and pour over meat. Simmer uncovered 10 minutes then cover and bake at 350 degrees for 1 hour or until tender. Add liquid if necessary to keep from drying out. Serves 6.

Kathryn L. Van Wick, Mendenhall

BAKED ROUND STEAK

1 (2 pound) round steak,	3 tablespoons oil
1 inch thick	1 (6-ounce) can tomato paste
1 clove garlic	1½ cups water
½ teaspoon salt	¼ teaspoon thyme
dash pepper	1 large sliced onion
¼ cup flour	1 green pepper, cut in rings

Cut steak into serving pieces. Trim off fat. Rub with garlic and sprinkle with salt and pepper. Pound flour into steak. Heat oil in large skillet. Brown steak on both sides, using moderate heat. Remove meat and place in casserole. Drain oil from skillet. Mix tomato paste, water and seasonings together and heat in the same skillet. Arrange onions and pepper rings over meat in casserole. Pour tomato mixture over all. Cover tightly with lid or aluminum foil. Bake in moderate oven (350 degrees) 1½ to 2 hours. Serves 6.

Mrs. Jeanne D. Williams, Bay St. Louis

BUSY DAY DINNER

1 round steak, size to fit	1 onion, sliced
family	1 (10½-ounce) can mushroom
meat tenderizer (optional)	soup
2 tablespoons flour	Worcestershire sauce (optional)
2 to 4 tablespoons cooking oil	salt and pepper to taste
1 potato for each person served	

Cut round steak in serving pieces. Pound, (or use a meat tenderizer) flour, and brown in 2 to 4 tablespoons cooking oil. Lower heat to simmer. Add 1 inch thick sliced potatoes. Slice a peeled onion over all. Add salt and pepper to taste. Pour mushroom soup over all, adding ½ can of water and Worcestershire sauce. Cover and simmer until fork tender (1½ to 2 hours). Several times during cooking, raise meat with spatula to prevent sticking.

Mrs. Larry Alexander, Carthage

BARBECUED ROUND STEAK

1 (2 pound) round steak
¼ cup seasoned flour
3 tablespoons shortening
1/3 cup minced onion
1/3 cup minced celery
1 small clove garlic
1 (10½-ounce) can tomato
   soup

2 tablespoons brown sugar
2 tablespoons Worcestershire
   sauce
2 tablespoons lemon juice
2 teaspoons prepared mustard
¼ teaspoon Tabasco sauce

Pound flour into steak. Melt shortening in skillet. Brown steak with onion, celery, and garlic. Combine remaining ingredients and pour over steak. Cook covered in oven at 350 degrees for about 1½ hours or until tender. Serves 6.

Mrs. Tressie Bonds, Iuka

BEEF STROGANOFF

1 (3 pound) sirloin steak,
   cubed
3 tablespoons shortening
1 large onion, chopped
4 tablespoons flour
1 can beef consomme
1 can tomato soup
1 (8-ounce) can mushrooms
   (optional)

1½ teaspoons Worcestershire
   sauce
1½ teaspoons Accent
½ teaspoon salt
½ teaspon black pepper
1 teaspoon paprika
1 cup sour cream

Remove gristle, fat, and bone from beef and cube. Brown beef in shortening. Add onion and cook for 2 or 3 minutes. Sprinkle flour over beef and mix well. Add consomme and tomato soup. Cook, stirring constantly, for a few minutes. Add mushrooms, Worcestershire sauce, Accent, salt and black pepper. Simmer for 1½ to 2 hours. (if roast is used, simmer until tender) stirring occasionally. When ready to serve, stir in paprika and sour cream and serve over rice. Serves 6 to 8.

    This dish freezes well. It may be frozen with the sour cream and paprika in, or frozen, thawed and heated and then the paprika and sour cream stirred in when ready to serve. This may also be served without the sour cream. Sirloin roast or rump roast may be used.

Mrs. M. A. Rowzee, State College

HAMBURGER STROGANOFF

½ cup chopped onion
1 clove garlic, minced
¼ cup oleo or butter
1½ pounds of ground beef
2 tablespoons flour
¼ teaspoon black pepper

2 teaspoons salt
1 (10½-ounce) can cream of
   chicken soup
1 (10½-ounce) can cream of
   mushroom soup
1 cup sour cream

Sautè onion and garlic in oleo until golden. Stir in meat, flour, and seasonings and cook for five minutes. Add soups and simmer, uncovered, for fifteen minutes. Stir in sour cream. Serve with rice, mashed potatoes or noodles. Serves 8.

Mrs. C. D. Morgan, Smithdale

BARBECUE BEEF PATTIES

1 cup soft bread crumbs
½ cup sweet milk
1 pound ground beef
½ cup chopped onion
2 teaspoons salt
¼ teaspoon pepper
2 tablespoons fat
¾ cup tomato juice
1 cup catsup

2 dashes Tabasco sauce
1½ cups water
1/3 cup Worcestershire sauce
1 tablespoon vinegar
1 teaspoon prepared mustard
2 tablespoons sugar
1 teaspoon chili powder
1 teaspoon salt

Moisten crumbs with half the milk listed in recipe then add beef, remaining milk, onion, 2 teaspoons salt and pepper. Mix well and shape into large patties. Brown on both sides in hot fat. Mix a sauce of the remaining ingredients and simmer on low heat for 15 minutes. Place patties in a 1½ quart casserole dish and pour basting sauce over them. Cook for 15 minutes longer in oven at 350 degrees.

Mrs. Freeman Livingston, Louisville

Y'ALL COME MEAT LOAF

3 pounds ground beef
1 package dried onion soup mix
3 whole eggs, beaten
12 crackers, crumbled
½ cup drained canned tomatoes
1 small can evaporated milk

3 tablespoons Worcestershire
   sauce
1 (10½-ounce) can cream
   of mushroom soup
1 soup can hot water

Mix beef, soup mix, eggs, crumbs, tomatoes, milk, and Worcestershire sauce together until ingredients are well mixed. Make into several loaves and place in baking dish. Bake in a 450 degree oven until well browned. Blend the can of mushroom soup with 1 soup can of hot water. Mix well and pour over meat loaf. Return to oven and bake until the sauce is brown, basting at intervals. Serve hot.

Mrs. E. B. Wray, Sr., Duck Hill

15-MINUTE MEAT LOAF

1½ pounds ground beef
1½ teaspoons salt
1⅛ teaspoons pepper
2 tablespoons chopped onion
2 tablespoons chopped green
   pepper

2 cans tomato sauce
2 tablespoons sugar
¼ tablespoon Worcestershire
   sauce

Combine beef, salt, pepper, onion, green pepper, and ½ can tomato sauce. Press into greased 9 x 12 x 2-inch baking dish and bake on lowest shelf in hot oven (450 degrees) for 10 minutes. Then broil 5 minutes longer. While meat is cooking, combine remaining ingredients and bring to boil for about 3 minutes. Add meat drippings, if desired. Cut meat in half crosswise, arrange sandwich fashion on a platter, pour tomato sauce mixture between and on top of meat loaf. Serves 6.

Mrs. A. T. Barrentine, Greenwood

APPLE POTATO MEAT LOAF

1 pound ground beef
1 medium apple, grated
¼ cup chopped green pepper
½ teaspoon black pepper

1 medium potato, grated
¼ cup chopped onion
½ teaspoon salt
1 egg

Mix all ingredients. Turn into a foil-lined loaf pan. Bake in 350 degree oven for 1 hour. Turn onto serving platter. Serves 6.

Miss Wilma Roberts, Carriere

MEAT LOAF

1½ pounds ground beef
1 cup medium bread crumbs
1 package onion soup mix
2 eggs, beaten
¼ cup catsup

¼ cup water
1 small can evaporated milk
1 (10½-ounce) can cream of
   mushroom soup
1½ cups grated cheese

Place the first 7 ingredients in a large mixing bowl and mix well. Shape meat mixture into 2 long loaves and place in a greased baking dish or foil casserole pan. Cover loosely with foil and bake at 350 degrees for 40 minutes. Remove foil and continue baking 15 minutes longer. Heat mushroom soup and cheese until cheese is melted. Slice meat loaf on platter. Just before serving pour cheese mixture over loaf. Serve hot. Serves 6 to 8.

This meat loaf can also be baked on top of range using a heavy cookware. Make in small loaves, turning once, and cook on low heat for one hour.

Mrs. Leola Childers, Ashland

APPLESAUCE MEAT LOAF

2 pounds ground beef
3 eggs, beaten
2 teaspoons salt
1 teaspoon seasoning salt
1 teaspoon garlic salt
1 tablespoon steak sauce
1 tablespoon Worcestershire
  sauce
¼ teaspoon black pepper
1 cup tomato juice
¼ cup catsup
½ cup chopped onion
¼ cup chopped bell pepper
1 cup rolled wheat
¾ cup applesauce
1/3 cup catsup

Leave ground beef in the refrigerator until all other ingredients are mixed in a large bowl. Place 1/3 cup catsup in dispenser and set aside. Measure carefully and combine all ingredients except applesauce. Remove the ground beef from the refrigerator and mix thoroughly with the other mixture. Add applesauce last and mix gently. Divide the mixture into two equal parts and pack firmly into two foil lined 3 x 5½ x 9½-inch loaf pans. Using the catsup dispenser, squeeze a design onto the top with the additional catsup. Bake in 350 degree oven for one hour. Remove from pans and peel away the foil and place onto platter, or platters, and garnish with spiced apple rings or spiced crab apples. Each loaf pan will serve 8 to 10.

Mrs. Edna E. Cupit, Meadville

MEAT LOAF

2½ pounds ground meat
1 cup shredded cheese
½ cup chopped green pepper
1 cup chopped onions
2½ cups crushed bread
  crumbs
4 eggs, beaten
2½ cups tomato paste
½ teaspoon black pepper
1 teaspoon salt

Mix meat, cheese, green pepper, onions and bread crumbs; then eggs, tomato paste and seasonings. Mix all ingredients and make into loaf. Put into greased 9 x 13-inch loaf pan, and bake 1 hour at 350 degrees. Serves 12.

Mrs. U. G. Richmond, Walnut Grove

SWEDISH MEAT BALLS

1 pound ground round steak	2 tablespoons margarine
¼ cup cracker crumbs	2 beef bouillon cubes
2/3 cup finely chopped onion	1½ cups boiling water
1 teaspoon salt	1 cup evaporated milk
dash pepper	1 tablespoon flour
2/3 cup evaporated milk	juice of one lemon

Dissolve bouillon cubes in boiling water and set aside. Mix beef, cracker crumbs, onion, salt, pepper, and 2/3 cup milk. Form into small balls. (Balls will be juicy but they should be!) Heat margarine in heavy skillet. Add meat balls to this and brown slowly. Next, add the dissolved bouillon broth. Cover skillet securely and simmer on low heat for 15 minutes.

To the 1 cup of evaporated milk, add the flour. Mix until dissolved. Add to skillet of beef balls and broth. Stir in milk-flour mixture until well mixed. Cook until gravy thickens (approximately 10 minutes). Add lemon juice at end of cooking period. Serve on hot egg noodles.

Mrs. Mary S. Parkman, Monticello

PARTY MEAT BALLS SERVED WITH DUNKY SAUCE

1 pound ground beef	½ cup catsup
½ cup corn flake crumbs or crackers	2 tablespoons brown sugar (or more)
½ cup evaporated milk	2 tablespoons finely cut onion
¼ cup finely chopped onion	2 tablespoons pickle relish, drained
¼ cup catsup or chili sauce	
1 tablespoon Worcestershire sauce	2 tablespoons water
1 teaspoon salt	2 tablespoons Worcestershire sauce
1 teaspoon pepper	1 tablespoon vinegar
1 (8-ounce can) tomato sauce	a few grains of pepper

Mix first 8 ingredients well in a 2-quart bowl. With wet hands, shape meat ball mixture into 36 small meat balls using about a teaspoon for each. Place in 13 x 9 x 2-inch pan. Bake in 400 degree oven 12 to 15 minutes, or until as brown as desired.

Mix all remaining ingredients in a 2-quart saucepan. Cook slowly until onions are tender. Sauce may be served separately or add to the meat balls.

Mrs. J. K. Worrell, Greenwood

BARBECUED MEAT BALLS

1½ pounds ground beef
2 teaspoons salt
½ cup milk
¼ teaspoon black pepper
1 cup catsup

¼ cup Worcestershire sauce
3 tablespoons chopped onion
1 teaspoon sugar
2 tablespoons vinegar
1 tablespoon water

Mix ground beef, salt, milk and black pepper. Shape into sixteen meat balls. Brown in saucepan in small amount of fat. Drain off excess fat. Mix catsup, Worcestershire sauce, onion, sugar, vinegar and water. Pour over meat balls. Cover tightly and simmer for ten minutes. Serves 4.

Mrs. Joseph M. White, Hazlehurst

MEAT BALL SUPREME

2 eggs
1 cup applesauce
1 cup dry bread crumbs
2 teaspoons salt
¼ teaspoons pepper
2 pounds ground beef
2 tablespoons chopped onions

¼ cup finely chopped celery
2 tablespoons grated carrots
2 tablespoons plain flour
2 cups tomato juice
¼ teaspoon salt
2 teaspoons sugar

Beat eggs in large mixing bowl. Stir in applesauce, bread crumbs, salt and pepper. Then add ground beef and mix thoroughly. Shape into 1 ½-inch balls. Brown in ½-inch deep fat in a heavy skillet. Remove browned balls to a 2-quart casserole dish. Leave 2 tablespoons fat in skillet and add vegetables. Cook until tender but not brown. Stir in flour and add tomato juice, ¼ teaspoon salt, and 2 teaspoons sugar. Cook until it thickens. Pour this mixture over the meat balls and bake in 350 degree oven for 30 to 35 minutes. This may be kept frozen. Serve with crisp salad and baked potatoes for a complete meal.

Mrs. Mae Betty Kelso, Calhoun City

BEEF WITH EGG DUMPLINGS

2 pounds beef chunk
1 cup diced celery
1 cup diced onion
2 medium potatoes, diced
(about 1½ cups) (optional)
2 teaspoons salt
⅛ teaspoon pepper
1 teaspoon monosodium
glutamate

3 or 4 quarts water, as needed
2 cups flour
½ teaspoon salt
1 teaspoon baking powder
½ cup shortening (not butter
or margarine)
3 eggs
½ cup butter

Remove fat, bone and gristle from beef and cut into bite-size pieces. Combine first 8 ingredients in dutch oven or large saucepan. Cover with water and simmer, do not boil, for about 2 hours until meat is fork tender. With slotted spoon remove meat from broth. Cover and keep warm while preparing dumplings.

Sift together flour, ½ teaspoon salt, and baking powder. Cut in shortening. Make well in center. Add whole, unbeaten eggs and stir with fork until dough forms a ball. A little water may be added, depending upon size of eggs; however, if eggs are small, it would be better to add an additional egg. Knead dough in hands if it seems dry at first, and it will become pliable. Divide dough into four pieces for easier rolling. Roll into a rectangle, about the thickness for pie dough. Sprinkle flour over each piece. Place one on top of the other with flour in between. Cut into ¼-inch strips, shaking loose as you cut.

Add ½ cup butter to boiling broth. Drop dumplings into liquid slowly. Reduce heat to simmer and cook 30-45 minutes, until dumplings are very tender. Time depends upon the thickness of strips, which resemble thick noodles; but do not dry before using. Stir occasionally to prevent sticking. Do not cover pan. After dumplings are tender, return meat to top of dumplings. Cover and reheat as necessary over low heat. Serves 6 to 8.

Leftover dumplings are good fried. To fry: Lightly brown ½ cup chopped onions in skillet with ½ cup butter, margarine, or drippings. Cube 1 cup soft bread and add to butter and onions. Stir until crisp and lightly browned. Add leftover dumplings and fry until brown, using spatula to turn when bottom is browned. Any leftover meat may be diced, and added before serving. It is not necessary to drain dumplings unless a great deal too much water has been added in the beginning. Broth on dumplings thickens as it cools. Serve fried dumplings with cream gravy.

Mrs. V. T. Kissel, Sr., Biloxi

SOUTHERN BURGERS

2 pounds ground beef
4 tablespoons catsup
1 onion, chopped
4 tablespoons mustard

1 (10½-ounce) can chicken
    gumbo soup
toasted buns

Brown beef and onions in a little fat, stir in catsup, soup and mustard. Cover and simmer until mixture has thickened, about 15 minutes. Spoon over toasted split buns.

Mrs. Magnolia Brown, Pachuta

MOCK FILET

1 pound ground beef
1 cup cracker crumbs
1 egg, beaten
1/3 cup catsup
¼ cup lemon juice

1 cup grated cheese
¼ cup chopped green pepper
2 tablespoons chopped onion
salt and pepper to taste
bacon slices

Combine all ingredients except bacon. Preheat oven to 300 degrees. Make into patties and wrap ½ slice of bacon around each patty. Bake 15 to 20 minutes.

Mrs. Charles Rayburn, Pontotoc

CHILI HAMBURGER

3 pounds ground beef
3 onions, chopped
1 button garlic
½ bunch celery
½ can tomato paste (sauce)
salt and pepper to taste

2 tablespoons catsup
2 (no. 2) can tomatoes
2 teaspoons Worcestershire
    sauce
3 teaspoons chili powder

Fry ground meat in skillet until brown or done. In another vessel, combine remaining ingredients. Cook until done, about 30 minutes. Add to meat mixture and cook a little longer, or to right consistency to spread between buns.

This is better if cooked ahead of time and heated to serve. Makes enough for 36 buns.

Nancy R. Bush, Raleigh

LIZ'S SPAGHETTI SAUCE

1 pound ground beef
2 tablespoons shortening
½ cup chopped onions
1 (2½-ounce) package of Chef
    Boyardee spaghetti sauce mix
1 tablespoon chili powder
½ teaspoon red pepper and
    cayenne
½ teaspoon garlic salt
½ teaspoon onion salt
1½ teaspoons oregano
1 teaspoon salt
½ teaspoon black pepper
2 (16-ounce) cans stewed
    tomatoes
1 (8-ounce) can tomato sauce

Brown ground beef and onions in shortening. Drain off excess shortening. Add spaghetti mix, chili powder, red pepper, cayenne, garlic salt, onion salt, oregano, salt, pepper, stewed tomatoes and tomato sauce. Bring to a boil and simmer from 45 minutes to 1 hour (stirring often to prevent sticking). A little water may be added if it becomes too thick. Serve over long spaghetti (cooked according to directions on package) and sprinkle with Parmesan cheese. Serves 6.

Mrs. Clyde Ray Lazarus, Meadville

SPAGHETTI

½ pound chopped bacon
2½ pounds ground beef
2 cups finely chopped onion
1 cup finely chopped green
    pepper
6 garlic cloves, finely chopped
3 (2-pound 3-ounce) cans
    Italian plum tomatoes
3 (6-ounce) cans tomato paste
1 cup dry red wine
4 teaspoons oregano
4 teaspoons basil
1½ cups water
½ cup chopped parsley
2 teaspoons thyme
1 bay leaf
2 teaspoons salt
½ teaspoon black pepper

Fry bacon until crisp in a wide 6-quart saucepan. Remove bacon and all but a teaspoon of fat. Save bacon and extra fat. Add ground beef, breaking with a spoon, and cook until brown, stirring occasionally. Stir in onion, green pepper, and garlic and cook 10 minutes. Add more bacon fat if needed. Mash plum tomatoes with spoon and stir in tomatoes, tomato paste, and bacon. Add wine, oregano, basil, and all other ingredients. Bring to boil, reduce heat and simmer 3 hours. Serve over hot spaghetti. Serves 12.

Gayle Harpe, Carthage

QUICK & EASY SUPPER DISH

2 tablespoons butter or
  margarine
1 cup elbow macaroni
2 cups tomato juice
½ pound ground beef

¼ cup chopped onion
1 teaspoon salt
½ teaspoon black pepper
1 cup grated cheese

Melt butter or margarine in large fry pan over medium heat. Add macaroni and stir, thoroughly coating with fat. Add tomato juice, bring to rapid boil, stir in ground beef, onion, salt and pepper. Cover, reduce heat to low for 15 minutes. Stir, and sprinkle cheese over mixture. Then remove from heat, cover, and let cheese melt. Serves 6 to 8.

Mrs. Everett Westmoreland, Tupelo

BEEF SKILLET FIESTA

1 pound beef stew meat
1 tablespoon salad oil
¼ cup diced onion
2 teaspoons salt
1 teaspoon chili powder
¼ teaspoon black pepper
1 (1 pound) can tomatoes

1 (12-ounce) can whole kernel
  corn
1¼ cups bouillon or 1 bouillon
  cube dissolved in 1¼ cups
  boiling water
1/3 cup thin strips green
  pepper
1 1/3 cups minute rice

Brown meat in oil over high heat in skillet, leaving meat in coarse chunks. Add onion, and reduce heat to medium. Cook until onion is tender but not brown. Add seasonings, tomatoes, corn, and bouillon and bring to boil. Stir in green peppers, then boil again and stir in rice. Remove from heat, cover and let stand 5 minutes. Fluff with fork. Serves 4.

Mrs. Eugene Boutwell, Newton

STUFFED BELL PEPPERS

8 bell peppers
1 pound ground beef
1 (no. 2) can tomatoes
2 tablespoons Worcestershire
  sauce
1 cup minced onion

1 tablespoon bacon drippings
½ pound sharp cheddar
  cheese, grated
1 teaspoon salt
¾ cup minute rice

[101]

Cut peppers in half, lengthwise. Remove top and seeds then cover with water and bring to a boil. Boil 3 minutes. Drain. Meanwhile, sautè beef and onions in bacon drippings until brown. Add tomatoes, sauce and salt. Simmer for 20 minutes. Add rice, cover, and simmer 5 minutes. Remove from heat. Add 1 cup grated cheese. Stuff the peppers with the mixture and put in baking dish. Cut remainder of cheese in strips and put on each pepper. Bake at 350 degrees for 15 to 20 minutes. Serve hot.

Mrs. Spence Townsend, Winona

TAMALE PIE

1 pound lean ground beef	2½ cups yellow cornmeal
1 medium onion, chopped	2 teaspoons salt
1 medium green pepper,	1 teaspoon chili powder
chopped	1 large can red beans, drained
1 clove garlic, minced	1 (12-ounce) can whole kernel
2 (8-ounce) cans tomato sauce	corn, drained
1½ tablespoons chili powder	½ cup sharp cheddar cheese,
salt and pepper to taste	shredded
5 cups water	stuffed green or ripe olives

In a large skillet lightly brown beef with onions, green pepper and garlic. Pour off fat. Stir in tomato sauce, chili powder, salt and pepper. Simmer, uncovered, 20 minutes. Meanwhile combine water, cornmeal, 2 teaspoons salt and 1 teaspoon chili powder in heavy saucepan. Bring to a boil over medium heat. Cook about 10 minutes, stirring constantly, until thickened. Lower heat and continue cooking. Stir occasionally until very thick. With back of spoon press two-thirds of cornmeal mixture against sides and bottom of a greased 13 x 9 x 2-inch baking dish. Reserve remaining cornmeal mixture for top crust. Stir beans and corn into meat mixture, and pour into cornmeal crust. Spoon remaining cornmeal mixture around edge of casserole. Sprinkle with cheese. Bake at 350 degrees for 40 minutes. Garnish with olives. Serves 8 to 10.

Mrs. Gertrude B. Broadus, Purvis

CORN CHIP PIE

1 pound ground meat	1 can white hominy
1 medium onion, chopped	¾ cup water
1 package Chili-O	corn chips
1 can tomatoes	cheese

Brown ground meat and onion. Add Chili-O and stir well. Add tomatoes, hominy and water and stir well. Cover and cook over low heat for 30 minutes. Pour into greased casserole dish, sprinkle corn chips over top, and grate cheese over corn chips. Place in 400 degrees oven for 10 minutes or until mixture bubbles and cheese melts. Serves 6 to 8.

NOTE: Chili-O is a package of chili mix. If this is not available, chili powder may be substituted. Use the amount suggested for chili on the container.

Mrs. Ginger Crowell, Picayune

CHINESE HAMBURGER CASSEROLE

1 pound ground beef
2 tablespoons salad oil
1 large onion, chopped
1 (10½-ounce) can cream
of mushroom soup
1 (10½-ounce) can cream
of chicken soup

1½ cups warm water
½ cup uncooked rice
2 tablespoons soy sauce
¼ teaspoon black pepper
1 (3-ounce can) chow
mein noodles

Brown ground beef in hot salad oil until slightly crumbly. Add chopped onion, mushroom and chicken soups. Rinse out the soup cans with the warm water and add the water to mixture. Stir in rice, pepper and soy sauce. Pour into lightly greased 1½-quart casserole dish. Cover and bake in 350 degree oven for 30 minutes. Remove cover and continue baking for 30 minutes longer. Cover mixture with chow mein noodles and bake for another 15 minutes. Serves 6 to 8.

Mrs. Charles Patterson, Kosciusko

CORNED BEEF CASSEROLE

1 (8-ounce) package noodles
1 (12-ounce) can corned beef,
flaked
½ pound diced American
cheese

1 (10½-ounce) can cream of
mushroom soup
1 cup milk
½ cup chopped onion
1 cup buttered bread crumbs

Cook noodles according to directions on package. Drain well. Add corned beef, cheese, soup, milk and onion. Pour into buttered 2-quart casserole dish. Top with buttered crumbs. Bake at 350 degrees for 45 minutes. Serves 6 to 8.

Mrs. Hershall Stephens, Booneville

TALLERINE

1 large onion, chopped
1½ pounds ground beef
1 package egg noodles
1 can whole kernel corn

1 (no. 2) can tomato juice
1 (10½-ounce) can cream of
  mushroom soup
½ pound cheese, grated

Brown onion in skillet, add ground beef, and cook until done. Cook egg noodles as directed on package, then add to ground beef. Add remaining ingredients, reserving part of the cheese to sprinkle on top. Bake at 350 degrees for 30 minutes in a 8 x 8 x 2-inch baking dish.

Mrs. B. F. Clements, Black Hawk

TEXAS HASH

3 large onions, sliced
1 large green pepper, minced
3 tablespoons fat
1 pound ground beef
1 cup uncooked rice

2 cups cooked tomatoes
1 teaspoon chili powder
1 teaspoon salt
⅛ teaspoon black pepper

Cook onion and green pepper in fat until yellow. Add ground beef and fry until mixture falls apart. Stir in rest of ingredients. Pour into a greased 2-quart casserole. Cover and bake 1 hour at 350 degrees. Remove cover the last 15 minutes of cooking. Serves 8 to 10.

Mrs. F. F. Bynum, Mendenhall

LAMB—CARROT BALLS

1 pound lamb (ground)
1 cup ground raw carrots
1 egg, beaten
1 teaspoon salt
⅛ teaspoon pepper

2 teaspoons minced onions
shortening
2 tablespoons flour
1 1/3 cups meat stock or water

Mix ground lamb and carrots together real well. Add egg, salt, pepper and minced onions. Shape into balls. Roll in flour and fry in skillet until browned. (Melt enough shortening to cover bottom of skillet for frying the balls.) Cover skillet and cook slowly 10 minutes. Remove to serving dish. Stir 2 tablespoons flour into drippings left in skillet. Add 1 1/3 cups meat stock or water and cook until thickened. Serve with the meat balls. Serves 4.

Mrs. Henry Steller, Bay St. Louis

CHICKEN SPAGHETTI

1 large hen
1 large onion, chopped
1 stem of celery, chopped
salt and pepper
2 pounds onions, chopped and
  lightly browned in butter
2 (no. 2) cans tomatoes
1 can tomato paste or 2 cans
  tomato sauce
4 large cloves garlic, minced
salt to taste (about 1½
  teaspoons)
red pepper to taste
2 cans button type mushrooms
½ pound sharp American
  cheddar cheese, grated
1 package spaghetti

Cover hen in water to which is added one large onion and stem of celery, salt and pepper. Cook hen until meat falls off bone easily. Add about 1 cup water to remainder of ingredients except spaghetti and cheese. Cook slowly until cooked down fairly low. Add cooked chicken in medium sized pieces (remove skin). Add grated cheese and simmer 30 minutes. In water where chicken was cooked, boil spaghetti. Bring stock to rolling boil, add spaghetti, cover tightly, turn off heat, and let steam for about 30 minutes. Add to chicken stock mixture, simmer for 20 minutes or just keep hot.

Mrs. Nettie Dyess, Hickory

TURKEY MONAY

2 cups milk
¼ cup flour
1 teaspoon paprika
½ teaspoon salt
2 tablespoons butter or
  margarine
1 (4-ounce) can mushroom
  slices, drained
½ cup grated cheddar cheese
¼ cup grated Parmesan cheese
1 (10-ounce) package pie crust
  mix
1 (10-ounce) package broccoli
  spears
8 slices cooked white
  turkey meat

Heat 2 cups milk in double boiler set over hot water. Mix together flour, paprika, and salt. Knead flour mixture into softened butter or margarine. Add enough milk to blend thoroughly and then add to remaining milk. Cook about 20 minutes or until sauce is thickened and has lost any trace of flour taste. Add mushroom slices, cheddar cheese, and Parmesan cheese. Stir until all cheese is melted. Leave sauce in covered double boiler till ready to serve.

Meanwhile, prepare the pie crust mix. Roll out to ⅜-inch thickness, slice into 8 diamond shapes about 3 inches long and 2 inches wide. Bake on ungreased cookie sheet at 400 degrees for 7 minutes until golden color.

Cook the frozen broccoli spears as directed on package. Drain and place a pastry diamond on each plate. Cover with a broccoli spear and white turkey. Pour sauce over each serving. Serves 8.

Mrs. Luther Johnson, Starkville

LIVER AND ONIONS

¼ cup cooking oil
1 pound liver
1 teaspoon salt
⅛ teaspoon pepper

¼ cup flour
½ cup water
4 large onions, sliced
1 cup tomato juice

Cut liver into ½ inch slices. Roll in seasoned flour. Brown in oil. Pour tomato juice over onions and liver. Reduce heat and cook about 30 minutes or so. Add more water if need to keep liver from sticking. Serves 6.

Mrs. C. L. Tunnell, Pontotoc

SPICED BEEF

10 pounds round of beef
3 tablespoons salt peter
2 cups salt
2 cups molasses

2 tablespoons ground allspice
2 tablespoons ground cloves
1 tablespoon ground nutmeg

Rub beef with salt peter, then place in a large crock. Pour the remaining ingredients over it. Let beef stand in the mixture in a cool place for 21 days, turning it each day.

Remove beef from marinade and tie closely with cloth. Put in a kettle of cold water and bring to a boil. Boil until the meat is tender, which will take several hours. Let cool in the water it was cooked in. Slice spiced beef paper thin and serve with rye bread or biscuits.

If a rolled roast is used, you need not treat the meat over 7 days, but follow same cooking instructions. Serves 20.

Mrs. M. P. Moore, Senatobia

TACOS

1 pound ground beef
1 to 2 pods hot pepper
½ of small can tomato sauce

1/16 teaspoon garlic powder
grated cheese to cover
taco shells

Chop peppers and add with salt and garlic powder to ground beef. Mix in tomato sauce. Simmer covered for 30 minutes or until meat is done. Stir often. Place meat into taco shells. Sprinkle with grated cheese and place on a cookie sheet. Place in a 350 degree oven for 3 or 4 minutes. Serve with tomatoes and lettuce. Makes 7 or 8 tacos.

Mrs. George Tuberville, Sr., Vaiden

CALHOUN COUNTY BRUNSWICH STEW

1 large baking hen
1 large fryer
5 pounds ground beef
5 pound ground pork
6 squirrels
½ cup oil or ½ pound of butter
2 small packages of spaghetti
5 pounds Irish potatoes
2 pounds onions
2 (no. 303) cans of corn

2 (no. 303) cans of English peas
1 (no. 303) can of lima beans
1 (32-ounce) bottle tomato catsup
1 gallon tomato juice
3 tablespoons hot sauce
3 tablespoons Worcestershire sauce
6 pods of red pepper
1 teaspoon black pepper

Pressure cook all meat until it is well done. Let cool and take out all bones. Season with salt to taste.

Cook spaghetti according to directions on package and drain in colander. Cook potatoes and onions and salt to taste. Dice in small pieces. Mix all ingredients in large container and simmer for 6 hours stirring frequently to prevent sticking or scorching.

More hot sauce may be added if desired after it finishes cooking. Makes from 4 to 4½ gallons.

Mrs. W. B. Griffin, Calhoun City

CABBAGE ROLLS

½ pound ground beef
½ cup uncooked minute rice
1 tablespoon diced onion
1 head of cabbage
½ teaspoon salt
2 teaspoons paprika

½ teaspoon sage
1 (10½-ounce) can tomato soup
¼ cup sweet milk
½ cup brown sugar

Sautè meat, rice, onion together in skillet. Boil cabbage head to loosen leaves, then remove from water and drain. Add seasonings to skillet and remove from heat. Mix ½ can of soup to meat mixture. Pile about a tablespoon full of meat mixture on end of leaf. Roll and tuck ends in and fasten with toothpicks. Place cabbage rolls in pan. Mix remainder of soup with milk, pour over rolls. Sprinkle brown sugar over top. Cover with foil. Put in 350 degree oven. In ½ hour check, and baste with juice. Continue to cook for 45 minutes. If necessary, remove cover to cook out juice.

Mrs. Kelly Ivy, Jackson

HUNGARIAN GOULASH

1 pound boneless beef stew meat
cooking oil or other fat
1 clove garlic, minced
2 medium onions, sliced
2 teaspoons paprika
1 teaspoon salt
½ teaspoon pepper
2 beef bouillon cubes
3 cups boiling water
2 cups cubed potatoes

Dissolve beef cubes in 2 cups hot water. Cut meat into 1 inch cubes. Brown in hot oil. Add garlic, onions, seasonings, and bouillon to meat. Cover and simmer for 2 hours. Add remaining 1 cup hot water and potatoes. Cook for 20 minutes, or until potatoes are tender. Add more seasoning if needed. If necessary, thicken with small amount of cornstarch or flour blended in broth; stir in. May be served over rice, parsley noodles or cornbread squares.

Mrs. Jacqueline Mikell, Port Gibson

CHILI

1½ pounds ground beef
1 large onion, chopped
2 garlic buds, minced
1 tablespoon butter or
  margarine
1 (8-ounce) can tomato
  sauce
2 tablespoons chili powder
1 (1 pound) can tomatoes
1 tablespoon paprika
1 teaspoon cumin
1½ teaspoons minced hot red
  pepper
salt to taste
1 large can red beans
  (optional)

Sautè ground beef, onion, garlic buds in butter until ground beef is no longer pink. Add other ingredients. Cook slowly for 2 hours or longer. Cooked or canned red kidney beans may be added after chili is cooked.

Mrs. Harold H. Robertson, Booneville

NEW ENGLAND DINNER

1 pound stew meat, about ¼ fat   ½ medium cabbage
3 medium Irish potatoes   3 stalks celery
3 medium onions   1 tablespoon flour
3 medium carrots

Boil stew meat until almost tender. Add vegetables and cook until tender, about 20 minutes. Arrange on platter, the stew meat in center and vegetables around. Thicken broth with 1 tablespoon flour and season with pepper, bay leaf and spices. If desired, pour over dinner. Serves 4.

Mrs. Robert Riley, Indianola

⸭Poultry⸭

Fried chicken is a speciality that appears frequently in Southern menus. A certain brand of shortening, a particular spice, a method of cooking— each homemaker has her own secret for delicious fried chicken.

Chicken and turkey are good sources of high-quality protein, plus iron, thiamine, riboflavin and niacin. Weight watchers are partial to chicken and turkey because an average serving contains fewer calories than the same serving of most other meats. Ducks and geese are delicious whether roasted on a spit over hot coals or cooked to a golden brown in the oven.

Chilled and frozen poultry are sold whole or cut in halves, quarters or serving pieces. There are numerous frozen and canned poultry products on the market also. The class name on poultry usually suggests the cooking method. In addition to the basic methods of cooking, there is a wide variety of recipes that feature poultry in main dishes, casseroles, salads, sandwiches and snacks.

CHICKEN BREASTS

6 whole chicken breasts
4 tablespoons butter
1 large onion, chopped
1 garlic clove, minced
1 tablespoon flour
¾ cup brandy

½ cup consommé
¾ teaspoon salt
⅛ teaspoon pepper
1 (8-ounce) carton sour cream
1 (2-ounce) can mushrooms

Sautè chicken in butter, place in casserole. In skillet where chicken was browned, put onion and garlic. Add flour, mix well until brown. Add brandy, consommé, salt and pepper and stir until smooth. Turn off heat and add sour cream and mushrooms. Pour over chicken; cover and bake at 350 degrees for 1 hour. Serves 6.

Mrs. L. A. Rather, Jr., Holly Springs

STUFFED CHICKEN BREAST

8 halves of boned chicken breast
8 thin slices of cooked ham
8 thin slices cheese
8 teaspoons drained mushroom
bits
salt
seasoned pepper
toothpicks

1 cup evaporated milk
1 cup cracker meal
2 cups cooking oil
2 (10¾-ounce) cans steak
gravy with mushrooms
butter

Bone chicken breast with small sharp knife. Place in center of each chicken breast 1 slice ham, 1 slice cheese, 1 teaspoon mushroom bits, salt and seasoned pepper to taste. Pull edges of meat and skin over and fasten with a couple or three toothpicks. Dip the stuffed breast in the undiluted evaporated milk, roll in cracker meal until well coated. Drop in hot oil just long enough to sear over and lightly brown. Place in a fairly deep casserole dish. Pour over the steak gravy with mushrooms. Dot lightly with butter and cover casserole tightly with foil. Place in a 325 to 350 degree oven and let cook undisturbed for 1 hour and 45 minutes. If extra large chicken breast or the entire breast is used, cook an additional 30 minutes. Serve piping hot with a little gravy spooned over each breast. Serves 8.

Mrs. Margaret Clark, Columbia

BAKED CHICKEN BREAST SUPREME

6 chicken breasts, large
2 cups sour cream
¼ cup lemon juice
4 teaspoons Worcestershire
   sauce
2 teaspoons celery salt
2 teaspoons paprika
4 cloves garlic, finely chopped
4 teaspoons salt
½ teaspoon pepper
1¾ cups bread crumbs or
   dried croutons
½ cup margarine
½ cup shortening

Cut breasts in half; remove skin. In a large bowl, combine the next 8 ingredients. Layer chicken into mixture, covering well. Cover and stand in refrigerator overnight. Next day set oven at 350 degrees. Remove chicken from mixture and roll in crumbs, covering completely. Arrange closely in single layer in a large shallow baking pan. Melt margarine and shortening in small saucepan and spoon half over chicken. Bake chicken uncovered 45 minutes. Spoon rest of margarine and shortening over chicken and bake 10 to 15 minutes longer. Serves 12.

Mrs. Hazel H. Bequette, Mayersville

PRETTY POPPY CHICKEN DINNER

5 whole chicken breasts
½ cup all-purpose flour
1 teaspoon paprika
1 tablespoon Parmesan cheese
½ cup salad oil
½ teaspoon salt
¼ teaspoon black pepper
1 cup water
1 (10½-ounce) can cream of
   chicken soup
1 (16-ounce) can chopped
   onions, drained
1 (3½-ounce) jar sliced mushrooms, drained
2 cups pancake or waffle mix
1 tablespoon poppy seed
1 tablespoon celery seed
3 tablespoons onion flakes
½ cup grated sharp cheese
¾ cup sweet milk
2 cups soft bread crumbs
1 cup melted oleo or butter
1 (10½-ounce) can cream
   of mushroom soup
1 cup sour cream

Cut chicken off bone and cut into 2-inch pieces. Coat with flour, paprika and Parmesan cheese. Brown in salad oil. Add salt, pepper and water. Simmer 30 minutes, or until chicken pieces are tender. Put into a deep 2½-quart ungreased casserole dish. Coat well with chicken soup. Add onions and mushrooms and mix well.

Sift pancake mix with poppy seed and celery seed. Add onion flakes

[113]

and cheese and mix well. Add milk and mix until all ingredients are moistened. Drop dumplings by tablespoons into bread crumbs and roll in butter. Cover contents in casserole with 14 to 16 poppy seed dumplings and bake 15 to 20 minutes at 375 degrees until dumplings are brown. Combine cream of mushroom soup and sour cream and bring to a boil. Serve in gravy boat. Serves 8.

Mrs. Herbert R. Brown, Mendenhall

CHICKEN'N'EIGHT

meaty pieces of 2 to 3½ pound broiler-fryer (legs, thighs, wings and breast)
½ cup cooking oil
2 tablespoons Durkee's famous sauce
1/3 cup all-purpose flour
2 teaspoons salt
⅛ teaspoon pepper
1/3 cup chopped onion
1 cup chopped celery
2 (6-ounce) cans V-8 vegetable juice
1 teaspoon brown sugar
2 teaspoons Worcestershire sauce
2 drops Tabasco sauce
1 clove garlic

Cut chicken into handy, eating-size pieces. Pat the pieces of chicken dry with paper towels. Put salad oil in electric skillet; set thermostat at 350 degrees. With a pastry brush, coat each piece of chicken well with Durkee's famous sauce. Put the flour, salt and pepper in a paper sack. Drop chicken, two pieces at a time, into the paper sack, and shake, coating each piece well; when the skillet has reached the proper temperature, drop in the chicken and brown well on all sides. Take chicken out of skillet and pour off ¼ cup of salad oil. Add onions and celery to the oil remaining in the skillet and cook until clear, but not brown. Add V-8 vegetable juice, brown sugar, Worcestershire sauce, Tabasco and clove of garlic with a toothpick stuck through it. Stir sauce and put chicken back in the skillet. Cover the skillet close the steam vent, turn control to "simmer' and let cook 30 to 45 minutes or until chicken is tender and sauce has thickened. If sauce becomes too thick before the chicken is tender, add a little hot water. When the chicken is done, remove the garlic on the toothpick and discard. Serve chicken and sauce with hot rice. Serves 4 to 6.

Mrs. W. T. Coker, Bude

CHICKEN—"DANNY"

1 (5-pound) hen
1 (10-ounce) package noodles
1 cup chopped onions
1 cup chopped celery
1 cup chopped bell pepper
1 cup chopped mushrooms
1 stick oleo
1 (8-ounce) package cream cheese
1 (10½-ounce) can mushroom soup
10 to 12 large green stuffed olives, chopped

Boil 5-pound hen until tender. Cut meat into bitesize pieces. Boil noodles in chicken stock until almost tender. Let stand in broth. Sautè onions, celery, pepper, mushrooms in oleo. Melt cream cheese in this mixture. Add to chicken. Add soup. Add olives. If needed, add 1 cup chicken stock. Use 1 large or several small casseroles. Bake in pre-heated oven 300 degrees about 45 minutes or until well heated. Serves approximately 20.

Mrs. J. Henderson Young, Jackson

CHICKEN IN WHITE WINE SAUCE

3 (2-pound) chickens
2 teaspoons monosodium glutamate
1½ teaspoons salt
freshly ground black pepper
4 tablespoons olive oil
½ cup plus 2 tablespoons dry white wine
¼ pound sliced mushrooms
1 cup sour cream
½ teaspoon Tabasco sauce

Season chicken with monosodium glutamate, 1 teaspoon salt and pepper. Sautè in olive oil for 10 minutes or until golden brown. Add ½ cup wine, cover and simmer for 30 minutes. Remove chicken to serving dish and keep hot. Add mushrooms and remaining 2 tablespoons of wine to sauce remaining in skillet and simmer for 5 minutes, stirring frequently. Remove from heat, stir in sour cream, Tabasco and remaining ½ teaspoon salt. Return to heat and simmer gently for 2 minutes or until thoroughly blended, stirring constantly. To serve pour sauce over chicken. Serves 6.

Mrs. Kathryn Van Zandt, Jackson

[115]

GLAZED CHICKEN

1 (3-pound) cut-up chicken
½ cup packed light brown sugar
1 tablespoon honey
1 (8¼-ounce) can crushed pineapple
6 cloves
1 cup flour
¼ cup vegetable oil

Have chicken pieces dried on paper towel. Combine sugar, honey, pineapple and cloves. Dust chicken with flour. In large skillet, heat oil and brown chicken on all sides. Pour pineapple sauce over the fried chicken in the skillet and let simmer with cover on for 45 minutes. Serves 6.

Mrs. Louise Frasier, Fayette

SWEET AND SOUR BAKED CHICKEN

7 chicken breasts
1 cup flour
2 teaspoons salt
½ teaspoon pepper
2/3 cup salad oil
1 cup vinegar
6 tablespoons light brown sugar
2/3 cup chopped sweet pickles
2 tablespoons Worcestershire sauce
2 tablespoons catsup

Skin chicken and wipe well with damp paper towel. In clean bag combine flour, salt and pepper. Shake pieces of chicken in mixture. Heat oil slowly in skillet. Brown chicken on both sides. Place skin side up in 13 x 9 x 2½-inch baking dish. Preheat oven to 350 degrees. In small bowl combine vinegar and sugar, stirring to dissolve sugar. Blend in remaining ingredients. Brush chicken with sauce and pour the rest over chicken. Bake covered for 30 minutes. Baste with sauce and bake 15 minutes more. Serve with sauce spooned over. Serves 7.

Mrs. Hazel Smith, Picayune

TANGY CHICKEN

¼ cup olive oil
¼ cup vinegar
¼ cup lemon juice
¼ teaspoon garlic salt
¼ teaspoon thyme
¼ teaspoon pepper
1 (2-pound) chicken, cut-up

Mix olive oil, vinegar, lemon juice, garlic salt, thyme and pepper. Place chicken in greased 2-quart casserole dish. Pour mixed ingredients over chicken and bake uncovered at 350 degrees for about 1 hour or until chicken is a golden brown. Baste often while chicken is cooking. Serves 4.

Mrs. W. J. Ward, Louisville

EASY CHICKEN DELIGHT

1 stick oleo
1 (1⅜-ounce) package dry
   onion soup mix

1 cup rice, uncooked
fryer parts
salt and pepper

Melt oleo in skillet. Add remaining ingredients in order listed. Cover and bake at 350 degrees for 1 hour. Serves 6.

Mrs. H. L. Wells, Coila

CHICKEN DISH

chicken thighs or parts
salt and pepper
¼ cup oil
1 (10-ounce) can mushroom
   soup

1 (2-ounce) can mushrooms
½ cup rice (optional)
1 soup can of water (optional,
   for more gravy)

Salt and pepper chicken. Brown in oil. May be browned in oven, if preferred. Remove to 2-quart casserole dish. Combine soup, mushrooms and rice and pour over chicken. Bake at 325 degrees for 1 hour, or until tender. Serves 4 to 6.

Mrs. George Morley, Skene

DIRTY RICE WITH CHICKEN

1 chicken
3 large onions, chopped
1 large bell pepper, chopped
2 large pieces of celery, chopped
3 buds of garlic, chopped
3 tablespoons cooking oil

2 (10¾-ounce) cans beef
   gravy
2 cans broth from chicken
2½ cups uncooked rice
½ tablespoon crushed red
   pepper
salt to taste

Boil chicken until tender, remove bones. Cook onions, pepper, celery and garlic in a heavy pot until wilted. Add gravy and chicken broth and stir. Add rice, stir from bottom. Add chicken, red pepper and salt. Stir ingredients until they boil. Put lid on and reduce heat to simmer, let cook until rice is tender and dried out. More broth from boiled chicken may need to be added to cook rice. Stir often. Serves 6 to 8.

Mrs. O. A. Stovall, McComb

CHICKEN RICE CASSEROLE

1½ cups cooked, chopped
   chicken
1 cup chopped celery
1 tablespoon chopped onion
1 (10½-ounce) can cream of
   chicken soup
1 cup slivered almonds, toasted

2 cups cooked rice
1 teaspoon lemon juice
½ teaspoon salt
½ teaspoon pepper
½ cup mayonnaise
½ cup water
3 hard cooked eggs, chopped

Combine all ingredients and pour into buttered 2-quart baking dish or individual casseroles. Cover and bake for 20 or 30 minutes at 350 degrees. Serves 10 to 12.

Mrs. William Kirk, Louisville

CHICKEN RICE CASSEROLE

4 tablespoons butter
½ cup minced onion
1 cup sliced mushrooms
1 (10¼-ounce) can cream of
   chicken soup
½ cup light cream

¼ cup dry sherry
3 cups cooked rice
3 cups cooked, diced chicken
2 tablespoons chopped pimiento
salt and pepper to taste
3 tablespoons slivered almonds

Melt butter in skillet; sautè onion and mushrooms for 5 minutes. Mix together soup, cream and sherry. Stir in rice, chicken, pimiento and sautèd vegetables. Add salt and pepper to taste. Turn into a buttered 2-quart dish and sprinkle with almonds. Bake at 375 degrees for 20 minutes or until hot. Serves 6 to 8.

Mrs. R. H. Walters, Clarksdale

BAKED CHICKEN AND RICE

1 fryer, cut up
1 teaspoon salt
1 teaspoon paprika
¼ teaspoon pepper
1 cup uncooked rice

½ cup chopped onion
2 tablespoons butter
3 cups of chicken broth or
   boiling water
1 teaspoon celery salt

Sprinkle chicken with salt, pepper and paprika. Brown rice and onion in butter. Spread rice mixture in a 13 x 9 x 2-inch buttered baking dish. Add broth and celery salt. Place chicken on top of rice broth mixture.

Cover dish tightly with foil. Bake at 350 degrees for 1 hour. Remove cover and bake 15 minutes longer, or until meat is tender. Serves 5.

Mrs. Marvin Hogue, Yazoo City

QUICK CHICKEN CASSEROLE

¼ cup butter
1 cup uncooked rice
1 (10½-ounce) can onion soup

1 (2-pound) chicken, cut up
salt and pepper to taste

Place chopped butter in bottom of 2-quart casserole. Pour rice over butter and add soup. Place chicken on top. Sprinkle with salt and pepper. Bake at 325 degrees for 1 hour. Serves 5.

Mrs. Caroline Anderson, Brookhaven

BARBECUED CHICKEN

1 quartered chicken
salt and pepper
1 stick oleo

¼ cup vinegar
1 (5-ounce) bottle Worcestershire sauce

Salt and pepper chicken to taste. Place in baking pan and dot with oleo. Add vinegar and Worcestershire sauce. Cook in oven at 450 degrees for 45 minutes to 1 hour, basting often. Chicken will be very brown and sauce thick. Serves 4.

Lynette Perkins, Marks

BARBECUED CHICKEN IN A SACK

2 (3-pound) broiler-fryers
2 clean, medium brown paper bags

¼ cup salad oil
¼ cup chili sauce
¼ cup bottled barbecue sauce

If possible, salt chickens ahead and leave them in refrigerator 2 or 3 hours, or overnight. Rub paper bags, inside and out with salad oil. Place a chicken in each bag and place in a covered roaster or shallow roasting pan. Stir chili sauce and barbecue sauce together. Pour half over each chicken, right in bags; close bags with twist'ems. Place cover on roaster or cover shallow roasting pan with foil. Bake 1½ to 2 hours at 375 degrees or until they are fork-tender. For smaller chickens, cook less time.

Mrs. Genevieve Harris, Hazlehurst

ROAST CHICKEN IN A BAG

1 (5-pound) roasting chicken	½ teaspoon pepper
1 lemon, halved	paprika
¼ cup butter, softened	½ cup cooking oil
1½ teaspoons salt	

Rinse and dry chicken; rub with lemon. Combine butter with salt and pepper. Coat chicken well with mixture, covering back lightly. Sprinkle with paprika; chill. Stuff chicken lightly with desired stuffing. Pour oil into brown paper bag; shake until bag is well oiled. Put bag in pan; put chicken in bag, breastside up. Twist end of bag shut; turn end under. Cook at 325 degrees for 4 hours. Do not open bag while cooking.

Mrs. Ethel A. Richardson, West Point

TURKEY COOKED IN BROWN PAPER BAG

1 small turkey	3 or 4 teaspoons paprika
1 cup peanut oil	salt and pepper
2 tablespoons hot water	1 heavy brown paper sack

Wash turkey. Mix oil, water and paprika well. Rub onto turkey inside and out with your hand. Pour remaining oil mixture into the bag and let it run all over and coat it well. Put turkey, breast side up in the bag and tie bag tight with a string (string and bag will not burn.) Place in shallow pan or roaster. Cook 15 to 20 minutes per pound in a preheated 325 degree oven. Be careful in opening bag to prevent being burned by steam.

Mrs. S. L. Ball, Greenwood

CHICKEN IN THE JUG

1 frying size chicken	salt and pepper

Cut up the fryer. Salt and pepper generously. Put chicken in clean, dry, large bean pot (large caserole dish may be used). Seal with foil and put top on tightly. Bake 3 hours in 300 degree oven. Serves 5.

Mrs. Hal DeCell, Rolling Fork

HERBED OVEN FRIED CHICKEN

1 (2½ or 3-pound) chicken	¼ teaspoon black pepper
1 1/3 cups cornflake crumbs	2/3 teaspoon salt
1½ teaspoons herb seasoning	1 egg, beaten slightly
⅛ teaspoon onion salt	1 teaspoon milk

Cut chicken into serving pieces. Place crumbs and seasonings in paper bag. Shake thoroughly. Mix egg and milk. Dip chicken pieces into egg mixture and then into seasoned crumb mixture. Line shallow baking pan with heavy duty foil. Slightly grease foil. Place chicken pieces on foil. Do not crowd. Bake in 350 degree oven 45 to 50 minutes or until tender. For a less crisp crust, lay a piece of foil over chicken.

Mrs. B. L. Jones, Kosciusko

OVEN FRIED CHICKEN

1 broiler-fryer chicken	1 teaspoon paprika
½ cup fine bread crumbs	¼ teaspoon pepper
2 teaspoons salt	¼ cup corn oil

Cut fryer into 8 pieces. Combine crumbs, salt, paprika and pepper. Brush each piece of chicken with corn oil; roll in crumb mixture. Place in shallow baking pan, skin side up. Bake at 425 degrees for 25 to 30 minutes or until chicken is tender.

Mrs. Bryan A. Prevost, McCool

FRIED CHICKEN

1 chicken, cut up in 4 or 6 pieces	1 teaspoon meat tenderizer
2½ cups all-purpose flour	1 tablespoon salt
¼ teaspoon baking powder	½ teaspoon black pepper
1 teaspoon Accent	¼ cup sweet milk
	1 egg yolk, slightly beaten

Add all dry ingredients together in a brown paper bag. Mix sweet milk and egg yolk; dip chicken in mixture. Dredge in dry ingredients and cook in deep very hot cooking oil until brown. Serves 4 to 6.

Mrs. Lou Emma Herring, Pope

OLD FASHIONED CHICKEN PIE

1 large fryer, cut up	1 egg
3 teaspoons salt	½ teaspoon salt
3 cups flour	black pepper
1 cup shortening	

Cook chicken with salt in water until tender. Remove from bone, if preferred. Place ½ of chicken and broth in bottom of baking dish. Have plenty of hot broth. Mix flour and shortening well. Beat egg. Add enough water to make ½ cup. Add this with salt to flour mixture. Do not overwork. Roll ½ of pastry on floured board, cut in strips and drop small pieces in broth, enough to cover chicken. Add remainder of chicken and broth. Add margarine evenly to each layer. Add pepper each time. Roll remainder of pastry to cover top. Place in oven, cook at 350 degrees for 1 hour. Serves 8.

Mrs. Selma Bostick, Belmont

CHICKEN POT PIE

1 (2-pound) cut up fryer
1 medium onion
4 cups water
1 chopped carrot
¾ of (1 pound) can English peas
¼ (2-ounce) can pimiento

1 tablespoon chopped green pepper
salt and pepper
2 cups flour
4 tablespoons baking powder
5 tablespoons shortening
2/3 cup milk

Cook chicken with onion and water until done. Remove from broth and chop into small pieces. Set aside. Add carrot, English peas, pimiento, and green pepper to broth; cook until done. Add chopped chicken and season with salt and pepper to taste. Thicken with flour and water paste. Place in a 1½ x 9 x 11-inch casserole dish. Mix flour, baking powder, shortening, 1 teaspoon salt and milk. Roll out and place on top of chicken mixture. Bake at 500 degrees until crust is brown. Serves 8.

Mrs. Caroline Anderson, Brookhaven

CHICKEN PIE

1 (3-pound) chicken
3 cups stock
½ cup chopped celery
1 small onion, chopped
2 diced medium carrots
1 diced medium potato
2 cups English peas

4 tablespoons butter
4 tablespoons flour
2 chopped hard boiled eggs
3 cups sifted flour
1½ teaspoons salt
1 cup shortening
5 to 6 tablespoons ice water

Cook chicken covered in water with salt to taste, until it is tender. There should be about 3 cups of stock when done. Cut chicken into bite size pieces. Boil all vegetables together about 20 minutes. While vegetables are cooking, melt butter in a large skillet. Add flour and brown. To this add the 3 cups of stock and simmer until thickened. Add vegetables, chicken and eggs to sauce. Season with salt and pepper.

Stir flour and salt into mixing bowl. Blend in shortening with fork until mixture resembles coarse meal. Add water and blend. Divide pastry into 1/3 and 2/3 parts. Roll out the 2/3 part to fit a quart casserole. Pour chicken mixture into lined casserole and cover with the 1/3 part of dough. Prick top with fork. Bake at 425 degrees for 25 to 30 minutes or until crust is brown as you desire. Serves 4.

Mrs. Ruel Ewing, Brooksville

CHICKEN DIVINE

½ cup uncooked rice
2 whole chicken breasts
1 (10-ounce) package frozen broccoli
3 tablespoons butter

3 tablespoons flour
½ teaspoon salt
1 cup chicken stock
1 cup evaporated milk
½ cup grated cheese

Cook rice. Steam chicken breasts in small amount of water until tender. Cook broccoli according to directions on package. Line a 9-inch square casserole dish with rice. Place boned chicken breast on top of rice. Place broccoli spears on top of chicken breast. Melt butter over low heat in saucepan. Stir in flour and salt. Gradually add 1 cup chicken stock. Add evaporated milk. Stir in grated cheese until smooth. Pour cheese sauce over ingredients in casserole dish. Bake in 350 degree oven for 30 minutes or until bubbly. Serves 2.

Mrs. Stewart Vail, Booneville

TURKEY DIVINE

1 (10-ounce) package frozen asparagus spears
4 servings of sliced turkey

1 (10¾-ounce) can cream of mushroom soup
1/3 cup milk
½ cup grated cheese

Preheat oven to 450 degrees. Cook asparagus by directions on package and drain. In 1½-quart baking dish place asparagus and arrange turkey slices on top. Pour soup and milk in a bowl and blend together. Pour over turkey and sprinkle with cheese. Bake 15 minutes. Serves 3.

Mrs. Fran Noble, Fayette

CHICKEN SALAD SUPREME

1 (2½ to 3-pound) cooked
   hen
1 cup seedless white grapes or
   seedless red grapes
1 (5-ounce) can water chestnuts
   (optional)
1 cup slivered almonds

1 cup diced celery
1½ cups mayonnaise
1½ teaspoons curry powder
1 tablespoon soy sauce
1 tablespoon lemon juice
½ cup toasted slivered almonds

Remove chicken from bone and cut in bite-size pieces. Mix chicken, grapes, chestnuts, celery and the cup of slivered almonds. Then mix mayonnaise, curry powder, lemon juice and soy sauce, and add to the chicken. Mix well. Serve on pineapple slices or crisp lettuce leaves. Top with mayonnaise and ½ cup toasted slivered almonds. This will serve 12 to 15.

Mrs. John Mahaffy, Booneville

CHICKEN SALAD

3 cups chopped cooked chicken
1½ cups diced celery
3 hard cooked eggs, chopped

½ cup sweet pickle relish
½ cup chicken broth
mayonnaise

Cook chicken in water, salted to taste, till tender. Cool; remove from bone. Chop fine. Combine chicken, celery, eggs, pickle, broth; moisten with mayonnaise. Chill. Serve on lettuce. Garnish with stuffed olives. Serves 8.

Mrs. J. C. Jenkins, Kosciusko

HOT CHICKEN SALAD

2 cups chopped cooked
   chicken (2 whole breasts
   will do)
¾ cup mayonnaise
1 (10½-ounce) can cream of
   chicken soup
¼ cup water

2 tablespoons grated onion
salt and pepper to taste
¼ cup chopped green pepper
⅛ teaspoon cayenne (optional)
2 boiled eggs, chopped
1½ cups cooked rice
½ cup crushed potato chips

Mix chicken with mayonnaise and soup. Add other ingredients, except potato chips. Pour into a greased 2-quart casserole and top with crushed potato chips. Cook about 25 minutes or until bubbly hot in a 350 degree oven. May be made the day before for the seasonings to really meld. Serves 6 to 8.

Mrs. Kathryn Drane, Clarksdale

HOT CHICKEN SALAD

2 cups cubed cooked chicken
2 cups chopped celery
½ cup chopped pecans
½ teaspoon salt
2 tablespoons grated onions
½ cup chopped green pepper
½ cup mayonnaise

2 tablespoons chopped pimiento
2 tablespoons lemon juice
½ (10½-ounce) can undiluted
  cream of chicken soup
½ cup grated American cheese
1½ cups crushed potato chips

Mix all ingredients except cheese and chips. Put into a 2-quart casserole dish. Mix cheese and potato chips and spread over top of first mixture. Bake at 350 degrees for 25 minutes. Serves 8.

Mrs. Webster Cleveland, Jr., Booneville

HOT TURKEY SALAD SOUFFLE

6 slices bread
2 cups chopped turkey or
  other fowl
½ cup chopped onion
½ cup chopped green pepper
½ cup chopped celery
½ cup mayonnaise

¾ teaspoon salt
2 eggs, beaten
1½ cups milk
1 (10½-ounce) can cream of
  mushroom soup
½ cup grated cheese
½ cup slivered almonds

Cube 2 slices of bread and place in bottom of 8 x 12-inch baking dish. Combine turkey, onion, green pepper, celery, mayonnaise, salt and spoon over bread cubes. Top mixture with 4 slices of bread which has been cubed.

Combine beaten eggs and milk; pour over mixture. Cover and chill 1 hour or overnight. Spoon cream of mushroom soup over top and bake in 300 degree oven 1 hour, or until set. Sprinkle cheese and almonds over top last few minutes of baking. Serves 6 to 8.

Mrs. Leonard Edwards, Greenville

SMOTHERED CHICKEN

2 fryers
salt and pepper
flour
juice of ½ lemon

2 tablespoons Worcestershire
  sauce
½ cup boiling water,
  more if needed
½ stick oleo

Cut up chicken. Salt and pepper. Dust generously with flour. Put in big baking pan, 2 inches deep. Do not crowd chicken. Mix lemon juice and Worcestershire sauce with boiling water and pour over the chicken (do not cover chicken with water). Dot with oleo. Bake at 400 degrees for 1 to 1½ hours (according to size of fryer.) Baste occasionally.

Mrs. Margaret Cresswell, Jackson

CHICKEN CACCIATORE

½ cup flour
2 teaspoons salt
¼ to ½ teaspoon black
  pepper
1 fryer, cut up
½ cup oil

2 medium sized onions,
  chopped
1 (16-ounce) can tomatoes
1 (8-ounce) can tomato sauce
2 cloves garlic
1 teaspoon celery seed
1½ teaspoons oregano

Put flour, salt and pepper into bag and shake well. Put in two or three pieces of chicken at a time; shake sack to distribute coating. Brown in oil in a deep pan. Remove chicken; add onions, cook until soft; add chicken and the other ingredients. Cover and simmer over low heat for 40 to 50 minutes. Turn often without puncturing the chicken. Makes 4 to 6 servings.

Mrs. William McCaleb, Carlisle

CHICKEN SPAGHETTI

1 (3½-pound) chicken
1 (10-ounce) package thin
  spaghetti
1 cup chopped celery
1 cup chopped onion
1 cup chopped green pepper
½ cup cooking oil
salt and pepper to taste
¼ stick margarine

3 tablespoons flour
1 large can mushrooms, stems
  and pieces (8 ounces)
1 (3 or 4-ounce) can pimientos,
  diced
2 tablespoons snipped parsley
½ pound processed cheese,
  grated

Cook chicken in salted water until tender. Remove chicken from broth and debone; dice meat. Strain chicken broth and measure; add water to make 3 quarts, if needed. Heat to boiling. Add spaghetti to broth and cook 15 minutes. Cook celery, onion and green peppers in oil until tender but not brown; add to spaghetti.

Make thick white sauce, using margarine, flour and the liquid drained from mushrooms. Add white sauce to spaghetti; mix in chicken, pimiento, mushrooms and parsley. Fill individual casseroles or large casserole and top with grated cheese. Heat in oven until hot and bubbly, or freeze for use at a later time. Serves 8 to 10.

Mrs. Dorothy Fox, Ovett

CHICKEN CRUNCH

½ cup chicken broth or milk
2 (10½-ounce) cans
    condensed cream of
    mushroom soup
3 cups diced cooked chicken
1 (7-ounce) can tuna drained
1 (5-ounce) can water
    chestnuts, sliced

¼ cup chopped onion
1 cup diced celery
1 (3-ounce) can chow mein
    noodles
1/3 cup toasted almonds,
    chopped

Blend broth into soup in 2-quart casserole. Add all ingredients, except almonds and mix well. Bake in slow oven, 325 degrees, 40 minutes. Just before serving, sprinkle with almonds. Serves 8.

Mrs. Thomas Pearson, West Point

CHICKEN A-LA KING

4 tablespoons butter
3 tablespoons green pepper,
    chopped
½ cup diced celery
3 tablespoons flour

¾ teaspoon salt
1 tablespoon pimiento
2 cups rich milk
2½ cups diced cooked chicken
1 (2-ounce) cans mushrooms

Melt butter in skillet and cook pepper and celery in butter until soft; stir in flour and seasonings. Add milk slowly, stirring constantly. When it reaches boiling point, set pan in double boiler, add chicken and mushrooms. Serve on toast points. Serves 6 to 8.

Mrs. Charles Ames, Holly Springs

CHICKEN CHOW MEIN

2 cups cooked cubed chicken
2 tablespoons salad oil
2 cups sliced celery
1½ cups sliced onion
½ cup sliced green sweet
  pepper
¼ teaspoon black pepper
salt to taste

2 cups chicken broth
1 No. 2 can bean sprouts
1 (4-ounce) can mushrooms
3 tablespoons soy sauce
2 tablespoons cornstarch
2 (3-ounce) cans fried noodles

Sear diced chicken slightly in hot oil. Add celery, onions, green pepper, salt and black pepper; then the broth. Boil slowly, covered, until vegetables are tender. Add drained bean sprouts and mushrooms. Heat to boiling. Mix cornstarch with soy sauce and blend into hot mixture. Simmer until slightly thickened, stirring constantly. Serve over fried noodles. Serves 6.

Mrs. Jim Buck Ross, Pelahatchie

CHICKEN LOAF

1½ cups milk
1½ cups chicken broth
4 eggs, well beaten
2 firmly packed cups of soft
  bread crumbs
4 cups diced cooked chicken
1 cup cooked rice
¾ cup diced celery
2 tablespoons chopped pimiento
1 teaspoon salt
¼ cup butter or margarine

6 tablespoons all-purpose flour
2 cups chicken broth
1 tablespoon chopped parsley
  (optional)
1 teaspoon salt
½ teaspoon paprika
1 teaspoon lemon juice
1 (3-ounce) can mushrooms,
  drained
1 cup light (Single X) cream
  (half and half may be used)

Combine in a bowl the milk and 1½ cups chicken broth. Blend in the beaten eggs. Then add the bread crumbs. Let this mixture set for several minutes to give the bread crumbs a chance to soak up the liquids. Then add the chicken, rice, celery, pimiento and salt. Spread this evenly into a greased pan or dish that measures 13 x 9 x 2-inches. This is much better if it is allowed to season overnight in the refrigerator, so at this stage cover with foil and put in the refrigerator. The next day bake it in a 350 degree oven for 1 hour and serve it hot with this sauce: Melt the butter in a saucepan or top of a double boiler. Add the flour and blend well. Then add 2 cups chicken broth. Cook this, stirring constantly until thick. Then add the parsley, salt, paprika, lemon juice, mushrooms, and cream. Serve hot over the chicken loaf. This recipe will make 12 generous servings. A 5 to 6 pound hen, stewed, gives about the right amount of chicken and broth.

Mrs. J. P. Box, Booneville

JAVA CHICKEN

2 (3-pound) chickens,
   quartered
¼ cup lemon juice
½ cup vegetable oil

2 tablespoons soy sauce
1 teaspoon garlic powder
½ teaspoon Accent
1 teaspoon sesame seeds

Place washed and dried chicken quarters in large pan. Pour lemon juice over chicken. Combine oil, soy sauce, garlic powder and Accent and pour over chicken. Let set for 45 minutes in refrigerator. Preheat oven to broil and place chicken on broiler rack. Broil 15 minutes not too close to the flame to burn. Sprinkle sesame seeds on chicken, turn, and sprinkle seeds on other side. Broil at least 15 minutes longer, or until chicken is fork tender and brown. Serves 6.

Mrs. Mary Geoghegan, Fayette

MEXICAN CHICKEN

1 cut-up fryer
½ cup butter
4 tablespoons sugar
2 teaspoons salt
½ teaspoon red pepper
4 tablespoons vinegar
1 teaspoon Tabasco sauce

2 tablespoons Worcestershire
   sauce
2 teaspoons black pepper
1½ tablespoons dry mustard
2 teaspoons chili powder
2 cups water
2 tablespoons chopped onions
2 cloves garlic, minced

Salt chicken pieces and brown in butter. Mix together rest of ingredients for a sauce and cook 4 or 5 minutes. Pour over chicken. Bake 1½ hours in moderate oven, 350 to 375 degrees. Baste often. Serves 6.

Mrs. Fulton Harris, Chunky

CORN BREAD DRESSING

3 quarts poultry broth
1½ to 2 (11 x 7 x 1½-inch)
   pans cornbread
6 slices white bread
6 eggs, beaten
¾ cup chopped onion
1 cup chopped celery
1 teaspoon sage (or to taste)

½ stick margarine, melted
1 (10½-ounce) can cream of
   chicken soup
2 cups poultry broth
2 tablespoons all-purpose flour
baked hen liver and gizzard,
   chopped
2 hard cooked eggs, chopped

Bake a 3 or 4 pound hen in 3 quarts of water in a roaster. Reserve 2 cups broth for giblet gravy. Make cornbread by favorite recipe. Mix first 9 ingredients in order listed. Stir until combined. Do not beat. Pour dressing into 14 x 9½ x 2½-inch pan. Cover and bake at 350 degrees for 1 hour. Remove cover and bake approximately 10 minutes longer or until slightly browned.

To make giblet gravy, combine small amount of cold poultry broth and flour to make a paste. Stir this paste into remainder of 2 cups poultry broth. Cook in a saucepan over medium heat. Simmer 5 minutes. Stir in chopped liver, gizzard and hardcooked eggs. Serve hot over cornbread dressing. Serves 12 to 15.

Mrs. Travis Gray, Dorsey

CHICKEN AND DRESSING

1 (4-pound) dressed hen
water to cover hen
1½ tablespoons salt
4 cups crumbled cornbread
4 biscuits or 4 slices bread
3 to 4 cups hot chicken broth
2 tablespoons butter or
   margarine
2 raw eggs
1 cup finely chopped celery
2 boiled eggs, chopped

1 teaspoon sage
3 tablespoons minced onions
¼ teaspoon black pepper
¼ cup butter
¼ cup flour
½ teaspoon salt
2 cups chicken broth
1 gizzard
1 liver
1 hard cooked egg

Bring hen to a boil and cook slowly until almost tender. Remove from broth and bake 40 minutes at 400 degrees until well browned and tender. Crumble bread and biscuit into large mixing bowl. Add butter and boiling broth to cover. Let stand 5 minutes. Add next 6 ingredients in order given. Pour into greased baking dish and bake 1 hour at 400 degrees. To make giblet gravy, melt butter, add flour and salt. Blend well and add 2 cups of chicken broth. Add gizzard, liver and hard cooked egg. Cook gravy until thick, stirring constantly. Serve the dressing with chicken and giblet gravy. Serves 10 to 12.

Mrs. Eula Webb, Wiggins

CORNBREAD STUFFING

3 cups slightly dry bread cubes
5 cups coarsely crumbled
　cornbread
1 teaspoon poultry seasoning
1 teaspoon salt
dash of pepper

1 cup finely chopped celery
½ cup finely chopped onion
½ cup butter or margarine
2 beaten eggs
¼ cup chicken broth or
　water

Toss together bread cubes, crumbled cornbread crumbs and seasonings. Cook celery and onion in butter till tender, but not brown; pour over bread. Add eggs and toss lightly to mix. Moisten with broth and toss. Makes 6 cups or enough for two 5-pound roasting chickens. To cook separately in pan, add more broth to be consistency or cornbread batter. Bake in greased 8 x 11-inch loaf pan at 400 degrees until golden brown.

Mrs. L. L. Bethay, Booneville

CHICKEN AND DUMPLINGS

½ hen, boiled or pressure
　cooked
1 fryer
1 cup shortening

5 cups plain flour
1 teaspoon salt
2 cups cold water

Boil or pressure cook the hen until tender. Cook fryer until tender; then remove the bones from broth, and set meat aside. Put the broth from both the fryer and hen in a large roaster or pot and bring to a boil. Mix shortening, salt, flour and water. Add more flour if needed for the dough. Roll out on floured board in small amounts, real thin, and cut in slices; add to boiling broth. Cook until the dumplings are done. Add margarine or butter if needed, and pepper if desired. Now add the meat and enough milk to make the whole real juicy. Serves 12 or 15.

Mrs. J. K. Rowell, Heidelberg

CHICKEN LIVERS MARYLAND

¼ cup butter
2 tablespoons minced onion
1 pound chicken livers
1 (10½-ounce) can cream of
    mushroom soup

1/3 cup milk
dash of black pepper
2 hard cooked eggs, chopped
½ cup sour cream

Sautè butter and minced onion in skillet until golden. Add chicken livers. Simmer until tender, about 4 minutes, stirring occasionally. Combine cream of mushroom soup with milk and black pepper. Stir into chicken livers along with chopped eggs. Heat thoroughly. Stir in sour cream. Serve at once over hot buttered toast triangles or rice. Serves 4.

Mrs. Jane Gunter, Tupelo

OYSTER DRESSING

3 strips of chopped bacon
4 shoots of chopped green
    onion
1 large chopped onion
1 medium chopped green
    pepper
2 or 3 stalks celery, chopped

1/3 cup chopped parsley
2 pints chopped oysters and
    oyster water
3 cups of bread crumbs
¼ teaspoon thyme
salt and pepper

Fry bacon in a large skillet. Add onions, green pepper, celery and parsley. Cook till tender over medium heat. Add chopped oysters and oyster water. Cook until oysters "curl." Combine bread crumbs and water and mix well. After oysters have curled, add the moistened bread crumbs and thyme. Add salt and pepper to taste. Cook over medium heat until the mixture has thoroughly browned. Stir frequently. Yields enough dressing to stuff a 12- to 14-pound turkey.

Mrs. Coleen Parker, Summit

⁒⟦Fish⟧⁒

Fish is a popular main dish for Mississippians. There's the annual shrimp festival on the Gulf Coast and seafood jamborees that feature a wide variety of salt water fish. In the springtime residents throughout the state are seen stringing their fishing poles and heading to the nearest lake or stream to bring home catches of bass, bream and crappie. In recent years Mississippi has become a center for catfish farming, and its cooks have developed new ways for cooking this fish.

Fish is one of the most nutritious foods—an excellent source of high-quality proteins, minerals and vitamins. It's also a weight-watcher's favorite because of the low calorie content. Fishery products can help you balance your food budget since they are among the most economical protein foods you can buy and serve.

BAKED STUFFED FISH

3 cups cracker crumbs	½ teaspoon salt
2/3 cup butter	¼ teaspoon pepper
¾ cup chopped celery	¼ cup hot water
¼ cup finely chopped onion	4 or 5 pounds fish
2 tablespoons lemon juice	1 tablespoon salt
3 teaspoons minced parsley	3 tablespoons cooking oil

Put the crumbs in a bowl. Heat butter in a skillet; add celery and onions. Cook slowly until onion is transparent, stirring occasionally. Add to the crumbs along with lemon juice, parsley, salt and pepper. Add hot water and mix thoroughly. Rinse body cavity of fish with cold water, drain and pat dry with paper towel. Rub cavity with salt. Place stuffing into fish; skewer or sew the opening. Place in a shallow 10 x 15-inch baking pan lined with aluminum foil. Brush surface with oil. Bake at 350 degrees 45 to 50 minutes or until fish flakes easily. Serves 8.

Mrs. Georgia Mason, Clarksdale

GOLDEN BAKED FISH

2 teaspoons salt	1½ cups slightly crushed
½ cup milk	corn flakes
6 fish steaks	3 tablespoons melted butter or
	margarine

Dissolve salt in milk. Dip fish into milk, then into corn flakes and place in baking dish. Pour butter or margarine over fish. Bake at 400 degrees about 20 minutes. Serve with tartar sauce. Serves 6.

Mrs. Fred D. Ferguson, Ovett

BAKED CREOLE FISH

2 tablespoons chopped onion	¼ cup sliced olives
¼ cup minced green pepper	1½ teaspoons salt
2 tablespoons butter	¼ teaspoon pepper
1½ cups cooked tomatoes	2 tablespoons sherry
¼ cup sliced mushrooms	1½ pounds fish fillets or steaks

Cook onion and pepper in butter until tender. Add tomatoes, mushrooms and olives and cook two minutes. Add salt and pepper and sherry. Place fish in a greased 7 x 12 x 2-inch baking dish. Pour the sauce over the fish. Bake in a 400 degree oven for 25 to 30 minutes. Serves 5.

Mrs. T. E. Neill, Clarksdale

BAKED RED SNAPPER OR BASS

¼ cup flour
½ cup cooking oil
3 cups hot water
1 cup onion, chopped
1 cup bell pepper, chopped
1 cup celery, chopped
1 (16-ounce) can tomatoes
1 (12-ounce) can V-8 juice
2 tablespoon Worcestershire
   sauce
1 teaspoon Tabasco sauce
1 tablespoon lemon juice
½ cup cooking wine

salt and pepper to taste
½ teaspoon sage
1 tablespoon Season All
½ teaspoon thyme
1 tablespoon garlic powder
4 large bay leaves
2½ pounds peeled shrimp
2 (6½-ounce) cans crab meat
1 cup green onions, chopped
½ cup parsley, chopped
1 large red snapper
   (10 to 12 pounds)

Brown flour in oil and add hot water, onions, bell pepper, celery, tomatoes, V-8 juice and all condiments. Let this cook for about 1½ hours. Add shrimp and crab meat and cook for about 30 minutes. Add green onion and parsley and cook for about 15 minutes. This sauce must be stirred frequently all through the cooking.

Pour the sauce over a 10 to 12 pound snapper and bake in a 350 degree oven until tender when tested with a fork, or approximately 2 hours. Baste frequently.

Mrs. J. B. Gathright, Oxford

BAKED RED SNAPPER WITH
SAVORY TOMATO SAUCE

3 pound red snapper or bass
½ cup flour
1 teaspoon salt
¼ teaspoon black pepper
6 tablespoons butter
½ cup chopped onion
2 cups chopped celery
¼ cup chopped green pepper
3 cups canned tomatoes
1 tablespoon Worcestershire
   sauce

1 tablespoon catsup
1 teaspoon chili powder
½ finely sliced lemon
2 bay leaves
1 minced clove of garlic
1 teaspoon salt
¼ teaspoon of red pepper
1 tablespoon chopped parsley
additional lemon slices

Dredge fish inside and out with flour, salt and pepper. Place in a 9 x 13 x 2-inch baking dish. Melt the butter in a saucepan. Sautè onion, celery,

[135]

and green pepper until very tender. Add the tomatoes, Worcestershire, catsup, chili powder, lemon slices, bay leaves, garlic, salt and red pepper to sautèd ingredients. Pour the sauce around the fish. Bake in a moderate oven, 350 degrees, for about 45 minutes. Baste frequently with the sauce. Garnish with parsley and additional lemon slices. Serves 4 to 6.

Mrs. Farar M. Truly, Fayette

BROILED CATFISH

6 catfish
1 cup melted fat or oil
¼ cup chopped parsley
2 tablespoons catsup
2 tablespoons wine vinegar

2 cloves garlic finely chopped
2 teaspoons basil
1 teaspoon salt
¼ teaspoon pepper

Place fish in a single layer in a shallow 9 x 13-inch baking dish. Combine remaining ingredients. Pour sauce over fish and let stand for 30 minutes, turning once. Remove fish, reserving sauce for basting. Place fish on a well-greased broiler pan. Brush with sauce. Broil about 3 inches from source of heat, 5 to 7 minutes or until lightly browned, basting twice. Turn carefully and brush other side with sauce. Broil 5 to 7 minutes longer, basting occasionally, until fish is brown and flakes easily when tested with a fork. Serves 6.

Mrs. Thomas Hamblin, West Point

CRISPY CATFISH

6 skinned catfish or other fish
½ cup evaporated milk
1 tablespoon salt
dash pepper

1 cup flour
½ cup yellow cornmeal
2 teaspoons paprika
12 slices bacon

Clean, wash and dry fish. Combine milk, salt and pepper. Combine flour, cornmeal and paprika. Dip fish in milk mixture and roll in flour mixture. Fry bacon in a heavy pan until crisp. Remove bacon, reserving fat for frying. Drain bacon on absorbent paper. Fry fish in hot fat for 4 minutes. Turn carefully and fry for 4 to 6 minutes longer or until fish is brown and flakes easily when tested with a fork. Drain on absorbent paper. Serve with bacon. Serves 6.

Mrs. Thomas Pearson, West Point

FISH IN WINE SAUCE

2 pounds fish fillets
1¼ cups white wine
2 tablespoons lemon juice
¼ cup butter
2 egg yolks
1 cup heavy cream

1 (3-ounce) can sliced
  mushrooms
1 tablespoon chopped parsley
1 teaspoon salt
⅛ teaspoon pepper

Poach fish fillets in wine and lemon juice until tender. Sautè mushrooms in 1 tablespoon butter. Remove fish to hot platter and keep warm. Heat wine in which fish was cooked to boiling and continue cooking for 10 minutes. Beat egg yolks and add cream. Pour wine into mixture stirring constantly. Add remaining butter, mushrooms, parsley, salt and pepper. Heat. Pour over hot fish and serve. Serves 8.

Mrs. Robert Carter, Clarksdale

FILLETS FLORENTINE

2/3 cup raw rice
⅛ teaspoon pepper
1 (10-ounce) can mushroom
  soup
½ cup milk
1½ cups cooked drained
spinach
salt to taste

1 pound fish fillets
⅛ teaspoon pepper
½ teaspoon salt
2 tablespoons lemon juice
1 cup grated sharp cheese

Cook rice according to instructions on package; then spread in greased casserole. Sprinkle with ⅛ teaspoon fresh ground black pepper. Mix soup and milk and pour ½ over the rice. Season spinach to taste and spread over rice and soup. Cut fillets into serving size pieces. (Use halibut, whiting, ocean perch or sole haddock.) Arrange fish over spinach. Sprinkle with ⅛ teaspoon pepper and ½ teaspoon salt. Sprinkle with lemon juice. Spread with remaining soup mixture. Cover with grated cheese. Bake at 375 degrees for 25 minutes. Place under broiler until cheese bubbles. Serves 4.

Mrs. Vernon Seals, Madison

PERCH FILLETS

¼ cup shortening
1 tablespoon chopped onion
¼ teaspoon salt
⅛ teaspoon pepper
3 cups (½ inch) soft bread
cubes

½ cup grated sharp cheese
¼ cup water
4 (4-ounce) butterfly perch
fillets

Melt shortening in a skillet; add onion and sautè until tender. Combine with salt, pepper, soft bread cubes, cheese; add water. Place ½ cup stuffing on skin side of each perch fillet. Roll up fillet, crosswise, with skin side turned in. Place in a greased shallow baking pan, arranging fillets so overlapping edges are down. Bake in a hot oven, 400 degrees, for 30 minutes. Serves 4.

Spencena Russ, Prentiss

SPECKLED PERCH AND SAUCE

6 medium size cleaned speckled
perch
½ cup cooking oil
¾ pound butter
10 tablespoons Worcestershire
sauce

4 tablespoons vinegar
4 tablespoons lemon juice
1 clove garlic, chopped
salt to taste

Swab fish with cooking oil and broil on each side about 20 minutes. To prepare sauce, brown butter lightly and add other ingredients; simmer for very few minutes. Remove garlic and serve sauce over fish. Serves 6.

Mrs. John Crigler, Fayette

OVEN-FRIED FISH

1 pound fish fillets
½ cup milk
3 teaspoons salt

1 cup corn flake crumbs
4 teaspoons salad oil or
melted butter

Cut fish into serving pieces allowing about ¼ pound for each serving. Combine milk and salt. Dip fish in milk, then in corn flake crumbs. Arrange on well-oiled baking sheet or shallow pan. Sprinkle fish with salad oil. Bake in extremely hot oven, 500 degrees, about 15 minutes or until tender. Serve immediately accompanied by lemon slices or tartar sauce. Serves 4.

Spencena Russ, Prentiss

SAVORY FISH LOAF

2 cups flaked cooked fish
  or 14-ounce can
1½ cups soft bread crumbs
¾ cup cooked or canned
  tomatoes
1 beaten egg

2 tablespoons melted fat or
  oil
1 tablespoon minced onion
¼ teaspoon savory seasoning
salt and pepper to taste

Combine all ingredients, pack into greased loaf pan. Bake at 350 degrees until firm, about 45 minutes. Serves 6.

Mrs. Clyde Holladay, Newton

·:⟦Seafood⟧:·

Deviled crab meat delight, scalloped oysters, shrimp creole, whatever the recipe, seafood deserves a place of honor in those special occasion meals.

Fresh and frozen seafood from the Mississippi Gulf Coast is available throughout the state and goes into delicious recipes of cooks in every town. Also valued in meal planning are the many varieties of fresh water fish that can be caught state-wide.

Canned products such as tuna, salmon and crab meat make appealing salads, casseroles and dips. To surprise your family and please your guests, try a tempting seafood dish in your next meal.

SHRIMP ON RICE

3 tablespoons bacon fat
1 medium onion, chopped
1 (10½-ounce) can cream of
    mushroom soup
2 tablespoons sherry

1 (10½-ounce) can mushrooms,
    sliced
2 cups cooked shrimp
1 cup rice, cooked

Sautè onion in bacon fat; add soup and sherry. Mix well. Add mushrooms and shrimp and heat thoroughly. Serve over cooked rice. Serves 6 to 8.

Mrs. W. M. Poynter, McLaurin

SHRIMP AND RICE PIE

2 cups cooked rice
2 cups peeled shrimp
½ teaspoon salt
½ teaspoon black pepper
dash of cayenne pepper

1½ cups milk
2 tablespoons vinegar
4 tablespoons butter or
    margarine

Mix cooked rice and shrimp with fork and place in baking dish. Mix salt and pepper with milk and pour over shrimp and rice. Sprinkle vinegar over the surface. Divide the butter into small pieces and dot over top of pie. Bake at 350 degrees for 30 minutes or until lightly browned. Serves 6 to 8.

Mrs. Emmerson Ladner, Poplarville

SHRIMP-GUMBO PIE

1 tablespoon margarine
¼ cup chopped onion
2 tablespoons flour
¼ teaspoon salt
½ teaspoon sugar
1/16 teaspoon Tabasco
1/16 teaspoon lemon pepper
1 (1-pound) can stewed
    tomatoes

1 (8-ounce) can cut okra,
    drained
1 stick piecrust mix
2 cups cooked shrimp
1 (12-ounce) can whole
    kernel corn, drained

Preheat oven to 450 degrees. Sautè onion in hot margarine until brown. Remove from heat and blend in flour, sugar, salt, Tabasco and pepper.

Stir in tomatoes and okra. Place back on heat and bring to boil, stirring until mixture thickens. Reduce heat and let simmer for 5 minutes.

Make pie crust as directed on package. Place shrimp in layer in 8¼-inch baking dish and top with corn. Add tomato mixture. Place rolled out pie crust on top of baking dish and trim overhang. Prick steam vents in top. Bake 20 minutes. Serves 6.

Mrs. Woodie Thomas, Fayette

SHRIMP CREOLE

½ cup onion, chopped
½ cup celery, chopped
1 clove garlic, minced
3 tablespoons vegetable oil
1 (1-pound) can tomatoes
1 (8-ounce) can seasoned
    tomato sauce
1½ teaspoons salt
1 teaspoon sugar
½ to 1 teaspoon chili powder
1 tablespoon Worcestershire
    sauce
dash of Tabasco sauce
2 teaspoons cornstarch
4 teaspoons cold water
1 pound raw, cleaned shrimp
½ cup green pepper, chopped
½ cup fresh parsley, chopped

Cook onion, celery and garlic in hot oil until tender, but not brown. Add tomatoes, tomato sauce and seasonings. Simmer, uncovered, for 45 minutes. Mix cornstarch and water; stir into sauce. Cook and stir until mixture thickens. Add shrimp, green pepper and parsley. Simmer for 5 minutes or until shrimp are just done. Serve with cooked rice. Serves 5 or 6.

Mrs. Maurice C. O'Keefe, Jr., Long Beach

SHRIMP CREOLE

1/3 cup fresh drippings or
    shortening
¼ cup flour
½ cup chopped onion plus
    two green onions
½ cup diced green pepper
½ cup sliced celery
¼ cup minced fresh parsley
4 garlic cloves, chopped
1 cup water
1 (8½-ounce) can tomato sauce
1½ teaspoon salt
2 bay leaves
½ teaspoon crushed thyme
⅛ teaspoon cayenne pepper
1 lemon slice
2 (4½-ounce) cans shrimp or
    1½ cups fresh cooked
    shrimp
4 cups cooked rice

Heat shortening in a heavy pan and blend in flour. Cook over medium heat until golden brown, stirring constantly. Add vegetables and cook 2 minutes. Add water, tomato sauce, dry seasonings and lemon. Turn heat low, cover pan closely and simmer 20 minutes, stirring occasionally. Add shrimp and heat. Serve on fluffy rice. Serves 4.

Mrs. Sam Barrentine, McCarley

CURRY OF SHRIMP

3 tablespoons bacon fat
3 tablespoons curry powder
1 teaspoon paprika
4 sliced onions
1 clove garlic, crushed

4 tablespoons flour
2 tomatoes, sliced
1 pint chicken or beef stock
2 tablespoons fresh coconut
3 pound cooked shrimp

Heat bacon fat. Add curry powder and paprika. Let brown. Stir in onions and let brown. Add garlic. Stir in flour. Cook well. Add tomatoes and simmer 5 minutes. Pour in stock and let boil slowly. Add coconut and shrimp. Serves 7 to 9.

Mrs. Edgar E. Moody, Hollandale

SHRIMP CURRY

5 tablespoons margarine
½ cup minced onion
¼ cup minced green pepper
1/3 cup all-purpose flour
1 tablespoon curry powder
¼ teaspoon salt

¼ teaspoon ground ginger
1 (14-ounce) can chicken broth
2 cups milk
2 cups cooked, cleaned shrimp
cooked rice

Sautè onion and green pepper until golden in margarine. Stir in flour, curry powder, salt and ginger. Gradually stir in broth and milk to keep from lumping. Cook, stirring, until thickened. Add shrimp, mix gently, and heat through. Serve with rice. The shrimp may be left out of this sauce and it can be used as a gravy over rice and served with fried chicken, if desired. Leftover chicken or turkey may be added to the sauce instead of shrimp. Serves 8.

Mrs. Conrad F. Nordholm, Hattiesburg

[144]

NOEL SHRIMP BAKE

¾ to 1 pound fresh mushrooms
¼ cup butter or margarine
2 cups cleaned, cooked or
   canned shrimp
2 cups cooked rice
1 cup chopped green pepper
1 cup chopped onion
½ cup chopped celery

¼ cup chopped pimiento
1 (No. 2) can (2½ cups)
   tomatoes, drained
¾ teaspoon salt
½ teaspoon chili powder
½ cup butter or margarine,
   melted

Cook mushrooms in ¼ cup butter just till tender. Combine with shrimp, rice, vegetables and seasonings. Place in greased 2-quart casserole. Pour ½ cup butter over. Bake in slow oven, 300 degrees, 50 to 60 minutes. Rim with wreath of parsley and stuffed olive slices. Serves 6 to 8.

Mrs. Marian H. Quinn, Canton

SHRIMP CASSEROLE HARPIN

2½ pounds large raw shrimp,
   shelled, deveined
1 tablespoon fresh, frozen or
   canned lemon juice
3 tablespoons salad oil
¾ cup raw regular or
   processed rice
2 tablespoons butter or
   margarine
¼ cup minced green pepper
¼ cup minced onion

1 teaspoon salt
1 teaspoon pepper
¼ teaspoon mace
dash cayenne pepper
1 (10½-ounce) can condensed
   tomato soup, undiluted
1 cup heavy cream
½ cup sherry
¾ cup slivered blanched
   almonds

Cook the shrimp several hours before (or the day before) then drain and place in 2-quart casserole. Sprinkle with lemon juice and salad oil. Cook rice as directed on package; drain. Refrigerate all. About 1 hour before serving, melt butter in skillet, sautè green pepper and onion. Add with rice, salt, pepper, mace, cayenne pepper, soup, cream, sherry and ½ cup almonds to shrimp in casserole. Several shrimp may be kept out to garnish casserole on top. Toss well all ingredients. Use 350 degree oven. Bake, uncovered, 35 minutes. Then top with shrimp for garnish and ¼ cup almonds. Bake about 20 minutes longer or until the mixture is bubbly and shrimp are slightly brown. Serves 6 to 8.

Mrs. H. Paul England, Baldwyn

SHRIMP CASSEROLE

¾ pound cooked shrimp
½ cup chopped celery
¼ cup chopped green pepper
3 tablespoons chopped onion
¼ cup butter or other fat, melted
6 tablespoons flour
1 teaspoon salt
1 (10½-ounce) can condensed mushroom soup
1½ cups milk
1 tablespoon butter or other fat melted
¼ cup dry bread crumbs

Cut large shrimp in half. Cook vegetables in butter until tender; blend in flour and salt. Combine soup and milk; add to vegetable mixture and cook until thick, stirring constantly. Add shrimp and pour into a well-greased casserole. Combine butter and crumbs; sprinkle over top of casserole. Bake in a hot oven, 400 degrees, about 10 minutes or until brown. Serves 6.

Mrs. Marilyn J. Bailey, Prentiss

BARBECUED BILOXI SHRIMP

5 pound headless raw shrimp, peeled
1 pound melted butter or margarine
5 cloves garlic, minced
paprika
salt
pepper
5 tablespoons Worcestershire sauce
2 teaspoons Tabasco
juice of 1 or 2 lemons, to taste

Combine all ingredients, seasoning as desired. Sautè over low heat for 1½ to 2 hours in a heavy skillet or in the oven in a shallow, heavy open pan.

Good with cocktails dipped in red sauce or served as main entree. This recipe has been served at the Biloxi Shrimp Festival banquet for many years.

Mrs. Ronald Meaut, Biloxi

SHRIMP STROGANOFF

1½ to 2 pounds shrimp (shelled and deveined)
6 tablespoons butter
1½ cups mushrooms, sliced
2 tablespoons onion, minced
1 clove garlic, minced
3 tablespoons flour
1 cup chicken consommé
1 teaspoon catsup
½ teaspoon Worcestershire sauce
1 cup sour cream
1 tablespoon dill seed

Cook shrimp in half the butter for 3 to 5 minutes. Turn off. Remove and keep warm. Add mushrooms to remaining butter, sautè for 2 minutes. Add onions and garlic. Sautè until tender. Add more butter if needed. Stir in flour and consommé. Stir and cook until thickened. Add catsup and Worcestershire sauce. Remove from heat and quickly blend in sour cream and dill. Season to taste, add shrimp to mixture. Serve on rice. Use wild rice or half and half mixture. Chicken broth can be used in place of consommé. Serves 4 to 6.

Mrs. Curtis Hines, Saulsbury

BAKED SEAFOOD CASSEROLE

1 (6½-ounce) can white
crab meat
1 (4¼-ounce) can deveined
shrimp
1 (7-ounce) can white tuna
1 cup mayonnaise
½ cup chopped green pepper

1/3 cup minced onion
1½ cups finely chopped celery
½ teaspoon salt
1 tablespoon lemon juice
1 can French fried onions
1 cup crushed potato chips
paprika

Mix all ingredients as for a salad. Save about one-half of the can of French fried onions for the topping. Fill a 3-quart baking dish with mixture and sprinkle with paprika. Bake at 400 degrees for 20 to 25 minutes. Just before removing from oven, sprinkle the rest of the French fried onions on top and let heat. Serves 12.

Mrs. Myron Allgood, Brookhaven

SEAFOOD CASSEROLE

4 tablespoons chopped onion
4 tablespoons chopped pepper
2 tablespoons butter
1 (10½-ounce) can celery soup
1 cup cooked shrimp (2 cans)

1 (4-ounce) can sliced
mushrooms
1 (6½-ounce) can crab meat
2 tablespoons pimiento
mashed potatoes

Sautè onion and pepper in butter. Add celery soup and mix well. Add shrimp and half of mushrooms to soup mixture. Add crab meat and pimiento. Mix well. Turn into a greased casserole dish. Top with mashed potatoes. This adds a pretty finish when the potatoes are put through a cake decorator or a cookie press. Sprinkle remaining mushrooms in center. Bake at 375 degrees for 25 minutes. Serves 4 to 6.

Mrs. Joy Frizell, Lexington

SEASHELL CASSEROLE

1 pint oysters	1/3 cup all-purpose flour
2 cups uncooked shell macaroni	2 cups milk
½ cup butter or margarine	2 teaspoons salt
1 clove garlic or 3 tablespoons	¼ teaspoon pepper
onions	2 cups grated cheddar cheese

Drain oysters, reserving 1 cup of liquid. Cook macaroni as directed on package. Meanwhile melt butter in saucepan. Peel garlic or onion, dice and brown in butter. Remove pan from heat. Discard garlic. Stir in flour until smooth. Gradually add oyster liquid and milk. Stir until well blended and return to heat and cook until thick. Stir in salt, pepper and grated cheese. Pour macaroni into buttered 2-quart casserole. Make a well in center and pour in oysters. Bake at 350 degrees about 30 minutes. Serves 6 to 8.

Mrs. Forrest D. Copeland, Newton

SEAFOOD GUMBO

3 tablespoons fat	4 cups water
1 (10-ounce) package frozen	6 crabs, cleaned and broken in
cut okra	pieces
1 large chopped onion	½ pint oysters
1 medium green pepper,	2 pounds cleaned shrimp
chopped	2 bay leaves
2 cloves garlic, chopped	1 tablespoon gumbo filè
1 (8-ounce) can tomato sauce	salt and pepper to taste
2 tablespoons flour	½ teaspoon red pepper

Sautè okra, onions, green pepper and garlic in fat in a 4-quart cooker for about 10 minutes. Add tomato sauce and mix well. Mix flour with ½ cup water to make a smooth paste. Add with remaining ingredients to mixture. Cook slowly for 1 hour. Use more or less water for desired thickness. May be served with rice. Serves 8 to 10.

Mrs. Caroline Anderson, Brookhaven

SEAFOOD GUMBO

4 tablespoons bacon drippings	2 cups water
4 tablespoons flour	2 chicken bouillon cubes
2 (1-pound) cans tomatoes	salt and pepper
1 large green pepper, chopped	red pepper
1 cup celery, chopped	1 teaspoon gumbo filè
1 (15½-ounce) can cut okra	dry mustard

Worcestershire sauce
1 (6½-ounce) can crab meat

3 pounds cleaned shrimp
1 cup raw oysters

Combine all ingredients except seafood. Cook slowly for 1 hour and 30 minutes. Add seafood. Cook slowly until done. Serves 8 to 10.

Mrs. Margaret Dawsey, Picayune

PICKLED SHRIMP

½ cup celery tops
¼ cup pickling spice
1 tablespoon salt
7 or 8 bay leaves
1 pod of hot pepper (if desired)
2½ pounds fresh or frozen
  shrimp

2 cups sliced onion
1¼ cups salad oil
¾ cup white vinegar
2½ tablespoons capers
2½ teaspoons celery seed
½ teaspoon salt
dash Tabasco sauce

To cook shrimp, use a 5-quart pot with 2½ quarts water. Add shrimp to boiling water containing celery tops, pickling spice, salt, bay leaves, and hot pepper. Cover shrimp and boil 5 to 7 minutes. Drain, cool under running water, peel, and devein. Place alternate layers of shrimp and onions in casserole. Use marinade made with salad oil, capers, white vinegar, celery seed, salt and Tabasco sauce. Mix well. Pour over shrimp, place in refrigerator. Drain on paper towels. Will keep in refrigerator a week.

Mrs. A. L. Nettles, Macon

PICKLED SHRIMP

2½ pounds shrimp
1½ tablespoons pickling spice
tops of 1 bunch celery
¾ tablespoon red pepper
¼ cup vinegar
1 tablespoon salt
15 thin slices of onion
9 thin slices of lemon

2 bay leaves
1 cup vegetable oil
¾ cup tarragon or
  white vinegar
2 tablespoons celery seed
2 tablespoons caper juice
Tabasco to taste
½ tablespoon salt

Cover shrimp with water and add pickling spice, celery tops, red pepper, ¼ cup vinegar and 1 tablespoon salt. Cook for 20 minutes. Cool and clean shrimp. Put in a bowl in layers with onion and lemon slices. Mix remaining ingredients and pour over shrimp layers. Cover and put in the refrigerator. Keep 24 hours before eating.

Walter White, Yazoo City

[149]

SEAFOOD DELIGHT

2 dozen fresh shrimp
2 dozen fresh oysters
1 (4½-ounce) can crab meat
6 fresh mushrooms, sliced
½ large green pepper,
  chopped fine
½ can pimiento, chopped fine

4 tablespoons butter or oleo
2 tablespoons flour
1 pint fresh cream
1½ teaspoons salt
¼ teaspoon paprika
2 cups cooked white chicken
  meat, diced

Cook shrimp 20 minutes in boiling water, peel and devein. Cook oysters slowly in their juice until edges curl. Add crab meat. Combine mushrooms and green pepper. Sauté for 3 minutes in butter. Make white sauce from the remaining butter, cream, flour and seasonings. Combine with other ingredients. Mix well. Serve on toast. Serves 8.

Miss Jerry Lack, Magee

SAUCEY SEAFOOD ROLL

2 cups buttermilk pancake
  mix
¼ cup butter
2/3 cup milk
1 (7-ounce) can crab meat,
  drained and flaked
1 (4½-ounce) can shrimp,
  drained and deveined

¼ cup dairy sour cream
2 tablespoons fresh or
  canned parsley
1 (10½-ounce) can cream of
  celery soup
½ cup milk
1 (10-ounce) package of
  frozen mixed vegetables

Combine first 3 ingredients, roll out to make a rectangle 8 x 15 inches. Combine crab meat, shrimp, sour cream and parsley. Spread over rolled dough; starting from long end, roll up as you would a jelly roll. Package and freeze. When ready to use slice into 2-inch rounds. Place on greased cookie sheet, bake 20 to 30 minutes at 400 degrees. Cook and drain the mixed vegetables. Add celery soup and milk. Heat thoroughly but do not boil. Serve over baked seafood rounds.

Mrs. John D. McCraine, Woodville

SALMON LOAF

1 cup flaked canned salmon
1 cup bread crumbs soaked in
1 cup scalded milk
1 teaspoon salt
½ teaspoon onion juice

1 tablespoon butter
2 egg yolks, beaten
1 teaspoon lemon juice
2 egg whites, stiffly beaten

Combine ingredients in order given, folding in the stiffly beaten whites last. Place mixture into a well-greased and crumbed pan and bake in a moderately hot oven, 375 degrees to 400 degrees. Serve immediately with white sauce with hard boiled eggs or stuffed olives chopped fine. Also good with a tomato sauce. Serves 4.

Mrs. Carl Bethea, Indianola

SALMON LOAF

1 (1-pound) can (pink or red) salmon
1 cup corn flakes
¼ cup catsup or chili sauce
2 teaspoons Worcestershire sauce
1 large egg, well beaten

Flake salmon and mix juice from can with meat. Crush cornflakes and mix well with salmon. Add catsup, Worcestershire sauce and egg. Mix thoroughly. Place in oiled baking dish and bake at 350 degrees for 30 minutes or until set and browned on top. Serve hot. Serves 6.

Mrs. Roy Harter, West Point

SALMON LOAF

½ cup chopped celery
½ cup chopped green pepper
¼ cup chopped onion
2 tablespoons butter
½ cup chopped black olives
1 (1 pound) can red salmon
1 (10½-ounce) can creamed chicken soup
2 cups biscuit mix
2/3 cup milk
1 egg
1 tablespoon water
1 tablespoon lemon juice

Sautè celery, pepper and onion in butter until tender. Add olives. Drain salmon, reserving liquid. Add salmon with ¼ cup chicken soup to the vegetables and set aside. Combine biscuit mix and milk. Turn onto floured surface. Knead 12 times. Roll dough into 9 x 12-inch rectangle. Set aside trimmings. Cover dough with salmon mixture and roll up as for jelly rolls. Place on baking sheet, seam side down. Combine egg and water and brush the roll to glaze. Bake at 400 degrees for 25 minutes or until golden brown. For the sauce to serve with the loaf, add milk to reserved salmon liquid to make ½ cup. Combine with remaining chicken soup and lemon juice in small sauce pan. Heat to boiling. Spoon over individual servings. Serves 6.

Mrs. Jim Moore, Wiggins

[151]

SALMON CROQUETTES

1 (16-ounce) can of pink salmon   ½ teaspoon salt
3 whole eggs   ¼ teaspoon cayenne pepper
¼ pound crackers, crumbled

Flake fish and add eggs. Mix well. Add cracker crumbs, salt and cayenne pepper. Mix well and form into balls the size of a tablespoon. Fry in deep hot fat, 375 degrees, until golden brown. Serves 6 to 8.

Mrs. Marvin Smitherman, Booneville

SALMON CROQUETTES

1 pound can salmon   8 ounces mild cheddar cheese
1 tablespoon lemon juice   6 tablespoons milk
½ teaspoon salt   3½ cups crushed cornflakes
½ cup chopped celery

Mix the salmon, lemon juice, salt and celery and set aside. To make cheese sauce; grate and melt cheddar cheese on low heat, then add sweet milk to melted cheese. Add cheese sauce to salmon mixture and then 3 cups crushed cornflakes and shape into croquettes. Roll in ½ cup crushed cornflakes. Bake on cookie sheet at 375 degrees for 20 minutes. Serves 6.

Mrs. Bo Livingston, West Point

DEVILED PACIFIC SALMON

3 tablespoons butter   ¾ teaspoon Worcestershire
½ cup celery, chopped   sauce
½ large onion, chopped   ½ teaspoon salt
3 tablespoons flour   ⅛ teaspoon pepper
1½ cups milk   ¼ cup fine buttered bread
1 (1 pound) can salmon   crumbs
3 hard cooked eggs

Sautè celery and onion in butter in heavy skillet. Remove celery and onion from skillet; add flour to make white sauce. Stir until well blended, add milk and heat until thick and smooth, stirring constantly. Remove from heat and add flaked salmon, chopped hard cooked eggs, celery and onion. Then add seasonings. Pour into buttered 1½-quart casserole;

top with crumbs. Bake at 450 degrees about 20 minutes or until delicately browned. Serves 6.

Mrs. Earl H. Moore, Port Gibson

TUNA BAKE

½ bell pepper, chopped fine
½ onion, chopped fine
1 tablespoon butter
2 tablespoons flour
½ cup milk
1 (10½-ounce) can mushroom
  soup
1 (no. 2) can green peas

2 (6½-ounce) cans tuna
2 tablespoons Worcestershire
  sauce
½ teaspoon hot sauce
salt and pepper to taste
grated sharp cheese
cracker crumbs

Sautè pepper and onion in butter. Add flour, milk and mushroom soup. Cook until thick. Add peas, tuna, Worcestershire, hot sauce, salt and pepper. Put in ramekins, top with cheese, cracker crumbs and butter. Bake at 350 degrees for 20 minutes. Serves 4 to 6.

Mrs. Stovall Milam, Leland

ROCKY CLAM MACARONI

3 green onions, minced
2 cloves garlic, minced
2 tablespoons olive oil
  or peanut oil
1 (10½-ounce) can Progresso
  Italian style sauce with
  rock lobster
1 package Kraft spaghetti
  sauce mix

1 teaspoon sugar
salt to taste
1 bay leaf
dash of Tabasco
dash of monosodium glutamate
1 (7-ounce can) minced clams
1 (12-ounce) package shell
  macaroni, cooked and drained
Parmesan cheese (optional)

Sautè onions and garlic in oil. Add Italian style sauce with rock lobster, spaghetti sauce mix, sugar, salt, bay leaf, Tabasco, monosodium glutamate and clams. Simmer for 30 minutes over low heat. Serve this sauce over the macaroni or mix sauce and macaroni together. May be served with Parmesan cheese sprinkled over if desired. Serves 6.

For variation, tomato sauce with mushrooms may be substituted for the rock lobster sauce, or oysters or shrimp or a combination may be substituted for the clams. Good served with garlic bread, salad and dessert.

Mrs. E. O. Newmon, Gulfport

[153]

LOBSTER NEWBURG

2 cups coarsely chopped
  cooked lobster
¼ cup butter
1 teaspoon minced green
  pepper
2 tablespoons each, cognac and
  sherry wine

½ cup cream
2 egg yolks, well beaten
¾ teaspoon salt
⅛ teaspoon cayenne pepper
½ teaspoon powdered nutmeg
pastry shells or toast

Melt butter and sautè green pepper 3 minutes over low heat. Add lobster, sherry and cognac. Cook 1 minute. Add cream and remove from heat. Slowly blend in egg yolks and add salt, cayenne and nutmeg. Cook over low heat 1 or 2 minutes. Stir constantly, just long enough to heat the yolks. Serve in pastry shells or on toast. Serves 4.

Spencena Russ, Prentiss

EPICUREAN CHEESED OYSTERS

1 (16-ounce) package of
  cheese-it crackers
½ teaspoon paprika
¼ teaspoon rubbed oregano

fat, oil or shortening for frying
2 eggs
2 tablespoons water
1 pint frying oysters

Crush crackers with rolling pin into very fine crumbs between waxed paper. Mix with paprika and oregano and set aside. Beat eggs with water. Dip oysters into eggs and roll in crumbs. Lay on flat surface at least 30 minutes to set crust. Fry in moderately hot fat, 375 degrees, until crusty, about 4 to 5 minutes. Drain on paper towels. Garnish with lemon wedges and dill pickles. Serve with tartar sauce. Serves 5.

Mrs. C. K. Carroll, Indianola

CRAB OR SHRIMP THERMIDOR

¼ cup chopped onion
2 tablespoons chopped
  green pepper
2 tablespoons butter or oleo
1 (10¼-ounce) can frozen
  condensed cream of potato
  soup
¾ cup light cream

½ cup shredded sharp cheese
2 tablespoons lemon juice
1½ cups drained crab meat,
  or 1½ cups cooked or
  canned shrimp (split
  lengthwise)
puff-pastry shell

Cook onion and green pepper in butter till tender, but not brown. Add soup and cream; heat slowly, stirring constantly, till blended. Bring just to boiling. Add cheese, stir to melt. Add lemon juice and crab meat. Heat through. Serve in pastry shells. Serves 4 to 5.

Mrs. J. E. Edwards, Cedar Bluff

CRAB MEAT CASSEROLE

2 cups bread crumbs (reserve ½ cup for topping)
½ cup milk
2 cups (2 [8-ounce] cans) crab meat
4 hard boiled eggs, mashed
1 medium onion, grated

1 cup mayonnaise
4 tablespoons Worcestershire sauce
2 pimientos, chopped
½ teaspoon salt
dash red pepper
dash black pepper
small can chipped mushrooms

Soften bread crumbs in milk (except crumbs reserved for topping). Combine all other ingredients well. Place in 2-quart casserole and top with bread crumbs. Bake at 350 degrees for 40 minutes. Serves 8.

Mrs. J. H. Burt, Sr., Wayside

CRAB MEAT CASSEROLE

5 tablespoons butter
3 tablespoons flour
2 cups milk
2 tablespoons minced onion
½ teaspoon celery salt
1 tablespoon grated orange rind
1 tablespoon minced parsley
1 pimiento, minced
2 tablespoons sherry

1 egg, beaten
½ teaspoon hot sauce
1 teaspoon salt
1 teaspoon black pepper
1 pound fresh crab meat
bread crumbs
1 tablespoon butter
1 tablespoon minced green pepper

Make white sauce of butter, flour and milk; then add next 6 ingredients. Remove from heat, add sherry. Add hot sauce to egg; then add egg to rest of sauce. Add salt, pepper and crab meat. Place in 1½-quart casserole, sprinkle with bread crumbs mixed with 1 tablespoon melted butter. Bake at 350 degrees for 15 or 20 minutes. Garnish with green pepper. Serves 7.

Mrs. Otto Browning, Yazoo City

STUFFED GULF CRAB

1 stick butter
1 onion, minced fine
1 stalk celery, minced
½ large bell pepper, minced
3 cloves garlic, minced fine
1 teaspoon parsley, minced
½ teaspoon thyme
9 slices bread, cubed

1 cup milk
2 eggs
Tabasco
salt
pepper
3 cups crab meat
bread crumbs

Cook onion, celery, bell pepper, garlic, parsley and thyme in butter until transparent. Combine cubed bread with milk and mix well. Add eggs, seasonings, crab meat and sautèd vegetables. Mix well. Fill clean crab shells. Sprinkle with bread crumbs. Bake 45 minutes in a 350 degree oven. Serves 6 to 8.

Mrs. Maurice C. O'Keefe, Jr., Long Beach

DEVIL CRAB

4 tablespoons butter
1 tablespoon minced onion
3 tablespoons flour
1 cup scalded milk
2 cups crab meat

1 teaspoon Worcestershire
  sauce
1 teaspoon prepared mustard
1 teaspoon salt
grated rind of 1 lemon
2 diced hard cooked eggs

Melt butter in frying pan. Add onions, cook slowly until brown. Add flour and brown. Add scalded milk. Cook until sauce is smooth. Cool— add crab meat and all seasonings. Add eggs. Put bread crumbs on top and brown in oven at 400 degrees. Serves 6.

Mrs. V. W. Spell, Braxton

CRAB MEAT SALAD

½ cup cold water
2 tablespoons unflavored gelatin
1 (10½-ounce) can tomato
  soup
1 (3-ounce) package cream
  cheese
1 cup chopped celery

1 medium bell pepper,
  chopped
1 teaspoon onion, minced
½ teaspoon salt
1 (6½-ounce) can flaked
  crab meat

Dissolve gelatin in cold water. Heat soup, do not boil, and stir in gelatin. Dissolve thoroughly. Add softened cream cheese and beat mixture until smooth. Chill until partially set, then add remaining ingredients. Pour into a 1½-quart salad mold and congeal. Serves 8.

Mrs. G. B. Barnard, Clarksdale

OYSTER CASSEROLE

2 cups cracker crumbs
1 stick oleo, melted
1 quart oysters

1 cup chopped celery
1½ cups milk
salt and pepper to taste

Mix cracker crumbs and melted oleo. Put a layer of crumbs in bottom of casserole. Cover with oysters and celery. Sprinkle with salt and pepper. Repeat layers until all is used. Be sure to end with a layer of cracker crumbs. Add milk. Bake at 350 degrees for 30 minutes or until lightly browned. Serves 8.

Mrs. Gertrude Dale, Port Gibson

SHRIMP OR CLAM DIP

2 cups shrimp or clams,
   minced (fresh or canned)
¼ cup French dressing
6 tablespoons salad dressing

1 teaspoon Worcestershire
   sauce
1 (8-ounce) package cream
   cheese
grated onion, if desired

If canned shrimp or clams are used, drain thoroughly. Blend all ingredients well and chill. Serve with potato chips, crackers, etc. Makes about 3 cups of dip.

Mrs. Andy Snider, Senatobia

SHRIMP DIP

1 (4½-ounce) can shrimp
1 cup mayonnaise
1 (3-ounce) package
   cream cheese

2 tablespoons of green onions
   or onion puree
2 teaspoons lemon juice

Mash or finely chop shrimp and mix all ingredients together. Serve as a dip for chips or hors d'oeuvres.

Mrs. Rachel Tramel, Raleigh

COME BACK SAUCE

1 cup mayonnaise
¼ cup chili sauce
¼ cup catsup
1 teaspoon mustard
½ cup vegetable oil

1 teaspoon Worcestershire
   sauce
1 teaspoon black pepper
1 tablespoon minced onion
   and garlic
juice of 1 lemon

Shake well in jar. Let set overnight before using.

Mrs. Mary Jean Saulters, Prentiss

REMOULADE SAUCE

1 medium onion, grated
1 pint mayonnaise
3 to 4 tablespoons
   finely chopped parsley
3 to 4 tablespoons finely
   chopped Kosher dill pickles
1 finely chopped hard-cooked
   egg

3 to 4 tablespoons dry mustard
juice of 1 lemon
minced garlic, to taste
salt to taste
5 ounces Zatarains
   remoulade sauce

Grate onion on paper towel, let stand until moisture is absorbed. Add to mayonnaise with remaining ingredients. If too thick, add pickle juice. Serve cold with seafood. If to keep a long time, omit egg. As a dressing for head lettuce: mix 1/3 cup sauce, 1/3 cup tomato catsup and 1 hard-cooked egg cut in coarse pieces. Yield: 1½ pints.

Mrs. Jacqueline Mikell, Port Gibson

⸙[Eggs]⸙

From an early morning eye-opener to a late-at-night snack, eggs add goodness to eating on each occasion.

Eggs have protein, two of the B vitamins plus vitamins A and D to help protect health. The egg yolk contains a rich store of iron for red blood cells plus phosphorus and other minerals needed for the body.

Eggs can be prepared a multitude of ways for a quick breakfast entrée. The egg is the main ingredient for a number of main dishes. Salads become more colorful garnished with hard cooked eggs. Soups and sauces are enriched by the addition of eggs, and most popular desserts depend on the egg for their flavorful goodness.

Eggs should be stored clean, covered and cold. The most important rule in cooking eggs, whether in water, frying pan or oven, is to cook them with low to moderate, even heat. Like all protein foods, eggs cooked at too high a temperature get tough and leathery.

GRANDMOTHER'S BOILED CUSTARD

1 quart sweet milk	4 egg yolks
¾ cup or 1 cup sugar	1 teaspoon lemon flavoring,
1 teaspoon flour	vanilla flavoring or nutmeg

Heat milk in top of double boiler. When water underneath boils, add sugar mixed with flour. Beat egg yolks until thick and lemon colored. Gradually add the hot milk, then return the whole mixture to double boiler. Continue cooking to thickness desired. Remove from heat and pour through wire strainer into bowl. Cool. Add flavoring. Store in refrigerator to chill thoroughly. Serve as is or on plain cake. Serves 6 to 8.

Mrs. J. W. Ward, Jackson

EGG CUSTARD PIE

3 eggs	2 tablespoons butter
1 cup sugar	2 cups sweet milk
1 teaspoon vanilla	9-inch unbaked pie shell

Beat eggs and add sugar. Beat well and add flavoring, butter and milk. Then pour into an unbaked 9-inch pie shell and bake about 45 minutes at 350 degrees. Pie will still be soft and shakey when done, but will gel when cool. Serves 6.

Mrs. Bob Addy, Chunky

HARD MERINGUES

1 teaspoon cream of tartar	4 egg whites
½ teaspoon salt	1 cup sugar

Add cream of tartar and salt to egg whites and beat until stiff peaks form. Add sugar, 1 tablespoon at a time, beating well after each addition. Shape meringues with a rim using a spoon or pastry bag, on several thicknesses of ungreased paper placed on a baking sheet. Bake in a 225 degree oven for 70 minutes. Let meringues cool thoroughly before removing from paper. Yields 10 to 12 individual meringue shells.

Mrs. LaVerne Y. Lindsey, Lexington

PICKLED EGGS

1½ dozen hard-cooked eggs	½ teaspoon salt
1 medium size onion	¼ teaspoon garlic salt
1¾ cups white vinegar	5 whole peppercorns

¾ cup water
3 tablespoons brown sugar

1 whole clove
few dill seed

Cook, peel and cool eggs. Thinly slice onion, place in saucepan then add all other ingredients except eggs. Set over medium heat, bring to boil. Reduce heat, simmer 5 minutes. Put eggs into two quart jars. Pour half of vinegar mixture into each jar. Cover. When cold, place in refrigerator. Let set a day or so before serving. Beet juice may be added for color. Serves 12 to 18.

Mrs. Johnnie Baker, Port Gibson

PICKLED EGGS

2 cups vinegar
3 tablespoons sugar
1½ teaspoons salt
1 teaspoon pickling spice,
    tied in bag

1 clove garlic, peeled
    (optional)
whole cloves (optional)
1 dozen hard-cooked
    eggs, peeled

Pour vinegar, sugar and salt into saucepan. Drop in spice bag, garlic and cloves. Simmer 5 minutes. Pour over eggs in a jar and put in refrigerator for several days before using. Serves 12.

Mrs. Marian H. Quinn, Canton

STUFFED EGGS

12 hard-cooked eggs
1 (3-ounce) package cream
    cheese, softened
1 tablespoon salad mustard
1 teaspoon vinegar
1 teaspoon vegetable oil

1 tablespoon Worcestershire
    sauce
½ teaspoon salt
⅛ teaspoon black pepper
¼ cup finely chopped
    sweet pickles

Peel and cut eggs in halves, lengthwise. Remove yolks and blend with remaining ingredients. Spoon back into egg whites. Chill until serving time. Serves 24.

Miss Joan Moore, Wiggins

DEVILED EGGS

6 hard-cooked eggs, halved
½ teaspoon salt
½ teaspoon pepper
½ teaspoon dry mustard
2 teaspoons minced parsley

2 tablespoons chopped sweet
    pickles
about 3 tablespoons
    mayonnaise

Mash egg yolks and mix in other ingredients. Refill whites with yolk mixture. Serves 6.

Myrtie Mae Horton, Port Gibson

HOT DEVILED EGGS

1 tablespoon butter
4 tablespoons sifted all-purpose flour
¼ teaspoon dry mustard
⅛ teaspoon paprika
½ teaspoon salt, pepper to taste
¼ teaspoon Worcestershire sauce
2 cups milk
1 bay leaf
6 hard-cooked eggs
½ cup chopped ripe olives
1/3 cup grated Parmesan cheese

Melt butter, blend in flour, mustard, paprika, salt, pepper and Worcestershire sauce. Add milk and bay leaf. Cook and stir until thickened. Remove bay leaf. Cut eggs into halves and remove yolks. Mash yolks and blend with a little of the sauce. Season to taste. Heap into whites and arrange eggs in an ungreased 8 x 8 x 2-inch baking dish. Add olives and half of the cheese to remaining sauce and pour over and around eggs. Top with remaining cheese and bake at 350 degrees for 15 to 20 minutes or until thoroughly heated. Serves 4.

Mrs. Fred Carroll, Lyon

EGG SOUFFLE SALAD

1 (3-ounce) package lemon gelatin
1 cup hot water
½ cup cold water
2 tablespoons vinegar
½ cup mayonnaise
salt and pepper to taste
3 diced hard-cooked eggs
1 cup chopped celery
1 tablespoon finely chopped onion
2 tablespoons pimiento
4 tablespoons pickled relish
2 tablespoons chopped bell pepper

Dissolve gelatin in hot water. Add cold water, vinegar, mayonnaise, salt and pepper. Beat with rotary beater. Pour into tray and chill until it is firm one inch from edge of pan. Whip. Fold in eggs, celery, onion, pimiento, relish and bell pepper. Pour into an ungreased 8 x 12 x 2-inch pan and chill 30 to 60 minutes before serving. Serve with sour cream dressing. Serves 12.

Mrs. Danny Hartley, Clarksdale

MOLDED EGG SALAD RING

4 tablespoons unflavored
  gelatin
½ cup cold water
¼ cup hot water
2¼ cups mayonnaise
1½ cups chili sauce
¾ cup catsup
1 teaspoon sugar

2 tablespoons Worcestershire
  sauce
1 tablespoon red hot sauce
juice of 1 grated onion
1½ cups diced celery
½ cup diced green pepper
9 hard-cooked chopped eggs
salt to taste

DRESSING:

2 cups mayonnaise
2 tablespoons chili sauce
1 tablespoon horseradish

1 tablespoon horseradish
  mustard
1 tablespoon grated onion
1 crushed button garlic

Dissolve gelatin in ½ cup cold water, add hot water and dissolve. Blend mayonnaise, chili sauce, catsup, sugar, Worcestershire sauce, hot sauce and onion juice. Add celery, pepper, eggs and salt. Then add gelatin. Pour into a 3-quart ring mold. Mix last 6 ingredients into a dressing and pour over salad when firm. Boiled shrimp is delicious served in center of this salad. Serves 12 to 15.

Mrs. J. P. Fisher, Jonestown

EGG–MACARONI SALAD

1 cup cooked macaroni
1 cup raisins
½ cup diced sweet
  cucumber pickles

½ cup diced celery
4 hard-cooked eggs, chopped
½ cup mayonnaise

Combine and toss together lightly the above ingredients. Serve in lettuce lined bowl or as individual salads. Serves 6 to 8.

Mrs. Zula Thompson, Louin

CREOLE EGGS

2 tablespoons cooking oil
2 tablespoons chopped onion
3 cloves finely chopped garlic
6 tablespoons flour
1 pound can tomatoes, mashed
  fine
⅛ teaspoon salt

⅛ teaspoon pepper
3 tablespoons finely
  chopped parsley
1½ dozen eggs, hard-cooked,
  chopped fine
cracker crumbs
butter

Sautè onion and garlic in oil until light brown. Add 3 tablespoons of flour. Cook until thickened, then add tomatoes, the other three tablespoons of flour, parsley and the seasonings. Cook slowly until well done, about 45 minutes to 1 hour. Mix eggs with sauce, put in greased casserole. Cover with cracker crumbs and dots of butter. Brown in oven and serve hot. Serves 5.

Mrs. Walter White, Indianola

CREOLE EGGS

¾ cup chopped onion
1 cup chopped celery
1 large bell pepper, chopped
bacon drippings
1 (8-ounce) can tomato sauce

1 (10½-ounce) can cream of celery soup
8 hard-cooked eggs (or 1 per person)

Sautè onion, celery and bell pepper in bacon drippings. Do not let brown. Add tomato sauce and celery soup. Simmer until well blended. Then, in a casserole, spread a layer of the sauce and a layer of sliced hardcooked eggs. Repeat layers with sauce as top layer. Heat in 300 degree oven for 30 minutes before serving. This is good with broiled chicken or ham and may be made in the morning before serving at evening meal. Serves 8.

Mrs. T. A. Gamblin, Jackson

EGG CASSEROLE

6 hard-cooked eggs
3 tablespoons dairy sour cream

2 teaspoons prepared mustard
¼ teaspoon salt

SAUCE:

2 tablespoons butter
½ cup chopped green pepper
1/3 cup chopped onion
¼ cup chopped pimiento

1 (10½-ounce) can condensed cream of mushroom soup
1 cup dairy sour cream
½ cup shredded cheddar cheese

Shell eggs and cut lengthwise. Remove yolks and set whites aside. Mash yolks and blend in sour cream, mustard and salt. Fill whites with yolk mixture. In large skillet melt butter. Sautè green pepper and onion in butter until tender. Remove from heat, stir in pimiento, soup and sour cream. Place one half the soup mixture in shallow baking dish (1½-quart), add eggs, cut side up, in single layer. Pour remaining soup mixture over top. Sprinkle with cheddar cheese and bake 20 minutes in 350 degree oven. Serves 6 to 8.

Mrs. Morris Agnew, Guntown

STUFFED EGG CASSEROLE

1 dozen hard-cooked eggs
¼ pound soft margarine
   or butter
salt to taste
1 (10¾-ounce) can tomato
   soup, undiluted

1 (10½-ounce) can cream of
   mushroom soup, undiluted
1 (4½-ounce) can deviled ham
1½ teaspoons chili powder

Peel eggs. Cut in half lengthwise, and remove yolks. Cream egg yolks with butter. Salt to taste. Stuff into whites. Place in 1½-quart casserole. Make sauce with soups, deviled ham and chili powder. Pour over eggs. Bake 25 minutes at 350 degrees. Serves 12.

Mrs. John Irving, Canton

HAM 'N EGGS

1 cup diced ham
2 cups milk, scalded
2 tablespoons melted butter or
   margarine

2 cups soft bread crumbs
1 teaspoon salt
¼ teaspoon black pepper
6 eggs, separated

Combine ham, milk, butter, bread crumbs, salt and pepper. Stir in egg yolks. Beat egg whites until stiff and fold into other mixture. Pour into buttered 12 x 8 x 2-inch baking dish. Bake at 325 degrees for 20 to 25 minutes until firm to touch. Serve at once. Serves 6.

Mrs. S. F. O'Neal, Wiggins

CREAMED EGGS

¼ cup flour
¼ cup butter or margarine
2 cups milk

6 hard-cooked eggs,
   quartered
salt and pepper

Blend flour thoroughly with melted butter or margarine. Add milk and cook over low heat, stirring constantly until thickened. Add eggs to sauce, season, heat, and serve on toast. If desired, add to the butter 2 teaspoons Worcestershire sauce or grated onion, or ¼ to ½ teaspoon curry powder. Serves 6.

Mrs. W. D. Stovall, Wayside

CRUMBS AND EGGS

2 cups bread crumbs	3 tablespoons grated cheese
1½ cups milk	½ teaspoon salt
4 beaten eggs	⅛ teaspoon pepper
1 tablespoon butter	1 tablespoon finely chopped onion

Heat bread crumbs and milk in saucepan until hot. Using fork, mash crumbs with milk until a thin paste is formed. Add other ingredients and cook until thick and creamy. Serves 6.

Mrs. Jessie Bush, Fayette

EGGS WITH PEPPER

3 green peppers	3 tomatoes
1 onion, chopped	salt and pepper
3 tablespoons corn oil	4 eggs

Slice peppers and onion thinly. Sautè in oil. When half cooked, add peeled and cut up tomatoes. Salt and pepper. Simmer until it is a soft puree, crushing ingredients with a fork. Add eggs, stirring quickly and constantly until eggs are creamy. Serve at once on toast triangles. Serves 4.

Mrs. Ethel A. Richardson, West Point

SAVORY HAM AND EGGS

4 slices bread, toasted	dash of pepper
1 cup chopped boiled ham	1 cup milk
2 tablespoons butter or margarine	¾ cup grated sharp cheddar cheese
2 tablespoons flour	4 eggs
½ teaspoon salt	parsley

Spread toast with chopped ham and keep warm. Melt butter. Blend in flour, salt and pepper. Add milk. Cook, stirring until thickened. Stir in cheese. Poach eggs, and put one on each slice of toast with ham. Top with cheese sauce and garnish with parsley. Serves 4.

Mrs. Mary B. Marks, McComb

SWISS POACHED EGGS

1 tablespoon fat
¾ cup cream
6 eggs

3 tablespoons grated cheese
6 slices toasted bread

Melt fat in saucepan. Add cream. When hot, gently pour in eggs. When egg whites are desired consistency (3 to 9 minutes) sprinkle cheese on top. Lift eggs onto toast and spoon cream around toast. Serves 6.

Mrs. Helen Bullen, Fayette

POACHED EGGS—FAMILY STYLE

water
2 teaspoons salt or vinegar

7 eggs

Pour water into a large deep skillet to a depth of at least 1½ inches. Add salt or vinegar. Heat until water simmers around edge of pan and tiny bubbles cover the bottom. Break 7 eggs into a bowl. Do not break yolks. When water simmers, reduce heat. Stir water well with a large spoon until it swirls rapidly around the pan. When it is evenly swirling carefully slip the eggs into center of skillet. Cook eggs over medium heat until whites are firm and a film forms over the yolks. Cooking time is approximately 3 to 5 minutes. Separate eggs with a knife and remove from water, using a greased slotted spoon. Place eggs on buttered toast. Serve at once. Serves 7.

Mrs. Leta Slade, Poplarville

OMELET

4 eggs
½ teaspoon salt
⅛ teaspoon pepper

¼ cup milk
4 teaspoons butter

Separate eggs. Beat yolks with salt, pepper and milk until creamy. Beat egg whites until stiff and fold into yolks. Have hot skillet ready with

[167]

butter melted and bubbling. Turn omelet into skillet lightly so as not to scatter the butter. Spread omelet gently with fork. Prick bubbles and smooth top to ensure even cooking. Shake skillet to keep omelet loose on the bottom. Do not cook too fast. When it is set, turn one half over onto other half. Do not shake skillet too much as omelet may fall. Slip onto hot dish and serve at once. Cooking time 12 minutes. Serves 6.

Mrs. Willard Smith, Fayette

EGG FLAPJACKS

4 eggs
1 tablespoon grated onion
  (optional)
1/3 cup flour
½ teaspoon salt
¼ teaspoon pepper

1 teaspoon baking powder
1 1/3 cups grated cheddar
  cheese
1/3 cup salad oil

Beat eggs. Add onion, sift in flour, salt, pepper and baking powder. Blend well. Stir in cheese. In skillet, heat part of oil. Drop in large spoonfuls of egg mixture, turn, browning on both sides. Add more oil as needed. Serve at once with marmalade, syrup, or a favorite jelly. Yields 8 large flapjacks.

Mrs. Russell Bryson, Tupelo

FEATHERWEIGHT PANCAKES

3 eggs, separated
¼ teaspoon salt
¼ cup flour

¾ cup creamed cottage
  cheese

Beat egg whites until stiff but not dry. With same beater, beat egg yolks until light and lemon colored. Stir into yolk mixture, salt, flour and cottage cheese. Fold in whites. Drop by small spoonfuls onto hot, lightly greased griddle. Cook until golden brown on both sides. Serve hot with butter and maple syrup. Yields about 16 small pancakes.

Mrs. Russell Bryson, Tupelo

❧[Cheese]❧

Cheese is one of the most versatile of foods. It's good in main dishes, salads, sauces or as a dessert served with fruit.

A lot of food value is found in cheese. It contains most of the nutrients of milk including protein, riboflavin and calcium. Like meat, eggs and fish, cheese has satisfying flavor and staying power. It is one of the most popular meat substitutes.

There are more than 400 varieties of natural cheese on the market today in addition to pasteurized process cheese and related products.

Cheese is a concentrated food and should be used in small amounts, grated or in combination with other foods. It is a protein food, and must be cooked at a low temperature. Cooked too quickly, cheese gets tough and stringy.

NEVER–FAIL CHEESE SOUFFLE

1 cup milk
1 tablespoon minute tapioca
1 cup grated yellow cheese
3 eggs, beaten separately

few drops Worcestershire
  sauce
1 teaspoon salt
sprinkling of paprika
  (optional)

Scald milk in double boiler, add the tapioca. Stir and cook 12 minutes. Add cheese and let it melt. Add beaten egg yolks and when thickened, remove from heat. Add Worcestershire sauce, salt and paprika. Let mixture cool, then add the stiffly beaten egg whites. Pour into a buttered glass baking dish. Bake the souffle in a 350 degree oven for 30 minutes. Serves 4 to 6.

Ada Dee McClamroch, Corinth

CHEESE FONDUE

3 eggs, separated
1 (10¾-ounce) can cream of
  vegetable soup

1 cup shredded cheddar
  cheese
¼ teaspoon dry mustard
2 cups bread crumbs

Beat egg whites until stiff. Beat egg yolks until thick. Blend into beaten yolks the soup, cheese and mustard. Stir in bread crumbs. Fold in egg whites carefully. Spoon into ungreased 1½-quart casserole. Bake at 325 degrees for 1 hour. Serves 4 to 6.

Mrs. Robert Young, West Point

CHEESE FONDUE

4 slices buttered bread
½ pound sharp cheese
2 beaten eggs
1 cup milk

¼ teaspoon salt
1 teaspoon Worcestershire
  sauce
1/16 teaspoon red pepper

Remove crust from bread and cut in cubes. Place half the bread in buttered 1½ quart casserole. Cover with half the cheese. Repeat. Beat eggs, add milk and seasonings. Pour over bread and cheese and chill several hours before baking. Bake in 300 degree oven for 45 minutes. Serves 6.

Mrs. Eugenia Scott, Fayette

CHEESE GRITS

1 cup uncooked grits
¼ pound butter
1 (6-ounce) bacon-cheese
  roll

3 eggs
2/3 cup milk
½ cup grated cheddar cheese

Cook grits according to instructions on package. While hot add butter and cheese roll. Let cool. Beat eggs. Add milk to eggs, stir well into grits mixture. Pour into greased 2-quart casserole. Sprinkle top with grated cheese. Bake in 300 degree oven for 30 minutes. Serve topped with bacon curls. Serves 4.

Mrs. Tommie Childress, Raleigh

SCALLOPED PEPPER

2 bell peppers—1 red, 1 green
¼ pound crumbled saltine
  crackers

8-ounces mild cheddar cheese,
  cubed
milk
1 tablespoon margarine

Cut peppers into ½-inch pieces. Boil 10 minutes in salted water. In a deep 1½-quart casserole, make a layer of cracker crumbs. Add layer of pepper and layer of cheese. Repeat layers. Cover with milk and dot with margarine. Bake at 350 degrees for 45 minutes, stirring deep every 15 minutes. Serves 8.

Mrs. John A. Evans, Jackson

CHEESY POTATO SALAD

¼ cup finely chopped onion
1 tablespoon cooking oil
1 tablespoon all-purpose flour
1 tablespoon sugar
1 teaspoon salt
¼ teaspoon dry mustard
¼ cup water

3 tablespoons vinegar
2½ cups diced cooked potatoes
½ cup chopped celery
2 tablespoons chopped green
  pepper
2 ounces (½ cup) shredded
  process American cheese

In small saucepan, cook onion in oil till tender. Blend in flour, sugar, salt, and mustard. Combine water and vinegar; add to onion mixture. Cook and stir until thickened. In bowl, combine potatoes, celery, green pepper, and cheese; add to hot onion mixture and toss to coat. Chill. OR, turn mixture into 1 quart casserole; cover and bake in 350 degree oven for 25 to 30 minutes. Serves 4.

Mrs. John H. Price, Booneville

PEPPERY GREEN BEAN–CHEESE CASSEROLE

4 cups (2 [15½-ounce] cans) French style green beans with mushrooms (If green beans with mushrooms are unavailable, use small can of chopped mushrooms, drained, to mix with beans)

1 cup (8-ounce jar) mild flavored imported Italian pepperoncini, drained

16 slices (12-ounce package) pasteurized process American cheese

Drain liquid from beans with mushrooms. Spread ½ of the beans with mushrooms over bottom of lightly greased 1½-quart baking dish. Remove stems from the little sweet peppers and arrange ½ of them over beans. Overlap 4 double slices of cheese on top of sweet peppers. Repeat layers with remaining ingredients, ending with cheese slices on top. Bake in 400 degree oven for 20 minutes or until cheese begins to melt and is lightly browned. Serves 8.

Mrs. Richard Davis, Wayside

MACARONI AND CHEESE

1 (7-ounce) package macaroni, cooked and drained
¼ cup chopped onion
1 cup mayonnaise
1 pound grated hoop-sharp cheese

¼ cup chopped pimiento
1 (10½-ounce) can cream of mushroom soup
½ cup milk
½ cup cracker crumbs

Cook and drain macaroni. Combine all other ingredients except milk and cracker crumbs together and mix with macaroni. Reserve some cheese for top. Pour milk around and over ingredients. Top with cheese and cracker crumbs. Cook at 350 degrees about 30 minutes or until cheese is bubbly. Serves 6 to 8.

Mrs. Kam Quinn, Louisville

CHEESE PUDDING

2 cups soft bread crumbs
2 cups coarsely grated sharp cheese
2 well beaten eggs
2 cups milk

1 teaspoon salt
1 teaspoon prepared mustard
pepper to taste
¼ cup bread crumbs

Place layer of crumbs, then a layer of grated cheese in buttered 2-quart casserole. Continue alternating layers of crumbs and cheese, ending with crumbs. Pour mixture of beaten eggs, milk, salt, mustard, and pepper over crumb-cheese layers. Sprinkle ¼ cup crumbs over top. Bake in 350 degree oven for one hour or until firm like a custard. Good for lunch or supper. Serves 4.

Mrs. M. H. Arnold, Sessums

CHEESE BAKE

8 slices bread	3 slightly beaten eggs
2 tablespoons butter	2 cups milk
2 cups ground cooked ham	¼ teaspoon salt
2 tablespoons prepared mustard	⅛ teaspoon pepper
2 cups grated American cheese	

Remove crust from bread. Spread with butter. Cut on the diagonal. Arrange 4 slices in greased 8-inch square baking pan or dish. Mix ham and mustard and spread over bread. Sprinkle with cheese. Cover with remaining bread slices. Combine eggs, milk, and seasonings. Pour over all. Chill 1 hour. Bake in slow oven (325 degrees) for 1 hour. Serves 4.

Mrs. Reggio O. Simmons, Inverness

HAM AND CHEESE MEAL

2 cups cooked macaroni (4-ounce uncooked)	¼ cup chopped onion
1 cup cubed cheddar cheese	2 tablespoons chopped green pepper
1 cup diced cooked ham	½ teaspoon prepared mustard
1 (10½-ounce) can cream of chicken soup	dash of Tabasco sauce
¼ cup chopped celery	dash pepper

Gently combine all ingredients and chill. Serve with tomato wedges and crackers. Serves 4 to 6.

Mrs. V. K. Carpenter, Greenville

CHEESE CROQUETTES

3 tablespoons butter	1 cup mild grated cheese
½ cup sifted all-purpose flour	½ cup sharp grated cheese
2/3 cup milk	½ teaspoon dry mustard
¼ teaspoon Worcestershire sauce	salt and pepper to taste
2 beaten egg yolks	1 beaten egg
	1½ cups cracker crumbs

Mix all ingredients except the 1 beaten egg and crumbs. Shape into croquettes. Dip into crumbs, beaten egg and crumbs again. Chill. Fry in deep hot fat and drain. Yields 2 dozen small croquettes.

Mrs. Danny Hartley, Clarksdale

CHEESE LOAF

3 cups sifted enriched
  self-rising flour
¼ cup sugar
1 cup grated sharp cheese
  (4-ounces)

½ teaspoon minced onion
1 egg, beaten
1½ cups milk
¼ cup melted shortening

Sift together flour and sugar. Stir in cheese and onion. Combine egg, milk and shortening. Add to flour mixture, stirring just until all flour is moistened. Turn into greased 5¼ x 9½-inch loaf pan. Bake in 350 degree oven for 50 to 60 minutes. Cool a few minutes before turning from pan. Slice in large pieces and serve warm. Makes 1 loaf.

Mrs. V. L. Sandifer, Hollandale

CHEESE DREAMS

3 pounds grated American
  cheese
1 cup finely chopped nuts
2 tablespoons Worcestershire
  sauce
½ teaspoon cayenne pepper

2 medium grated onions
1 cup mayonnaise
1 teaspoon Tabasco
1 teaspoon salt
1 cup finely chopped celery
sliced bread, crust removed

Mix all ingredients except bread together to a smooth paste. Spread generously on thin sliced bread. Roll from corner into cone. Fasten with toothpicks. Place on ungreased cookie sheet. Preheat oven at 500 degrees. Bake quickly. Serves approximately 12.

Mrs. G. H. Hairston, Sr., Silver City

CHEESE TURKS

¾ cup cooked turkey, finely
  diced
½ pound sharp cheese, grated
½ pound soft butter

1 cup nuts, chopped
2 cups flour
¼ teaspoon red pepper
1 teaspoon Worcestershire sauce

Combine turkey, cheese and butter. Add remaining ingredients. Shape mixture into balls about 1 inch in diameter. Bake on ungreased cookie sheet in 250 degree oven for 20 minutes. Yields 4 dozen.

Mrs. J. T. Kerr, Rolling Fork

CHEESY SNACK

1 cup of pancake mix
¼ teaspoon of garlic powder
dash of cayenne
½ cup of grated cheddar
   cheese

2 tablespoons of mayonnaise
1/3 cup of milk
1 tablespoon chopped parsley

Combine pancake mix, garlic powder and cayenne. Beat in cheese, mayonnaise and milk. Shape into 30 small balls. Roll each in chopped parsley. Bake on ungreased cookie sheet in preheated 375 degree oven 8 to 10 minutes. Yields 2½ dozen.

Mrs. Thomas Pearson, West Point

CHEESE CRACKERS

2 cups grated sharp cheese
2 sticks softened margarine
2 cups sifted all-purpose flour
2 cups Rice Krispies
1 teaspoon Worcestershire sauce

1 teaspoon salt or ½ teaspoon
   garlic salt
1 teaspoon Tabasco sauce or
   1 teaspoon cayenne pepper
½ cup imitation bacon bits
   (optional)

Mix all ingredients together well. Work dough into small balls, 1 inch in diameter. Place on ungreased cookie sheet, press top of ball with fork. Bake at 300 degrees for 25 minutes or until golden brown. Yields about 60 crackers.

Mrs. John L. Webb, Clarksdale

SWISS CHEESE FONDUE

1 tablespoon margarine or
   butter
1 pound Swiss cheese,
   shredded
2 cups dry white wine

salt and pepper to taste
baked ham, cut into 1 inch
   cubes
French bread, cut into 1 inch
   cubes

Melt margarine in heavy skillet. Begin to add small amounts of shredded cheese and white wine, allowing time for each to melt before adding more. Stir while adding until smooth. Continue this until all cheese and wine are used. If cheese mixture should be too thick, add more white wine as needed. Transfer to fondue dish and keep hot. Add salt and pepper to taste. Serve ham and French bread cubes with the cheese fondue. Each person may pick up ham or bread with fondue forks and dip into cheese mixture. Serves 4.

Mrs. J. D. Landin, Jr., Utica

CHEESE FONDUELLA

6 tablespoons lemon juice	1 teaspoon Worcestershire sauce
½ pound grated Swiss cheese	⅛ cayenne pepper
½ pound grated Gruyere cheese	½ teaspoon salt
3 tablespoons all-purpose flour	bread cubes
1 cup milk	apple wedges

Heat lemon juice to boiling point. Mix cheeses together. Sprinkle with flour and mix. Add cheese to lemon juice a little at a time until it melts. Add milk slowly, stirring constantly. Add all other ingredients, except bread cubes and apple wedges. Add additional milk as required until the consistency of white sauce. Heat to boiling point. Remove from heat and pour into ungreased earthenware fondue pot. Spear bread cubes and apple wedges on fondue forks; dip into the cheese fonduElla, swirl and eat. For variation: add ¼ teaspoon curry powder instead of the cayenne pepper for curried Cheese FonduElla. Serves 6.

Jim Ella Wells Aden, Rolling Fork

·⟦Game⟧·

Wild game cookery is something that should be mastered by every Southern homemaker. If the men in her family enjoy the outdoor sport of hunting, she'll soon be called on to prepare a venison steak, squirrel stew or some other wild delicacy.

Hunting clubs are popular in Mississippi and many members prefer to do their own cooking. A pot of brunswick stew simmering over an open camp fire at dusk can be mighty tempting.

Some game are mild-flavored and are delicious prepared by a simple recipe such as country fried quail or baked pheasant. Other meats like deer, duck and squirrel have a stronger flavor and need more seasonings and pre-cooking preparation to enhance their taste. The strong flavor of venison (deer meat) can usually be removed by soaking the meat overnight in salt water or a water and vinegar mixture.

For the best quality, it's important that wild game be dressed as soon as possible after killing. Big game such as deer, antelope and elk must be bled and dressed immediately. Game meat freezes well but should be adequately wrapped and used in six to nine months.

VENISON STEAK

3½-inch thick loin or	salt and pepper
round steaks	2 medium onions, sliced

Trim all fat from meat, blot dry with paper towel. Rub salt into meat to taste; sprinkle on black pepper generously (the more pepper the better flavor). Place in skillet with ¼ inch deep cooking oil. Cover top of steak with sliced onions, careful not to let onion touch skillet. Cover and cook over medium heat. Remove onions from skillet to turn steaks over, replace onion and cook until tender. Best when served hot.

Mrs. Harold R. Tyner, Canton

DEER STEAKS

meat tenderizer	½ teaspoon salt
4 (5-inch) round deer steaks	¼ teaspoon pepper
2 cups milk	¼ cup flour

Sprinkle meat tenderizer on steaks and pound on both sides. Cover steaks with milk and let soak for 3 hours. Remove from milk and season with salt and pepper and dredge with flour. Fry in deep fat. Serve hot. Serves 4.

Mrs. Robert Geoghegan, Fayette

GRILLED VENISON

1 bottle red wine	3 thinly sliced small onions
½ cup wine vinegar	3 thinly sliced carrots
1 tablespoon salt	3 minced garlic cloves
several cloves	3 bay leaves
1 teaspoon coarsely ground	½ teaspoon thyme
black pepper	

Combine all ingredients and mix well. In a cool place, turning often, marinate either venison roast or steaks in sauce. Allow six days for marinating a roast and two days for a steak. Then grill or roast venison as usual. Although roasting in the oven is satisfactory, it cannot be compared to preparation on an outdoor grill.

Mrs. Kerry Kinder, Macon

VENISON, SMOTHERED STEAK

2 to 3 pound venison steak   ¼ teaspoon salt
¼ cup vinegar   ¼ teaspoon black pepper
1 teaspoon Worcestershire sauce   flour
¼ teaspoon garlic salt

Trim off fat and any other undesirable parts from steak. Rinse well.
Slice to desired thickness. Place on chopping board and pound or hack
with butcher knife on each side. Mix remaining ingredients except
flour. Saturate each piece and place in refrigerator until ready to cook.
Dredge in flour before browning; brown in hot fat. Cover with water to
make gravy and cook covered, in a 350 degree oven for 1 hour.

Mrs. Lynward Baker, Duck Hill

DEER POT ROAST

2 to 3 pound deer roast (frozen   ¼ cup diced celery or
    or unfrozen)   green pepper
3 tablespoons shortening   1 clove garlic
1 teaspoon table salt   2 medium diced onions
1 teaspoon spiced salt   ¾ cup water
1 teaspoon pepper   6 medium potatoes, cubed
1/3 cup flour

Place shortening in dutch oven over medium heat. Sprinkle meat with
salt and pepper and dredge in flour. Add diced celery or green pepper,
garlic and onions. Brown in dutch oven, turning meat until evenly
browned. Add water. Cover, reduce heat to low and continue to cook
for 3 to 3½ hours. Add potatoes and cook an additional ½ hour, or
until done. Serves 6.

Laura Inez Richardson, Magnolia

VENISON ROAST

4 or 5 pound vension roast   salt and pepper
½ cup vinegar, or more   5 narrow slices beef suet,
water   1-inch thick

Soak vension roast in vinegar water for several hours. Take out and
place in cool water for an hour. Drain, Salt and pepper roast on all sides,

[179]

rubbing in well. Place the sliced suet on the roast, holding in place with toothpicks. Place on sheet of heavy duty foil, wrap well. Place in 325 degree preheated oven. Bake 30 minutes per pound, or until done. Just before removing it from oven, uncover, let brown. The drippings from roast will be like beef drippings. Makes good gravy. Serves 8 to 10.

Mrs. Johnnie Baker, Port Gibson

VENISON ROAST

1 (5-pound) roast	1 (10½-ounce) can cream of
2 teaspoons salt	mushroom soup
2 bay leaves	2 tablespoons sherry

Cover roast in cold water and soak overnight. Salt roast. Place roast and bay leaves in a large boiler on moderate heat and cook for several hours in enough water to cover. When meat is tender, remove top from boiler and cook the water down to 1½ cups. Add the mushroom soup and sherry. Simmer 15 minutes longer. Serves 10.

Mrs. A. J. Gregory, Bay Springs

QUICK VENSION CAMP ROAST

4 or 5 pounds venison	2 (10½-ounce) cans onion
½ cup vegetable oil	soup
2 heaping tablespoons flour	2 soup cans medium hot water

Braise venison on all sides. Take meat out, add flour to fat, stir and brown to a medium brown. Place venison back in roux. Pour onion soup and water on top of roast leaving onions on top. Cook in pressure cooker at 15-pound pressure for 30 minutes. This is for quick thawed meat; cook longer if meat is frozen, 40 to 50 minutes. Serves 8 to 10.

Mrs. L. P. Ratliff, Sr., Brookhaven

REFRIGERATOR–CURED VENISON

4 to 6 pound venison shoulder	Kitchen Bouquet (optional)
or rump roast	salad oil (optional)
1 cup Morton's sugar cure mix	glass, enamel or stone crock
3 cups water	container
1 teaspoon salt	

Wash meat and place in container. Using curing mix and water, make enough brine to completely cover meat. Cover and place in refrigerator from 9 to 12 days, turning meat 2 or 3 times. After curing time is completed, drain meat and place in cooking utensil. Cover with water, add salt and boil until tender. Serve with horseradish or other suitable sauce. May be cooked in oven in open pan at 300 degrees until tender. If oven roasted, brush several times during baking with equal parts Kitchen Bouquet and salad oil. Serves 6 to 8.

Note: Morton's sugar cure mix is necessary for success of recipe.

Mrs. B. L. Berry, Vicksburg

VENISON STEW

2 pounds, cubed venison meat	1 cup diced celery
6 cups salted water	2 cups diced potatoes
1 (8-ounce) can tomato sauce	1 large onion, diced
1 (6-ounce) can tomato paste	1 large bell pepper, diced
1 cup diced carrots	salt and pepper to taste

Marinate venison in vinegar water (1 part vinegar and 3 parts water) 3 hours before cooking. Rinse, and cook in approximately 6 cups of salted water until tender. Add tomato sauce and tomato paste, stir well. Add vegetables, season to taste, cook until done. Serves 4.

Woodrow W. Ware, Raleigh

DAVID COLEMAN'S ROAST DUCK

6 ducks, with broth	6 cloves garlic
salt	garlic salt
black pepper (coarse ground)	3 teaspoons Tabasco sauce
red pepper (coarse ground)	1½ dozen fresh lemons
1½ pounds real butter	1 (10-ounce) bottle Lea &
3 onions	Perrin Worcestershire sauce
6 small tart apples	3 bay leaves
3 small Irish potatoes	

Rub ducks inside and out with salt, black pepper and red pepper and place in roaster. Have butter at room temperature and rub generously inside and outside of ducks. Fill the cavity with onions, apple and potato. Place 1 garlic clove in the cavities. Pour other ingredients over. Add one-half bay leaf for each duck. Cover roaster. Stuff ducks and let stand in

[181]

marinade overnight. Begin roasting at 150 degrees. Increase temperature 25 degrees each hour until it reaches 300 degrees or until ducks are tender. This will take about five hours.

When using the broth to make dressing, add at least an equal amount of hot water, as the broth is very rich. It will be necessary to add only eggs, cooked onion, celery and sage to cornbread and broth for the dressing.

Note: When David Coleman returned to Mississippi after having lived in South Louisiana for several years, he started growing ducks on *Lakeland*, his plantation near Thornton. At the end of the harvest season of his first year, he had a duck supper for about 20 of his friends. As the size of his flock grew, so did the size of the crowd at the duck suppers. In 2 years it had to be moved to a larger camp and many ranges and roasters borrowed to handle the cooking. The second site was the Bailey Place on Pluto Plantation, owned by Bobby Thompson. From there the duck supper was moved to the Yazoo City Elks Club where some 600 men from at least six states were served.

An interesting outgrowth of the men's duck supper was a ladies duck supper. Mr. Coleman cooked and served his female ducks for the ladies in the area. At the last ladies' duck supper, about 150 were served. Mr. Coleman was chief cook for this event too.

This recipe came from a South Louisiana Cajun who was a cook at Frank Lindsay's Duck Hunting Camp on Catahoula Lake. It was originated for cooking wild ducks, but is delicious for any kind of fowl.

David Coleman, Yazoo City

ORANGE DUCK

1 duck	1 tablespoon orange marmalade
salt and pepper	2 livers of duck or chicken,
1 stick butter	chopped fine
½ cup soy sauce	1 tablespoon flour
2 oranges	1 tablespoon curacao

Rub duck inside and out with salt and pepper; then brush with melted butter and soy sauce. Grate peel from oranges and set aside. Slice oranges, remove seeds, and stuff duck with orange slices and orange marmalade. Place in roaster, sear at 450 for 10 minutes. Cover and cook for 1½ hours, basting occasionally. Meantime, simmer finely chopped livers in enough salted water to cover until tender. Pour off pan juice from duck, discarding excess fat. Simmer juices gently and add grated orange peel and chopped livers with their broth. Thicken with flour. Put curacoa in gravy boat, add gravy and serve immediately. Serves 4.

Mrs. L. B. Morris, Macon

BRANDIED DUCK

2 or 3 Mallard ducks,	1 teaspoon parsley
cut in serving pieces	¼ teaspoon thyme
1 bay leaf	3 jiggers brandy
2 large onions, cut up	¼ cup olive oil
2 cups claret	½ pound mushrooms
1 clove garlic	

Marinate ducks for 4 hours in a deep dish with bay leaf, onions, claret, garlic, parsley, thyme and brandy. After 4 hours, place olive oil in a casserole and heat. Brown duck then add marinating liquid and mushrooms. Cover casserole and cook over low flame until duck is tender.

Mrs. Otto Browning, Yazoo City

WILD DUCK

5 to 6 pounds of duck (cut into	½ teaspoon thyme
serving pieces)	1 bay leaf
salt and pepper	¼ teaspoon marjoram
½ cup brandy (optional)	¼ teaspoon ground allspice
2/3 cup claret	2 tablespoons bacon fat
1 medium orange, sliced	1 tablespoon olive oil
2 large onions, chopped	½ pound sliced mushrooms
1 tablespoon parsley, minced	1 clove garlic

Wipe pieces of duck with damp cloth, rub with salt and pepper. Put in deep bowl. Mix brandy, claret, sliced orange, onions, parsley, thyme, bay leaf, marjoram, allspice and pour over duck. Let stand for several hours or overnight. Stir occasionally to be sure all pieces of duck are soaked in marinade. When ready to cook, drain, saving the marinade. Heat bacon fat and olive oil in skillet and brown duck well. Place, when browned, in roaster or large casserole. Remove skillet from heat and stir in the liquid in which duck was marinated, scraping all the brown glaze from the bottom. Pour this over duck, add garlic (stuck on toothpick) and the mushrooms. Cover closely and cook in 325 degree oven for 1 to 1½ hours or until duck is tender. Remove garlic. Serves 4 to 6.

Mrs. Robert Aldridge, Estill

BAKED WILD DUCK AND DUCK SAUCE

2 large ducks	1 large sliced Irish potato
2 teaspoons soda	1 tablespoon salt
3 tablespoons vinegar	2 tablespoons pepper
1 large sliced onion	butter
¼ cup of salt	flour

SAUCE:

½ cup melted butter or oleo	2 tablespoons vinegar
juice of 2 lemons	1 cup chopped celery
1 tablespoon prepared mustard	1 (14-ounce) bottle catsup

Soak ducks overnight in cold tap water to which has been added the soda, vinegar, onion, ¼ cup salt and potato. Use large container (not aluminum) and cover with a cloth. For more ducks, simply increase amount of ingredients. Wash and see that ducks are clean before putting in the above solution. Remove from solution and wipe with cloth. Rub inside and out with 1 tablespoon salt and 2 tablespoons pepper, then rub with butter and sprinkle with flour. Put breast down in baking dish or roaster, cover with sauce made from remaining ingredients. Cook for 2 hours in a 350 degree oven, with dish covered. Baste often and add hot water as needed. Serves 8.

Mrs. Frank Stuart, Rolling Fork

BAKED DUCK

4 ducks	1 onion
4 tablespoons salt	2 apples
2 teaspoons pepper	4 stalks celery

Sprinkle ducks on outside and inside with salt and pepper. Place ¼ of an onion and ½ of an apple in the cavity of each. Place on a rack in a 12 x 16-inch roaster with two inches of water in the bottom. Chop one stalk of celery over each duck. Cover with foil then place the lid over all. Cook at 350 degrees until meat will leave the bones. Remove rack from the roaster and let ducks cool. Remove meat from bones keeping breasts in halves. Return meat to broth in roaster. Place over low heat and keep warm until time to serve. Serves 8.

Mrs. Homer A. Greene, Tutwiler

BAR-B-QUED DOVES

6 cleaned doves	¼ teaspoon pepper
½ teaspoon salt	¼ teaspoon Accent

SAUCE:

½ pound margarine	½ teaspoon salt
6 lemons, juice and rind	¼ teaspoon pepper
½ bottle Heinz 57 sauce	1/16 teaspoon Accent
½ bottle Worcestershire sauce	

Rub doves with salt, pepper and Accent. Place in roaster, with very little water in the bottom. Put in 450 degree oven and brown on both sides. To make sauce, melt margarine, add lemon juice and rind, Heinz 57 sauce, Worcestershire sauce and seasonings. Pour the sauce over the doves; reduce heat to 350 degrees and bake, covered, 1½ hours. Baste 3 or 4 times. Serves 6.

Mrs. Robert Phillips, Fayette

BRAISED DOVES

1 stick margarine	10 dove breasts
juice of 1 lemon	salt and pepper to taste
3 tablespoons Worcestershire sauce	

Melt margarine in heavy pan on very low heat; add lemon juice and Worcestershire sauce. Salt and pepper doves and place in butter mixture. Cover with tight fitting top. Simmer (very low heat) for 2 hours without lifting top. Recipe may be doubled and cooked in roaster in 250 degree oven. Serves 2 to 3.

Mrs. Laura Sumrall, Brookhaven

DOVE OR QUAIL PAPRIKA

12 dove or quail	1 (6 or 7-ounce) package egg noodles
¾ cup all-purpose flour	salt to taste
2 teaspoons salt	water
½ teaspoon pepper	¼ stick margarine
1 teaspoon paprika	2 cloves garlic, minced
1½ sticks margarine	
½ cup cooking oil	

Wash birds and make sure all feathers and pellets are removed. Mix flour, salt, pepper, paprika and pour into a paper bag. In meantime, heat the 1½ stick margarine and cooking oil in a 12 x 17 x 2¼-inch pan in a 350 degree oven. Place a few birds at a time in the sack, shake and coat thoroughly. Place birds in the hot melted margarine and oil. Place in oven and cook at 350 degrees for 45 minutes, turning once. *Do not cook until dry and hard.* The length of cooking time will depend upon the age and tenderness of the birds. While the birds are cooking in the oven, place the package of noodles in a 2-quart saucepan, cover with water salted to taste. Cook until noodles are tender. Sautè garlic in ¼ stick melted margarine. Remove the garlic buds. When the birds are tender, drain the noodles, pour warm garlic-margarine sauce on noodles. Remove birds from pan and place on platter. Pour all scrapings and drippings from the pan in which the doves were cooked, over noodles also. Mix well and place around birds on platter. Serves 6.

Mrs. Joseph L. Hurst, Booneville

BAKED DOVES

8 doves
flour, salted and peppered
hot fat
1 (10½-ounce) can
consomme

1 teaspoon Worcestershire sauce
1 teaspoon onion juice
½ cup sherry wine

Roll doves in seasoned flour, brown in hot fat as for fried chicken. Remove doves and place in a roaster or dutch oven. Make gravy, using consomme added to liquid in which doves were browned. Add the Worcestershire sauce and onion juice. Pour over doves. Add sherry wine and bake in a slow oven, 250 degrees. Baste frequently and add water and wine as needed. Serves 4.

Mrs. Hugh Moseley, Pheba

DOVE WITH WINE

12 doves
salt and pepper to taste
flour for dredging
½ cup oil for browning
½ cup water

1 (10½-ounce) can cream of
mushroom soup
½ cup chopped celery
½ cup red wine

[186]

Shake doves in seasoned flour. Brown in oil in skillet. Pour off excess oil. Place in 2-quart casserole. Combine water, soup, chopped celery and wine. Pour over doves. Cover and bake at 350 degrees for 2½ hours. Serves 6.

Mrs. L. E. Gholston, Starkville

BARBECUED RABBIT

1 rabbit	¼ cup salad oil
1½ teaspoons salt	1 tablespoon paprika
4 teaspoons sugar	1 tablespoon Worcestershire
2/3 cup catsup	sauce
½ cup vinegar	1 medium onion, chopped
1 tablespoon pepper	1 cup water
1 clove garlic	

Brown rabbit in hot fat and place in a heavy container. Combine all ingredients and blend well. Pour sauce over rabbit and bake uncovered at 325 degrees for 1½ to 2 hours. Baste every 15 to 20 minutes.

Walter White, Yazoo City

MARINATED RABBIT (OR VENISON)

2 cups water	1 teaspoon mashed pepper-
½ cup salad oil	corns
1 coarsely cut carrot	2 large or 3 small rabbits,
2 stalks of celery	cut into serving pieces
2 bay leaves	1 cup flour
1 tablespoon dried parsley	2 teaspoons salt
2 cups good white wine	½ teaspoon nutmeg
2 medium onions	½ teaspoon pepper
3 teaspoons salt	4 tablespoons bacon drippings
	2 cups sour cream

For marinade, liquify in blender water, salad oil, carrot, celery, bay leaves, and parsley. Add liquified mixture to wine, onions, salt and peppercorns. Bring this to a boil and simmer for 5 minutes, cool. This will make 5 to 6 cups of marinade which will keep in the refrigerator for 1 month. *Do not keep this in a metal container!* Place rabbit with marinade in a plastic, glass, or earthenware container. Refrigerate for 48 hours, turning 2 or 3 times. Remove meat from marinade, wipe dry.

Strain remaining marinade and set aside. Also reserve the onion after you strain the marinade. Mix flour, salt, nutmeg and pepper in a paper bag. Place rabbit in bag and shake. Heat bacon drippings in a large skillet or dutch oven, slowly sautè meat until golden brown. When nearly done add onion slices from marinade. Add 2 cups strained liquid marinade. Cover tightly and simmer over low heat, 325 to 350 degrees for 1 hour or until tender. Remove rabbit to a hot serving dish. Skim off excess fat. Stir in sour cream, more marinade, if needed, and blend. Pour this gravy over meat. Serve very hot. Serves 6.

Mrs. Joseph L. Hurst, Booneville

BAKED SQUIRRELS

4 squirrels, cleaned and
  dressed
flour
1 can bouillon
¼ teaspoon Worcestershire
  sauce
2 tablespoons parsley,
  chopped

2 tablespoons onion juice
1 clove garlic, minced
1 small bay leaf
salt, seasoned salt and pepper
  to taste

Dredge squirrels in flour and brown in roasting pan. Add all ingredients and bake at 350 degrees for 45 minutes. Reduce temperature to 300 degrees and bake slowly for another 45 minutes or until tender. Serves 4.

Mrs. L. T. Potter, Wayside

QUAIL SAUTERN

12 dressed quail
1 teaspoon black pepper
2 teaspoons paprika
3 teaspoons salt
1 cup chopped onion
1 cup sautern wine

½ pound margarine
2 cups warm water
2 tablespoons flour
2 (4-ounce) cans mushroom
  stems and pieces

Sprinkle quail with salt, pepper and paprika. Put margarine in iron dutch oven then lightly brown quail and remove. Put onion in dutch oven, cook until lightly browned and remove. Add water and flour, stirring until smooth for gravy. Add wine, drained mushroom stems, pieces of quail and onions. Mix all together with quail on top. Place in a 350 degree oven for 2 hours with top on dutch oven. To brown quail place in large baking dish uncovered and baste with gravy in 400 degree oven for 45 minutes. Serves 6.

Mrs. Floyd Mobley, Jackson

FRIED QUAIL

4 quails	1 teaspoon salt
¼ cup flour	⅛ teaspoon pepper

Roll quail in a dry mixture of flour, salt and pepper until they are completely covered. In a deep frying pan half filled with hot shortening, brown quail on both sides then reduce heat and slowly cook quail for 15 to 20 minutes or until they are tender. Don't overcook. Serves 2 to 4.

Georgia L. Williams, Hazlehurst

PEGGY'S QUAIL

salt and pepper	1 tablespoon Worcestershire
8 quail	sauce
2 sticks margarine	½ cup onion finely chopped
1 can chicken broth	½ teaspoon garlic juice
2 tablespoons of cream	

Brown salted and peppered quail in 1 stick of margarine in skillet on top of range. Put quail breast down in pyrex dish or roasting pan containing the remaining ingredients. Cover and bake in 300 degree oven for at least 2 hours or until tender. Serves 8.

Mrs. Ray (Peggy) Cannada, Edwards

SMOTHERED QUAIL

6 quail, dressed	½ cup sherry
6 tablespoons butter	salt and pepper
3 tablespoons flour	cooked rice
2 cups chicken broth	

Prepare quail, brown in heavy skillet or dutch oven in butter. Remove quail to baking dish. Add flour to butter in skillet and stir well. Slowly add chicken broth, sherry, salt and pepper. Blend well and pour over quail. Cover baking dish and bake at 350 degrees about 1 hour. Serve with cooked rice. Serves 3.

Hazel H. Bequette, Mayersville

[189]

QUAIL

8 quail
salt and pepper
1 stick butter
juice of 1 lemon
¼ medium onion, sliced

¼ cup Lea and Perrin sauce
½ lemon, sliced
1½ cups water
salt and pepper

Season birds with salt and pepper. Brown birds in lightly browned butter. In a saucepan, put lemon juice, onion, Lea and Perrin sauce, lemon slices, water and salt. Pepper to taste. Bring to boil, reduce to simmer. Remove onion and lemon slices; pour mixture over birds. Put lid on skillet and cook about 1 hour at 300 degrees or over very low heat. Serves 4.

It goes without saying that quail are better if not cooked the day of the hunt. Cleaned quail should be refrigerated at least 4 days before cooking for best flavor. This is one dish where there should be no substitute for butter. This method of cooking quail, snipe or other shore birds was introduced to this country by the Theroits when they moved into Attala County to open a cafe 80 years ago. The French love of good food resulted in this recipe.

Chatwin Jackson, Kosciusko

PHEASANT IN CASSEROLE

1 pheasant
1 cup flour
1 teaspoon salt
½ teaspoon pepper
1 cup cooking oil or butter
½ cup mushrooms

½ cup white wine (or ¼ teaspoon nutmeg, ½ teaspoon thyme and 1 tablespoon chopped parsley)

Cut pheasant in serving pieces (4th's). Roll in seasoned flour (flour, salt, pepper). Brown lightly in hot butter or oil. Place in casserole or pan. Add mushrooms and ½ cup white wine. Cover, and bake in slow oven at 350 degrees about 2 hours. The wine may be omitted and use nutmeg, thyme and chopped parsley. Serves 4.

Mrs. L. B. Morris, Macon

PHEASANTS IN SOUR CREAM

2 pheasants
2 teaspoons salt
1 teaspoon pepper
½ cup sifted all-purpose
   flour

1 cup salad oil
1 (10½-ounce) can
   mushroom soup
1 cup sour cream
1 cup French onion sour cream

Cut pheasants into serving pieces. Sprinkle with salt and pepper, dredge in flour. Fry in oil until brown. Remove to an ungreased 8 x 12 x 2-inch casserole. Pour off excess oil after browning the pheasants. Make gravy by mixing soup, sour cream and French onion sour cream in the skillet where pheasants were browned. Heat and pour over pheasants. Bake in a 325 degree oven for 1 hour. Serves 8.

Mrs. B. J. Haney, Tutwiler

BRUNSWICK STEW

3 pounds chuck beef roast
3 pounds pork roast
3 pounds chicken
3 squirrels
1 rabbit
1 quart butter beans
1 (No. 2) can English peas
1½ pound package
   spaghetti

1 quart raw cubed potatoes
1 cup chopped onions
1 quart corn, cream style
1 (14-ounce) bottle catsup
1 (6-ounce) can tomato paste
add Louisiana hot sauce to
   taste

Boil each kind of meat separately, salt to taste. Save all liquid. Boil until meat is tender. Remove from bones. Put all meat together with liquid in a 20-quart container. Start cooking on low heat. Add hard-to-cook vegetables to meat first; then add others according to time interval for cooking. Cook all ingredients together about 1 hour or until thick. Serve with crackers and salad. Yield: 2 gallons.

Mrs. Thomas Bufkin, Port Gibson

⁖⟦Breads⟧⁖

Nothing smells better than the aroma of homemade bread baking in the oven. It's an invitation to sit down and enjoy the warm hospitality and good food of a homemaker who enjoys her work.

Certain breads are traditional in Mississippi, and it's hard to resist a serving of golden cornbread, hush puppies or buttermilk biscuits—"take two and butter 'em while they're hot."

The history of bread-baking is life itself. Once enjoying the status of an art, it has become an enthusiastic hobby for those who pride themselves on their culinary skills. Our bread-making grandmothers used to get up at the crack of dawn and work all day to turn out a tantalizing loaf of bread.

Today it's easier than ever to make good bread. Flour is standardized, better yeast is available, and we are more informed about the chemical factors involved in combining ingredients. We also have better cooking equipment.

Breads are usually divided into two classes, yeast breads and quick breads. Yeast breads are raised by a leavening agent that produces a gas, causing the dough to be light and porous. Quick breads like biscuits, waffles and muffins are raised by the chemical action that takes place when baking powder is combined with water or sweet milk and soda is mixed with sour milk or other acid ingredients.

The secret of good bread-baking is practice. With practice and a little imagination, a basic recipe can produce many delicious variations for mealtime pleasure.

SALT RISING BREAD

1 cup sweet milk
½ cup sifted home ground
  corn meal
1 quart sweet milk
1 tablespoon sugar
4 pounds sifted all-purpose
  flour less ¾ cup

¾ cup shortening
½ cup sugar
1 tablespoon salt
shortening to brush tops of
  loaves
oleo to brush tops of loaves

Scald 1 cup milk. Add sifted corn meal and cook until thick. Place in a quart jar with top and place in warm place to sour overnight. (Save a tablespoon of the soured mixture for a starter for your next batch of bread. This starter will shorten the souring time of the next meal mixture. Starter can be stored in the refrigerator for 2 weeks.) When bubbles form, it is ready to use. Mix 1 quart of milk and 1 tablespoon sugar and scald. Cool slightly and add to first mixture. Gradually add 6 cups of flour. Set in warm place to rise double (approximately 2 hours). Next, add shortening, ½ cup sugar and salt. Mix well. Gradually add 6 cups flour and work in. Put remaining flour on board and turn dough mixture onto board. Work in more flour and knead for about 20 to 30 minutes. Divide into four equal parts and put in greased and floured 9½ x 5½ x 2¾-inch loaf pans. Brush tops of loaves with shortening and place in warm place to rise double (takes approximately 2 hours). Place in preheated 200 degree oven. Gradually turn heat to 300 degrees. Bake for 45 minutes. Take loaves out and brush top with oleo. Bake until done. Turn out on rack to cool. Total cooking time is approximately 1 hour to 1 hour and 15 minutes. Yields 4 loaves.

    This recipe is over 150 years old. It was handed down by the families of Mrs. Gordon Smith and Mrs. Andrew A. Tays.

Miss Mildred Tays, Booneville

CRACKLIN' BREAD

2 cups plain corn meal
½ teaspoon soda
½ teaspoon salt

1 cup ground cracklin's
1 egg
1½ cups buttermilk

Mix all the ingredients. Stir well. Pour in a hot greased pan. (A no. 6 skillet is good to use if you have one.) Bake in 400 degree preheated oven about 30 minutes or until brown. Yields 8 servings.

    This recipe was handed down from Mrs. Michael's grandmother. She used it during the Civil War and baked it in a covered skillet on the fireplace with hot coals underneath the skillet and on top of the lid.

Mrs. Quay Michael, Booneville

OLD TIMEY HOT WATER BREAD

2 cups plain corn meal   2 cups or more hot water
1 tablespoon salt

Mix corn meal and salt together in a pan. Pour boiling water over salted corn meal and stir until mixed thoroughly and soft enough to handle easily. Dip hands into cold water. Pick up enough hot meal mixture to handle and form into oblong ball. Lay on hot greased baker. Dip hands in cold water and repeat the process until all of the mixture is used. Brush and smooth tops with spoon dipped in melted oleo. Bake about 15 minutes or until brown at 425 degrees. Yields 3 small "pones" of bread.

Mrs. R. D. Pittman, Montrose

ANNADAMA BREAD

½ cup corn meal   1 package dry yeast
3 tablespoons shortening   ¼ cup warm water
¼ cup molasses   1 egg, beaten
2 teaspoons salt   3 cups sifted all-purpose
¾ cup boiling water   flour

Combine the first 5 ingredients in a large bowl. Let stand until lukewarm. Sprinkle the yeast over warm water to dissolve. Stir in yeast, beaten egg, and half of the flour into the corn meal mixture and beat vigorously. Stir in the remaining flour. Mix until the dough forms a soft ball. Transfer to a greased 9 x 5 x 3-inch loaf pan and cover with a cloth. Set in a warm place until dough rises about 1 inch above the pan. Sprinkle the top with a little salt and corn meal. Bake in 350 degree oven for 50 to 55 minutes. Cool before slicing. Yields 1 loaf.

Miss Somerville was owner-hostess of the popular Tea Hound in Oxford from 1926 to 1945. This was the social center for Ole Miss fraternity, sorority and other organizational parties. Miss Somerville recommends this bread as a tasty complement to country cured ham.

Miss Ella Somerville, Oxford

SOUTHERN SPOON BREAD

3 cups milk	1 teaspoon salt
1 cup white corn meal	1 teaspoon sugar
1 teaspoon butter	3 eggs, separated

Scald milk in double boiler and gradually add corn meal. Cook 5 minutes stirring to make smooth. Cool slightly and add butter, salt and sugar. Beat egg yolks and add to mixture. Then fold in stiffly beaten egg whites. Bake in greased 1½ quart size baking dish in a moderate oven (350 degrees) about 45 minutes. Serve hot from dish in which it was baked with plenty of butter. Yields 6 servings.

Mrs. Reuben Smith, Fayette

SOUTHERN CORN BREAD

1½ cups sifted plain white corn meal	1 tablespoon bacon drippings or cooking oil
½ cup sifted, self-rising flour	1 egg, unbeaten
¼ teaspoon baking soda	¾ cup buttermilk
½ teaspoon salt	¼ cup water
1 teaspoon sugar	

Put all dry ingredients in a large bowl and mix well. Add bacon drippings, egg and milk in the order given. Mix well. Add water and blend mixture thoroughly. Pour batter into a hot, greased 9-inch iron skillet. Bake at 425 degrees 12 to 15 minutes. (For a fancier bread, bake in a hot, greased corn stick pan.) Yields 16 servings about 2 inches square.

Mrs. Clyde Richmond, Walnut Grove

MEXICAN CORN BREAD

2 slightly beaten eggs	1 teaspoon salt
1 cup sour cream	2 tablespoons chopped green pepper
¼ cup oil	2 hot peppers, chopped
1 cup cream-style corn	1 cup grated cheese
1½ cups self-rising meal	

Mix all ingredients together except cheese. Pour half into hot greased 9 x 12 x 2-inch pan and sprinkle with half of cheese. Add remaining mixture and top with remaining cheese. Bake 25 minutes in 450 degree oven. Yields 10 to 12 servings.

Mrs. Everett Smith, Chunky

HUSH PUPPIES

1 package yeast	¾ cup plain flour
¼ cup warm water	¾ cup buttermilk
1½ cups white corn meal, self-rising	1 egg, beaten
	1 large onion, chopped fine

Dissolve yeast in ¼ cup warm water. Place corn meal and flour in bowl. Add buttermilk and stir until mixed thoroughly. Add beaten egg, onion, and dissolved yeast mixture. Mix thoroughly and drop from teaspoon into deep hot fat. Cook until golden brown. Serve immediately. Yields 10 servings.

Mrs. Murray Ray, Madison

HUSH PUPPIES

½ cup flour	½ cup diced onion
2 teaspoons baking powder	1 egg
1 teaspoon salt	½ cup milk
1½ cups plain corn meal	3 tablespoons cooking oil
½ cup drained whole kernel corn	hot pepper flakes (to taste)
	dash garlic powder

Combine all ingredients and drop (by teaspoonfuls) into hot fat in which fish has been fried. When golden brown, remove from fat and drain on paper towels. Serve hot. Yields 10 servings.

Mrs. Joe Fife, Port Gibson

SOUR DOUGH BREAD

STARTER:

- 1 package yeast
- ½ cup warm water
- 2 cups lukewarm water
- 2 cups sifted all-purpose flour
- 1 tablespoon sugar
- 1 tablespoon salt

BREAD:

- 1 package yeast
- ¼ cup warm water
- 1 cup milk
- 1/3 cup shortening
- 1/3 cup sugar
- plain flour

Make the starter one week before you expect to make the bread. Dissolve yeast in ½ cup warm water. Add 2 cups lukewarm water, flour, sugar and salt. Beat until smooth. Let stand (uncovered) at room temperature for 4 days to one week. Stir 2 or 3 times a day to prevent drying. Starter should have a yeasty, not a sour, smell. Store covered

THE MISSISSIPPI COOKBOOK

in refrigerator until ready to make bread. The longer it stands the better it is.

To make the bread, soften yeast in warm water in a large mixing bowl. Heat milk with shortening and sugar. (Do not boil). When cool, add to yeast and 1 cup starter batter. Put in enough flour to make a stiff dough. Stir well. Let stand until double in bulk. Knead enough to handle the dough, adding as little flour as possible. Make out into rolls and place on ungreased baking sheet. Let stand until double in size. Bake at 375 degrees about 30 minutes. The baked rolls keep well in freezer. Yields 3½ dozen rolls.

Mrs. Eula G. Webb, Wiggins

WHITE BATTER BREAD

1 cup milk
3 tablespoons sugar
1 tablespoon salt
2 tablespoons margarine
1 cup warm water (temperature
   105-115 degrees)

2 packages yeast
4 ¼ cups unsifted
   all-purpose flour

Scald milk. Stir in sugar, salt and margarine. Cool to lukewarm. Measure warm water into large warm bowl. Sprinkle or crumble in yeast. Stir until dissolved. Add lukewarm milk mixture. Stir in flour (batter will be fairly stiff). Beat until well blended, about 2 minutes. Cover and let rise in warm place, free from draft, for about 40 minutes or until more than doubled in bulk. Stir batter down. Beat vigorously about ½ minute. Turn into a greased 9¼ x 5¼ x 3-inch loaf pan, or casserole. Bake in moderate oven (375 degrees) about 50 minutes. Yields 1 loaf.

Mrs. A. M. Vandevere, Jr., Yazoo City

WHITE BREAD

1 cake yeast
2½ cups milk
½ cup plus 1 teaspoon sugar
about 7½ cups flour
2½ teaspoons salt

½ cup lard or other
   shortening
1 egg
melted butter

Dissolve yeast in ½ cup of lukewarm heated milk. Add 1 teaspoon sugar and ½ cup of the flour. Mix well and let rise for 30 minutes in a warm place. The mixture will become light and full of bubbles. Sift 6 cups of flour with salt. Heat ½ cup sugar, ½ cup lard (or other shortening) and 2 cups of milk over low heat, stirring well until sugar and shortening

[198]

are dissolved. Cool this to lukewarm. Meanwhile, add 1 well beaten egg to yeast mixture and beat well. Pour in the lukewarm milk mixture and add enough flour to make dough. The amount of flour required will vary from 6 to 7 cups. Grease dough lightly and cover. Place in refrigerator overnight. Next morning, knead dough on lightly floured board. When the dough is smooth and elastic, divide it into halves and shape into 2 loaves. Place loaves in well-greased 9 x 5 x 3-inch pans and let rise until doubled in bulk. Loaves may be brushed with melted butter before rising. Bake at 375 degrees for 45 minutes. Melted butter may be brushed on the bread at intervals during the baking. Remove from the pans as soon as the bread is cooked. This bread may be frozen with great success. The dough also makes delicious rolls. Yields 2 loaves.

Mrs. Powell Dungan, Port Gibson

DILL CASSEROLE BREAD

1 package active dry yeast	1 tablespoon dill seed
¼ cup warm water	1 teaspoon salt
1 cup creole cream cheese	¼ teaspoon soda
2 tablespoons sugar	1 egg, unbeaten
1 tablespoon minced onion	2¼ to 2½ cups all-purpose
1 tablespoon butter	flour

Soften yeast in water. Heat creole cream cheese to lukewarm and combine with sugar, onion, butter, dill seed, salt, soda, egg and softened yeast. Mix until smooth. Add flour to form stiff dough, beating well after each addition. Cover and let rise in warm place until light and double in bulk. Stir dough down, then turn into well greased 8-inch round casserole. Let rise in warm place about 30 to 40 minutes or until light. Bake at 350 degrees for 40 to 50 minutes or until golden brown. Brush with soft butter and sprinkle with salt. Serve while warm with butter and jam or jelly. Yields 1 round loaf.

Mrs. Clem R. Butler, Summit

FRENCH RAISED DOUGHNUTS

1 cup boiling water	½ cup lukewarm water
¼ cup shortening	2 eggs, well beaten
½ cup sugar	7½ cups sifted flour
1 teaspoon salt	(about)
1 cup evaporated milk	melted butter
1 package yeast	

Pour boiling water over shortening, sugar and salt. Add milk and cool to lukewarm. Dissolve yeast in lukewarm water and stir into cooled mixture. Add beaten eggs. Stir in 4 cups flour, beat. Add enough flour to make a soft dough. Place in greased bowl. Brush with melted butter and cover bowl with damp cloth. Chill until ready to use. Roll dough to ⅛ inch thickness. Cut into squares about 2½ inches in diameter and fry in hot fat (360 degrees) until brown. Do not let dough rise before frying. Drain on absorbent paper. Sprinkle with confectioners sugar or glaze. Yields about 3 dozen.

Mrs. David Street, Eden

RIZ BISCUITS

2½ cups self-rising flour
¼ teaspoon soda
¼ cup sugar

1 package yeast
1 cup buttermilk
1/3 cup shortening

Sift together flour, soda, and sugar. Dissolve yeast in lukewarm buttermilk. Cut shortening into flour mixture, (as done for biscuits). Stir buttermilk into dry ingredients quickly. Turn dough out on floured cloth and knead just until smooth. Roll to ¼ inch thickness and cut with a biscuit cutter. Brush top of each round with melted butter. Place one biscuit on top of another making double biscuits. Cover and place in a warm place to rise until light and doubled, about 1 hour. Bake at 375 degrees for 12 to 15 minutes. Yields about 1½ dozen.

Mrs. Joe Hughes, Monticello

ONE BOWL CHEESE PUFFS

1 to 1½ cups unsifted flour
1 tablespoon sugar
1½ teaspoons dry mustard
1 package active dry yeast
½ cup (1 stick) softened
   margarine
½ cup very hot water

1 2/3 cups grated sharp
   cheddar cheese (at room
   temperature)
2 eggs (at room temperature)
1 egg white, slightly beaten
salt

In a large bowl thoroughly mix ½ cup flour, sugar, dry mustard and undissolved yeast. Add softened margarine. Gradually add very hot tap water to dry ingredients and beat 2 minutes at medium speed of electric mixer, scraping bowl occasionally. Add cheese, 2 eggs and ½ cup flour. Beat at high speed 2 minutes scraping bowl occasionally. Stir in enough additional flour to make a stiff batter. Drop mixture by slightly rounded teaspoonfuls, about 2 inches apart, onto greased baking sheets. Let rise, uncovered, in warm place, free from draft, until light and spongy, about 1 hour. Brush puffs very gently with egg white, sprinkle lightly with salt. Bake in moderate oven (375 degrees) about 12 to 15 minutes, or until golden brown. Remove from baking sheets and cool on wire racks. Yields 3 dozen puffs.

Miss Sally Rosell, Lexington

SPOON ROLLS

1 package dry yeast
2 cups very warm water
1½ sticks oleo, melted
¼ cup sugar

1 egg
4 cups unsifted self-rising
    flour

Place yeast in 2 cups warm water. Cream oleo and sugar together in a large bowl. Add egg and cream a little more. Add yeast and water mixture, stir and add flour. Mix well with electric mixer. Place in air-tight bowl and keep in refrigerator. To cook, drop by spoonfuls into well-greased muffin tins and bake at 350 degrees about 20 minutes or until well-browned. Will keep in refrigerator about 1 week. This is the ideal roll recipe for the working woman who doesn't have time to set rolls out for rising. These go directly from refrigerator to oven and are delicious. Yields 2 dozen.

Mrs. Carolyn Ellard, Kosciusko

SWEET DOUGH ROLLS

5-6 cups flour
2 packages active dry yeast
½ cup sugar
1½ teaspoons salt

½ cup soft margarine
1½ cups very hot tap water
2 eggs (at room temperature)

Spoon flour into dry measuring cup. Level off and pour measured flour onto wax paper. Combine 2 cups flour, undissolved yeast, sugar and salt in large bowl. Stir well to blend. Add soft margarine. Add hot tap water to ingredients in bowl all at once. Beat with electric mixer at medium speed for 2 minutes. Scrape sides of bowl occasionally. Add eggs and 1 cup more flour. Beat with electric mixer at high speed for 1 minute or until thick and elastic. Scrape sides of bowl occasionally. Stir in remaining flour gradually, using wooden spoon. Use just enough flour to make a soft dough which leaves sides of bowl. Turn out onto floured board. Round up into a ball. Knead 5 to 10 minutes or until dough is smooth and elastic. Cover with plastic wrap, then a towel. Let rise for 15 to 20 minutes on board. Punch down. Shape into rolls. Place close together, smooth-side up in greased 8-inch square pan, for ½ of the rolls. Refrigerate 2 to 48 hours at moderately cold setting. When ready to bake, remove from refrigerator. Uncover. Let stand for 10 minutes. Preheat the oven. Bake at 375 degrees for 30 to 35 minutes or until done. Bake on a lower oven rack for best results. Remove from pan immediately. Cool on rack. Yields 32 rolls.

Nancy Loague, Dorsey

YEAST ROLLS

2 cakes yeast	1 cup lukewarm mashed
1½ cups lukewarm water	potatoes
2/3 cup sugar	2 beaten eggs
1½ teaspoons salt	6 cups sifted flour
2/3 cup melted shortening	

Dissolve yeast in ½ cup lukewarm water and set aside. In a large mixing bowl put 1 cup lukewarm water, sugar, salt, shortening, mashed potatoes and beaten eggs. Mix well. Add dissolved yeast and mix again. Stir in flour to make a soft dough. Cover and place in refrigerator for two hours. Take out and make into rolls. Place on ungreased baking sheet in a warm place for two or three hours. Bake at 400 degrees about 20 minutes or until golden brown. To freeze rolls, place dough in the refrigerator two hours as directed. Remove, shape into rolls and freeze. Yields about 5 dozen.

Mrs. Harry Williams, Holly Springs

REFRIGERATOR ROLLS

½ cup boiling water	1 egg, beaten
½ cup shortening	1 package dry yeast
½ cup sugar	½ cup lukewarm water
¾ teaspoon salt	3 cups unsifted flour

Pour boiling water over shortening, sugar and salt. Blend and cool, then add beaten egg. Sprinkle yeast into lukewarm water and stir until dissolved. Combine with egg mixture. Add flour and blend well. Cover and place in refrigerator for at least 4 hours. Will keep about 10 days.

Prepare amount of rolls needed. Roll out dough and cut. Place on greased pan and let rise 1½ to 2 hours. Bake at 425 degrees for 12 to 15 minutes. Yields 2 dozen rolls.

Mrs. Mary M. Jones, Lexington

ONE HOUR ROLLS

2 cups flour	¼ cup shortening
2 tablespoons sugar	1 package yeast
1 teaspoon baking powder	¼ cup warm water
1 teaspoon salt	¾ cup buttermilk

Sift dry ingredients together. Cut in shortening until fairly fine. Dissolve yeast in warm water; add to the buttermilk and mix well. Stir yeast mixture into dry ingredients. Turn out dough on a floured board, and knead until smooth and blistered. Roll ¼ inch thick and cut with biscuit cutter. Spread with melted butter (if desired) and fold double. Place on ungreased baking sheet, and let rise one hour. Bake in 400 degree oven (moderately hot) for 12 to 15 minutes until golden brown. Yields 2 dozen rolls.

Mrs. John W. Bramlett, Pontotoc

SUGARPLUM RING

1 package frozen rolls (2 dozen)	about 10 green candied cherries
½ cup melted butter	for color (optional)
½ cup sugar	¾ cup whole nut meats
1 teaspon cinnamon	½ cup white or dark corn
¾ cup whole red candied	syrup
cherries	

Cut rolls in half to make smaller rolls about size of walnuts. Coat cut rolls with melted butter. Mix sugar and cinnamon together. Then shake cut rolls in sugar mixture. Place rolls loosely on the bottom of a well greased 10-inch tube pan. Sprinkle whole cherries (both red and green) and whole nut meats over rolls. Continue in layers until pan is about half full. Mix left over sugar, butter and syrup together and drizzle over top. Let rise until double in bulk. Bake in preheated 350 degree oven 35 minutes or until done. Let set in pan 5 minutes. Turn out and allow syrup to drip onto bread before removing pan. Decorate the upside-down ring with cherries and nuts to give more color, if desired. Let cool. Yields about 10 servings.

Mrs. Robert C. Morris, Leland

ANGEL BISCUITS

5 cups unsifted all-purpose
   flour
¼ cup sugar
3 teaspoons baking powder
1 teaspoon soda
1 teaspoon salt

1 cup shortening
1 package dry yeast
2 tablespoons warm water
2 cups buttermilk
melted butter

Sift dry ingredients together. Cut in shortening. Dissolve yeast in warm water and add with buttermilk to dry mixture. Mix well. Turn out on lightly floured board. Add more flour, if necessary. Roll to ¼ inch thickness. Cut with floured cutter, then dip in melted butter and fold to make pocketbook rolls or rolls may be stacked together. Place on greased baking sheet. Bake at 400 degrees for 15 minutes. Yields about 2 dozen biscuits.

Mrs. Harry Sugg, Amory

SOUTHERN BUTTERMILK BISCUITS

2 cups flour
½ teaspoon soda
1 teaspoon salt

1 teaspoon baking powder
1/3 cup shortening
1 cup buttermilk

Sift dry ingredients and cut in shortening. Add milk and mix to a soft dough. Roll about ½ inch thick. Cut with biscuit cutter or pinch off uniform size rolls and shape into biscuits. Bake in a 450 degree oven for about 12 to 15 minutes. Yields 12 large biscuits.

Mrs. Caroline Anderson, Brookhaven

EASY MIX BISCUITS

2 cups sifted flour
3 teaspoons baking powder
1 teaspoon salt

1/3 cup corn oil
2/3 cup milk

Mix and sift flour, baking powder and salt. Combine corn oil and milk. Pour all at once over entire surface of flour mixture. Mix with fork to make a soft dough. Shape lightly with hands to make a round ball. Place on waxed paper and knead lightly ten times or until smooth. Pat out to ½ inch thickness or roll between 2 squares of waxed paper. Remove top sheet of paper; cut biscuits with unfloured 2-inch biscuit cutter. Place biscuits on ungreased baking sheet. For soft biscuits, place biscuits close together with sides touching. For crusty biscuits, place well apart. Bake in hot oven (450 degrees) 12 to 15 minutes. Yields about 20 biscuits.

Spencena Russ, Prentiss

HERB BISCUITS

2 cups flour
1 teaspoon baking powder
½ teaspoon soda
½ teaspoon salt
½ teaspoon sage

2 teaspoons dry mustard
2½ teaspoons caraway seed
4 tablespoons shortening
2/3 cup plus 2 tablespoons
buttermilk

Sift flour and measure. Add all dry ingredients and sift together. Add shortening and cut into dry mixture with blender or two knives. Add buttermilk and stir. Turn onto a floured board and knead. Roll, cut, and place on ungreased baking sheet. Bake 8 minutes at 450 degrees. To freeze, cool and package in aluminum foil. To serve, thaw and heat in foil wrapping for 15 minutes in 375 degree oven. Yields 2 dozen.

Miss Edna Hicks, Pontotoc

CRUNCHY BISCUITS

1½ cups sifted flour
4 teaspoons baking powder
1 teaspoon salt
½ cup enriched white
hominy grits, uncooked

½ cup shortening
¼ cup chopped onion
1 cup grated sharp cheese
½ cup milk

Sift flour, baking powder and salt together. Stir in grits. Cut in shortening until mixture resembles coarse crumbs. Stir in onion and cheese. Gradually add milk, stirring lightly until just dampened. Shape dough into ball and turn out on lightly floured board. Knead gently a few times. Sprinkle board with 1 tablespoon grits. Roll dough to form a 9 X 8-inch rectangle. Using a sharp knife, cut dough into eight 1-inch wide strips and cut each strip into three pieces. Place about 1 inch apart on ungreased cookie sheet. Bake at 425 degrees for 10 to 12 minutes or until lightly browned. Serve hot. Serve these rectangular-shaped biscuits with a soup and salad or with bacon and egg supper. Yields 2 dozen biscuits.

Mrs. W. B. Hulsey, Gloster

BRAN MUFFINS

2 cups Nabisco Bran
2 cups boiling water
3 cups raisins
1 cup shortening
3 cups sugar

4 eggs
1 quart buttermilk
5 cups all-purpose flour
5 teaspoons soda
4 cups Kellogg's All Bran

Mix Nabisco bran, boiling water, and raisins. Let cool. Cream shortening and sugar, then add one egg at a time and beat well. Add buttermilk, the sifted flour, and soda. Stir in Kellogg's All Bran. Mix well. Then add the Nabisco Bran, water, and raisin mixture. This will keep a long time in the refrigerator. Put this in a wide mouth jar and be sure to keep tightly covered. This will get rather thick, but will turn out well. *Do not* stir this after it has been refrigerated. Just dip out what you need. To bake, grease bottom of muffin pan, fill muffin cups about half full, then bake at 350 degrees for about 25 minutes or until desired degree of brown-ness.

Mrs. E. B. (Grace) Tinsley, Scooba

JACK FROST MUFFINS

½ cup butter
½ cup brown sugar
¼ cup white sugar
¼ teaspoon salt
2 egg yolks, well beaten
1 cup flour
½ teaspoon baking powder
⅛ teaspoon nutmeg

1 tablespoon maraschino cherry juice
2 egg whites
1½ cups finely chopped nut meats
1 (2-ounce) bottle maraschino cherries

Cream butter, sugars and salt well. Add egg yolks. Sift flour, baking powder and nutmeg together. Add to butter mixture. Stir in cherry juice. Fold in stiffly beaten egg whites. Grease bottom only of 12 cup muffin pan and cover bottom of cups with nut meats. Place tablespoon of batter over nuts. Place cherry in center of batter, then cover with another tablespoon of batter. Sprinkle nut meats on top. Bake in a 350 degree oven for 25 minutes. Freezes well. Yields 12 muffins.

Mrs. Anthony Garst, Clarksdale

SPICED MUFFINS

1 cup margarine
2 cups sugar
2 eggs, well beaten
4 cups flour
3 teaspoons cinnamon
2 teaspoons allspice

1 teaspoon cloves
small pinch salt
2 teaspoons soda
2 cups hot applesauce
1 cup chopped nuts

Cream margarine and sugar together. Add well beaten eggs. Sift together flour, spices, salt and soda. Add flour mixture to margarine mixture alternately with heated applesauce. Beat after each addition. Add nuts last and stir well. Grease bottom only of small muffin tins. Dip batter into pans. Bake at 350 degrees for about 20 minutes. Fill tins only ½ full of batter. This batter will keep several weeks in refrigerator, to be used when desired. Yields 84 small muffins.

Mrs. Boswell Stevens, Macon

BACON MUFFINS

2 slices bacon
2 cups all-purpose flour
½ teaspoon salt
2¼ teaspoons baking powder
2 tablespoons sugar
1 egg, beaten

1 cup milk or 1/3 cup
   evaporated milk and 2/3
   cup water
2 tablespoons melted bacon
   drippings

Chop bacon and pan-broil until done. Drain thoroughly. Sift flour and measure. Re-sift twice with salt, baking powder, and sugar. Add crisp bacon and stir until well distributed. Beat egg. Combine egg with milk and melted fat. Add to dry ingredients all at once, and stir quickly until they are just dampened. Then give 3 or 4 more stirs. Do not stir until smooth. Grease bottom of muffin pans. Spoon into muffin pans, filling cups 2/3 full. Bake in a hot oven (425 degrees) 20 minutes or until nicely browned. Serve piping hot with butter. Yields 12 medium size muffins.

Mrs. Geneva Forte, Louin

BLUEBERRY MUFFINS

2 cups all-purpose flour
3 teaspoons baking powder
1/3 cup sugar
1 egg
1 cup milk

¼ cup salad oil
2 teaspoons lemon juice
1 cup of fresh blueberries,
   OR ¾ cup drained canned or
   frozen blueberries

Sift flour and baking powder. Add sugar. Mix and set aside. Beat 1 egg. Stir in milk, oil and lemon juice. Stir briefly into presifted dry ingredients. Fold in blueberries. Grease bottom of muffin pans. Fill muffin tins 2/3 full. Bake 20 or 25 minutes at 425 degrees. Yields 15 muffins.

Mrs. M. L. Dilworth, Booneville

CARROT BREAD

2 well beaten eggs
1 cup sugar
¾ cup salad oil
1½ cups sifted all-purpose
  flour

1 teaspoon cinnamon
½ teaspoon salt
1 teaspoon soda
1½ cups grated raw carrots

Beat eggs and sugar until creamy. Add salad oil. Sift dry ingredients and add to this mixture. Mix well. Add grated carrots and mix. Fill 2 greased 7½ X 3½ X 2¼-inch loaf pans half full. Bake at 325 degrees for one hour. Serve hot or cold. Makes delicious and attractive sandwiches; or just spread with a bit of butter and eat. Will stay moist for a week. Yields 2 loaves.

Mrs. T. E. Neill, Clarksdale

CRANBERRY LOAF

2 cups flour, unsifted
½ teaspoon salt
1½ teaspoons baking powder
½ teaspoon soda
1 cup sugar
1 orange rind, grated
juice of the orange and enough
  water added for ¾ cup
  liquid

2 tablespoons oil
1 egg, beaten
1 cup chopped nuts
1 cup cranberries, quartered

Sift together first four ingredients. Add sugar, orange rind, liquid, oil and beaten egg. Mix thoroughly. Stir in nuts and cranberries. Pour into a greased 9 X 5-inch loaf pan. Bake 1 hour at 350 degrees. Yields 1 loaf.

Mrs. Frances Evans, Kosciusko

CRANBERRY BREAD

1 cup cranberries
1¼ cups sugar
3 cups plain flour
4½ teaspoons baking powder
1 teaspoon salt
3 tablespoons grated orange
  rind

1 cup milk
3 tablespoons butter, melted
1 egg, slightly beaten
½ cup chopped nuts

Coarsely grind cranberries. Mix in ¼ cup sugar and set aside. Sift together 1 cup sugar, flour, baking powder and salt. Add grated orange rind. Blend in milk, melted butter, egg and nuts. Fold in sweetened cranberries. Pour into greased 9½ X 5½ X 2¾-inch pan. Bake in 350 degree oven 1 hour. Turn out on rack and cool. Yields 1 loaf.

Mrs. Frank Allen, West Point

APRICOT NUT BREAD

1 cup sugar
2 tablespoons shortening
1 medium egg
¾ cup milk
¾ cup orange juice
4 teaspoons grated orange rind

3 cups sifted all-purpose flour
3½ teaspoons baking powder
1 teaspoon salt
1 cup dried apricots, finely
   chopped
1 cup chopped pecans

Cream sugar, shortening and egg thoroughly. Stir in milk, orange juice and orange rind. Sift together and stir in the flour, baking powder and salt. Last, add apricots and nuts. Pour into 2 greased loaf pans (7½ X 3½ X 2¼-inch) or one regular loaf pan. Let stand 20 minutes before baking at 325 degrees for 50 to 55 minutes in the small pans or 70 minutes for large loaf. Yields 2 small loaves or 1 large loaf.

Mrs. J. E. Collins, Jr., Utica

PUMPKIN BREAD

3 cups sugar
1 cup corn oil
4 eggs, well beaten
1 (no. 2) can pumpkin
   (2 cups)
3½ cups all-purpose flour

2 teaspoons soda
1½ teaspoons salt
1 teaspoon nutmeg
1 teaspoon cinnamon
1 cup chopped pecans or 1 cup
   white raisins (optional)

Cream sugar and oil well. Add eggs and beat vigorously. Add pumpkin and stir. Mix dry ingredients together and add to first mixture, stirring well after each addition. May add 1 cup chopped pecans and/or 1 cup white raisins, if desired. Fresh pumpkin may be substituted for canned. Put in greased and floured 9 X 5 X 3-inch loaf pan. Bake 1 hour at 350 degrees. Yields 1 loaf.

Mrs. Claude Tynes, Jackson

BANANA NUT BREAD

1½ cups whole wheat flour
1/3 cup non-instant powdered
  milk, OR 1/3 cup plus 2
  tablespoons instant dry milk
1 teaspoon salt
2 teaspoons double-acting
  baking powder

1 cup broken pecans or
  walnuts
1½ cups honey (or molasses)
3 tablespoons vegetable oil
½ cup wheat germ
1¼ cups mashed bananas
grated rind of ½ lemon

Sift into a large mixing bowl the wheat flour, powdered milk, salt and baking powder. Add nuts and mix until well covered with flour mixture. Add remaining ingredients and stir with not more than 40 strokes. To make Banana Date Bread, substitute dates for nuts. Line bottom of a loaf pan with heavy paper and grease well. Pour batter into 9 X 5 X 3-inch pan, forcing it into the corners. Make indentation lengthwise through center. Bake at 350 degrees for 45 minutes. Yields 24 slices 1/3-inch thick.

Mrs. George L. Carr, Hattiesburg

BANANA NUT LOAF

2/3 cup sugar
1/3 cup soft shortening
2 eggs
3 tablespoons buttermilk
1 cup mashed ripe bananas
  (2 or 3)

2 cups sifted self-rising flour
¼ teaspoon soda
½ cup chopped nuts

Heat oven to 350 degrees. Cream sugar, shortening and eggs thoroughly together. Stir in buttermilk, mashed bananas and flour, then stir in soda and fold in chopped nuts. If using plain flour, use 2 teaspoons soda and ½ teaspoon salt. Bake in greased 8½ X 4½ X 2½-inch loaf pan for 50 to 60 minutes. Yields 1 loaf.

Mrs. Marilyn J. Bailey, Prentiss

TROPICAL APPLE DATE BREAD

3 cups sifted all-purpose flour
1 cup sugar
1 tablespoon baking powder
1½ teaspoons salt
1 cup flaked coconut, toasted

1½ cups milk
1 egg, beaten
1 teaspoon vanilla
1 (8-ounce) package diced dates
1 cup finely chopped apples

Mix and sift flour, sugar, baking powder and salt. Stir in coconut. Add combined milk, egg and vanilla. Stir well. Blend dates and apples into mixture. Spread into greased and floured 9 X 5 X 3-inch loaf pan. Bake at 350 degrees for 1 hour and 15 minutes. Yields 1 loaf.

Mrs. George Arthur Bailey, Prentiss

CHERRY BREAD

1 pound can red tart cherries, drained
2 cups sifted all-purpose flour
¾ cup sugar
1½ teaspoon baking powder
½ teaspoon salt
½ teaspoon soda
½ cup chopped nuts
1 egg, beaten
¾ cup cherry juice
2 tablespoons melted butter

Chop cherries coarsely, using kitchen shears. Let cherries continue to drain. Sift together flour, sugar, baking powder, salt and soda. Stir in the well drained cherries and nuts. Combine egg, cherry juice, and butter. Add to first mixture and mix only until flour is moistened. Pour into 2 greased 7⅜ X 3⅝ X 2¼-inch loaf pans. Bake in a 350 degree oven for 35 to 40 minutes or until done. Yields 2 loaves.

Mrs. Jewel Starkey, Iuka

SWEET POTATO BREAD

2 eggs
1½ cups sugar
½ cup oil
½ cup water
1 cup mashed sweet potatoes
1¾ cups flour
¼ teaspoon baking powder
1 teaspoon salt
1 teaspoon soda
½ teaspoon nutmeg

Beat eggs. Beat in sugar. Add oil, water, and potatoes. If using uncanned potatoes, cook raw potatoes and mash, removing strings or veins. Mix dry ingredients. Stir into egg mixture and blend well. Pour into waxed paper lined 9 X 5 X 3-inch loaf pan. Bake in 325 degree oven for 1 hour and 30 minutes. Yields 1 loaf.

Mrs. Rosa Simmons, Tylertown

PUMPKIN BREAD

3 cups flour
1 teaspoon cinnamon
1 teaspoon nutmeg
2 teaspoons soda
1½ teaspoons salt
3 cups sugar
1 cup vegetable oil
4 eggs
1 cup canned pumpkin
2/3 cup water

Sift flour with cinnamon, nutmeg, soda and salt. Cream sugar with oil. Beat eggs. Add pumpkin and water to eggs. Mix all ingredients well. Grease and flour 3 one pound coffee cans (tall type). Divide into equal parts and bake for one hour at 350 degrees. When cool, slice thin and spread with cream cheese, butter or margarine. (This bread freezes well.) Yields 3 round loaves.

Mrs. Otto Browning, Yazoo City

GOLDEN BATTER BREAD

1 cup milk	½ cup warm water
¼ cup margarine or butter	1 beaten egg
¼ cup sugar	4½ cups sifted plain flour
2 teaspoons salt	1 (3½-ounce) can crumbled
2 packages dry yeast	onion rings

Scald milk until it bubbles. Remove from heat. Add margarine, sugar and salt. Cool to lukewarm. Sprinkle yeast in warm water. Stir until dissolved then add to milk mixture. Stir in beaten egg and 3 cups flour. Spoon beat until smooth. Stir in remaining flour to make a stiff batter. Let rise until double in bulk. Stir in crumbled onion rings. Put in 2 well greased 13 X 4½ X 2½-inch loaf pans. Let rise again until double in bulk. Bake at 350 degrees for 30 to 40 minutes. Yields 2 loaves or approximately 2 dozen slices.

Mrs. Hilton Royster, Clarksdale

CHEESE AND POPPY SEED BREAD

3¾ cups biscuit mix	1 cup shredded cheese
1 tablespoon minced fresh or	2 teaspoons poppy seed
dehydrated onion	1 slightly beaten egg
1 teaspoon garlic salt	1½ cups milk

Pour biscuit mix into large mixing bowl. Add onion, garlic salt, cheese and 1 teaspoon poppy seed. Add egg and milk. Stir to blend and beat by hand about 50 strokes. Pour into 2 greased 8½ X 4½ X 2½-inch loaf pans and sprinkle remaining teaspoon of poppy seed over the tops of dough. Bake in 350 degree preheated oven 35 to 40 minutes. For metal loaf pans, increase temperature to 375 degrees. Yields 1 loaf.

Mrs. Esther K. Gunn, Laurel

BISHOP'S BREAD

2¾ cups sifted all-purpose flour
3 teaspoons baking powder
1 teaspoon salt
½ cup butter or margarine

1 cup firmly packed light
  brown sugar
2 eggs
1 cup milk

TOPPING:
½ cup granulated sugar
¼ cup sifted all-purpose
  flour

1 tablespoon cinnamon

Preheat oven to 375 degrees. Then lightly grease a 13 X 9 X 2-inch baking pan. Sift flour, baking powder, and salt. In a large bowl of electric mixer, beat at medium speed the butter, brown sugar, and eggs until mixture is very light and fluffy. At low speed, blend in milk and then the flour mixture. Beat until ingredients are combined. Turn batter into greased 10-inch square pan. Spread evenly. Make a topping of the last three ingredients. Mix until crumbly and sprinkle over batter. Bake at 375 degrees for 25 minutes or until a cake tester inserted in the center comes out clean. Let cool slightly in pan on wire rack. Serve bread warm. Yields 16 servings.   *Mrs. Clem Butler, Summit*

QUICK GRAHAM BREAD

½ cup brown sugar
¾ cup cold water
½ cup melted shortening
¾ cup milk

1 cup all-purpose flour
1½ teaspoons salt
1 teaspoon baking soda
2 cups graham flour

Dissolve sugar in water; add shortening and milk. Sift all-purpose flour and measure. Sift flour with salt and baking soda. Add to first mixture. Add graham flour. Mix thoroughly. Bake in well oiled 8½ X 4½ X 2½-inch loaf bread pan in moderate (375 degrees) oven for 1 hour. Yields 1 loaf.   *Norah B. Hales, Mendenhall*

CINNAMON–RAISIN LOAF

½ cup melted shortening
½ cup sugar
2 teaspoons salt
2 beaten eggs
1 cake fresh yeast

½ cup lukewarm water
2 cups scalded milk
7 cups enriched flour
2 cups seedless raisins
1 tablespoon cinnamon

Combine shortening, sugar, salt and eggs. Soften yeast in lukewarm water, then add to egg mixture. Cool milk to lukewarm and add alternately with flour. Add raisins and cinnamon. Turn onto lightly floured surface. Cover and let stand ten minutes. Knead until smooth and elastic. Place in greased bowl. Cover with damp cloth. Let rise in warm place until double. Punch down. Form into 2 loaves. Place in greased 6½ X 19½-inch loaf pans. Cover. Let double. Bake in moderate (350 degrees) oven for 45 minutes. When bread is taken out of oven, brush top lightly with cream. Yields 2 loaves.

Mrs. Charles Leon, Canton

DESSERT WAFFLES

1 cup plain flour	2 whole eggs
3 teaspoons baking powder	1 cup heavy cream
½ teaspoon salt	2 stiffly beaten egg whites

Sift dry ingredients together. Beat whole eggs very lightly. Add cream. Stir into dry ingredients. Fold in egg whites. Bake in hot waffle iron. Yields 8 large waffles.

Mrs. Gerald Ratliff, Kokomo

NANCY JANE WAFFLES

1 egg	1⅛ cups milk
1 tablespoon sugar	⅜ cup cooking oil
1¼ cups sifted self-rising flour	

Beat egg light and fluffy. If desired, egg may be separated and white beaten stiffly to be folded in later. Sift sugar with flour. Measure milk to 1⅛ cups level. Add ⅜ cup oil to make 1½ cups liquid. Combine liquid with beaten egg. Add dry ingredients stirring just enough to combine. Bake in preheated waffle iron until light brown. Recipe may be doubled and leftover waffles frozen. To reheat frozen waffles, place in toaster on lightest setting. To make dessert waffles, add ½ cup chopped pecans to batter. Serve dessert waffles with 2 scoops of a favorite ice cream. Yields 8 large 3-inch waffles.

Mrs. Lawrence R. Stokes, Alligator

DUMPLINGS

2 cups sifted all-purpose flour
1 teaspoon baking powder
1 teaspoon salt

¼ cup margarine
1 cup liquid (½ cup
   milk and ½ cup ice water)

Sift dry ingredients together. Cut in margarine. Add liquid and mix until moistened. Roll out dough on floured board and cut in strips. Drop in hot broth and cook, covered, for 8 to 10 minutes. Yields about 1 dozen dumplings.

Mrs. George R. Davis, Heidelberg

FRITTER BATTER

2 cups all-purpose flour
3 teaspoons baking powder
½ teaspoon salt

1 egg, beaten
2/3 cup sweet milk

Sift together dry ingredients; add beaten egg and milk. Beat well. Drop by spoonfuls into deep hot fat at 375 degrees and fry until golden brown. Yields about 10 servings.

Mrs. Gaston Womack, Mendenhall

PUFFS

1 teaspoon salt
2 teaspoons baking powder
2 cups flour

1 teaspoon lard
¾ cup milk
1 egg

Sift dry ingredients together. Add lard. Then add milk and egg and mix. Roll out on floured board. Cut in pieces 2 inches long and 1 inch wide. Fry in deep fat. Yields 12 to 15 puffs.

Mrs. O. C. Hutto, Montrose

⁖[Vegetables]⁖

In Mississippi an abundance of fresh vegetables can be grown the year round. They are readily available in supermarkets, roadside stands and even a neighbor's private garden. When a particular vegetable is not in season, it is always available in a canned or frozen form.

Vegetables give beauty, zest and variety to meals every day. Each of us needs four or more servings of vegetables daily.

Knowing how to prepare vegetables to retain their nutritive value and appetite appeal is a test of any good cook. To help you improve your skill with vegetables, remember to: (1) boil vegetables in as little water as possible. Losses in vitamins and minerals will be less, the less water you use. Serve the cooking liquids with your vegetables, or make them into sauces, gravies or soups. (2) Cook vegetables until just tender and serve them immediately. They will taste better and retain more nutrients. (3) Trim leafy vegetables like lettuce and cabbage sparingly. Use the dark outer leaves as they are especially rich in nutrients.

Serve vegetables in new and different ways so your family will not tire of them. Try adding a pinch of herbs or a tablespoon of minced onion, green pepper or chives before cooking fresh vegetables. Make salads out of vegetables you usually boil. Use a creamed sauce on some vegetables. Try combining several vegetables in a casserole. Add chopped nuts, pimiento strips, celery cubes, mushroom pieces or crumbled bacon to vegetables for color and texture.

The following recipes are favorites of Mississippi cooks from the Delta to the Gulf Coast.

RANCH STYLE BAKED BEANS

2 tablespoons butter
1 pound ground chuck
1 (1⅜-ounce) envelope
onion soup mix.
2 (1-pound cans) pork and
beans in sauce

1 (1-pound) can kidney beans,
drained
1 cup catsup
½ cup cold water
2 tablespoons prepared mustard
2 teaspoons cider vinegar

Preheat oven to 400 degrees. In large skillet, melt butter and brown meat. Stir in soup mix, beans, catsup, water, mustard, and vinegar. Pour into 2½ quart casserole or bean pot. Bake 30 to 45 minutes. Serves 8 to 10.

Mrs. Henry D'Aquilla, Long Beach

BARBECUED BAKED BEANS

1 (31 ounce) can baked
beans
1 tablespoon Worcestershire
sauce
1 teaspoon prepared mustard

½ cup white sugar
½ cup barbecue sauce with
onions
¼ cup chopped onions
3 slices bacon

Mix all ingredients except bacon; place in 1¾ quart casserole dish. Top with bacon. Bake at 350 degrees for one hour. Serves 6.

Mrs. Wyvona Scarbrough, Perkinston

LUZON'S BAKED BEANS

4 to 6 strips chopped bacon
2 medium-size onions, chopped
1 medium bell pepper, chopped
1 clove garlic, chopped
1 (28-ounce) can pork & beans
½ cup brown sugar

2 teaspoons Lea & Perrin Sauce
1/16 teaspoon red pepper
salt and pepper to taste
1 teaspoon liquid smoke
1 (8-ounce) can tomato sauce

Fry chopped bacon until crisp. Remove from grease and reserve. Sautè onions, pepper and garlic in bacon grease. Cook slowly until tender, pour in beans, add brown sugar, Lea & Perrin sauce, salt, pepper and red pepper, liquid smoke, tomato sauce and fried bacon crisps.

Pour into uncovered bean pot and bake at 350 degrees for 45 minutes, stirring twice while baking. Serves 8.

Mrs. Luzon Truly, Fayette

SUMMER SQUASH CASSEROLE

2 pounds tender yellow
   summer squash
½ stick margarine
2 tablespoons finely chopped
   green onion tops
½ teaspoon nutmeg
1 tablespoon Worcestershire
   sauce

dash Tabasco
½ teaspoon onion salt
1½ cups grated sharp cheese
1 cup bread croutons
melted margarine
garlic salt

Wash and scrub squash and remove stem and blossom ends. Steam in large saucepan in as little water as possible to tender the squash. When done, drain very thoroughly; mash coarsely. Mix in margarine, chopped onion tops (use only very tender tops), nutmeg, Worcestershire sauce, Tabasco and onion salt. Fold in grated cheese. Use a "light hand" in mixing ingredients, to make for a fluffier product. Place in a buttered casserole and cook uncovered at 350 degrees until bubbly, about 20 minutes or so. Meanwhile, dice enough lightly toasted bread to make 1 cup of croutons. Toss gently in melted margarine until all croutons are coated with margarine; sprinkle fairly generously with garlic salt. As casserole begins to bubble, cover top with croutons and finish cooking, until bread is nicely browned. Serve hot. Serves 8.

Mrs. Kate Woods, Starkville

COUNTRY CLUB SQUASH

6 or 8 tender, small squash
salt and pepper to taste
2 tablespoons butter
1 chicken or beef bouillon cube
1 tablespoon grated onion

1 egg, well beaten
1 cup sour cream
¾ cup bread crumbs
½ cup grated cheese
dash of paprika

Cut and cook squash until tender, drain, mash. Add salt, pepper, butter, bouillon cube and onion. Add well beaten egg, and sour cream. Pour into a one quart casserole dish. Combine bread crumbs, grated cheese and paprika, and sprinkle on top of squash. Bake at 350 degrees for 30 minutes. Serves 6.

Mrs. Ruth H. Green, Leakesville

SQUASH FRITTERS

1 cup cooked squash
1 cup flour
1 egg
½ cup milk

chopped onion or onion powder
   (optional)
2 teaspoons baking powder
½ teaspoon salt

Cook squash first. Mix ingredients until just moistened. Drop by spoonfuls (try an ice cream dipper) into deep hot fat following the frying of chicken. Makes an ideal accompaniment for fried chicken. Serves 6.

Mrs. J. E. Richardson, Enterprise

SQUASH CASSEROLE

1 pound squash
1 large onion
1/3 cup milk
¼ cup butter
½ cup grated cheese

¾ cup bread crumbs or crackers
1 teaspoon salt
1 egg, well beaten
¼ cup bread crumbs

Boil squash and chopped onion until tender. Drain off all water and mash. Add milk, butter, cheese, crumbs and salt. Pour in greased baking dish. Pour well-beaten egg over top. Sprinkle a few bread crumbs over top of egg. Bake in moderate (350 degrees) oven until done or 30 minutes. Serves 6.

Mrs. J. P. Barnett, Macon

SQUASH CASSEROLE

2 cups cooked yellow squash
¼ cup butter or oleomargarine
¾ cup herb seasoned croutons
1 chopped small onion

1 beaten egg
1 cup cream of mushroom soup
salt and pepper to taste

Cook squash until tender; drain. Add butter or oleo and croutons; mix lightly. Add onion, egg, mushroom soup and salt and pepper. Mix thoroughly. Pour in buttered 1 quart casserole. Bake at 350 degrees for 30 to 40 minutes, or until top is slightly brown and center bubbles. Serves 6.

Mrs. Eugene Holcombe, Macon

FRIED SUMMER SQUASH

4 beaten eggs
¾ cup milk
1¼ teaspoons salt

7 medium squash, thinly sliced
2½ cups flour
oil

Combine eggs, milk and salt to make batter. Dip squash in batter, roll in flour and fry in deep fat until done.

Mrs. Bonnie Cooper, McNeill

SQUASH AU GRATIN

2 cups cooked squash
2 tablespoons butter or
    margarine, melted
1 teaspoon onion juice

salt and pepper to taste
2 eggs, beaten
1 cup buttered breadcrumbs
1/3 cup grated cheese

Combine squash, melted butter, seasonings and beaten egg. Arrange mixture in alternate layers with breadcrumbs and cheese and bake at 375 degrees 10 to 15 minutes. Serves 4. For *variation*, use crushed cheese ritz crackers, instead of breadcrumbs and cheese.

Mrs. Joyce Clark, Greenville

SWEET POTATO SURPRISE

1 (1-pound 1-ounce) can whole
    sweet potatoes
1½ cups brown sugar
1½ tablespoon cornstarch
¼ teaspoon salt
⅛ teaspoon cinnamon

1 teaspoon shredded orange peel
1 pound can (2 cups) apricot
    halves
2 tablespoons butter or
    margarine
½ cup pecan halves

Half sweet potatoes and place in greased 10 x 6 x 1½ inch baking dish. In saucepan, combine brown sugar, cornstarch, salt, cinnamon and orange peel. Drain apricots, reserving syrup. Stir 1 cup apricot syrup into cornstarch mixture. Cook and stir over medium heat until boiling. Boil 2 minutes. Add apricots, butter or margarine, and pecan halves. Pour over sweet potatoes. Bake, uncovered, at 375 degrees for 25 minutes. Serves 6.

Mrs. Robert Agnew, Guntown

[221]

SWEET POTATOES & MARSHMALLOWS

6 medium sweet potatoes
¾ cup butter
½ to ¾ cup sugar (depending
  on sweetness of potatoes)
½ teaspoon salt (scant)
½ teaspoon cinnamon

¼ teaspoon nutmeg
⅛ teaspoon ginger
1 teaspoon vanilla extract
½ teaspoon grated orange rind
marshmallows

Boil potatoes in enough water to cover. When tender (do not overcook), drain and place in electric mixer bowl and cream until smooth. Add butter, mix until butter has melted. Gradually add other ingredients, mixing thoroughly between each addition. Place mixture in greased two-quart casserole; bake in 350 degree oven 30 minutes. Remove from oven, cover top with marshmallows and return to oven until marshmallows have reached a golden brown and melted slightly. Serves 8 to 10.

Mrs. Everette Bruce, Vaiden

SWEET POTATO PONE

3 cups grated (raw)
  sweet potatoes
½ cup sugar
¼ cup flour
½ cup molasses

2 whole eggs
1 tablespoon nutmeg
1 teaspoon vanilla
½ stick oleo

In large mixing bowl, mix potatoes, sugar, flour, molasses, eggs, nutmeg and vanilla. In 8-inch iron skillet, melt oleo and drain into above mixture. Pour entire mixture back into skillet and bake for 50 minutes in preheated oven at 350 degrees. Serves 6.

Mrs. Nell Dennis, Fayette

CANDIED SWEET POTATOES

6 medium size sweet potatoes
⅛ teaspoon salt
¼ cup butter

½ cup orange juice
½ cup honey

Boil unpeeled sweet potatoes. When tender, drain, remove skins, cut in half and arrange in buttered baking dish. Salt. Heat butter, honey, orange juice, and add to potatoes. Bake in quick oven (400 degrees) until brown. Serves 6.

Mrs. J. D. Smith, Jr., Shaw

[222]

SWEET POTATO CROQUETTES

5 medium sweet potatoes
5 tablespoons sugar
2 tablespoons butter or
  margarine

1 teaspoon lemon juice
6 marshmallows
2 slightly beaten egg whites
2 cups crushed corn flakes

Cook potatoes in jackets. Peel and mash. Season with sugar, butter and lemon juice. Make croquettes by shaping potatoes around marshmallows. Chill one hour. Dip into egg whites and roll in corn flakes; fry in deep fat (375 degrees) until golden brown. Drain on absorbent paper and serve at once. Serves 6 to 8.

Mrs. Etta Shoemaker, Mendenhall

GRATED SWEET POTATO PUDDING

1 pint grated raw sweet
  potatoes
½ cup melted butter
1 pint sweet milk
3 eggs
1 cup sugar

1 teaspoon cinnamon
½ teaspoon cloves
1 tablespoon flour
1 tablespoon whiskey
  (optional)

Beat all together for three minutes. Pour into greased, shallow casserole or pan (1½ quart). Bake in 350 degree oven about 1 hour or until done. Serves 6.

Mrs. W. R. Hammett, Port Gibson

SWEET POTATO CASSEROLE

3 cups cooked sweet potatoes
1 cup sugar
½ teaspoon salt
2 eggs, beaten
½ stick butter
½ cup milk

½ teaspoon vanilla
1 cup brown sugar
1/3 cup flour
1/3 stick butter
1 cup nuts

Mix potatoes, sugar, salt, eggs, butter, milk and vanilla in order given. Pour into 2-quart casserole. Combine brown sugar and flour; add the butter and mix all together with fork or fingers. Add nuts and mix. Place topping over sweet potato mixture. Bake at 350 degrees for 35 minutes. Serves 8.

Mrs. Carl H. Craig, Brookhaven

[223]

FRENCH STYLE GREEN BEANS

1 (no. 2) can French green
  beans
1 (10½-ounce) can cream of
  mushroom soup, undiluted
½ cup slivered almonds
½ cup grated cheese
½ cup bread crumbs
2 tablespoons butter or oleo

Place half the beans in bottom of a casserole. Cover with half the mushroom soup. Sprinkle on half the almonds and half the cheese. Now layer remaining ingredients again in the same order. Put bread crumbs on top and dot with butter. Bake for 20 minutes at 350 degrees and sprinkle about ½ cup more grated cheese on top and bake 10 minutes longer. The last layer of cheese may be left off and used for the top if desired. Serves 6. English peas may be used instead of green beans, if preferred.

Mrs. Margaret Hart, Holly Springs

GREEN BEAN CASSEROLE

1 (no. 303) can green beans,
  French style
1 (10½ ounce) can mushroom
  soup, undiluted
1 cup grated cheese
1 (3½ ounce) can onion rings

Put drained green beans in a 9-inch shallow round oven-proof dish. Spread mushroom sauce over beans and sprinkle cheese over this. Cook 15 to 20 minutes at 350 degrees in oven. Place onion rings on top and return to the oven for 5 minutes. Serve hot. Serves 6.

Mary McCollum, Mendenhall

SNAP BEANS WITH SOUR CREAM DRESSING

1 pound fresh snap beans
1 cup commercial sour cream
1 teaspoon minced fresh onion
¼ teaspoon garlic salt
¼ cup crumbled cooked
  crisped bacon

Cover and cook beans in a small amount of boiling water until just tender. Drain if necessary. Combine sour cream, onion and garlic salt. Stir in bacon. Serve dressing over the beans. Serves 4.

Mrs. Minnie Harris, Magnolia

PICKLED GREEN BEANS

½ cup sugar
1 teaspoon whole pickling spice
1 large bay leaf
1 pound canned whole green
    beans

1 sliced pimiento
1 (3-ounce) can mushrooms,
    drained
1 teaspoon salt
1 onion, sliced into thin rings

Mix sugar, spices, liquids from vegetables and salt. Stir over low heat until sugar dissolves.

Bring to boil. Pour over mushrooms and onions, drained beans and pimiento. Mix well. Serves 6.

Mrs. G. E. Percival, Holly Springs

PICKLED BEANS

2 (no. 303) cans French
    style beans
onion rings
1 cup Italian dressing

2 tablespoons catsup
salt
pepper

Put layer of beans in dish. Add layer of onion rings. Mix dressing and catsup and pour over beans and onions. Marinate every few hours, keeping in refrigerator. Add salt and pepper to taste. Serve cold. Serves 8.

Mrs. J. R. Patterson, Pontotoc

EGGPLANT CASSEROLE

1 large eggplant
1 teaspoon grated onion
⅛ teaspoon salt and pepper to
    taste
4 tablespoons butter
4 tablespoons flour

1¼ cups milk
1 green pepper, chopped
¾ cup grated sharp cheese
2 eggs, beaten separately
4 tablespoons chili sauce

Cook peeled, cubed eggplant in boiling water with onion, salt and pepper until tender. Drain. Melt butter in double boiler. Add flour; blend. Add milk gradually, stir until blended. If needed, add additional salt. Add chopped pepper, cheese and slightly beaten egg yolks, chile sauce and egg plant. Fold in stiffly beaten egg whites. Bake in buttered casserole 40 minutes at 350 degrees. Serves 6.

Mrs. Harvey McCrosky, Holly Springs

[225]

EGGPLANT CASSEROLE

1 medium eggplant, peeled
3 slices loaf bread, toasted
½ cup sweet milk
2 eggs, slightly beaten
1 medium onion, chopped

3 tablespoons butter or
  oleo, melted
⅛ teaspoon pepper
1 teaspoon salt
2 tablespoons cream or ½ cup
  grated cheese

Boil eggplant in salted water until tender. Drain and mash. Soak bread in milk until soft; mix with mashed eggplant. Add eggs, onion, butter, pepper and salt. Pour mixture into 1 quart casserole dish which has been buttered. Pour cream over mixture or sprinkle on grated cheese. Bake in 350 degree oven for 30 minutes. Serves 6.

Mrs. Gerald E. Benoist, Longview

EGGPLANT COUNTRY SUPPER STYLE

1 medium size eggplant,
  peeled and cubed
3 tablespoons bacon drippings
  or butter
½ cup diced peeled onion
1 (no. 2½) can tomatoes
  chopped

1 tablespoon finely cut parsley
1 teaspoon sugar
½ teaspoon chili powder
1 teaspoon salt
⅛ teaspoon pepper
1 cup buttered coarse crumbs
½ cup cheese, grated

Start oven at moderate (350 degrees) heat. Grease 2-quart casserole. Sautè eggplant 5 minutes in drippings or butter in large frying pan. Pour mixture into prepared baking dish. Sautè onion 2 minutes in same pan. Stir in tomatoes, add parsley, sugar, chili powder, pepper, salt. Stir and let come to boil. Pour over eggplant. Sprinkle generously with crumbs and cheese. Bake 45 minutes at 350 degrees or until top is brown and bubbly. Serves 6.

Mrs. C. L. Weaver, Magnolia

STUFFED EGGPLANT

3 eggplants
6 slices toasted bread
2 whole eggs
1 chopped onion

1 cup chopped ham
½ cup chopped celery
½ cup water
buttered bread crumbs

Wash eggplant, cut in half lengthwise. Scoop out inside. Put eggplant shells in pot, cover with water, cook 5 minutes. Drain. Cook scooped out eggplant in a little water until tender; cool. Soak 6 slices of toasted bread in eggplant water. Add 2 whole eggs. Brown chopped onion in margarine or bacon drippings. Add chopped ham and eggplant mixture. Add ½ cup chopped celery. Cook until browned. Put mixture into eggplant shells, place in shallow pan or pyrex dish. Put ½ cup water in pan. Bake at 350 degrees for 30 minutes. Top with buttered bread crumbs until brown. Eat shells too. Serves 6.

Mrs. G. L. Disharoon, Port Gibson

FRENCH FRIED EGGPLANT

2 medium sized eggplants
pan of ice and water
1 tablespoon of salt

black pepper to taste (if desired)
4 tablespoons flour or meal
(optional)

Peel the 2 eggplants and cut like Irish potatoes to french fry. Place them in a pan of ice and water, add the 1 tablespoon of salt. Let them stand in the water 20 to 25 minutes. If the ice melts before the time is up, add more ice. Drain off water, and fry in deep fat. You can pepper and flour or meal them lightly before frying if you so desire. When you remove them from the skillet, drain on paper kitchen towels. Serves 4 to 6.

Mrs. J. C. Melvin, Florence

SPANISH CORN

1 (no. 2) can whole kernel
corn
2 tablespoons salad oil
¼ cup chopped green pepper
1 tablespoon oleo

2 tablespoons Worcestershire
½ cup catsup
⅛ teaspoon salt
⅛ teaspoon pepper
½ teaspoon paprika

Drain corn. Heat oil, add corn and pepper and sautè for 3 minutes in heavy 10 or 12 inch skillet. Remove from heat. Add other ingredients and cook in covered skillet over medium heat for 20 minutes. Serves 6.

Mrs. Ruby Hegwood, Forest

SCALLOPED CORN

2 cups cream style corn
1 cup milk
1 well beaten egg
1 cup cracker crumbs
¼ cup minced onion

3 tablespoons pimiento
¾ teaspoon salt
dash pepper
½ cup buttered cracker crumbs

Heat corn and milk. Stir in egg; then other ingredients; mix well. Pour in greased 8-inch dish. Sprinkle buttered crumbs over. Bake at 350 degrees for 20 minutes. Serves 4 to 6.

Mrs. Coburn Awtrey, Pheba

PLANTATION CORN PUDDING

1¾ cups milk
1 tablespoon butter or oleo
4 eggs
2 cups cream style corn
2 tablespoons chopped pimiento
2 tablespoons finely chopped
 green pepper

2 tablespoons grated onion
1 teaspoon salt
1 teaspoon sugar
½ teaspoon Accent
¼ teaspoon pepper

Scald milk, add butter or oleo. Beat eggs slightly and blend with corn, pimiento, green pepper, onion, salt, sugar, Accent and pepper. Stirring vigorously, gradually add the milk to the corn mixture and pour into greased 1½ quart casserole. Set a deep pan on oven rack and place the filled baking dish in pan. Pour boiling water into pan to level of mixture in baking dish. Bake at 300 degrees 45 to 60 minutes or until knife comes out clean when inserted halfway between center and edge of casserole. Serves 6.

Mrs. Glen McCullough, Tupelo

CORN FRITTERS

2 well beaten eggs
¼ cup milk
1 cup self-rising flour

1½ cups drained whole-kernel
 corn
2 tablespoons melted fat or oil

Mix eggs and milk and add to the self-rising flour. Blend until smooth. Stir in corn and fat. Drop by spoonfuls into hot fat 375 degrees and cook to desired degree of brownness. Drain on absorbent paper. Serves 15 to 16 fritters of average size.

Mrs. H. B. McNeill, Wesson

ZESTY BUTTER BEAN BAKE

2 tablespoons chopped onion
2 tablespoons chopped green
  pepper
1 tablespoon butter
1 (10¾-ounce) can
  condensed tomato soup

¼ cup water
1 tablespoon vinegar
1 tablespoon brown sugar
1 teaspoon prepared mustard
2 (1-pound) cans butter beans,
  drained

Brown onion and green pepper in butter. Add remaining ingredients except beans. Heat. Pour beans in buttered 1 quart casserole, pour sauce over. Bake in a 375 degree oven 45 minutes. Serves 6.

Mrs. Genevieve Harris, Hazlehurst

BUTTER BEAN CASSEROLE

¼ cup vegetable oil
1 cup chopped onion
1 cup chopped green pepper
1 clove garlic, minced
1 tablespoon cornstarch
1 teaspoon salt
1 tablespoon chili powder

1¼ cup liquid from beans,
  or water
3 (no. 303) cans small lima
  beans or use fresh beans
1 cup ripe olives, chopped
1 cup American cheese, grated

Heat oil in skillet; add onion, pepper and garlic. Cook until tender. Blend in cornstarch, salt, chili powder, and ¼ cup of liquid. Add remaining liquid, beans, olives and ½ cup cheese. Mix well and pour in 1½ quart greased casserole. Bake at 350 degrees about 30 minutes. Put remaining cheese on top just before serving, and put in oven long enough to melt cheese. Serves 8.

Mrs. Homer Gray, Kosciusko

BROCCOLI PARMESAN

2 (10-ounce) packages frozen
  broccoli florets or cuts
3 tablespoons butter
3 tablespoons flour

1½ cups milk
¼ cup mayonnaise
Parmesan cheese, grated

Cook broccoli as directed on package. Drain well and place in buttered 1½ quart casserole. Prepare white sauce by melting butter, blend in flour, and milk. Cook until quite thick and smooth, stirring constantly. Remove from heat. Blend in mayonnaise. Pour sauce over broccoli. Top with a generous layer of Parmesan cheese. Bake at 350 degrees for about 20 minutes or until hot and bubbling and lightly browned. Serves 6.

Mrs. Maurice C. O'Keefe, Jr., Long Beach

BROCCOLI WITH SOUR CREAM DRESSING

1 pound broccoli
1 cup sour cream
2 tablespoons brown sugar

2 tablespoons lemon juice
¼ teaspoon salt
½ teaspoon prepared mustard

Wash broccoli and trim off tip end of stems. If any stems are more than 1 inch in diameter, make lengthwise gashes through them almost to the florets. Drop prepared broccoli into a small amount of boiling salted water, cover and cook about 10 to 15 minutes or until just tender. Combine ingredients for dressing and mix well. Carefully remove broccoli from boiling water and drain; place in serving dish and cover with dressing. Serves 4.

Mr. H. T. Watts, Canton

GOLDEN BROCCOLI

2 (10-ounce) packages frozen
   broccoli
2 teaspoons salt
pepper to taste

2 tablespoons lemon juice
1 (10½-ounce) can cream of
   chicken soup
½ cup grated cheddar cheese

Cook broccoli in salted water as directed on package, or until tender. Drain. Place broccoli in a greased 9 x 12 x 2-inch baking dish. Sprinkle with lemon juice, pepper and cover with the soup. Sprinkle cheese on top and place under broiler for 10 minutes or until cheese is melted and bubbly hot. Serves 8.

Mrs. Anthony Garst, Clarksdale

QUICK AND EASY CREAMED CARROTS

1 medium onion, minced
2 tablespoons cooking oil
2 (1-pound) cans canned
   carrots, undrained (fresh
   carrots, if preferred)

2 heaping tablespoons sugar
2 tablespoons sifted flour
salt to taste

Cook onion in oil until done, but not brown. Add carrots and juices. Add sugar. Sift flour over mixture in pan and stir until smooth. Season to taste. Turn heat low and continue stirring until thick and creamy. Serves 6.

Mrs. Thomas J. Reid, Pass Christian

[230]

MARINATED CARROTS

5 cups sliced carrots
1 medium sweet onion
1 small green pepper
1 (10½-ounce) can cream of
   tomato soup
½ cup salad oil
1 cup sugar

¾ cup vinegar
1 teaspoon prepared mustard
1 teaspoon Worcestershire
   sauce
1 teaspoon salt
1 teaspoon black pepper

Cook carrots. Drain and cool. Cut onion and green pepper in round slices and mix with cooled carrots. Mix other ingredients together and pour over vegetables. Cover and marinate for 12 hours or more. Drain to serve. This will keep 2 weeks in refrigerator. Serves 12.

Mrs. Herman Smith, Water Valley

MINTED CARROTS

1 bunch (5 to 6 carrots,
   cut in strips)
¼ cup butter or margarine

3 tablespoons honey
2 teaspoon chopped fresh mint
   leaves or parsley

Cook carrots in boiling salted water 15 minutes or until tender. Drain. Combine butter, honey and mint; heat to melt butter. Add carrots and heat over low heat, stirring occasionally, until glazed. Serves 4 to 5.

Mrs. Styton Proctor, Glen Allen

ONION FRIED POTATOES

2 medium size potatoes,
   peeled and sliced
salt and pepper to taste

¼ cup flour
3 tablespoons shortening
1 small onion, sliced

Salt and pepper potatoes and sprinkle lightly with flour. Brown potatoes in shortening and cook slowly, until almost done. Add sliced onion. Cover and cook until done. Serves 4.

Mrs. Samuel Skinner, Tylertown

REFRIGERATOR MASHED POTATOES

5 pounds Irish potatoes
2 (3-ounce) packages
   cream cheese
1 cup dairy sour cream

2 tablespoons onion salt
1 teaspoon salt
¼ teaspoon pepper
2 tablespoons butter or oleo

Cook peeled potatoes in boiling salted water until tender, drain. Mash until smooth (no lumps). Add remaining ingredients and beat until light and fluffy (cool, cover and place in refrigerator). May be used at any time within two weeks. To use, place desired amount in greased casserole, dot with butter and bake in 350 degree oven until heated through, about 30 minutes. Makes 8 cups or 12 servings.

Mrs. H. T. Watts, Canton

LUSCIOUS POTATO CASSEROLE

2 cups cream style cottage
   cheese
1 cup commercial sour cream
1/3 cup sliced green onions
1 minced small clove garlic

2 teaspoons salt
5 cups diced cooked potatoes
½ cup shredded American
   cheese

Combine the first five ingredients. Fold in potatoes. Pour into a greased flat 1½ quart casserole dish. Top with cheese. Sprinkle paprika over top. Bake at 350 degrees for 40 minutes. Serves 10 to 12.

Mrs. C. A. Wilson, State College

POTATO BATTER CAKES

5 medium size Irish potatoes
1 egg
1 or 2 tablespoons flour (plain)

1 teaspoon salt
½ cup shortening

Grate potatoes on medium size grates. Drain on paper towels. Beat egg and add to potatoes. Add flour and salt. The amount of flour depends on how watery the potatoes are. Put shortening in large skillet over high heat. When fat is hot, drop in mixture by heaping tablespoonfuls. Spread out thin. Brown on one side, turn and brown the other side. Serve hot with butter. Makes 8 or 9 batter cakes.

Mrs. T. C. Owens, Hazlehurst

CABBAGE ROLLS

½ pound ground beef
½ cup uncooked rice
½ teaspoon black pepper
¼ cup chopped cabbage

1 cup canned tomatoes
1 medium onion, chopped
1 teaspoon salt
cabbage leaves

Thoroughly mix all ingredients except cabbage leaves. Form mixture into small balls. Wrap cabbage leaves around balls; secure with toothpick. Place rolls in a dutch oven. Cover with water; place top on dutch oven and cook slowly for about 45 minutes. Serves 4 to 6.

Mrs. J. T. Kerr, Rolling Fork

RED CABBAGE WITH APPLE

1 head red cabbage
2 cooking apples, unpeeled
½ lemon, unpeeled
¼ cup water
1 onion, diced

salt and pepper to taste
1 cup wine vinegar
dash of cinnamon
2 tablespoons brown sugar
1 cup Claret wine

Wash and thinly slice the cabbage. Remove seeds and cores from apples and dice. Slice lemon thinly. Combine all ingredients in a large, heavy cooking vessel. Cover securely. Bring to boil quickly. Turn immediately to simmer. Simmer slowly for approximately 35 to 45 minutes. Serves 6 to 8.

Mrs. Mary S. Parkman, Monticello

BEEF BRISKET–CABBAGE–TOPPED WITH MUSTARD SAUCE

beef brisket
2 tablespoons butter
1 small head cabbage,
   shredded

½ cup chopped celery
salt to taste
½ cup chopped green pepper
¼ cup water

SAUCE:

1 tablespoon butter
2 eggs, beaten
¼ cup vinegar
¼ cup water

dash of paprika
1½ tablespoon sugar
½ teaspoon dry mustard
¼ cup coffee cream

Cook brisket one hour per pound on simmer. When tender, set aside to cool. Slice thinly across grain. Melt 2 tablespoons butter in skillet. Add shredded cabbage, chopped celery, salt, green pepper and ¼ cup water. Cover and cook on low heat for 5 minutes. Top with the slices of beef brisket. Cover and continue cooking until meat is well heated (10 to 15 minutes).

Melt the tablespoon of butter in saucepan; add beaten eggs with all other ingredients for sauce except coffee cream. Cook over low heat stirring until thickened. Remove from heat and add cream. Beat until smooth. Serve hot over beef and cabbage.

Mrs. Mary S. Parkman, Monticello

SPECIAL RICE

1 pound bulk pork sausage	½ cup slivered toasted almonds
1 cup chopped celery	2 (12½-ounce) cans chicken
1 cup chopped green pepper	broth
1 cup chopped onion	1½ cups raw rice

Fry sausage until browned. Drain well; reserve fat. Cook celery, green pepper and onions in ¼ cup sausage fat. Turn sausage, vegetables, and almonds into a 3-quart baking dish. Add rice and broth; mix well. Bake at 350 degrees for 1½ to 2 hours or until liquid is completely absorbed. Serves 8.

Mrs. Carlisle Moore, Holly Springs

COLESLAW

3 pounds cabbage	1 cup sugar
1 medium bell pepper	1 cup vinegar
1 medium onion	1 cup salad oil
2 carrots	

Shred cabbage; slice bell pepper in rings; slice onion in thin rings and carrots lengthwise. Toss vegetables.

Combine sugar, vinegar and salad oil. Bring to boil and pour over vegetable mixture. Cover and chill in refrigerator for 24 hours before serving. Slaw will keep in refrigerator for two weeks.

Mrs. M. C. Curtis, Tupelo

OLD FASHIONED GREEN PUMPKIN

3 cups green raw pumpkin	1 teaspoon salt
1 cup sugar	½ teaspoon pepper
½ stick margarine	

Peel, dice and steam pumpkin in small amount of water until tender. This does not take long. Drain. Add sugar, margarine and seasonings. Simmer in uncovered saucepan or bake in uncovered casserole in preheated 350 degree oven for 20 to 30 minutes.

A variety of things can be added, such as a favorite spice or spices, raisins, drained crushed pineapple, coconut, or topped with marshmallows. Use your imagination and taste. Serves 6.

Mrs. J. B. Graves, Gulfport

ENGLISH PEA CASSEROLE

3 celery stems, chopped
3 chopped green onions
½ stick oleo
1 (10½-ounce) can condensed
cream of mushroom soup
1 (5-ounce) can water
chestnuts, sliced

1 (2-ounce) can mushrooms
1 (no. 2) can English peas
1 tablespoon flour
½ teaspoon garlic powder
dash of Accent
½ cup cracker crumbs

Brown chopped celery stems and chopped onions in ½ stick oleo. Add mushroom soup, sliced water chestnuts and mushrooms. Thicken English peas with 1 tablespoon flour mixed with juice of mushrooms. Add Accent and garlic powder.

Mix all this in casserole dish and top with cracker crumbs and bake in 350 degree oven about 20 minutes or until hot through. Serves 4 to 5.

Mrs. Billy Fisackerly, Winona

DEVILED ENGLISH PEAS

1 pound can English peas,
drained
4 hard cooked eggs, sliced
1 cup grated cheese
½ cup chopped pimiento

1 (10½-ounce) can cream of
mushroom soup
½ can (no. 2 size) French
fried onion rings

Arrange a layer of peas, egg slices, pimiento and cheese in a 1½ quart casserole dish. Spread half of the soup over the top. Repeat layers. Bake at 350 degrees for 15 minutes. Cover with onions and heat until hot. Serves 6.

Mrs. Zelma Mitchell, Magnolia

HARVEST SPINACH RING

4 (10-ounce packages)
frozen chopped spinach
4 separated eggs
2 cups shredded sharp
cheddar cheese
3 tablespoons flour

3 tablespoons melted margarine
2 tablespoons grated onions
1 tablespoon lemon juice
½ teaspoon salt
¼ teaspoon black pepper

Cook spinach as directed on package; drain thoroughly. Beat egg yolks; combine with cheese, flour, margarine, onions, lemon juice and seasonings. Add spinach and mix well. Fold in stiffly beaten egg whites. Grease 6½ cup ring mold; line bottom with a strip of foil. Grease foil. Spoon spinach mixture into mold; place in large pan on oven rack. Pour boiling water to ½ depth. Bake at 350 degrees 30 to 35 minutes or until knife inserted comes out clean. Loosen sides of mold with knife. Unmold on serving plate. Remove foil. If desired, fill ring with small whole carrots, cooked. Serves 8 to 10.

Mrs. C. R. Vaughn, Olive Branch

CELERY CASSEROLE

4 cups diced celery, diagonally cut	1 (no. 2) can chicken broth
½ teaspoon salt	½ cup half & half cream
½ cup water chestnuts, sliced	½ cup canned mushrooms
¼ cup slivered almonds	½ cup Parmesan cheese
3 tablespoons flour	½ cup dry bread crumbs
3 tablespoons butter	2 tablespoons butter

Parboil celery and salt for 5 minutes. Drain, and put in buttered casserole with almonds and water chestnuts. Melt butter with flour. Cook slowly and add broth and cream. Simmer over low heat for 5 minutes. Add mushroom to sauce and pour over celery. Sprinkle with cheese. Dot with butter. Sprinkle with bread crumbs. Bake at 350 degrees till bubbly. Serves 10.

Mrs. Bob Anding, Jackson

CAULIFLOWER ROYAL

1 large head cauliflower	1 teaspoon lemon juice
1 (10-ounce) can frozen shrimp soup	¼ cup sweet milk
2 teaspoons fresh or dried parsley	¼ cup chopped almonds
	½ teaspoon paprika

Cook whole cauliflower in small amount of salt water (do not overcook). Melt shrimp soup in small sauce pan. Add 1 teaspoon parsley, lemon juice and milk. Pour over cauliflower. Sprinkle with remaining teaspoon parsley, almonds and paprika. Serve at once. Serves 6.

Mrs. R. W. Lipscomb, Como

CAULIFLOWER WITH PEAS IN CREAM SAUCE

1 head fresh cauliflower
1 cup water
1 teaspoon lemon juice
1 (1 pound) can petit pois peas
1½ cup liquid from peas and
  milk
3 tablespoons butter

2 tablespoons flour
1 teaspoon salt
¼ teaspoon Worcestershire
dash each cayenne, dry mustard,
  nutmeg
paprika

Wash cauliflower under running water and drain. Bring water to boil. Place cauliflower in pan, stem end down. Sprinkle with lemon juice. Simmer until crisp tender.

Drain liquid from peas and add milk to measure 1½ cups. Melt butter. Blend in flour until smooth. Add liquid. Cook over medium heat, stirring constantly, until smooth and thickened. Add salt, Worcestershire sauce, cayenne, mustard, and nutmeg. Blend in thoroughly. Add peas and heat thoroughly. Drain cauliflower, place in center of serving dish, pour peas over and sprinkle lightly with paprika. Serves 6 to 8.

Mrs. Maurice C. O'Keefe, Jr., Long Beach

FLUFFY TURNIP

2 cups mashed rutabaga turnips
1 beaten egg
1 tablespoon sugar

salt and pepper to taste
½ teaspoon baking powder
2/3 cup milk

Mix well and place in 1½ quart casserole. Bake at 350 degrees until set and brown. Serves 4.

Mrs. R. P. Goodman, Chunky

BEET CASSEROLE

1 cup sugar
¼ cup vinegar
1 tablespoon cornstarch
½ cup beet juice

¼ cup orange juice
grated rind from one orange
1 (no. 2) can sliced beets
1 cup raisins

Mix sugar, vinegar, cornstarch, beet juice, orange juice and rind. Add to beets and raisins. Pour into an ungreased 8 x 8 x 2-inch baking dish. Bake in a 350 degree oven for 1 hour. Serves 6 to 8.

Mrs. E. G. Davis, Lula

STUFFED GREEN PEPPERS

6 green peppers
2 cups cooked chicken,
  minced
¼ cup chicken broth
1 onion, minced
1 tablespoon butter

1 tablespoon parsley
1 teaspoon salt
¼ cup bread crumbs or rice
1 cup water or stock
1 egg unbeaten

Cut the peppers in halves crosswise, remove the seeds and cut off the stems. Chop the meat and onion together. Mix all the ingredients together except the water or stock. Fill the peppers, stand them in a pan, and put the hot stock or water around them. Bake at 350 degrees basting often, until peppers are tender, about 35 minutes. Serves 12.

Beatrice Hamilton, Raleigh

FIELD PEAS

1 quart of fresh field peas
2 quarts of water
2 teaspoons of salt

2 teaspoons of sugar
1 (2 x 4 inch) slice of bacon
2 teaspoons of flour

Put water, peas, salt, sugar and bacon in pressure saucepan. Pressure at 10 pounds for 20 minutes. Take a little of the juice and mix flour in it well to eliminate lumps and add to the peas to make a good thick juice. Cook 5 or 10 minutes more. Serves 8.

Mrs. J. T. Darnell, DeKalb

SOUTHERN OKRA

1 cup cut okra
1 small sized onion, chopped
½ green sweet pepper,
  chopped
¼ cup salad oil

1 cup thick tomato juice
1 tablespoon sugar
1 tablespoon flour
½ teaspoon salt
¼ teaspoon pepper

Cook okra in boiling salted water ten minutes. Drain. Brown onion and green pepper in salad oil. Add tomato juice, cook slowly five minutes. Add okra and remaining ingredients. Cook over low heat five minutes longer. Serves 4.

Miss Mable Dean, Iuka

SCALLOPED OKRA

1 (no. 303) can cut okra
salt and pepper to taste
3 slices bread with crusts,
   torn into small bits
1 beaten egg

1 cup milk
½ medium onion, chopped
½ green pepper, chopped
slivers of cheese, if desired

Mix all ingredients together. Pour into well buttered 1½ quart casserole. Add cheese slivers. Cover with crushed cereal and dot liberally with butter. Bake at 350 degrees until done. Can be made ahead. Serves 4 to 5.

Mrs. M. E. Brooks, Newton

STUFFED TOMATOES

6 ripe tomatoes, average size
1 cup ground beef or other
   meat, cooked and chopped
1 onion, chopped
1 bell pepper, chopped
1 teaspoon vinegar

2 cups bread crumbs
½ teaspoon salt
½ teaspoon black pepper
½ teaspoon spice
3 slices bacon, halved

Cut thin slice from stem end of tomatoes. Scoop out pulp, leaving a shell. Mix the pulp with the chopped meat, onion, pepper, vinegar, bread crumbs, salt, spice and black pepper. Mix thoroughly and fill tomato shell. Place filled tomato shells in greased baking dish or pan. Place one half slice of bacon on top of each tomato. Add 1½ cups of hot water in pan and bake 20 to 30 minutes at 350 degrees. Serves 6.

Mrs. Berta Mae Wasson, Ethel

MEXICAN HOT PEPPERS

6 or 8 whole banana peppers
3 large onions, thinly sliced
3 large carrots, chopped

3 tablespoons olive oil
1 bay leaf
2 cups vinegar, or little more

Using 3-tine fork, make one punch into each pepper. Leave whole; put in a one quart jar, add onions and carrots. In sauce pan add olive oil, vinegar and bay leaf. Heat just below boiling, pour over peppers, having enough to cover; seal; keep about two weeks before using. Very hot. Serve with Mexican Rice.

Mrs. Virginia Love, Poplarville

RED BEANS 'N RICE

1 pound red kidney beans	3 quarts water
2 chopped onions	1 tablespoon vegetable oil
2 cloves minced garlic	1 teaspoon salt
¼ pound pork meat (ham, salt shoulder, pickled pork or bacon)	½ teaspoon black pepper
	1½ teaspoons Tobasco
	1 cup raw rice, cooked

Wash and sort beans. Boil all ingredients except rice together in large pot. Cook on low heat with pot lid crooked on pot, stirring occasionally and adding more water if beans become too dry, for 3 hours. Serve over hot steamed rice. Serves 8 to 10.

Mrs. Gwen M. McKee, Brandon

·[Casseroles]·

It's no wonder cooks love casseroles. They can be prepared quickly, they provide the main dish of the meal, and finally while the casserole is cooking, the cook is free to put together a salad and dessert.

A popular type of fellowship in Mississippi is the "covered dish supper" where each family brings a different part of the meal. A casserole can be utilized on these occasions as the main dish, the vegetable, or even the bread.

Originally the term "casserole" implied a cooking utensil and not a cooked dish. Now it is regularly used to mean a mixture of food that is often precooked or consists of a combination of precooked and quick-cooking foods and is served in the utensil in which it is heated. Casseroles are a favorite type of self-service dish that graces so many American buffets.

Casseroles are time savers, economical, nutritious, and they add variety to your family meals

Casserole dishes freeze well too. You may freeze them right in the baking dish. If you need the container for another use, line it with foil, add the food and freeze. Then you can lift out the contents and wrap tightly in foil for keeping. For best quality, plan to use within a few weeks.

SCALLOPED OYSTERS

1 (½-pound) box Saltine
   crackers
1 pint oysters
1½ sticks butter
½ teaspoon salt

¼ teaspoon black pepper
1 cup finely cut celery
1 cup parsley
1 pint half and half cream

Rub bottom and sides of deep 2-quart casserole with butter. Break crackers into large pieces. Place layer of cracker pieces in bottom of casserole and cover with whole drained oysters. Dot generously with butter and sprinkle with part of the salt and pepper. Next add a generous sprinkling of finely cut celery and parsley. Repeat layers, beginning with crackers, until dish is two-thirds full, ending with cracker layer topped with butter. Pour cream over and bake in 375 degree oven for 40 minutes, or until it is set and lightly brown. Serves 6.

This may be made ahead and kept in refrigerator until ready to cook.

"This has become a traditional Christmas Eve supper dish in my house, because I can make it in the morning and keep it in the refrigerator until we come in from late afternoon and early evening delivering Christmas presents. It is *great* to have it ready to pop in the oven when everyone is starved. I usually buy extra oysters, and while the casserole is cooking we have either Oysters Rockefeller (I have a friend who gives me the sauce for Christmas!), or Oyster Cocktail—and this, with the casserole and a green salad is a perfect Christmas Eve supper!"

Mrs. Carroll Gartin, Laurel

RICE AND SALMON CASSEROLE

2 tablespoons butter or
   margarine
2 tablespoons diced green
   onion
2 tablespoons diced green
   pepper
2 tablespoons diced pimiento
2 (10½-ounce) cans cream of
   mushroom soup
⅛ teaspoon salt
1/3 cup dry sherry (optional)

1 teaspoon Worcestershire
   sauce
¼ teaspoon dry mustard
1 (16-ounce) can red salmon,
   well drained, cleaned,
   boned and flaked
4 hard cooked eggs
3 cups cooked rice
bread crumbs
Parmesan cheese

Add mushroom soup to onion, pepper and pimiento sautèd in the margarine. Add sherry and condiments. Fold in salmon. Cut eggs into fifths and fold into mixture. Lightly oil 2-quart casserole. Cover bottom with cooked rice. Spoon salmon mixture over rice. Sprinkle top generously with bread crumbs and grated Parmesan cheese. Place in 375 degree oven for 30 minutes. Serves 6.

Note: Any seafood may be substituted for salmon, such as shrimp, crab, lobster, etc.

Mrs. Mike Lundy, Merigold

CRAB–SHRIMP BAKE

1 medium pepper, chopped
1 cup chopped celery
1 (6½-ounce) can crab meat, flaked
½ teaspoon salt
1 cup mayonnaise

1 medium onion, chopped
1 cup cooked, cleaned shrimp
dash of pepper
1 teaspoon Worcestershire
1 cup butter crumbs

Combine ingredients, except crumbs; place in individual seashells, or bake in greased casserole. Bake in moderate oven, 350 degrees, about 30 minutes. Serves 8.

Mrs. R. B. Harris, Midnight

TUNA NOODLE CASSEROLE

1 (6-ounce) package noodles
1 teaspoon salt
1 can tuna, flaked
½ cup mayonnaise
1/3 cup chopped onion
¼ cup chopped pimiento
½ cup finely chopped celery

¼ cup chopped green pepper
1 (10½-ounce) can cream of celery soup
1 cup milk
1 cup shredded cheese
almonds (optional)

Cook noodles in salt water until tender. Drain. Combine noodles, flaked tuna, mayonnaise, onion, pimiento, celery and pepper. Blend soup and milk together and add to noodle mixture. Put in 1½-quart casserole and bake in 425 degree oven for 20 minutes. Remove from oven and sprinkle with cheese. Return to oven until cheese is melted. Top with almonds (optional). Serves 8 to 10.

Mrs. Joe C. Moak, Brookhaven

CHICKEN DUMPLINGS

1 large fryer, cut up
1 quart of cold water
1 (10½-ounce) can cream
  of chicken soup
3 tablespoons butter

salt to taste
½ teaspoon black pepper
1 box pie crust mix
1 cup all-purpose flour
1 cup sweet milk

Place chicken in a 4-quart boiler, add 1 quart of cold water, and cook slowly until chicken is tender. Remove chicken from broth, and add to the broth the soup, butter, salt and pepper. Reduce heat to simmer while preparing dumplings.

Blend pie crust mix and flour in a mixing bowl with enough cold water to mix, and roll out as for pie crust. Cut in pieces about 1-inch square. Bring broth mixture to a boil, and drop in the squares of dough. Continue to boil for 5 minutes, then add the milk, and cook 3 minutes longer. The boiled chicken may be served with the dumplings, or used as a separate dish. If served separately, dip chicken in a mixture of 1 egg, ½ cup sweet milk and ½ cup of flour beaten well together, then roll in flour. Cook quickly in hot grease. Serve with the dumplings.

Mrs. W. B. Jackson, Purvis

CASSEROLE OF CHICKEN AND STUFFING

1 (8-ounce) package
  herb-seasoned stuffing
3 cups cubed cooked chicken
½ cup margarine
½ cup flour
¼ teaspoon salt
4 cups chicken broth

4 eggs, slightly beaten
1 (10½-ounce) can mushroom
  soup
¼ cup milk
1 cup sour cream
¼ cup chopped pimiento

Spread stuffing in greased 13 x 9 x 2-inch baking dish. Top with layer of chicken. In large saucepan, melt margarine, blend in flour, add salt, then stir in chicken broth. Cook until mixture thickens, stirring slowly. Gradually stir some of hot mixture into beaten eggs, then add remaining hot mixture. Pour over chicken in casserole and bake 1 hour at 350 degrees until knife comes out clean. Let stand 5 minutes before cutting into squares. Combine remaining ingredients for sauce, and heat. Pour over casserole when serving. Serves 12.

Mrs. Hilman Wedgeworth, Laurel

CHICKEN WIGGLE

1 (6-pound) hen
2 tablespoons salt
10 peppercorns
1 (no. 2) can small green peas, drained
1 (5-ounce) bottle stuffed olives, chopped
1 (4-ounce) can mushrooms, chopped
2 sticks butter or margarine
3 large onions, chopped
1 large bell pepper, chopped
2 cups celery, chopped
1 (no. 2½) can tomatoes
2 cups uncooked rice
6 cups chicken broth
½ pound cheddar cheese, grated

Cover chicken with water, add salt, pepper, boil until tender. Remove chicken from bone, dice in small pieces. Add this to the peas, olives and mushrooms. Set aside. Sautè onions, bell pepper, and celery in butter or margarine till soft. To this mixture add tomatoes, rice and chicken broth. Cook until the rice is done. Add more chicken broth if necessary. Combine chicken, peas, mushrooms, olives, with the tomatoes and rice, pour into a 13 x 9-inch pan, top with grated cheese and bake for 30 minutes in 350 degree oven. Serves approximately 18 to 20.

Mrs. B. L. Bridges, Memphis, Tennessee

CHICKEN SPAGHETTI

1 boiled hen
3 medium onions, chopped
1 large bell pepper, chopped
2 (2-ounce) jars sliced pimientos
1 clove garlic
½ cup chopped celery
1 stick or ¼ pound oleo
2 (16-ounce) cans tomato sauce
1 (16-ounce) can water
3 (4-ounce) cans button mushrooms
1 (10-ounce) package Vermicelli spaghetti
1 pound hoop cheese, grated

Boil hen, remove meat and dice it. Reserve broth. Combine onions, bell pepper, pimientos, garlic and celery in melted oleo in a 2-quart saucepan. Cook covered at medium heat until mixture is clear, about 20 minutes. Add tomato sauce, water and mushrooms and cook, covered, 1 hour, until well seasoned. Add diced chicken to tomato mixture and set aside. Cook spaghetti in chicken broth. Drain and mix the tomato ingredients. Put mixture in two 2-quart well greased casserole dishes and top with cheese. Bake at 350 degrees 30 to 45 minutes. Yields 4 quarts and serves 12 people. May be prepared ahead of serving time and frozen. Will keep in freezer 6 months. *Mrs. Ronald O. Respess, Lambert*

CHICKEN AND WILD RICE DELIGHT

2 fryers, cut up
oleo
1 cup chopped celery
1 medium onion, chopped
1 package seasoned white
and wild rice
1 (10½-ounce) can cream of
mushroom soup

1 cup sour cream
1 small can mushroom pieces
¾ cup sherry
pimiento
ripe olives
paprika

Salt and pepper fryers. Cover with water and boil until tender. Cool and remove meat from bones. Save broth. Sautè celery and onion in small amount of oleo.

Cook one package seasoned white and wild rice according to instructions on package, using broth instead of water. Add mushroom soup, sour cream, mushroom pieces, cut up chicken and sherry. Put in casserole and garnish with pimiento and ripe olives. Sprinkle with paprika. Bake at 350 degrees until bubbly. Serves 8 to 10.

Mrs. Vernon Seals, Madison

CHICKEN CASSEROLE

2 cups cooked rice
6 chicken breasts (halves)
cooked and boned, or 3 cups
cooked chicken cut in
bite-size pieces
1 (10½-ounce) can cream
of chicken soup
½ cup mayonnaise
3 or 4 tablespoons lemon juice

3 teaspoons curry powder
1½ cups shredded sharp or
mild American cheese
1½ cups soft bread crumbs
(about the size of lima
beans)
3 tablespoons margarine,
melted

Spread rice in greased 9 x 13-inch baking dish. Place chicken on top. Combine soup, mayonnaise, lemon juice and curry powder and pour on top of chicken. Sprinkle with cheese. Mix bread crumbs with melted margarine and sprinkle over all. Bake at 350 degrees for 30 minutes, or until bubbly on sides and brown on top. Garnish with sliced olives or pimiento strips. Serves 6 to 8.

Mrs. M. A. Rowzee, State College

TURKEY PILAF

¼ cup butter or margarine
1 cup uncooked regular rice
1 cup chopped celery
2 cups chicken broth or
  bouillon
1 envelope onion soup mix
  (or one chopped onion)

1 teaspoon salt
¼ teaspoon marjoram
¼ teaspoon thyme
1/3 teaspoon pepper
2 cups diced cooked turkey
  or chicken
chopped parsley

In a 3-quart saucepan melt butter or margarine and sautè rice and celery until rice is golden brown. Add broth and stir in soup mix and seasonings. Bring to a boil, stirring occasionally. Cover, reduce heat, and simmer gently for 15 minutes. Stir in turkey. Simmer uncovered 10 more minutes or until liquid is absorbed. Remove from heat and let stand 10 minutes. Garnish with parsley. Serves 4 to 6.

Mrs. Marilyn J. Bailey, Prentiss

SZÉKLY KÁPOSZTA
(Transylvania Gulyas)

1 medium onion, chopped
2 tablespoons shortening
2 tablespoons red paprika
2 pounds pork shoulder,
  cut in 1-inch cubes

1 fresh green pepper, chopped
1 fresh tomato, cut up
1 can sauerkraut
2 tablespoons caraway seeds
sour cream (optional)

Chop the onion and brown it in the shortening in a deep skillet. Add the paprika. Right away put in the pork, the fresh green pepper and the fresh tomato and stir all together and simmer. Rinse the sauerkraut to remove some of the salt. Add the caraway seeds (and sour cream, if desired). Stir together with the meat and cook for 1 hour on medium low heat on top of the stove. Serves 6.

Mrs. Bencze owned the *Atlantic* the second largest restaurant in Budapest, Hungary. The Benczes escaped from Hungary in 1956 after the Hungarian Revolution. Mr. Bencze is now Artist in Residence at the University of Mississippi. In Budapest he was the leading Basso of the Budapest State Opera.

Mrs. Miklos Bencze, University

[247]

BEANS AND PORKCHOP CASSEROLE

2 cans pork and beans
6 pork chops
6 tablespoons mustard
6 tablespoons brown sugar

6 teaspoons catsup
6 slices onion
6 slices lemon

Place beans in bottom of casserole. Place the six pork chops on top. On top of each pork chop put 1 tablespoon mustard, 1 tablespoon brown sugar, 1 tablespoon catsup, thin slice of onion and a slice of lemon. Stick a toothpick in the center to hold in place. Place in oven and cook at 350 degrees for 1 hour, or until pork chops are tender. This is a delicious dish. Serves 6.

Mrs. L. Z. Tindoll, Kilmichael

PORK CHOPS CASSEROLE

4 pork chops
½ cup uncooked rice
1 large onion, sliced
1 green pepper, sliced

2 cups hot water
1 cup cooked tomatoes
2 teaspoons salt and pepper

Put chops in bottom of baking dish. Place rice over them. Slice onion and green pepper over rice and pour in hot water and tomatoes, add salt and pepper. Cover and bake 1 hour in medium oven, 350 degrees, until rice is cooked and chops are tender. Serves 4.

Mrs. Zell Barber, Carriere

INSIDE OUT RAVIOLI

1 pound ground beef
1 medium onion, chopped
1 clove garlic, minced
1 tablespoon salad oil
1 (10-ounce) package
   frozen chopped spinach
1 pound can spaghetti
   sauce with mushroom
1 (8-ounce) can tomato sauce

1 (6-ounce) can tomato paste
½ teaspoon salt
¼ teaspoon pepper
1 (7-ounce) package shell or
   elbow macaroni, cooked
1 cup shredded sharp cheese
½ cup soft bread crumbs
2 eggs, well beaten
¼ cup salad oil

Brown first three ingredients in the 1 tablespoon salad oil. Cook spinach according to package directions. Drain, reserving liquid; add water to make 1 cup. Stir spinach liquid and next 5 ingredients into meat mixture.

Simmer 10 minutes. Combine spinach with remaining ingredients. Spread in a greased 9 x 13 x 2-inch baking dish. Top with meat sauce. Bake at 350 degrees for 30 minutes. Let stand 10 minutes before serving. Serves 8 to 10.

Mrs. Robert Carter, Clarksdale

CHOP SUEY

1 pound ground beef
¼ cup slivered green pepper
1 tablespoon shortening
1 (10½-ounce) can condensed
  onion soup
1 (16-ounce) can drained
  chop suey vegetables

1 tablespoon soy sauce
1 tablespoon cornstarch
2 tablespoons water
1 (no. 2½) can Chinese
  noodles

Brown beef and cook green peppers in shortening until tender; stir and separate meat particles. Pour off fat. Add soup; simmer 10 minutes. Stir in vegetables and soy sauce. Blend cornstarch and water. Add to meat mixture. Cook until slightly thickened; stir occasionally. Serve on heated Chinese noodles with additional soy sauce. Serves 6.

Mrs. Lucille Betts, Houston

SOUR CREAM NOODLE BAKE

1 (8-ounce) package
  narrow noodles
2 pounds ground beef
1 tablespoon salt
½ tablespoon black pepper
½ tablespoon garlic salt
2 tablespoons oleo

1½ cups tomato sauce
1 cup creamed cottage cheese
1 cup sour cream
1 cup chopped green onions
  (about 2 bunches tops with
  roots)
1 cup grated American Cheese

Cook noodles according to package directions. Set aside. Sautè meat (with salt, pepper and garlic salt) in oleo over medium heat until meat loses red color. Add tomato sauce and stir well and simmer for several minutes. Remove from heat.

Drain cooked noodles and mix well with cottage cheese, sour cream and chopped onion. Spread in alternate layers in 3-quart greased casserole beginning with noodles and ending with meat. Top with grated cheese. Cook in 350 degree oven for 25 to 30 minutes until bubbly. Serves 12.

Mrs. Eli Ellis, Port Gibson

BAKED MACARONI AND CORNED BEEF

1 cup uncooked elbow
macaroni
1 (10½-ounce) can condensed
cream of mushroom soup
1 cup milk

1 teaspoon prepared mustard
½ cup grated sharp cheese
¼ cup chopped celery
1 (12-ounce) can corned beef,
unchilled, flaked

Cook macaroni according to package directions; drain. Combine soup, milk and mustard. Add macaroni and remaining ingredients, pour into a 1½-quart casserole. Bake at 350 degrees for 25 minutes. Serves 4.

Mrs. George Morley, Skene

GROUND MEAT CASSEROLE

1 tablespoon cooking oil
1 pound ground meat
1 large onion, chopped
1 green pepper, chopped
1 small bottle stuffed olives
1 can tomatoes

3 tablespoons Worcestershire
sauce
dash hot sauce
salt and pepper
1½ cups cooked macaroni
1 cup grated cheese
1 cup bread crumbs

Brown meat in cooking oil, add onion, green pepper, olives and tomatoes and all seasonings. Add macaroni, pour into greased baking dish. Cover with grated cheese and bread crumbs. Bake 25 minutes at 350 degrees. Serves 4.

Mrs. Ance Speights, Columbia

BEN–GETTI

1 pound ground beef
1 medium-size onion,
finely chopped
1 cup celery, finely chopped
1 (10¾-ounce) can
condensed tomato soup
1 (10½-ounce) can condensed
cream of mushroom soup

1 cup extra small English peas
1 soup can of water
1 (5-ounce) package egg
noodles
1 teaspoon salt
1 teaspoon garlic salt
½ teaspoon black pepper
2 cups grated cheddar cheese

In a large, heavy, covered skillet, cook slowly the beef, onions, and celery until tender. Add the soups, English peas and water. Let this simmer while the noodles are cooking by the directions on the package. When noodles are cooked, drain them and add to the meat and soup mixture. Add salt and pepper. Simmer a few minutes longer to blend all ingredients. Pour this into a deep 2-quart ungreased casserole or into two 1-quart casseroles. Cover with grated cheddar cheese. Bake at 350 degrees, until mixture bubbles and cheese is melted. Serves 6 to 8.

Mrs. J. Starr Howle, Macon

BEEF AND POTATO CASSEROLE

1½ pounds ground beef	1 (10½-ounce) can
3 average potatoes, thinly	mushroom soup
sliced	1½ cups grated cheese
½ cup chopped onion	salt to taste
½ cup chopped celery	

Cook beef in skillet until done, add a little water and stir as it cooks. Set aside. Cook potatoes until tender in salted water. Mix onion and celery in saucepan, add a little water and slowly cook until tender. Then add mushroom soup and stir until it is well blended. In a 2-quart casserole, rotate layers of beef, potatoes, soup mixture and cheese until all is used. Place dish in 350 degree oven and bake until cheese is melted, 20 to 30 minutes. Serves 8 to 10.

Marian H. Quinn, Canton

MEAT BALL CASSEROLE

1 pound ground beef	1 egg
¼ cup finely chopped onion	1 cup milk
¼ cup finely chopped	1 (10½-ounce) can
green pepper	mushroom soup
¼ teaspoon pepper	1/3 cup flour
1 teaspoon salt	½ cup chili sauce
1 cup fine cracker crumbs	

Preheat oven to 350 degrees. Combine the first 7 ingredients. Mix and blend well. Add milk to mushroom soup and stir until blended. Add one-fourth of the soup mixture to the first ingredients. Mix well and form into medium balls. Dip balls in flour and brown on all sides in hot fat. Place in a casserole dish. Combine chili sauce and remaining soup mixture; pour over meat balls. Bake in moderate oven, 350 degrees, 30 minutes. Serves 5.

Miss Lillian Heffner, Indianola

[251]

MEXICAN TORTILLA CASSEROLE

1½ pounds ground chuck
2 tablespoons chili powder
salt
pepper
1 package tortillas

3 medium onions, chopped
1 pound cheese, grated
1 can Rotel sauce, tomatoes
   and green chilies
1 can enchilada sauce

Brown meat and chili powder; salt and pepper to taste. In a 9 x 13-inch flat dish lay bottom with tortillas, then layer of meat, onion and cheese. Repeat for second layer. Any meat and onions left over after layers put on top and add remaining cheese.

Combine Rotel and enchilada sauce and pour over top and bake in 400 degree oven for 45 minutes or until cheese on top is brown.

Mrs. J. D. Fuller, Laurel

MEXICAN CHICKEN POT PIE

1 onion, chopped
1 clove garlic, chopped
1 (10½-ounce) can mushroom
   soup
1 can chicken broth
   (measured in soup can)

1 can enchilada sauce
1 hen, cooked until tender,
   deboned and chopped
1 large package Fritos
3 cups grated cheese

Sautè onion and garlic in small amount of butter. Mix mushroom soup, broth and enchilada sauce. In a buttered baking dish, put a layer of chicken, layer of Fritos, layer cheese, layer of sauce. Continue layering. Add grated cheese on top. Bake at 350 degrees until cheese is melted, approximately 30 to 40 minutes.

Mrs. J. T. Thompson, New Hebron

HOT TAMALE PIE CASSEROLE

1 large onion, chopped
½ cup chopped bell pepper
1 pound ground beef
1 (10½-ounce) can tomato
   soup
2 cups water
1 teaspoon salt

1 cup whole kernel corn,
   drained
¾ cup cornmeal
1 tablespoon flour
1 tablespoon sugar
½ teaspoon salt
1½ teaspoons baking powder

¼ teaspoon pepper
1 tablespoon chili powder

1 egg, beaten
1/3 cup milk
1 tablespoon corn oil

Sautè onions and bell pepper, add meat. When pink is gone from meat, add soup, water, salt, pepper, chili powder and corn. Simmer 15 minutes. For topping, sift dry ingredients. Add beaten egg and milk, stir until combined. Add melted fat. Place meat mixture in greased casserole, cover with cornbread topping. Bake at 425 degrees for 20 or 25 minutes or until brown. Serves 6 to 8.

Mrs. John Haley, Canton

FRITOS AND CHILI

1 (6-ounce) package Fritos
2 (15-ounce) cans of chili
   (no beans)

1 medium-size onion,
   finely chopped
1 cup grated cheddar cheese

Grease 2-quart casserole. Add package of Fritos and pour chili over Fritos. Add finely chopped onions on top of chili. Sprinkle grated cheese over top. Bake at 350 degrees until cheese melts. Serves 6.

Mrs. Bert Hearst, Hattiesburg

CORN CASSEROLE

2 tablespoons chopped bell
   pepper
3 tablespoons chopped onion
3 tablespoons margarine
2 tablespoons flour
1 teaspoon salt
⅛ teaspoon pepper

¼ teaspoon paprika
¼ teaspoon dry mustard
1¼ cups milk
2 cups cracker crumbs
2 cups creamed corn
1 egg, well beaten

Sautè bell pepper and onion in 2 tablespoons margarine in saucepan. Cook gently until tender. Add flour, seasonings and milk, stir until thickened, stirring constantly. Crush 1 cup of cracker crumbs. Add with corn and egg to creamed mixture. Turn into greased 1½-quart casserole. Melt remaining tablespoon margarine, pour over remaining cup of crushed crumbs. Toss lightly, sprinkle over top of corn. Bake in 400 degree oven 30 minutes. Serves 6.

Mrs. John Foster, Natchez

EGGPLANT AND SHRIMP CASSEROLE

3 medium eggplants
2 pounds fresh shrimp
(frozen shrimp may be
substituted)
3 (10½-ounce) cans
mushroom soup
1 large onion, minced

½ pound sharp cheese,
grated
1 cup bread crumbs
2 tablespoons butter
2 teaspoons salt
1 teaspoon pepper
1 tablespoon Worcestershire
sauce

Peel and slice eggplants and cook in salted water 8 to 10 minutes or until it begins to get limp. Drain off water. Peel shrimp and cut in bite-size pieces. In 2-quart greased casserole place a layer of shrimp, mushroom soup, minced onion, grated cheese and bread crumbs. Dot with butter. Then start with next layer and continue until all ingredients are used; ending with bread crumbs and butter on top. The salt, pepper and Worcestershire sauce should be divided equally between each layer. Cover casserole and bake in 350 degree oven for 1 hour. Uncover last 15 minutes and let brown. Serves 8 to 10.

Mrs. Goodwin Myrick, Columbus

EGGPLANT CASSEROLE

1 medium eggplant
¼ cup margarine
1 teaspoon salt
½ teaspoon pepper
1 tablespoon Worcestershire
sauce
1 tablespoon catsup
2 eggs, slightly beaten

¾ cup milk
¼ cup chopped onion
¼ cup chopped bell pepper
¼ cup chopped canned
pimiento
1 cup buttered cracker crumbs
1 cup sharp cheese, cubed

Boil eggplant until tender; drain. Mix remaining ingredients in order listed, reserving cheese and ¼ cup cracker crumbs. Place in greased 1½-quart casserole. Insert cubed cheese into mixture. Sprinkle reserved cracker crumbs over all and bake until brown in a 350 degree oven. Serves 8.

Mrs. W. Taylor Smith, Booneville

EGGPLANT CASSEROLE

2 or 3 cups cooked eggplant
1½ cups cheese cubes
1 (10½-ounce) can cream of
mushroom soup

2 eggs, beaten
1 can oysters (optional)
salt and pepper to taste
1 cup cracker crumbs

Mix all ingredients and pour into greased casserole dish. Cover with buttered bread crumbs. Bake slowly, 325 to 350 degrees, until done, about 30 minutes. Serves 8.

Mrs. Rosa Wade, Vaiden

EGGPLANT AND BEEF CASSEROLE

1 large eggplant	2 cups canned tomatoes
½ cup oil or bacon drippings	salt and pepper to taste
½ cup minced onion	2 tablespoons sugar
½ cup chopped green pepper	1 cup sharp grated cheese
½ pound ground beef	1 cup bread crumbs

Sautè eggplant (peeled and diced) in oil with onion, green pepper and ground beef for 10 minutes. Add tomatoes, salt, pepper and sugar and cook 10 minutes longer. Pour into buttered 2-quart casserole. Cover with cheese and bread crumbs. Bake at 400 degrees 20 minutes. Serves 8 to 10.

Mrs. Joe Elliott, Sr., Water Valley

CARROT CASSEROLE

2 cups cooked, mashed carrots	1 tablespoon baking powder
1 cup sugar, (½ brown, ½ white)	1 stick margarine
	3 eggs, beaten
2 tablespoons flour	cinnamon to taste

Mix and bake in 1-quart buttered casserole for 15 minutes at 400 degrees then at 350 degrees until firm. Serves 6.

Mrs. J. E. Richardson, Enterprise

BROCCOLI CASSEROLE

3 (10-ounce) packages frozen broccoli	1 cup grated sharp cheese
2 (10-ounce) cans frozen shrimp soup	¼ teaspoon Worcestershire sauce
1 cup dairy sour cream	¼ teaspoon Tabasco sauce

Cook broccoli in salted water until tender. Drain. Thaw soup in top of double boiler. Fold in sour cream, ½ cup cheese and broccoli. Add Worcestershire and Tabasco sauce. Pour into a buttered 2-quart casserole. Top with remaining cheese. Place in a 350 degree oven for 15 to 20 minutes or until just hot. Serves 12.

Mrs. J. P. Fisher, Jonestown

RICE AND BROCCOLI CASSEROLE

2 packages chopped frozen
  broccoli
1 cup rice, uncooked
2 cups water
1 stick margarine
1 onion, chopped

1 cup cream of chicken soup
½ cup milk
2 teaspoons salt
¼ teaspoon black pepper
1 cup grated cheddar cheese

Cook broccoli slightly (not done) and drain. Cook rice in 2 cups water until done, but not mushy. Sautè onion in margarine. Combine broccoli, soup, milk, rice, onion, salt, pepper and ¾ cup cheese. Sprinkle the remaining ¼ cup cheese on top. Fill two 2-quart greased casserole dishes and freeze one for an extra meal. Bake at 300 degrees for 30 minutes. Serves 8 to 10.

Mrs. Jerry Webb, Noxapater
Mrs. R. H. Crowder, West Point

ZUCCHINI SQUASH CASSEROLE

2 tablespoons cooking oil
1 onion, chopped
1 bell pepper, chopped
2 stalks celery, chopped
1 or 2 small to medium squash
1 (10½-ounce) can cream of
  mushroom soup

1 (10½-ounce) can cream of
  cheese soup
¼ pound crushed cracker
  crumbs
4 eggs, well beaten
salt and pepper to taste
½ cup grated cheese

In large saucepan place cooking oil, chopped onion, bell pepper and celery. Cook until tender but not brown, add squash which has been peeled and chopped. Cover and cook until tender. Remove from heat and add mushroom and cheese soups. Stir well. Add crushed cracker crumbs and eggs. Season to taste with salt and pepper. Pour into oiled or buttered casserole. Top with grated cheese and bake in 350 degree oven until cheese melts. Serves 8 to 10.

Mrs. Phillip Seburn, Hattiesburg

BAKED SPINACH CASSEROLE

2 (10-ounce) packages frozen
  spinach, cooked
1 teaspoon salt
¼ teaspoon nutmeg
¼ teaspoon pepper
2 cups milk
1 tablespoon oleomargarine

2 tablespoons all-purpose
  flour
2 tablespoons grated onion
½ cup grated American cheese
3 hard cooked eggs, sliced
½ cup cornflakes

Cook spinach with salt, nutmeg and pepper. Make white sauce by mixing 2 tablespoons all-purpose flour with small amount of milk, until smooth. Add remaining milk and oleomargarine. Cook until thickens. Mix spinach, white sauce and 2 tablespoons grated onion. Place in 9 x 13 x 1½-inch greased casserole dish. Top with ½ cup grated American cheese, sliced hard cooked eggs and cornflakes. Bake at 325 degrees for 20 minutes. Serves 8 to 12.

Mrs. Archie Magee, Mendenhall

SQUASH SUPREME

2 cups cooked squash
1 cup chopped onions
½ stick oleo
2 eggs, slightly beaten
1 teaspoon salt
½ teaspoon pepper
1 cup grated cheese
1 cup evaporated milk
2 cups cracker crumbs

Put squash and onion in 2-quart saucepan with enough water to cover. Boil until tender, drain and mash. Add other ingredients and mix well. Pour into a well-buttered 2-quart casserole dish and bake for 40 minutes at 375 degrees. Serves 6 to 8.

Mrs. Eal Johnson, McComb

SQUASH CASSEROLE

2 cups cooked yellow squash
1 cup crushed cracker crumbs
½ cup finely chopped bell
  pepper
1 tablespoon chopped parsley
  flakes
1 teaspoon salt
1 teaspoon sugar
½ teaspoon black pepper
¼ teaspoon garlic salt
1 egg, beaten
1 cup sweet milk
½ cup melted oleo
½ cup grated American cheese
¼ teaspoon paprika
1 tablespoon finely chopped
  fresh parsley

Mix all ingredients except cheese and paprika. Toss gently until well mixed. Place in greased 1½-quart casserole. Bake in 350 degree oven for 30 minutes. Remove from oven and sprinkle grated cheese on top and sprinkle paprika on top of cheese. Return to oven and bake another 10 minutes or until cheese is melted and "bubbly". Remove and sprinkle with chopped parsley before serving. Serves 6 to 8.

Mrs. Herbert D. Gillis, Mendenhall

ASPARAGUS–TUNA CASSEROLE

1 (5-ounce) package fine egg
noodles
1 (6½-ounce) can white
chunk style tuna
1 (14½-ounce) can whole
green asparagus spears

1 (10½-ounce) can undiluted
cream of mushroom soup
½ cup grated cheese
¼ cup bread crumbs
dots of butter

Line an 8 x 10-inch greased casserole dish with cooked, drained
noodles. Top the noodles with remaining ingredients, following the order
given. Place in a 375 degree oven for 30 minutes or until bubbly and
cheese is melted. Serves 8.

Mrs. Paul Nelson, Raleigh

ASPARAGUS CASSEROLE

1 (no. 2) can asparagus
4 hard cooked eggs, sliced
1 teaspoon salt
dash of pepper

1 cup cracker crumbs
1½ cups grated cheese
1 cup mushroom soup

Drain the asparagus. Place layers of asparagus and sliced hard cooked
eggs in buttered casserole, sprinkle with salt and pepper and cracker
crumbs. Cover with grated cheese. Pour one-half of mushroom soup over
this. Repeat layer—pour remainder of soup over contents of this dish.
Bake 1 hour at 325 degrees. Serves 4.

Mrs. Carrol Rowley, Foxworth
Mrs. Mildred Edwards, Indianola

ASPARAGUS CASSEROLE

3 eggs, beaten
1 cup bread crumbs
1 cup grated cheese
1 cup milk

salt to taste
1 large can asparagus
6 strips of pimiento
½ cup butter, melted

Mix beaten eggs, bread crumbs, cheese and milk; season to taste and
pour over one large can of asparagus (not drained) in a large baking
dish. Mix lightly and lay strips of pimiento across the top. When ready to
bake, pour ½ cup melted butter over the top and bake in a moderate,
350 degree, oven 30 minutes. Serves 6 to 8.

Mrs. Cross Savell, Philadelphia

DELECTABLE SPINACH CASSEROLE

½ pound sliced bacon
2 packages frozen spinach
2 eggs, slightly beaten
2 cups milk
1 teaspoon salt

2/3 cup soft bread crumbs
1½ cups shredded Provalone
  cheese
paprika

Dice bacon and pan fry until crisp; drain on paper. Cook spinach according to directions; but remove from heat somewhat prematurely. Beat eggs slightly. Add milk and salt. Stir in spinach, bread crumbs, bacon and half of cheese. Pour mixture into 1½-quart baking dish. Sprinkle remaining cheese on top. Sprinkle with paprika. Bake 30 to 35 minutes at 375 degrees. Serves 8.

Mrs. W. A. McDonald, Hazlehurst

SCALLOPED POTATOES

4 medium potatoes, sliced or
  coarsely grated
1½ teaspoons salt
½ teaspoon pepper
¼ cup minced onion
2 tablespoons butter or
  margarine

½ cup grated sharp cheese
2 tablespoons butter
2 tablespoons flour,
  all-purpose
¼ teaspoon salt
⅛ teaspoon pepper
1 cup milk

Arrange layers of thinly sliced or coarsely grated raw potatoes in greased 2-quart baking dish. Sprinkle each layer with salt, pepper and minced onion. Dot with butter. Make a white sauce of last five ingredients: melt 2 tablespoons butter over low heat in a heavy saucepan. Blend in 2 tablespoons flour and seasonings. Cook over low heat, stirring until mixture is smooth and bubbly. Remove from heat. Stir in milk, bring to boil, stirring constantly. Boil 1 minute. Pour white sauce over potatoes. Bake uncovered in moderate oven 350 degrees about 1 hour and 20 minutes. Sprinkle grated cheese over top and replace in oven until cheese becomes thoroughly melted. Serves 4 to 6.

Sandra L. Musgrove, Laurel

SWEETPOTATO SUPREME

6 pounds raw unpeeled
  sweetpotatoes
2 cups white sugar
½ cup water
1 stick margarine

¼ cup grated coconut
¼ cup raisins (optional)
½ cup crushed, undrained
  pineapple
8 slices lemon

Wash and boil potatoes until tender. Cool and peel, cut in fourths or halves. Place in 12 x 16-inch pan. Measure sugar, place in small pan, add water and oleo. Boil 5 minutes. Pour over potatoes, sprinkle coconut, raisins and pineapple over potatoes. Place lemon slices about on top. Bake 45 minutes at 350 degrees. Dip syrup and dribble over potatoes every 10 or 15 minutes, making sure that syrup covers potatoes in order to glaze them.

Mrs. Dwight V. Roberts, Raleigh

SWEETPOTATO CASSEROLE

4 cups cooked sweetpotatoes
1 cup butter or margarine
2 cups sugar
4 eggs, slightly beaten
½ teaspoon cinnamon

½ teaspoon cloves
½ teaspoon nutmeg
1½ cups undiluted evaporated
   or sweet milk
1 cup shredded coconut

Add butter, sugar, beaten eggs, spices, milk and ¾ cup coconut to the cooked potatoes. Save ¼ cup coconut for topping. Mix well. Pour into greased 7½ by 12-inch baking dish. Sprinkle remaining ¼ cup coconut on top. Bake at 375 degrees for 35 minutes. Serves 10.

Miss Bessie Jackson, Louisville

EASY BAKED BEANS

1 (15½-ounce) can kidney
   beans
1 (15½-ounce) can pork
   and beans
¼ cup honey
½ cup chopped celery

1 (2-ounce) can mushroom
   pieces
minced onion to taste
chopped bell pepper to taste
strips of bacon

Mix all ingredients except bacon and pour into 1½-quart baking dish or bean pot. Place several bacon strips on top. Bake in oven at 350 degrees, covered, for about ½ hour and then remove cover and bake for another ½ hour. Oven can be set on warm after baking and beans will remain warm until serving time. Cover to keep moist. Serves 6.

Use larger amounts of beans in equal parts and expand spices to suit for larger groups.

Mrs. Thomas P. Hall, Vicksburg

CARROT RING

2 cups cooked carrots, mashed
1 teaspoon grated onion
3 eggs, well beaten
1 cup sweet milk

2 tablespoons melted butter
1 teaspoon salt
¼ teaspoon pepper

Mix ingredients in order given and pour into well greased ring mold. Set mold in shallow pan of water and bake in moderate oven 350 degrees, 40 minutes or until firm. Remove from oven; let stand a few minutes. Loosen edges and turn out carefully. Fill center with green peas or French-style string beans. Serves 6.

Mrs. E. B. (Grace) Tinsley, Scooba

ENGLISH PEA CASSEROLE

1 stick butter or oleo
1 small onion, minced
2 tablespoons chopped green
  pepper
1 cup diced celery
2 (no. 303) cans English
  peas, drained

1 (5-ounce) can water
  chestnuts, sliced
2 slices pimiento, chopped
1 (10½-ounce) can mushroom
  soup

Melt butter in thick skillet. Add onion, pepper and celery. Sautè over medium heat, stirring until soft. Remove and add peas and chestnuts with 1 can liquid of peas. Fold in pimiento. Transfer contents to a 2-quart casserole dish. Top with soup, sprinkle with cracker crumbs. Bake at 350 degrees until bubbly. Serves 6 to 8.

Mrs. H. L. Barham, DeKalb

ENGLISH PEA CASSEROLE

1 (no. 303) can English peas,
  drained
3 hard cooked eggs, sliced
1 small jar pimiento, chopped
½ pound cheddar cheese,
  grated

1 (10½-ounce) can condensed
  mushroom soup
bread crumbs

In bottom of a greased 1-quart casserole put half of the peas, then half of the sliced hard-cooked eggs, half of the pimiento and half of the cheese. Repeat, using the rest of each of these four ingredients. Dilute the condensed soup according to the directions on the can for making a "sauce". Pour over the layers in the casserole, sprinkle the bread crumbs over the top and bake in a 350 degree oven for about 20 minutes, or until bubbly. Serves 6 to 8.

Mrs. J. L. Alexander, West Point

GREEN BEAN CASSEROLE

2 (16-ounce) cans French
    cut beans
6 tablespoons sugar
6 tablespoons vinegar
6 tablespoons bacon grease
¼ cup slivered almonds
6 strips of bacon, fried and
    crumbled

Place beans in baking dish. Mix sugar, vinegar and bacon grease. Pour over beans and let stand for 4 hours. Add almonds and crumbled bacon and bake uncovered in 325 degree oven for 40 minutes. Serves 8.

Mrs. Velma Hardin, Smithdale

GREEN BEAN CASSEROLE

2 (15½-ounce) cans French
    style green beans
1 (5-ounce) can water chest-
    nuts, sliced
1 (8-ounce) can mushroom
    stems and pieces
1 (10½-ounce) can cream of
mushroom soup, undiluted
1 tablespoon Worcestershire
    sauce
1 teaspoon salt
2 (5-ounce) packages frozen
    onion rings
1 cup grated cheddar cheese

Drain vegetables and combine with soup, seasonings and one package onion rings which have been cut into small pieces. Turn into a 1½-quart greased casserole. Top with remaining onion rings and cheddar cheese. Bake at 350 degrees for 30 minutes. Serves 8 to 10.

Mrs. Robert C. McMillan, Sr., Booneville

STRING BEAN CASSEROLE

3 (no. 2) cans French blue
    lake beans
1 onion, chopped
5 slices crisp bacon, chopped
1 (10½-ounce) can cream of
    mushroom soup
1 tablespoon sesame seed
1 tablespoon Accent
1 cup grated cheese
cheese cracker crumbs
butter
paprika

Cook beans in juice, strain and save 4 tablespoons of bean juice. Cook onion in bacon fat. Add crumbled bacon, soup and seasonings. Mix well, pour in baking dish, top with grated cheese and cheese cracker crumbs. Dot with butter. Sprinkle with paprika. Bake 30 minutes in moderate 350 degree oven. Serves 6 to 8.

Miss Addie Hester, Amory

CREOLE BUTTER BEANS

1½ cups frozen butter beans
1 tablespoon chopped onion
1/3 cup chopped green pepper
1 tablespoon oleo
1 cup cooked or canned
   tomatoes

½ teaspoon salt
dash of pepper
1 tablespoon cheese, grated
1 cup toasted buttered
   croutons

Cook butter beans. Brown onion and pepper in oleo. Add tomatoes and cook slowly for 15 minutes longer. Add beans; season with salt and pepper. Thoroughly blend, place in 1½-quart casserole, and heat completely. When ready to serve, toss croutons with cheese and sprinkle atop casserole. Serves 6.

Mrs. A. M. Aust, Macon

OKRA–SHRIMP CASSEROLE

1 can cut okra
1 (6-ounce) can shrimp
   (save stock)
½ cup bread crumbs
2 tablespoons lemon juice
1 teaspoon baking powder

1 teaspoon chili powder
½ teaspoon salt
1 teaspoon all-purpose
   seasoning
1 tablespoon mayonnaise

Place layer of okra on bottom of casserole dish and add shrimp. Cover with half of bread crumbs. Place remainder of okra on top of bread crumbs. Add lemon juice and shrimp stock mixed with baking powder, chili powder, and salt. Add all-purpose seasoning. Dot with mayonnaise and sprinkle with remainder of bread crumbs. Bake at 450 degrees for 20 minutes. Serves 4 to 6.

Viola Smith, Brookhaven

OKRA CASSEROLE

1 pound okra, sliced thin	½ teaspoon sugar
1 medium onion, chopped	1 small bell pepper, chopped
2 fresh tomatoes, chopped	salt and pepper to taste

Put a small amount of salad oil into a skillet. Add all ingredients and cook slowly, stirring constantly, until all vegetables are done and okra is cooked thoroughly. Put in greased casserole and add tomato slices and pepper strips to make attractive. Bake at 350 degrees about 25 minutes. A pleasing surprise for people who like only fresh okra! Serves 6.

Mrs. Ray Leeper, Pontotoc

SWEET AND SOUR ONIONS

¼ cup margarine, melted	¼ cup sugar
4 large onions, sliced	¼ cup hot water
¼ cup cider vinegar	

Melt margarine in 1½-quart baking dish, arrange onion slices, vinegar, sugar and water over onions. Bake at 300 degrees for 1 hour. Serves 4 to 6.

Mrs. Clyde Cox, Corinth

BAKED FRUIT CASSEROLE

1 (no. 2½) can peaches or apricots	¾ cup brown sugar
1 (no. 2½) can pears, sliced	1/3 cup margarine
1 (no. 2½) can chunk pineapple	1 teaspoon ground ginger

Drain fruit and cut in bite-size pieces. Place in 3-quart casserole. Combine brown sugar, margarine and ginger and stir over low heat until melted. Pour over fruit and bake at 325 degrees about 30 minutes or until hot and bubbly. Serves 8.

Mrs. Gordon Clayton, Ripley

HOMINY AND ALMOND

1 (10½-ounce) can cream of
  mushroom soup
½ cup milk
⅛ teaspoon cayenne pepper
1 teaspoon Worcestershire
  sauce
1 teaspoon celery seed
½ teaspoon black pepper
1 (no. 2½) can hominy
1 cup almonds, blanched,
  cut in half
1 cup buttered bread crumbs

Mix soup with milk and seasoning. Simmer over low heat until well blended. Drain hominy. Place in casserole. Add almonds to soup mixture. Pour over hominy. Cover with buttered crumbs. Bake in 350 degree oven for 30 to 40 minutes. Serves 6 to 8.

Mrs. Lanelle Montgomery, Yazoo City

CHILI AND HOMINY CASSEROLE

1 (15-ounce) can chili
1 (1 pound 14-ounce)
  can hominy
1 medium size onion, grated
1 (10½-ounce) can mush-
  room soup
½ cup grated cheese

Place half can of the chili in 8-inch baking dish. Cover with half the hominy. Grate the onion over this. Put rest of the hominy in and cover with remainder of chili. Spread the mushroom soup over this. Next, sprinkle with the ½ cup of cheese. Bake 25 minutes at 375 degrees. Serves 8.

Mrs. James M. Murphy, Carthage

GRITS CASSEROLE

1 cup regular grits
3 cups water
1 teaspoon salt
¾ pound sharp cheese, grated
1 stick margarine
1 clove garlic, crushed
1 tablespoon Worcestershire
dash of Tabasco sauce
2 egg yolks, beaten
2 egg whites, beaten

Cook grits in water with salt. Mix all ingredients, except eggs, with hot grits. Add beaten egg yolks, cool. Fold in beaten egg whites. Bake in buttered casserole at 350 degrees 25 to 30 minutes until golden brown. Serves 6.

Mrs. Spence Townsend, Winona

MEXICAN RICE

1 large 3 or 4-pound fryer
  or hen
3 medium size carrots,
  chopped
3 tablespoons cooking oil
1 large whole clove garlic
1 small package converted rice

1 large onion, chopped
1 large can tomatoes
1 large jar pimientos, cut
  in strips
salt and pepper
1 small can tiny peas, drained

Boil chicken until tender; about 20 minutes before chicken is done, add carrots. Remove chicken from stock, cool, skin, cut meat in medium size pieces and set aside. In 3 tablespoons oil in heavy dutch oven add garlic, rice and onion. Brown slowly until rice is only a light golden brown, stirring constantly. Add tomatoes, 3 cups stock with carrots, chopped pimiento, salt, pepper and chicken. Cover and let simmer slowly about 45 minutes or until all moisture is absorbed and rice is dry. Add peas, turning over in rice very gently with 2-tine fork so that rice is not broken.

Mrs. Virginia Love, Poplarville

CONSOMMÉ RICE

1 stick oleo
1 cup celery, chopped
½ cup onion, chopped
  (¼ cup minced dry onion
  may be used)
½ cup bell pepper, chopped
  (¼ cup dry bell pepper
  may be used)

1 can consommé
1 cup water
1 teaspoon salt
1 tablespoon Worcestershire
  sauce
1 cup rice, uncooked
1 small can mushroom
  stems and pieces (optional)

In a large skillet melt the oleo. Simmer in the oleo until half done, the celery, onion and pepper. In a deep heavy aluminum vessel, mix the consommé, water, salt, Worcestershire sauce and rice. Cover and simmer until the rice is partially done. Stir to prevent sticking. Combine the vegetable and rice mixtures. Add the mushrooms. Mix gently. Pour into an ungreased 2-quart casserole. Bake about 15 minutes in a 350 degree oven. Serves 6.

Note: If the dry onion and pepper are used, add them to the consommé mixture and rice rather than simmering in the oleo. With the exception of the celery, the ingredients can be kept on hand for a last minute dish, or the dish can be prepared ahead and reheated at the last minute.

Mrs. Jean Allen Young, Oxford

MISSISSIPPI DIRTY RICE

6 tablespoons cooking oil
finely chopped giblets
   from 3 chickens
2 large onions, diced
1 cup celery, diced
2 dozen oysters, chopped
¼ cup oyster liquid

½ cup parsley, diced
½ cup green onions, diced
2 cloves garlic, minced
1 cup raw rice, cooked
salt, black pepper and cayenne
   pepper to taste

Pour oil into heavy skillet or Dutch oven and add chopped giblets, onion and celery. Cook on medium heat, stirring as needed, until giblets are browned and onions and celery are soft. Add oysters and liquid, parsley, green onions and garlic, cover and simmer for 10 minutes. Stir in cooked rice, salt and pepper and heat to steaming. Makes 8 to 10 servings.

Note: 1½ cups of ground beef, veal or pork may be substituted for the giblets. The flavor is better if the oysters, giblets and vegetables are ground and not just chopped. Seasonings may be varied according to personal preference. Worcestershire sauce may be added. Tabasco sauce can be used instead of cayenne pepper.

This may be used as a stuffing in a turkey or large hen. It may also be put in a greased casserole dish and baked in a 350 degree oven for 20 minutes.

Mrs. Esther K. Gunn, Laurel

°❡Make-Ahead Dishes❡°

Today's homemaker is an active woman who may hold down a job outside of the home or spend many hours doing volunteer work, taking part in civic clubs, or mastering a new hobby. She's concerned about nutrition and wants an attractive, well-balanced meal for her family. Sometimes however, there just isn't enough time for elaborate preparation.

There are many convenience foods on the market that are good just as they are, or altered slightly with special seasonings or additional ingredients. These foods are more expensive because you pay not only for the ingredients but the preparation as well.

Many dishes can be made ahead of time with one or two ingredients left out and either frozen or stored until just before cooking. Use your cooking skill, your imagination, and the recipes in this section for make-ahead dishes which will save you time and money.

ICE CREAM RIBBON CAKE

angel food cake
1 pint chocolate ice cream
1 pint peppermint ice cream
1 pint whipping cream

4 tablespoons confectioners
  sugar
1 teaspoon vanilla
1 (3½-ounce) box shredded
  coconut

Cut cake lengthwise in three layers. Spread chocolate ice cream between first layer and peppermint ice cream between second layer. Place cake in freezer. Whip cream; add sugar and vanilla and blend. Ice top and sides of cake with whipped cream. Cover with shredded coconut and return to freezer until whipped cream is frozen. Wrap and store in freezer until ready to serve. Storage time: 1 month. Serves 8.

Mrs. Ethel A. Richardson, West Point

FREEZER CAKE

1 cup shortening
1 cup sugar
6 mashed bananas
1 (8½-ounce) can crushed
  pineapple, drained
1 cup miniature marshmallows

1 (4-ounce) bottle cherries,
  chopped
4 egg whites, stiffly beaten .
1/3 of (1-pound) box finely
  crushed graham crackers

Cream shortening and sugar; add bananas, pineapple, marshmallows and cherries. Fold in egg whites to mixture. Alternate layers of cracker crumbs and mixture. Set in freezer for 24 hours. Cut in squares and serve. For holiday festivities, add 1 package of chopped dates and 1 cup of chopped pecans. Serves 12.

Mrs. Hilman Wedgeworth, Laurel

CREPES HUNGARIAN

1 cup dried apricots
1 cup water
¼ teaspoon grated lemon rind
1 cup sugar
¼ cup sherry wine
3 eggs
1½ cups cold water
3 tablespoons melted butter

¾ cup sifted all-purpose
  flour
¾ teaspoon salt
1 teaspoon sugar
½ teaspoon baking powder
additional melted butter
½ pint sour cream
½ cup finely chopped walnuts

Rinse and drain apricots; chop finely and place in saucepan with water. Cook about 20 minutes until apricots are tender and water is evaporated. Add lemon rind and sugar; stir until sugar is dissolved. Remove from heat, cool to lukewarm and stir in sherry wine. Set aside.

Beat eggs with water and melted butter. Sift flour, salt, sugar and baking powder together. Add flour mixture to liquid ingredients; blend thoroughly. Melt a small amount of butter in skillet over medium heat. Pour in about 3 tablespoons batter. Cook until firm and slightly brown; turn, brown other side. Spread crepes with apricot filling and roll up. Arrange in shallow baking pan and refrigerate. Reheat in a 325 degree oven about 20 minutes before serving. Top each serving with a spoonful of sour cream and sprinkle with chopped walnuts. Serves 12 to 14.

Kathleen Daniel, Jackson

24–HOUR FRUIT PARFAITS

¾ cup whipping cream
2 eggs
2 tablespoons sugar
2 tablespoons lemon juice
2 tablespoons pineapple juice
1 tablespoon butter or margarine
⅛ teaspoon salt
1 (1 pound 4-ounce) can
  pineapple chunks, drained

1 (1 pound) can pitted red
  cherries, drained
1 (11-ounce) can mandarin
  orange segments, drained
½ cup flaked coconut
1 cup miniature marshmallows
maraschino cherries

Whip cream; set aside. Combine eggs, sugar, lemon juice, pineapple juice, butter and salt in saucepan and beat well. Cook over low heat stirring constantly until just boiling. Remove from heat. Cool. Fold in whipped cream. Set dressing aside.

Combine pineapple chunks, red cherries, orange segments, coconut and marshmallows. Fold in cooled dressing, blending well. Chill several hours or overnight. Serve as a dessert in parfait glasses, garnished with maraschinos. Serves 6 to 8.

Mrs. Dilcie McCoy, Lexington

APPLE CASSEROLE

5 sliced apples
6 tablespoons water
1 teaspoon lemon juice
¾ cup sugar

½ cup flour
1/3 teaspoon cinnamon
¼ cup butter
¼ pound sharp cheddar cheese

Grease dish. Mix apples with water and lemon juice. Mix sugar, flour, and cinnamon. Cut in butter and lightly mix in grated cheese. Make 2 layers of apples and dry mixture, alternately. Bake in 300 degree oven 40 minutes. Serves 6.

Miss Mary Wanda Stebbins, Canton

STRAWBERRY SALAD

2 (3-ounce size) packages
   strawberry gelatin
1 envelope plain gelatin
1 cup boiling water
2 (10-ounce) packages frozen
   strawberries, drained

1 (1 pound 4 ounce) can
   crushed pineapple
3 mashed medium size
   bananas
1 cup chopped pecans
1 pint sour cream

Melt strawberry and plain gelatin in water until completely dissolved. Add all other ingredients except sour cream. Put ½ mixture in long pyrex pan and refrigerate until set. Spread with sour cream and top with other ½ of mixture that has been left at room temperature.

Mary Frances Littlejohn, Olive Branch

FROSTED CRANBERRY MOLD

1 (8½-ounce) can crushed
   pineapple
1 (16-ounce) can whole
   cranberry sauce
2 (3-ounce) packages
   raspberry gelatin
1 (8-ounce) package
   cream cheese

2 tablespoons salad dressing
1 (2-ounce) package dessert
   topping mix, whipped
½ cup coarsely chopped
   walnuts
1 peeled and chopped apple

Drain pineapple and cranberries, reserving liquid. Add water to make 2 cups. Bring to boil. Dissolve gelatin in hot liquid. Chill until partially set. Beat softened cream cheese and dressing together until fluffy. Gradually beat in gelatin; fold this mixture into topping mix. Set aside 1½ cups of this mixture. Add drained fruit, nuts and apple to remaining cheese-gelatin mixture. Pour into a 12 x 7½ x 2-inch glass dish and refrigerate until surface sets (about 20 minutes). Ice with reserved topping; refrigerate several hours. (Or salad may be frozen; move from freezer to refrigerator an hour before serving.) Serves 12.

Mrs. Walter Dilworth, Rienzi

SAUERKRAUT SALAD

1/3 cup water
2/3 cup vinegar
1/3 cup salad oil
1¼ cups sugar
2 (No. 303) cans or 1 large
    can sauerkraut
1 cup diced celery

1 cup chopped green pepper
1 (4-ounce) jar chopped
    pimiento
1 cup or less chopped onion
1 (5-ounce) can water
    chestnuts, sliced thin

Mix and heat together water, vinegar and salad oil. Add sugar and stir until dissolved. Make 3 or 4 cuts with scissors through the sauerkraut, before adding other ingredients. Mix vegetables, pour dressing over vegetables. Mix well. Cover and chill. Serves 8.

Mrs. M. E. Brooks, Newton

CORNED BEEF SALAD

1 (3-ounce) package
    lemon gelatin
1 beef bouillon cube
2 cups boiling water
dash Worcestershire sauce

1 (12-ounce) can corned beef
1 heaping cup chopped celery
3 chopped, hard-cooked eggs
1 medium onion, chopped
1 cup whipped topping

Dissolve lemon gelatin and bouillon cube in two cups boiling water. Add a good dash of Worcestershire sauce. Set aside to cool. While it cools, butter an 8 x 8 x 2-inch pan. Set aside. In a four-quart bowl, mix the corned beef, which has been cut in thin slices and rubbed between fingers until every tiny lump is removed, (this works best at room temperature) chopped celery, chopped eggs, chopped onion and whipped topping. Add gelatin, beef bouillon, water and Worcestershire sauce to this mixture. Pour into pan and chill. Good when served with potato chips, fruit salad and/or hot cheese sandwiches. May be served in half an hour, but decidedly better if made 1 to 2 days ahead so flavors can blend. Serves 8 to 10.

Mrs. M. E. Brooks, Newton

OVEN CHICKEN SALAD

2 cups diced cooked chicken
¾ cup diced celery
1 tablespoon chopped pimiento
1 (5-ounce) can water
    chestnuts, drained and sliced
1 (3½-ounce) can french fried
    onions

1 tablespoon mayonnaise
1 (1-ounce or ¾-ounce)
    package dry chicken gravy
    mix
1 cup milk

Combine chicken, celery, pimiento, chestnuts, half of the onions and mayonnaise in a large mixing bowl. Make chicken gravy according to directions, using 1 cup milk instead of water. Pour hot gravy over salad mixture; blend. Pour into 1-quart baking dish; top with remaining onions. Bake at 400 degrees for 10 to 15 minutes, until heated through. If chicken mix is not available, make gravy with broth from chicken. Serves 6 to 8.

Mrs. Jacqueline Mikell, Port Gibson

AMBROSIA SALAD

1 (No. 303) can fruit cocktail
1 (No. 303) can chunk
  pineapple
1 (No. 303) can white grapes
1 cup coconut, flaked

2 cups miniature
  marshmallows
2 (8¾-ounce) cans mandarin
  oranges
½ pint sour cream

Combine all ingredients, stirring well. Store in refrigerator until ready for use. Serves 10 to 12.

Mrs. Lucille Smith, Jackson

FROZEN FRUIT SALAD

2 (3-ounce) packages
  cream cheese
2 tablespoons mayonnaise
2 tablespoons pineapple syrup
1 (No. 2) can pineapple bits,
  drained

2 small bananas, sliced
1 pint frozen strawberries,
  thawed
1 cup heavy cream

Soften cream cheese and blend with mayonnaise. Beat in the pineapple syrup. Mix in the bananas, pineapple bits and strawberries. Whip cream and fold in the above mixture. Pour into a 1-quart refrigerator tray. Freeze until firm. Cut into squares. Separate layers of squares with several layers of waxed paper. Wrap in freezer packaging material and store in home freezer. Can be stored up to three months. When ready to serve, garnish with fresh or frozen strawberries. Serves 12.

Mrs. Curtis Orman, West Point

BEAN SALAD

1 cup vinegar
1 cup sugar

1 large red or sweet
  ringed onion

½ cup salad oil
1 (No. 2) can kidney beans
1 (No. 2) can green beans
1 (No. 2) can yellow wax beans

1 green pepper, chopped
½ cucumber, chopped and
    peeled
salt and pepper to taste

In large bowl combine vinegar, sugar and salad oil. Drain beans. Add beans, onion, green pepper and cucumber. Marinate for 24 hours tightly covered in refrigerator. Drain off marinade and salt and pepper to taste before serving. Serves 12.

Mrs. M. E. Brooks, Newton

STUFFED POTATOES

6 large baking potatoes
1/3 cup milk
¼ cup melted margarine

1 teaspoon salt
⅛ teaspoon pepper
grated cheese

Wash and dry potatoes. Bake potatoes 50 to 60 minutes in 425 degree oven. (It will shorten cooking time to let potatoes stand in very hot water for at least 15 minutes before baking.) Remove a thin oval slice from across the top of each potato and scoop out pulp being careful not to break skin. Reserve skins. Whip potato pulp with milk, margarine, salt and pepper at low speed in electric mixer. If potatoes are dry add a little more milk. Spoon the whipped potatoes back into skins and sprinkle with cheese. Cover and refrigerate. When ready to serve place in 375 degree oven, uncovered, for 25 to 30 minutes. Will refrigerate 1½ days. Serves 6.

Mrs. Mary Geoghegan, Fayette

ENGLISH PEA CASSEROLE

2 medium onions, chopped
1 stick oleo
2 (16-ounce) cans English
    peas, drained
½ cup slivered almonds

5 hard-cooked eggs,
    chopped
2 cups grated cheese
1 cup chopped pimiento
1 tablespoon Worcestershire
1 cup cream of chicken soup

Sautè onions in oleo. Mix this with all other ingredients in a 2-quart ungreased casserole dish. Let stand 4 to 5 hours. Bake at 325 degrees about 45 minutes. Serves 8.

Mrs. Ruby Hegwood, Forest

SPANISH CORN

1 (No. 2) can yellow cream
  style corn
2 (6-ounce) cans Spanish
  style tomato sauce
1 cup yellow corn meal
1 cup milk

1½ heaping tablespoons
  chili powder
2 eggs, beaten
1/3 cup cooking oil
chopped olives, if desired

Mix all ingredients together and pour in 2-quart casserole. Cook in 300 degree oven, over pan of water, about 1½ hours or until center is firm. This freezes well. Serves 8.

Mrs. Edgar E. Moody, Hollandale

GREEN RICE

2 cups rice
2 cups grated cheese
2 cups milk
1 cup dried parsley

2 beaten eggs
1 teaspoon salt
3 cloves garlic, chopped
2 or 3 spring onions, chopped

Cook rice, drain and mix with remaining ingredients, reserving ½ cup cheese. Pour mixture into casserole and sprinkle top with cheese. Bake in 300 degree oven for 1 hour. May be served cold and is delicious with outdoor barbecued chicken. Serves 8 to 10.

Mrs. Margaret H. Nichols, Tupelo

BAKED HAM SANDWICH

12 slices bread
1 tablespoon prepared mustard
2 cups grated cheddar or
  American cheese
½ pound cooked ham, ground
4 slightly beaten eggs

3 cups milk
½ teaspoon salt
1 (10½-ounce) can cream of
  mushroom soup
2 hard-cooked eggs, chopped

Grease an 8 x 12 x 2-inch baking dish. Cut crust from the bread. Place 6 slices in bottom of dish and brush top lightly with mustard. Cover with grated cheese. Place ham over cheese. Butter remaining 6 slices of bread and place butter side up on ham. Beat eggs; add milk and salt. Pour over sandwiches. Let stand in refrigerator overnight. Bake at 300 degrees for 1 hour. Let set a few minutes before serving so sandwiches will have time to firm. Place on plates with spatula. Serve with hot mushroom sauce made by combining the mushroom soup and chopped eggs. Serve hot sauce over sandwiches. Serves 6.

Mrs. Homer A. Green, Tutwiler

LEMON BUTTER SANDWICHES

juice of 2 lemons
grated rind of lemons
1 cup sugar
2 tablespoons butter

2 eggs, well beaten
1 (8-ounce) package cream
    cheese

Combine juice, grated rind, sugar, butter and eggs and cook over low heat, stirring constantly until smooth and thick. Cool. Spread thin rounds of white sandwich bread (about the size of a small biscuit cutter) with softened cream cheese. Then add a layer of the lemon butter to half the slices, and cover with rounds spread with cream cheese. Package for freezing. Let thaw about 15 minutes before serving. May be stored 2 weeks. Makes 45 party sandwiches.

Mrs. J. L. Alexander, West Point

PEPPER STEAK WITH CHEDDAR NOODLES

1½ pounds beef, round or
    sirloin tip
¼ cup butter
⅛ teaspoon garlic powder
1/3 cup chopped onions
1½ green peppers, cut in strips
1 (1-pound) can tomatoes
1 beef bouillon cube

1 tablespoon cornstarch
2 tablespoons water
2 tablespoons soy sauce
1 teaspoon sugar
½ teaspoon salt
3 cups wide noodles
1 cup shredded cheddar cheese

Cut beef into 2 x ½ x ⅛-inch strips. Melt butter in skillet. Add beef; sprinkle with garlic powder. Sauté on moderate heat, stirring constantly, until browned, remove meat from skillet. Add onion and green pepper; sautè for 2 minutes. Return meat to skillet with tomatoes and bouillon cube. If using round steak, simmer for 15 to 20 minutes; if using sirloin tips, simmer for 5 minutes. Blend cornstarch, water, soy sauce, sugar and salt; add to meat mixture. Cook, stirring constantly, until thickened. Reduce heat and cook 2 additional minutes. Cook noodles according to package directions, drain. Toss with cheddar cheese. Place in serving dish and spoon pepper steak over cheddar noodles. Serves 6.

Mrs. PonJola Andrews, Magnolia

CORN–STUFFED PORK CHOPS

4 double-rib pork chops	3 tablespoons chopped onions
salt	¼ teaspoon salt
½ cup whole kernel corn	dash thyme
Mexican-style	¼ teaspoon sage
½ cup soft bread crumbs	½ cup hot water

Have butcher cut a pocket in each chop, slitting from fat edge and cutting almost to the bone edge. Salt pocket lightly. Combine corn, crumbs, onion, salt and thyme for stuffing; fill pockets in chops. Close openings with toothpicks or lace with string. Wrap in moisture-vapor proof material, separating individual chops with 2 layers of paper; seal tightly. Freeze.

To serve, unwrap the pork chops and arrange in preheated skillet. Sprinkle with sage. Heat slowly till chops are thawed and lightly browned on both sides, about 40 minutes. Add hot water; cover skillet and simmer 40 minutes, or till tender. Add more water if necessary. Remove string and picks before serving. Serves 4.

Mrs. Howell G. Mims, Columbus

SHRIMP CREOLE

2 tablespoons olive oil	1 cup chopped green pepper
1½ pounds fresh shrimp,	½ cup diced celery
deveined	¾ teaspoon salt
½ cup thinly sliced onion	⅛ teaspoon garlic powder
1 (8-ounce) can tomato sauce	1/16 teaspoon chili powder

Heat oil in large skillet. Add shrimp and cook until shrimp turns pink. Stir frequently. Remove shrimp from skillet. Add onion to same skillet and cook until browned. Stir in tomato sauce, pepper, celery, salt, garlic powder and chili powder. Simmer over low heat uncovered about 10 minutes. Remove from heat and combine with shrimp and cool. Place into 1½-quart casserole that is lined with heavy foil, with enough overlap for a double-fold seal. Seal and freeze. When frozen, remove foil pack from casserole and return to freezer. When ready to cook, remove foil from frozen creole and slip creole into the casserole in which it was frozen. Cover with foil and bake 1 hour in preheated 400 degree oven. Serve over cooked rice or noodles. Will refrigerate about 2 days. Freezer storage, 3 months. Serves 3 to 4.

Mrs. Helen Lehmann, Fayette

SHRIMP CASSEROLE

1 (10-ounce) package frozen shrimp (or fresh shrimp)
1 (6-ounce) box wild rice with herbs
1 (10½-ounce) can cream of mushroom soup
1 onion, chopped
½ pound sharp cheddar cheese, cubed (more if desired)
1 clove garlic pressed
½ bell pepper, chopped
½ teaspoon prepared mustard (optional)
1 teaspoon Worcestershire sauce

Cook shrimp (bring water and salt to boil then drop shrimp in)—let water return to boiling point and set off stove. Let shrimp set in water for no longer than 3 minutes then drain well. Cook wild rice and herbs according to directions on box. Combine all ingredients and put into casserole. Cover with aluminum foil and put in refrigerator until ready for use. Can be left for a week. When ready to use, place casserole in 325 degree oven for 30 to 45 minutes. Done when bubbling. Serves 6.

Mrs. Robert Derrick, Forest

COMPANY CASSEROLE

1 (8-ounce) package noodles
1 pound fresh ground chuck
1 (8-ounce) carton creamed cottage cheese
1 (8-ounce) package cream cheese
1 (8-ounce) carton sour cream
½ teaspoon garlic salt
½ teaspoon paprika
½ cup finely chopped onion
½ cup finely chopped bell pepper
2 (8-ounce) cans tomato sauce

Cook noodles in boiling salted water until tender; drain. Cook meat in heavy skillet until pink color is gone, but not too dry. Mix cheeses and sour cream well. Add in garlic salt, paprika, chopped onion and bell pepper. Layer one half of the noodles into long loaf-type buttered baking dish to fit the quantity of ingredients. (Taste noodles to see if added salt is needed.) Spread all of the cheese mixture onto this layer and then the remaining half of the noodles. Last, layer on the meat and cover with one can of tomato sauce, carefully covering entire surface of the meat. With a spatula, cut down through contents of the casserole in several places, to allow seasoning to penetrate. Add on the second can of tomato sauce and bake uncovered at 350 degrees for about 30 minutes until the onions and pepper are cooked and the contents bubbling briskly.

This is better, the flavor more pronounced if made ahead, cooled and refrigerated overnight, covered well with plastic wrap. For serving, let come to room temperature again, cover with foil and reheat at 350 degrees until thoroughly hot through and through.

Mrs. Kate Woods, Starkville

SAUSAGE RICE CASSEROLE—ERLINE

2 pounds, mild or hot, bulk
    sausage
3 stalks chopped celery
1½ cups rice
2 large white onions, chopped

3 (1¾-ounce) packages dry
    chicken-noodle soup
9 cups water
1 (5-ounce) can water
    chestnuts, chopped

Crumble sausage and fry until crisp. Drain off grease and add all other ingredients. Bake at 400 degrees in covered casserole for 50 minutes, stirring occasionally. Serves 8 to 10.

Mrs. R. L. Hundaker, Clinton

MACARONI AND CHILI CASSEROLE

1 (7-ounce) package elbow
    macaroni
1 medium size onion
1 large green or
    red sweet pepper

black pepper to taste
1 cup grated hoop cheese
1 (No. 303) can chili—
    without beans

Cook macaroni in salted boiling water until tender. Drain. Place one half of the macaroni in baking dish. Place on this ½ thinly sliced onion and half of the green or red pepper. Sprinkle with black pepper. Sprinkle ½ cup cheese over this. Make second layer the same. Mix chili with ½ can of water and pour over entire ingredients in dish. Be sure chili settles to cover contents completely. Bake in 350 degree oven for 45 minutes. It is best to cover dish for entire cooking. Serves 6 to 8.

Mrs. P. A. Cockrell, Louin

VEAL CUTLET CASSEROLE

¼ cup margarine
1/3 cup chopped onion
1½ pounds veal cutlets,
  cut in 2-inch strips
1 (8-ounce) package egg
  noodles, cooked and drained

2 (10½-ounce) cans
  condensed cream of
  mushroom soup, undiluted
1 cup sour cream
3 tablespoons chopped
  pimiento
chopped parsley

Melt margarine in large skillet. Add onion and cook until almost tender and remove from skillet and reserve. Add veal cutlets to same skillet and cook until tender and brown. Mix veal, onion, noodles, soup, sour cream and pimiento. Turn into shallow 2-quart casserole and cover and refrigerate. Will keep in refrigerator 2 days. When ready to serve, place in 425 degree oven, covered, for 30 minutes and serve garnished with chopped parsley. Serves 6 to 8.

Mrs. Rennie Geoghegan, Fayette

BEAN SUPREME

2 pounds ground beef
1 large chopped onion
1 chopped green pepper
1 cup chopped celery
1 pound can red beans, drained
1 (1-pound) can pork and
  beans
1 (15-ounce) can tomato
  sauce

1 (15-ounce) can tomatoes
1 (4-ounce) can mushrooms
1½ teaspoons salt
3 tablespoons Worcestershire
  sauce
dash of Tabasco
grated cheese

Cook meat in skillet without fat until it loses its red color; remove from skillet with slotted spoon. In grease that cooks out of meat, cook until soft on low heat and covered; onion, pepper and celery. Add red beans, pork and beans, tomato sauce, tomatoes, salt, mushrooms, Worcestersire sauce and Tabasco. Pour into large shallow casserole. Cover with grated cheese just before baking. Cook 1 hour at 350 degrees. Freezes well. Serves 8 to 10.

Mrs. Jacqueline Mikell, Port Gibson

[281]

CHEESE MEAT LOAF

1½ pounds ground beef
1½ cups dry bread crumbs
2/3 cup diced process
   American cheese
½ cup chopped onion
2 tablespoons chopped green
   pepper

1 teaspoon salt
1 small bay leaf, crushed
dash thyme
dash garlic salt
2 beaten eggs
1¼ cups tomato puree

Combine beef, crumbs, cheese, onion, green pepper and seasonings. Mix thoroughly. Add eggs to tomato puree; blend into meat mixture. Form into 2 loaves in 9½ x 6½ x 1½-inch foil tray or shallow baking pan. Bake in moderate oven, 350 degrees, about 1 hour. Cool thoroughly; wrap; freeze. To serve: heat, unwrapped, in moderate oven until heated through, about 1½ hours. Serves 8 to 10.

Mrs. Ollie J. Lane, Yazoo City

A DIFFERENT GROUND BEEF CASSEROLE

2 small onions
1 pound lean ground beef
¼ cup shortening
5-ounce package pure egg
   noodles, medium size
1 teaspoon salt
4 cups boiling water
1 (10½-ounce) can cream
   of mushroom soup

¾ cup evaporated milk
4 to 8-ounces sharp
   cheddar cheese
1 (3-ounce) can fried
   Chinese noodles
¼ pound cashew nuts OR
   toasted pecans

Cook onion and ground beef in shortening over medium heat until onion is tender and beef has lost its color. Add noodles and salt to boiling water. Stir constantly for 2 minutes (water should be boiling vigorously). Remove from heat, cover and let stand 10 minutes. Drain and rinse with hot water. Combine soup and evaporated milk. Grate cheese. In a 2½-quart, or larger, casserole, put first a layer of ground beef; cover with a thin layer of noodles; add a layer of the soup mixture and then a layer of grated cheese. Repeat layers. Bake, uncovered, in a 350 degree oven 30 minutes. Sprinkle Chinese noodles and cashew nuts (halved the long way, or ground) over top, or serve in side dish and sprinkle over each individual serving. Casserole can be prepared, ready for the final baking, a day before you plan to serve it. Serves 6.

Mrs. L. T. Potter, Wayside

TARLINI

1 clove garlic
1 large onion
1 green pepper
1 pound ground chuck
3 tablespoons olive oil
1 (No. 2) can tomatoes
1 (16-ounce) can whole
   kernel corn, drained

1 (½-pound) package
   noodles, cooked
1 (8-ounce) can mushrooms
   and liquid
2 tablespoons Heinz 57 sauce
½ pound American
   cheese, grated

Chop garlic, green pepper and onion together. Sautè meat in oil, add garlic, pepper and onions, cook 5 minutes. Add tomatoes and cook 10 minutes, add corn, noodles, mushrooms and liquid and half grated cheese. Mix and add Heinz 57 sauce. Mix thoroughly and place in greased 2½-quart baking dish. Place in refrigerator overnight to marinate. Let return to room temperature before placing in 350 degree oven for 1 hour. Some 5 minutes before baking is done, sprinkle with remaining cheese. Serves 4 to 6.

Mrs. A. D. Corban, Sr., Gloster

GROUND BEEF CASSEROLE

2 chopped medium onions
1 chopped bell pepper
2 pounds ground beef
1 cup tomato sauce
garlic salt and pepper to taste

1 cup grated cheese
2 (14½-ounce) cans
   asparagus spears
pastry

Sautè onion and pepper in small amount of oil. Add ground beef and cook until browned. Add tomato sauce and seasonings. In a greased 13 x 9 x 2-inch casserole put a layer of meat mixture then a layer of asparagus spears and a layer of grated cheese. Repeat layers. Top with latticed pastry strips from your favorite pastry recipe. Bake at 350 degrees for 45 minutes. This can be made early in the day and refrigerated until time to bake. If kept longer than this prior to baking, don't put the pastry on top until just before baking time. Serves 8.

Mrs. Betty Byrd, Grenada

QUICK HAMBURGER CASSEROLE

2 tablespoons cooking oil
¾ pound hamburger
3 medium potatoes, sliced
3 medium carrots, sliced

½ cup uncooked rice
1 onion, sliced
2 cups cooked tomatoes
buttered bread crumbs

Brown hamburger in the cooking oil. Place sliced potatoes in greased 2 to 3-quart baking dish. Place sliced carrots on top of potatoes. Season with salt and pepper. Sprinkle the raw rice over top of carrots. Spread hamburger over rice; slice onion over meat. Pour the tomatoes over all. Top with buttered bread crumbs. Bake uncovered at 350 degrees for 1 hour. May be prepared and refrigerated until ready to bake. Serves 6.

Mrs. Larry Alexander, Carthage

BEEF NOODLE BAKE

8-ounce package noodles
1 pound ground chuck
1 (14½-ounce) can
    Contadina tomato sauce
½ cup chopped onion
¼ cup chopped green pepper

1 teaspoon seasoned salt
⅛ teaspoon pepper
2 cups cottage cheese
1 (3-ounce) package softened
    cream cheese

Cook noodles. Brown chuck in skillet. Remove from heat, pour off excess fat. Stir in tomato sauce, onion, green pepper, salt and pepper. Blend cottage cheese with cream cheese till creamy. Spoon half of noodles into buttered 2-quart casserole. Cover with cheese mixture, add remaining noodles, then pour meat sauce over noodles. Place in refrigerator until 30 minutes before meal time. Then bake, uncovered, in a moderate oven 350 degrees for 30 to 35 minutes. Serves 6.

Mrs. Marian H. Quinn, Canton

CHICKEN BREASTS

8 chicken breasts
flour
salt and pepper
paprika
4 green onions
1 pound or 2 cans mushrooms

½ stick butter
2 cups mushroom soup
1 cup sour cream
¼ cup sherry
½ cup slivered almonds

Flour chicken and brown in shortening, salt and pepper. Place in a baking pan large enough for the pieces to lie flat in pan. Sprinkle with paprika. Bake at 350 degrees for 45 minutes. Sautè onions and mushrooms in butter. Add mushroom soup and sour cream. Mix well and add wine. Pour over chicken breasts. Spread almonds over the top and return to oven to bake until almonds are crisp. Serve over hot rice. This may be made a day before it is needed. Serves 8.

Mrs. Robert Estes Blount, Jackson

CHICKEN–SPAGHETTI CASSEROLE

1 (4-pound) hen
1 (10-ounce) package
  of thin spaghetti
1 cup chopped celery
1 cup chopped onion
1 cup chopped green peppers
½ cup of cooking oil

1 small can of diced pimiento
2 tablespoons snipped parsley
1 (4-ounce) can of mushrooms
1 teaspoon black pepper
salt to taste
½ pound Velveeta cheese

Cook chicken in salty water until tender. Remove meat from bones and dice. Strain broth and add water to make three quarts; add spaghetti to broth and cook 15 minutes. Cook celery, onion and pepper in oil until tender, not brown, and add to spaghetti. Mix chicken, pimiento, parsley, mushrooms, pepper and salt and add to spaghetti. Fill casserole and top with cheese. Heat in 350 degree oven until it bubbles. Can be frozen.

Mrs. Pearl Brock, Raymond

QUICK CHICKEN ON RICE

4 (12 x 12-inch) squares
  of foil
1 cup uncooked regular rice
4 chicken pieces, either
  breasts or thighs

1 (10½-ounce) can condensed
  cream of mushroom soup
1 teaspoon salt
2 cups water

Make shallow cup of each square of foil. Place ¼ cup rice in each square. Place 1 piece of chicken over the rice in each square. Add ½ cup water to each packet, pouring over chicken. Sprinkle each packet with ¼ teaspoon of salt then spoon ¼ of can of soup onto chicken. Fold foil, sealing each packet. If planning to cook immediately, preheat oven to 350 degrees. Lay packets on cookie sheet or jelly roll type pan in oven and cook for 1 hour. May be served right from foil or placed on dinner plates. These packets once prepared may be frozen before or after cooking. Just be sure to thaw thoroughly before cooking, or to heat thoroughly after having been cooked and frozen. Serves 4.

Mrs. J. D. Landin, Jr., Utica

CHICKEN STRATA

9 thin slices day old bread
3 cups cooked diced chicken
½ cup chopped onion
½ cup diced celery
½ cup mayonnaise
1 teaspoon salt

⅛ teaspoon pepper
2 well beaten eggs
2 cups milk
1 (10½-ounce) can
  mushroom soup
½ cup grated sharp cheese

Spread 2 slices bread with butter, set aside. Cut remaining bread into 1-inch cubes and arrange half of the amount in bottom of buttered 8 x 12 x 2-inch baking dish. Combine chicken, celery, onions, mayonnaise and seasonings; spoon chicken mixture over bread cubes in dish and sprinkle with remaining cubes. Beat eggs well, mix with milk and pour over ingredients in casserole. Chill 1 hour or overnight in refrigerator. When ready to cook, spoon soup over top. Top with 2 buttered pieces of bread cut into ½-inch cubes. Bake at 350 degrees for 50 minutes or until set. Just before removing from oven, sprinkle with shredded cheese and allow to melt. Serves 8 to 10.

Mrs. Floyd Shields, Clarksdale

CHICKEN LOAF

1½ cups milk
1½ cups chicken broth
4 eggs, beaten
2 cups soft bread crumbs
4 cups diced cooked chicken
1 cup cooked rice
¾ cup chopped celery
2 tablespoons chopped
  pimiento
1 teaspoon salt
¼ cup oleo or butter
6 tablespoons flour
2 cups chicken broth

1 tablespoon chopped
  parsley
1 tablespoon salt (taste
  before adding salt; may
  have to reduce or omit if
  broth is very salty.)
½ teaspoon paprika
juice of 1 lemon
1 (3-ounce can) mushrooms,
  drained
1 cup light cream or
  evaporated milk

Combine milk and 1½ cups broth and blend in eggs. Add bread crumbs. Let set until bread crumbs absorb milk and broth. Add diced chicken, rice, celery, pimiento and salt. Spread into greased 13 x 9 x 2-inch pan. Cover and put in refrigerator to season overnight (or may be frozen till ready to bake). Bake at 350 degrees for 1 hour.

Melt butter in saucepan. Add flour and blend well. Add chicken broth and cook, stirring constantly, until thick. Add remaining ingredients. Reheat and serve hot over chicken loaf. Add toasted slivered almonds, if desired.

Mrs. Carolyn Ellard, Kosciusko

"DO–AHEAD" CURRY

½ cup butter
½ cup flour
1 tablespoon salt
3 tablespoons curry powder
1½ teaspoons ginger
3 cups chicken broth

5 cups evaporated milk
1½ cups shredded coconut
6 cups cooked, diced
chicken
6 cups cooked rice

Melt butter in large saucepan. Stir in flour, salt, curry powder and ginger. Add chicken broth and evaporated milk. Cook over medium heat, stirring constantly, until mixture thickens. Add coconut. Simmer for 5 to 10 minutes. Add chicken. Heat to serving temperature. Spoon over hot rice. Serves 12.

Mrs. Hoyle Patton, Guntown

CHICKEN CHOW MEIN

¼ cup cooking salad oil
1 teaspoon salt
¼ teaspoon pepper
2 cups sliced cabbage
3 cups thinly sliced celery
1 (No. 303) can bean sprouts,
drained

1 (4-ounce) can water
chestnuts, sliced
2 teaspoons sugar
2½ teaspoons cornstarch
¼ cup cold water
¼ cup soy sauce
2 cups sliced cooked
chicken, thin slivers

Heat cooking salad oil, salt and pepper in deep skillet. Add cabbage, celery, bean sprouts, chestnuts and sugar. Blend together cornstarch, cold water and soy sauce. Add this blended mixture to vegetables and stir until entire mixture thickens. Then add cooked chicken and heat thoroughly. Serve over hot noodles. Serves 4.

Mrs. PonJola Andrews, Magnolia

[287]

DEVIL WALNUT—CHICKEN BON–BONS

1 chicken or turkey
1 cup coarsely ground toasted
    English walnuts or pecans
2 tablespoons finely chopped
    onion
2 tablespoons pimiento

¼ teaspoon salt
curry to taste
⅛ teaspoon Tabasco
½ cup cream of mushroom
    soup

Coarsely grind or chop meat from cooked chicken or turkey. Mix ¼ cup nuts with the other ingredients. Form into small balls (2 teaspoons to each ball). Roll balls in remaining nuts. Cover and chill for at least 1 hour before serving. To serve—spear with picks and stick in apple, orange or grapefruit.

Mrs. J. E. Richardson, Enterprise

RED DEVIL BALLS

1 (4½-ounce) can deviled
    ham

1 (8-ounce) package cream
    cheese
1 cup pecans, finely chopped

Blend ham and cheese. Chill. Form into balls. Roll balls in finely chopped nuts and serve on wooden picks.

Mrs. J. E. Richardson, Enterprise

CHEESE SOUFFLE

8 slices bread
4 tablespoons softened oleo
½ pound grated cheese
1 tablespoon dry mustard

pinch of salt
4 eggs
2½ cups sweetmilk

Cut off bread edges and spread each slice with softened oleo. Cut bread into finger bars, placing a layer of them in a 2-quart casserole dish. Mix grated cheese with the mustard and salt in a small bowl. Sprinkle some of the cheese mixture over bread layer. Repeat bread strip layer and cheese layer until all has been used.

Beat eggs and milk together. Pour over the bread and cheese. Refrigerate for 24 hours. Place casserole in pan of water and bake at 350 degrees for 1 hour. Serves 12.

Mrs. Doyle Varner, Jr., Coffeeville

CHEESE BREAD SOUFFLE

8 slices bread
½ pound sharp grated
　cheese
1 teaspoon dry mustard

1 teaspoon salt
4 whole eggs
2½ cups milk

Lightly grease a 9 x 13 x 2-inch casserole. Cut crust off bread. Butter, quarter and place bread into casserole. Sprinkle cheese over bread. Combine the remaining ingredients, mixing well. Pour liquid mixture over bread and cheese and cover with foil. Refrigerate overnight. Remove from refrigerator 1 hour before baking. Place casserole in pan of water. Uncover and bake in 350 degree oven for 1 hour. Serves 8.

Mrs. Julius Levy, Clarksdale

SPANISH SAUCE

1 (1-pound 12-ounce) can
　tomatoes
1 large thinly sliced onion
2 tablespoons Worcestershire
　sauce
1 tablespoon sugar

1 (10¾-ounce) can
　tomato soup
1 finely cut green pepper
2 tablespoons lemon juice
1 teaspoon salt
1 (8½-ounce) can tiny peas
1 (2-ounce) can mushrooms

Combine all ingredients in saucepan; cover and simmer for about 30 or 45 minutes. Serve over egg omelet.

Mrs. Virginia Love, Poplarville

AUNT EMMA'S MUSTARD PICKLE

1 gallon green tomatoes,
　medium size
6 green bell peppers
6 red bell peppers
6 medium size onions
2 or 3 hot peppers (optional)
½ cup salt
1 quart vinegar

1 quart water
4 cups sugar
2 cups flour
4 cups sugar
1 quart vinegar
1 quart water
1 cup prepared mustard

Grind tomatoes, green, red and hot peppers and onions. Add ½ cup salt and let mixture set for two hours. Drain this mixture in a jelly bag

[289]

to remove salt water. Place mixture in large pan. Add 1 quart vinegar, 1 quart water and 4 cups sugar, bring to a boil and cook for 25 minutes, remove from heat and let stand. Make a paste by mixing 2 cups flour and 4 cups sugar thoroughly, gradually add 1 quart vinegar and 1 quart water and mix well, then gradually add prepared mustard and stir until well blended. Now place mixture of tomatoes, peppers, etc. back on range, bring to a boil, then gradually add the paste mixture. Turn heat down low and simmer until the pickle is real thick. Pack hot into clean, hot pint jars and fill jars to ½ inch of top. Adjust lids. Process in boiling water bath for 5 minutes, counting processing time after water begins to boil. Remove jars and set them upright on rack to cool. Yield: 12 pints.

Mrs. Emma Brandon, Senatobia

PEPPER JELLY

¼ cup diced hot pepper   6 cups sugar
¾ cup diced bell pepper   1 cup Certo
1½ cups vinegar

Run peppers through blender with vinegar. Pour into boiler. Add sugar, stir to dissolve, and bring to a boil. Add Certo and bring to boil again. Skim off foam. Do not strain. Put in jars and seal. This is good with meats.

Mrs. C. H. Compton, Poplarville

·⟦Outdoor Cookery⟧·

Food just seems to taste better when it's prepared outdoors. Throughout Mississippi there are attractive parks and camping sites where tempting aromas of food frying over a campfire sharpen every appetite.

Cooking different types of meat on an outdoor grill is a hobby for many men. The smart homemaker can enhance this hobby by her own addition of special dishes which can be cooked right on the grill with the meat. A grill-side salad, bread and easy outdoor dessert make barbecues even more fun.

Summertime brings fresh air, sunshine and delicious food served in the outdoors. A velvety lawn, beach trip, walk through the woods, or carefree two-week vacation all call for a picnic. Most of the food can be prepared ahead of time, but it's also fun to fix one hot dish on the grill or open fire right at the picnic spot.

BRUNSWICK STEW

30 pounds chicken (fat
  hens preferred)
30 pounds pork shoulder,
  cubed
45 pounds venison or other
  game (squirrels, rabbits,
  etc.)
6 gallon tomatoes
6 gallons butterbeans
6 gallons corn
2 gallons tomato catsup
2 gallons sliced okra
1 gallon apple cider
  vinegar

30 pounds Irish potatoes,
  cubed
15 pounds onions, chopped
1 pound salt, or to taste
½ pound black pepper
4 (6-ounce) bottles
  hot sauce (more if
  desired)
4 (10-ounce) bottles
  Worcestershire sauce
2 pounds butter, unless
  enough fat is provided by
  meat
water (hot)

Boil chickens, squirrels, rabbits until tender, remove from bones, and chop. Cube large pieces of meat, pork, venison or beef, and boil until tender. Combine all meats and broth. Big black pots are ideal for cooking this stew.

Add all other ingredients and cook together *very slowly* for 10 hours or longer, stirring frequently (toward the last, stir constantly). A large wooden paddle is best. Add water as needed to prevent scorching. Long, slow cooking is essential for a desirable finished product. Taste occasionally to determine if additional seasoning is needed.

Makes approximately 50 gallons, or yields 200 to 250 individual servings.

Mrs. Allison White, Starkville

HOBO STEW

1 (4-ounce) piece meat
  (pork chop, steak, or
  hamburger)
¾ cup of water
salt to taste
pepper to taste

1 whole carrot, peeled
1 whole potato, peeled
1 whole ear corn cleaned
1 wedge cabbage
1 whole tomato

Use a 2-pound coffee or shortening can. Put meat in bottom of can. Add water. Salt and pepper vegetables as you arrange them in can. Seal the top with aluminum foil. Wrap wire around top of can and fasten. Cook over charcoals. If meat and vegetables are left whole, 1 hour cooking time is required. Open carefully because of steam. Yield: 1 serving.

Very good for picnics or beach. While you're having fun, food can cook with no attention. Food can be put in cans at home and be ready to cook when you get there. Servings are prepared in individual cans, with each person selecting his own combination of vegetables.

Mrs. Don Bigsby, Booneville

POCKET STEW

1 pound ground beef	1 large carrot
1 large onion	1 teaspoon salt
1 large Irish potato	⅛ teaspoon pepper

Make 4 hamburger patties. Slice onion into 4 parts. Slice potato into 4 parts. Cut carrot into 8 strips. Place each hamburger patty on a 12-inch square of double thickness heavy-duty aluminum foil. Top with slice of onion and slice of raw potato. Add two carrot strips. Sprinkle with salt and pepper. Seal foil securely. Place on hot grill and cook for 45 minutes, turning twice during cooking. Serves 4. For variations, pieces of chicken may be used instead of hamburger patties.

Mrs. W. B. White, Booneville

ONION POTATOES

6 medium baking potatoes	8 tablespoons softened
1 (1⅜-ounce) envelope dry	butter or margarine
onion soup mix	

Scrub potatoes. Cut each crosswise into ½-inch thick slices. Blend butter or margarine and onion soup mix; spread on one side of each potato slice. Reassemble potatoes. Wrap each in foil, sealing well. Bake on grill over coals for 45 minutes or 1 hour, turning once. Makes 6 servings.

Mrs. Joy Frizell, Lexington

POTATO–EGG SCRAMBLE

4 medium potatoes, boiled	4 eggs
6 slices bacon	1 teaspoon salt
1 bunch green onions, chopped	¼ teaspoon pepper

Dice 4 boiled medium potatoes. Dice 6 slices bacon and fry in skillet until crisp; pour off half the fat. Add potatoes and onions. Fry until lightly browned. Add 4 eggs. Season with salt and pepper. Stir gently until eggs are set. Yields 4 servings.

Mrs. Hilman Wedgeworth, Laurel

BEEF MARINADE

½ cup salad oil
¼ cup vinegar
¼ cup chopped onion
1 teaspoon salt
dash of pepper

2 teaspoons meat sauce or
  Worcestershire sauce
2 pounds lean beef, round
  or chuck, cut in 1-inch cubes

Combine all ingredients except meat; mix well. Add meat and let marinate 1 to 3 hours. Skewer meat and roast 6 to 8 minutes on each side. Serves 6.

Mrs. Joyce W. Clark, Greenville

GREAT BARBECUE SAUCE

3 tablespoons dry mustard
½ stick butter
2 teaspoons chili powder
½ cup vinegar
2 cloves garlic
salt and pepper to taste

3 tablespoons white
  corn syrup
2 tablespoons Worcestershire
  sauce
2 tablespoons liquid smoke
onions to taste

Combine all ingredients and simmer for 1 hour. Keeps well.

Mrs. Ronald Meaut, Biloxi

BARBECUE SAUCE

¾ cups catsup
½ cup water
¼ cup cider vinegar
2 tablespoons brown sugar
1 tablespoon minced onion
2 tablespoons Worcestershire
  sauce

1½ teaspoons salt
1 teaspoon dry mustard
¼ teaspoon pepper
3 drops red hot Tabasco
  sauce

Combine all ingredients in a sauce pan and simmer 10 to 15 minutes. This will be enough sauce for 1 chicken barbecued on a grill or in the oven.

Mrs. Hugh Moseley, Pheba

BARBECUE SAUCE

4 pounds onion, chopped
vegetable oil
1 gallon catsup
2 (10-ounce) bottles
  Worcestershire sauce
2 tablespoons vinegar
red hot sauce to taste
3 tablespoons concentrated
  lemon juice

1 quart prepared mustard
1 ounce black pepper
1 tablespoon minced garlic
salt to taste
1 cup sugar
2 tablespoons liquid
  hickory smoke

Cook onions in a little oil until tender. Add other ingredients. Simmer until thick. Then pour over sliced meat.

Mr. A. O. Turnage, Tylertown

BEEF & VEGETABLE KABOBS

½ cup salad oil
¼ cup lemon juice or
  vinegar
2 teaspoons monosodium
  glutamate
2 teaspoons salt
¼ teaspoon pepper

2 pounds beef (top round
  or sirloin)
24 medium mushrooms
2 large green peppers
2 tomatoes
8 small white onions

Cut meat in 1½-inch pieces, green peppers into 1-inch pieces, and tomatoes into eighths. Parboil onions. Blend together salad oil, lemon juice, monosodium glutamate, salt and pepper in a deep bowl. Add beef and vegetables; marinate 1 hour. Alternate pieces of beef on 8 (10-inch) skewers with mushrooms, green pepper and tomato wedges. Place whole onions on the end of each skewer. Place on outdoor grill which has been lined with aluminum foil. Grill 20 to 30 minutes, depending on desired degree of doneness, turning frequently and brushing occasionally with remaining marinade. Yield: 4 servings of 2 kabobs each.

Mrs. Marian H. Quinn, Canton

STEAK KABOBS

½ cup soy sauce
¼ cup packed brown sugar
½ teaspoon dry ginger
2 tablespoons oil

2 cloves minced garlic
½ cup orange juice
1½ pounds top sirloin
  steak

Combine all ingredients except steak. Mix well. Cut steak into 1 x ½-inch pieces. Add to sauce. Stir to coat. Marinate for 3 hours. Thread steak on skewers. Broil over hot coals for 10-12 minutes, turning frequently. Baste with marinade. Serves 4-5.

Mrs. John L. Webb, Clarksdale

HAM–K–BOBS

½ pound cooked ham
  (1 inch cubes)
½ cup barbecue sauce

2 medium zucchini, cut in
  chunks
1 (13¼-ounce) can pine-
  apple chunks, drained

The night before: Place ham cubes in medium bowl and pour barbecue sauce over them. Cover and let soak overnight in refrigerator.

15 minutes before cooking: Prepare grill. On 6 skewers alternate zucchini chunks, pineapple chunks and ham cubes. Brush with remaining sauce. Grill 10 minutes turning occasionally. Serves 6.

Miss Rennie Geoghegan, Fayette

MEAL–IN–A–BUNDLE

2 pounds lean chuck
6 carrots
6 medium potatoes
6 tablespoons chopped onion
½ cup chopped parsley
2 (10½-ounce) cans con-

densed golden mushroom
  soup
heavy duty aluminum foil
red hot sauce
6 tablespoons water
salt and pepper

Cut meat into 1-inch cubes, carrots into ¼-inch slices. Peel and dice potatoes. Chop onions and parsley. Divide chuck, potatoes, onions, carrots, parsley, and soup into 6 equal portions. Place each portion on an 18-inch square of heavy duty aluminum foil. Add a couple of dashes of hot sauce and a tablespoon of water to each portion. Season with salt and pepper. Bring up corner of foil and twist at top to close bundles. Place bundles on grill 6 inches above hot grey coals. Cook about 1 hour. Remove bundles from grill and serve in the foil. Serves 6.

Mrs. LaVerne Y. Lindsey, Lexington

CHICKEN BUNDLES

2 frying size chickens
8 slices peeled sweet potatoes
8 slices canned pineapple, drained
8 slices green pepper (optional)

½ cup butter or margarine
2 teaspoons salt
½ teaspoon pepper
heavy-duty aluminum foil

Cut chicken into quarters. For each serving, place individual portions of chicken, skin side down, in center of piece of foil large enough to cover and seal chicken. Top with slice of sweet potato, pineapple, pepper, and 1 tablespoon butter, ¼ teaspoon salt and dash of pepper. Bring foil up over food; seal edges with double fold seal to make airtight package. *Be sure there are no holes in the foil.* Cook on the backyard grill over medium heat about 50 minutes. Serves 8.

Mrs. W. D. Stovall, Wayside

BARBECUED CHICKEN

2 medium sized broilers
½ cup catsup
¼ cup water
¼ cup butter
2 tablespoons packed brown sugar
2 tablespoons Worcestershire sauce

1 teaspoon ginger
1 teaspoon red hot sauce
1 teaspoon dry mustard
¼ teaspoon pepper
1½ teaspoons salt
1 small onion, diced

Quarter broilers. Remove tips of wings and break joints to make chicken lie flat on grill. Combine all ingredients for sauce in a pan and heat slowly, stirring occasionally until butter is melted and mixture comes to a boil. Brush chicken with barbecue sauce. Place skin side down on grill. Keep lid on sauce while chicken is cooking. Turn chicken and mop with sauce several times as it cooks. Serves 8.

Mrs. T. E. Neill, Clarksdale

BARBECUED DRUMSTICKS

1/3 cup catsup
3 tablespoons lemon juice
2 tablespoons Worcestershire
   sauce

¼ cup salad oil
½ teaspoon garlic salt
   (optional)
12 chicken drumsticks

Mix all ingredients, except chicken. Add drumsticks and coat. Refrigerate in marinade overnight. Place in wire basket. Grill over slow coals about 25-30 minutes, basting occasionally. Turn and grill other side 20 minutes. Baste. Serves 6.

Mrs. Jack Crawford, Utica

LEMON GRILLED CHICKEN

¼ cup margarine
1 teaspoon grated lemon
   peel
2 tablespoons lemon juice
¼ teaspoon salt

¼ + ⅛ teaspoon paprika
⅛ teaspoon ground ginger
⅛ teaspoon red pepper sauce
1 (3-pound) fryer, quartered

Melt butter or margarine in small saucepan over moderately low heat. Stir in lemon peel, lemon juice, salt, paprika, ginger and red pepper sauce. Remove from heat. Brush chicken with lemon-butter sauce and place skin side up on grill about 12 inches from heat. Grill 1 to 1¼ hours, turning and brushing occasionally. Chicken is done when leg twists easily out of thigh joint or when fork-tender. Serves 6.

Mrs. Mary Geoghegan, Fayette

GRILLED CHICKEN

6 chicken halves
1 tablespoon lemon and
   pepper seasoning

1 tablespoon seasoned salt
1 stick margarine
lemon juice (optional)

Generously sprinkle each half of chicken with seasoned salt and place on outdoor grill or broiler rack of oven. Preheat oven to 400 degrees, or have coals three or four inches apart in grill. Let cook about 30 minutes; then turn. Mix together melted margarine, lemon and pepper seasoning and seasoned salt. After chicken has cooked 30 minutes on each side, start basting with margarine mixture. Turn and baste often for another hour. The juice of 1 lemon may be added to baste if desired.

Mrs. Thomas Pearson, West Point

GRILLED PORK CHOPS

1-inch pork chops
  (1 to 2 per person)
½ stick butter or margarine
¼ cup lemon juice

2 tablespoons Worcestershire
  sauce
¼ teaspoon salt
¼ teaspoon seasoned pepper

Start fire in grill about 45 minutes before cooking time. Have glowing coals. Melt butter. Add other ingredients except pork chops and mix well. Bring to a boil. Turn off heat. Place chops on grill when coals are ready. Grill 15 minutes on each side, brushing with sauce during cooking.

Mrs. Jacqueline Mikell, Port Gibson

HICKORY SMOKE RIBS

pork ribs (4 to 5 rib size)
barbecue sauce

large pieces hickory wood or
  chips

Prepare barbecue grill for indirect cooking. Cut ribs in pieces, about 4 or 5 ribs to a piece, and place on grill with inside of rib down.

Place large pieces of hickory wood at the edge of the coals. Smoke slowly for about 3 hours or until tender (not necessary to turn ribs). Watch coals closely to keep them glowing. Coat with a favorite barbecue sauce and cook 5 minutes longer. Ribs will be a bright pink.

Mrs. Tom Montgomery, Greenville

BABY TURKEY HALVES

2 (4-5 pound) baby turkeys,
  cut in half

1 (8-ounce) bottle garlic
  salad dressing
1 cup chicken broth

Marinate turkeys in large bowl with the salad dressing and broth for 1 hour, at room temperature. Turn several times. Place each half in foil and pour ¼ cup of the marinade over each. Reserve remaining marinade. Seal each foil package. Place packages 4 inches from coals and cook at least 45 minutes. Open packages and cook over coals for at least 30 minutes or until golden brown. During last cooking, baste with remaining marinade. Serves 6 to 8.

Mrs. Betty Jean Anders, Fayette

[299]

SMOKED FISH

6 dressed fish (1 pound
   each), fresh or frozen
1 cup salt

1 gallon water
¼ cup salad oil
1 pound hickory chips

If frozen fish are used, thaw before beginning preparation. Have fresh fish at room temperature. Remove the head just below the collarbone. Cut along the backbone almost to the tail. The fish should lie flat in one piece. Clean and wash fish. Add salt to water and stir until dissolved. Pour brine over fish and let stand for 30 minutes. Remove fish from brine and rinse in cold water. To smoke the fish, use a charcoal fire in a barbecue grill with a cover or hood. Let charcoal fire burn down to a low, even heat. Cover with 1/3 of the wet chips (Soak 1 pound of hickory chips or sawdust in 2 quarts of water overnight). Place fish on a well-greased grill, skin side down, about 4 inches from the smoking coals. Cover and smoke for 1½ hours. Add remaining chips as needed to keep the fire smoking. Increase the temperature by adding more charcoal and opening the draft. Brush fish with oil. Cover and cook 15 minutes longer. Brush fish again with oil. Cover and cook 10 minutes longer or until fish is lightly browned. Serves 6.

Mrs. Mary Davis, Lumberton

SMOKED FISH

21 bream or crappie
½ pound oleo or butter
1 teaspoon salt
½ teaspoon pepper
½ teaspoon onion salt
½ teaspoon garlic

½ teaspoon Worcestershire
   sauce
1 teaspoon vinegar
juice of 1 lemon
1 large onion, chopped

Melt oleo or butter in saucepan, add remaining seasoning ingredients except onion. When coals are hot, arrange the fish on a greased pan and place on grill over hot coals. Cook fish 30 minutes, basting with sauce each 15 minutes. Baste again, add chopped onion and cook 15 minutes longer. Remove and serve.

Mrs. Stewart Vail, Booneville

PATIO CATFISH

6 catfish
¾ cup butter or margarine
1/3 cup lemon juice

2 teaspoons salt
paprika

Clean, wash, and dry fish. Make a sauce by combining butter, lemon juice, and salt. Cut 6 pieces of heavy-duty aluminum foil. Grease lightly. Place 2 tablespoons of sauce on foil. Place fish in sauce. Top each fish with 2 tablespoons sauce and sprinkle with paprika. Bring the foil up over the fish and close all edges with tight double fold. Makes 6 packages. Place packages on a grill about 6 inches from moderately hot coals. Cook for 25 to 30 minutes or until fish flakes easily when tested with a fork. Serves 6.

Mrs. Thomas Pearson, West Point

MARINATED GRILLED ROAST

1 (3-pound) chuck roast	½ cup cooking sherry
4 cloves minced garlic	4 tablespoons catsup
4 tablespoons salad oil	1 teaspoon Worcestershire
½ teaspoon dry mustard	sauce
2 teaspoons soy sauce	1 tablespoon steak sauce
1 teaspoon crushed rosemary	1 teaspoon red pepper sauce
4 tablespoons wine vinegar	

Place roast in pryex dish. Sautè garlic in oil; remove from heat and add the next five ingredients. Pour mixture over meat and marinate 48 hours in refrigerator. Turn meat frequently. Remove meat from marinade mixture and place over hot coals. Add catsup, Worcestershire sauce, steak sauce and red pepper sauce to marinade. Baste meat while cooking. Cooking time is approximately 2 hours. Serves 8.

Mrs. Dudley Lester, Clarksdale

BARBECUED HAMBURGERS

1 pound ground beef	1 tablespoon butter
1 medium grated onion	½ cup chili sauce
½ teaspoon salt	½ cup sweet pickle relish
¼ teaspoon pepper	6 hamburger buns

Mix together thoroughly the ground beef, grated onion, salt and pepper. Place the meat mixture on a sheet of aluminum foil. Dot with butter, fold up the edges of the foil so the steam will not escape. Place foil pack on barbecue grill and cook for 30 minutes.

Open the foil pack and stir in the chili and relish. Stuff this mixture into hollowed out large round buns. Put buns in a large sheet of foil, fold edges tightly, heat on grill for 20 minutes and serve hot. Makes 6 servings.

Mrs. Mary B. Marks, Magnolia

"YOUR CHOICE" HAMBURGERS

1 pound hamburger
1 egg
1 teaspoon salt
pepper
¼ cup of breadcrumbs

onion, relish, mustard, catsup,
    horseradish or cheese
oil or lard for frying
5 buns for burgers

Mix together hamburger, egg, salt, pepper and breadcrumbs. Shape into ten thin hamburgers. Put "your choice" of onion, relish, mustard, catsup, horseradish or cheese on half the burgers. Top with second burger and seal the edges. Fry in skillet well coated with vegetable oil. Let every one have his favorite. The patties may be made ahead and covered with waxed paper. Serve with potato chips and coffee or cocoa.

Mrs. Mae Dossett, Picayune

PATIO OAT BURGERS

1½ pounds ground beef
1 cup rolled oats, uncooked
½ cup chopped onion
1 egg

2 teaspoons salt
⅛ teaspoon pepper
2/3 cup sweet milk or
    tomato juice

Combine and mix all ingredients. Shape into 8 patties. Grill or broil to desired doneness over low glowing coals, turning only once. Serve hot. Yield: 8 patties.

Mrs. Kimble Curtis, French Camp

MOCK FILET MIGNON

1 pound ground beef
1 tablespoon cooking oil,
    if meat is lean
1 garlic clove (minced)
1 teaspoon salt
½ teaspoon seasoned pepper
4 strips bacon

1 (4-ounce) can mushroom
    pieces
3 tablespoons butter or
    margarine
1 tablespoon Worcestershire
    sauce
dash of red pepper sauce
¼ teaspoon seasoned pepper

Combine meat, oil, garlic, salt and pepper. Mix well. Shape into 4 patties. Wrap each with bacon, fasten with toothpicks. Cook on grill 10-15 minutes on each side or to desired doneness. Serve with sauce made by sauting mushrooms in melted butter and adding seasonings. Yield: 4 servings.

Mrs. Jacqueline Mikell, Port Gibson

CORN DOGS

1 to 2 pounds wieners	2 tablespoons sugar
small sticks for wieners	1 egg
1 cup self-rising corn meal	1 cup sweet milk
1 cup self-rising flour	2 tablespoons melted fat

Mix all ingredients together thoroughly. Dip wieners with sticks inserted into mixture and fry in deep fat until golden brown. Serve hot.

Mrs. George G. Weaver, Wiggins

HOBO POPCORN

4 teaspoons cooking oil	heavy-duty foil
¼ cup popcorn	salt

Cut an 18-inch square of heavy-duty foil into 4 squares. In center of each, place 1 teaspoon oil and 1 tablespoon popcorn. Bring the 4 corners of foil to center, making a pouch. Seal edges well, allowing room for expansion of popcorn during cooking. With string, tie each pouch to a long handled barbecue tool or long stick. Place pouch directly on hot coals and shake constantly until corn is popped. Season with melted butter and salt to taste. Makes 4 servings.

Mrs. Joy W. Frizell, Lexington

⋅ː[Sandwiches]⋅ː

Ever since the Earl of Sandwich ordered that famous meal between two slices of bread so he wouldn't have to leave a card game, the sandwich has become a popular staple in most diets.

It's easy to prepare, easy to keep, and easy to eat. From the fancy tea sandwiches, the peanut butter and jelly favorite of youngsters, and the he-man sandwiches of the working husband's lunch, the variety is endless.

A sandwich can be a serving of empty calories or it can fit well into the day's food plan and provide needed protein, vitamins and minerals. The choice of bread, fillings and spreads is important in providing wholesome nourishment.

With nearly 100 million sandwiches eaten in America every day, a new recipe is always in demand.

[305]

TOT'S PARTY SANDWICHES

3 ounces of cream cheese	onion juice
1 bell pepper	2 pieces of white bread
mayonnaise	1 piece of brown bread

Fluff the cream cheese. Grate bell pepper. Mix together with enough mayonnaise and onion juice to season to taste. This amount of filling makes 4 whole sandwiches. Spread filling on the two pieces of white bread and put together with the one piece of brown bread in the center. Wrap and store overnight. Immediately before serving, cut into 8 pieces and place on serving tray to look like wedge shape sandwiches.

Mrs. Griffin Norquist, Yazoo City

CHEESE NUT LOGS

½ pound sharp cheese	whipped butter
mayonnaise	½ pound salted cashews,
15 slices of sandwich bread	chopped

Mix cheese and enough mayonnaise for spreading consistency. Cut crust from bread. Spread with cheese mixture and roll. Cut in half. Spread outside lightly with whipped butter and roll in finely chopped cashews.

Dr. Louise Burnette, University

MOCK CHICKEN SALAD SANDWICH

white and whole wheat bread	1 cup chopped pimiento
1 cup chopped celery	stuffed olives
1 cup chopped nuts	¼ cup or more mayonnaise

Cut white and whole wheat bread into circles with cookie cutter. Mix rest of ingredients. Spread mixture on white bread and top with whole wheat circle from which center has been cut out with a thimble. Place a slice of pimiento stuffed olive in center. Makes 12.

Mrs. Danny Hartley, Clarksdale

CORNED BEEF ROLL

1 (12-ounce) can corned beef	½ pound mild cheese
1 small onion, grated	2 tablespoons mustard
1 tablespoon Worcestershire sauce	½ cup mayonnaise

Mix all ingredients together thoroughly. Spread on trimmed slices of bread. Roll up, pin with toothpicks, and toast in moderate oven, 350 degrees. This may also be used as a sandwich. Makes approximately 2 dozen.

Mrs. W. M. Jolly, Cleveland

HOT TUNA SANDWICHES

2 (6½-ounce) cans tuna
1 cup chopped celery
1 cup American cheese, grated

½ cup minced onion
½ cup salad dressing

Mix ingredients in bowl and toss lightly. Fill 12 hamburger buns and wrap in foil. Place on cookie sheet and bake for 15 minutes at 350 degrees. Makes 12 sandwiches.

Mrs. Tom Montgomery, Greenville

HOT TUNA SANDWICHES

1 (7½ ounce) can light tuna
½ of (10½-ounce) can mushroom soup
4 hard cooked eggs, chopped
2 tablespoons salad dressing
¼ cup chopped bell pepper
¼ cup chopped pimiento
¼ cup minced onion

salt to taste
2 cups medium white sauce
1 (3-ounce) can mushrooms, stems and pieces
½ of (10½-ounce) can mushroom soup
1 cup grated cheddar cheese
salt and pepper to taste

Mix first 8 ingredients. Reserve the remaining half can of soup for the sauce. Spread mixture between slices of bread, wrap in waxed paper and refrigerate overnight. One hour before serving, take from refrigerator, butter top and bottom of sandwiches. Place on an ungreased cookie sheet, and bake at 350 degrees for 25 minutes. Meanwhile, mix white sauce, mushrooms, soup, cheese, salt and pepper together. Heat until cheese is melted and sauce is bubbly hot. Serve sandwiches topped with the hot sauce. Serves 5 to 6.

Mrs. Dudley Lester, Clarksdale

[307]

TUNA SANDWICHES

1 (7½-ounce) can tuna
½ cup chopped pecans
½ cup pimiento
1 large sour pickle, chopped

1 cup celery, chopped
2 hard cooked eggs
1 apple, chopped
¼ cup sandwich spread

Mix together all ingredients using enough sandwich spread for mixture to spread easily. Makes filling for approximately 12 sandwiches.

Mrs. James V. Gross, Woodville

TUNA SANDWICHES

1 (6½-ounce) can tuna
1 (8-ounce) package cream cheese

Worcestershire sauce to taste
onion juice to taste
mayonnaise

Mix all ingredients together well and spread on slices of buttered bread. Serve toasted or chilled. May be frozen, wrapped tightly in plastic wrap material.

Mrs. Griffin Norquist, Yazoo City

OPEN FACE SHRIMP SANDWICHES

1 cup shrimp, mashed very fine with a fork
1/3 cup celery, chopped very fine

salt and red pepper
juice of ½ lemon
mayonnaise

Combine flaked shrimp and celery and sprinkle with salt and pepper. Mix in lemon juice and enough mayonnaise to spreading consistency. Spread on thinly sliced bread and cut in desired shape for sandwiches.

Mary Jane Hall, Jackson

CORNED BEEF BUNWICHES

8 buns
1 (12-ounce) can corned beef, shredded
1 cup shredded sharp cheese
½ cup chopped stuffed olives

½ cup catsup
2 tablespoons Worcestershire sauce
2 medium onions, sliced

Split buns and remove some of the crumb from the centers. Combine corned beef, cheese, olives, catsup and Worcestershire sauce. Fill buns with mixture. Wrap each bun separately in foil. Freeze if desired. To serve, heat in moderate oven, 375 degrees, about 25 minutes or until well heated. Serve with slices of onion. Serves 8.

Mrs. Buck Adams, Macon

CORNED BEEF SANDWICHES

1 (12-ounce) can corned beef	½ pound cheese
1 small onion	1 dill pickle
1 small jar mustard	mayonnaise

Grind all together and spread on thin bread which has been brushed with mayonnaise. Roll and toast.

Mrs. Harold Hillebert, Canton

BEEF BARBECUE SANDWICHES

1 pound cubed pork	1/3 cup vinegar
1 pound cubed beef	1 cup water
1 (10¾-ounce) can tomato soup	1/3 cup Worcestershire sauce
1 onion	salt and pepper to taste
¼ cup sugar	

Mix all ingredients and cook 2½ to 3 hours in a 350 degree oven. Remove. Mash and blend meat well into the mixture. Makes 16 to 20 sandwiches.

Mrs. Clem Butler, Summit

QUICKIE HOT TAMALE SANDWICHES

1 pound hamburger meat	⅛ teaspoon pepper
¼ cup chopped celery	1 tablespoon cooking oil
¼ cup chopped onion	1 (10½-ounce) can tomato soup, undiluted
1 teaspoon salt	

Mix together the first 5 ingredients in order given. Brown in the cooking oil until meat loses its red color. Add tomato soup (do not use cream of tomato soup) and simmer about 10 minutes. Serve on hamburger or hot dog buns, or plain toasted bread. Makes about 8 sandwiches.

Mrs. Louis Udovich, Leland

SUPPER ON A BREAD SLICE

1½ pounds ground beef
2/3 cup (small can)
  evaporated milk
½ cup cracker meal
1 egg
½ cup chopped onion
1 tablespoon prepared
  mustard

1½ teaspoons salt
¾ teaspoon monosodium
  glutamate
⅛ teaspoon pepper
2 cups (8-ounces)
  grated cheese
1 loaf French bread

Combine all ingredients, except French bread, in a large bowl. Cut loaf bread in half lengthwise. Spread meat mixture evenly over top surface of bread. Wrap foil around crust side of each half, leaving top uncovered. Place on cookie sheet. Bake at 350 degrees for 25 to 30 minutes. Cut into serving-size pieces. Serves 6 to 8.

Carol S. Vandevere, Meadville

SLOPPY JOES

3 pounds hamburger
2 (10¾-ounce) cans
  tomato soup
1 tablespoon salt

1 cup sweet pickle relish
½ teaspoon pepper
24 hot frankfurter or
  hamburger buns

Put hamburger in large skillet and cook until brown, stirring to break up meat. Add soup, relish, salt and pepper. Cook 5 minutes or until blended. Serve a heaping spoonful on each bun. Serves 24.

Mrs. Clem Butler, Summit

PIZZA BURGERS

2 pounds ground beef
1/3 cup minced onion
1 teaspoon salt
½ teaspoon leaf oregano
¼ teaspoon pepper

1 (8-ounce) can pizza sauce
6 slices Mozzarella cheese
3 large English muffins, split
butter, softened
6 slices cheddar cheese

In a bowl, lightly mix ground beef, onion, salt, oregano, pepper and ½ cup pizza sauce. Shape into 6 patties, about 4½ to 5-inches in diameter. Broil one side; turn and broil other side to desired degree of doneness. Spoon remaining pizza sauce over patties. Top patties with slices of Mozzarella cheese; return to broiler just until cheese begins to melt.

Meanwhile, toast and butter muffins. Place a slice of cheddar cheese on each half-muffin. Top each with a beef patty. Serves 6.

Mrs. LaVerne Y. Lindsey, Lexington

CHEESE BUNS

1 cup crushed corn chips
6 tablespoons mayonnaise
¼ cup onion chopped fine

5 hamburger buns
5 slices cheese

Mix crushed corn chips with mayonnaise and onion. Slice buns, and spread mixture on lower halves. Top with slice of cheese. Heat in oven until cheese melts. Cover with top half of bun. Serves 5.

Mrs. Stennis Clardy, West Point

PIMIENTO CHEESE SANDWICH

1 (4-ounce) medium
  can pimiento
½ pound cheese, grated
½ cup vinegar
2 eggs, beaten
2 tablespoons flour

½ cup sugar
2 teaspoons dry mustard
pinch of salt
dash of pepper
½ cup water

Grind cheese and pimiento together. Mix all other ingredients and cook in double boiler until thick. Cool thoroughly, and mix well with the pimiento and cheese mixture.

Mrs. Ike Grisham, Pontotoc

CHEESE BOXES

½ pound American cheese,
  grated
1 cup mayonnaise
1 tablespoon Worcestershire
  sauce

1 teaspoon prepared mustard
1 tablespoon Durkee's salad
  dressing
salt and pepper to taste

Mix cheese and mayonnaise. Add seasonings. Cut crust from bread. Spread square of bread with mixture, place on greased cookie sheet and place slice of bread on top and spread mixture over all. (One teaspoon grated onion juice may be used in mixture.) When ready to serve, toast in a 400 degree oven for 10 minutes or until bubbly hot. This makes 1 pint of filling. Keep refrigerated. For smaller boxes cut bread in fourths.

Mrs. A. W. Rhyne, Coahoma

ROQUEFORT CHEESE AND APPLE SANDWICHES

1 cup Roquefort cheese
4 tablespoons butter
1 tart apple, grated

½ cup chopped pecans
mayonnaise

Cream cheese with butter. Add grated apple and chopped pecans. Add enough mayonnaise to spread well. Spread on trimmed whole wheat bread slices. Makes 1¼ cups of spread.

Mrs. Jessie Rollins, Port Gibson

CHEESE AND NUT SANDWICH FILLING

½ cup cream cheese
½ cup chopped nuts
2 tablespoons orange juice

¼ teaspoon salt
1 tablespoon butter
¼ teaspoon chopped pimiento

Blend ingredients in order listed. Chill thoroughly in refrigerator. This filling may be kept in a covered jar on your emergency shelf in the refrigerator.

Mrs. Prentiss Daniel, Booneville

DATENUT SANDWICH

1 (7¼-ounce) package pitted
   dates, chopped
½ cup chopped pecans

2 (3-ounce) packages
   cream cheese
1/3 cup light cream

Mix ingredients well. Spread on thin sliced, trimmed bread.

Mrs. Jessie Rollins, Port Gibson

HAWAIIAN HAM SANDWICHES

8 slices whole wheat bread
softened butter or margarine
1 cup ground cooked ham

½ cup crushed pineapple,
   drained
½ tablespoon brown sugar

Spread bread with butter or margarine. Blend together all other ingredients, and spread on 4 slices of bread. Top with remaining bread. Makes 4 sandwiches.

Mrs. Sammie Pearson, West Point

CRUNCHY HAM–CHEESE SANDWICHES

4 cups oven-toasted rice cereal	3 eggs, slightly beaten
4 thin slices cooked ham	2/3 cup milk
4 slices cheese	¼ teaspoon salt
8 slices day-old bread	¼ cup melted margarine

Measure oven-toasted rice cereal; then crush to 2 cups. Set aside. Place a slice of ham and a slice of cheese between 2 slices of bread. Cut sandwiches in half diagonally. Set aside. Combine eggs, milk and salt in shallow dish. Dip sandwiches in egg mixture, turning once. Coat evenly with crushed cereal. Place flat side in a single layer on well-greased baking sheet. Drizzle with melted margarine. Bake in hot oven, 450 degrees, about 10 minutes until crisp and lightly browned. Serve hot, garnished with olives, radishes and parsley. Serves 4.

Mrs. Hilman Wedgeworth, Laurel

MONTE CARLO SANDWICH

2 slices bread	2 slightly beaten eggs
mild mustard	½ cup milk
1 slice cheese	dash Worcestershire sauce
1 slice ham	2 tablespoons butter

Spread 2 slices of bread with mild mustard and put them together with a slice of cheese and a slice of ham. Cut in half. Mix egg, milk and Worcestershire sauce. Dip sandwich in mixture. Melt butter in skillet and fry sandwich until golden brown; turn and brown other side.

Mrs. Jim Tatum, Chunky

SURPRISE PACKAGE

¼ pound ham	½ cup chopped green olives
½ pound cheddar cheese	3 tablespoons mayonnaise
1/3 cup chopped onions	½ cup chili sauce
2 hard cooked eggs	salt and pepper

Chop all ingredients, mix in seasonings and spread into buns. Wrap buns in aluminum foil and heat in hot oven, 450 degrees, for about 10 minutes. Makes enough for 12 hamburger or hotdog buns.

Mrs. W. A. McDonald, Hazlehurst

HAM AND EGG SANDWICH

5 eggs	¼ teaspoon salt
¼ cup minced onion	dash of black pepper
¼ cup diced green pepper	½ cup milk
¾ cup minced cooked ham	4 buns, split, toasted
2 tablespoons margarine	and buttered

Beat eggs slightly. Mix onion, green pepper and ham. Melt margarine in a pan. Add eggs, salt, black pepper and milk. Cook over low heat, stirring constantly until mixture begins to get firm. Add other ingredients and serve hot on toasted buns. Serves 8.

Mrs. Christine Annis, Wiggins

FRANK AND EGG SANDWICH FILLING

½ cup chopped cooked frankfurters	1 tablespoon chili sauce or catsup
1 chopped hard-cooked egg	¼ teaspoon salt
1 tablespoon finely chopped onion	⅛ teaspoon pepper

Combine all ingredients and blend well. Makes about 2/3 cup sandwich filling.

Mrs. Charles Everett, West Point

SHRIMP AND EGG SANDWICH

1 cup cooked chopped shrimp	2 tablespoons pickle relish
½ cup chopped walnuts	3 tablespoons mayonnaise
3 hard cooked eggs, chopped	

Mix well and spread on thin sliced, trimmed bread, top with second slice of bread. Cut diagonally.

Mrs. Jessie H. Rollins, Port Gibson

EGG SALAD SANDWICHES

6 eggs, hard cooked, chopped	6 tablespoons mayonnaise
¼ cup celery, minced finely	½ teaspoon salt
¼ cup pickles, chopped	8 hamburger buns

Combine first 5 ingredients and spread on plain or toasted buns. Serves 8.

Eva Ruth Rowell, Perkinston

CUCUMBER SANDWICH SPREAD

1 (8-ounce) package cream
  cheese, softened
1 large cucumber, peeled,
  grated and drained
1 tablespoon grated onion

2 tablespoons mayonnaise
few drops lemon juice
dash of salt and pepper
green food coloring

Mix well and spread on thin sliced bread, using three slices for each sandwich. Wrap closely in foil, seal in plastic bag and freeze until needed. Then after thawing, remove crust of bread and slice thin into finger sandwiches. Each large sandwich yields 4 finger sandwiches. For a good cucumber dip use the above ingredients, add the juice of the cucumber and more mayonnaise.

Mrs. June Murray, Taylorsville.

CARROT SANDWICH

1 (3-ounce) package cream
  cheese
2 tablespoons soft oleo
½ teaspoon onion juice

½ teaspoon salt
¼ teaspoon sugar
1 cup grated raw carrots
mayonnaise to spread on bread

Blend all ingredients except carrots. Then fold in carrots and chill overnight. Use thin bread slices to make sandwich. Spread each slice very thinly with mayonnaise and then spread thin layer of mixture on 1 slice and top with other slice of bread. Cut in odd shapes to serve. Servings vary according to size of sandwiches.

Mrs. Herman Smith, Water Valley

BACON AND AVOCADO SANDWICH

soft butter or margarine
4 slices white bread
1 avocado, sliced thin

8 slices cooked crisp bacon
½ cup mayonnaise
1 tablespoon lemon juice

Spread butter lightly on bread. Place avocado equally on each slice. Place two slices of bacon on each slice. Mix lemon juice with mayonnaise and drizzle about 2 tablespoons of this mixture on each slice. Place on broiler pan in preheated 350 degree oven just long enough for the mayonnaise to lightly brown. Serve with fork. Serves 4.

Mrs. Lilly Lucas, Lorman

[315]

TURKEY SANDWICHES

1 cup boned turkey,
  minced fine
1/3 cup celery, chopped
  fine

1/3 cup chopped white grapes
1/3 cup chopped pecans
mayonnaise for spreading
12 slices sandwich bread

Mix and blend well all ingredients and spread the sandwiches. Makes 6 sandwiches.

Mary Jane Hall, Jackson

∘⦗Desserts⦘∘

The right kind of dessert provides the perfect ending to a good meal. There are many things involved in the planning and preparation of desserts. They should complement the other foods in the meal. If you serve a light main course, the dessert may be a substantial one such as pie, cake or pudding. After a high calorie main course, the dessert should be simple, such as fruit, gelatin, sherbet or plain cookies.

Desserts are more attractive and acceptable when their form varies from that of other foods on the menu. A contrast of color, texture or flavor is good. After soups, serve something solid; after a hot meal, something cool; and after a bland meal, something spicy.

Usually the dessert is sweet. However, if the main course has included a number of foods that are sweet and rich in fat, desserts such as sherbet, grapefruit or other sour fruits may be more agreeable. They are certainly lower in calories.

When preparing your next dessert, select from any one of the following favorites.

BOILED CUSTARD ICE CREAM

3 quarts milk	dash of salt
6 eggs, separated	2½ cups sugar
2 tablespoons flour	1 tablespoon vanilla

Scald milk, less 1 cup, in a double boiler. Sift flour, sugar, (less ½ cup) and salt together in a bowl. Into this mixture stir egg yolks, well beaten, to which 1 cup of cold milk has been added. When milk is scalded stir egg mixture into it. Cook until slightly thickened, stirring constantly. Let cool.

Fold in beaten egg whites to which ½ cup sugar has been added. Add vanilla. Pour into freezer. Pack 8 parts ice to 1 part ice cream salt. Turn until frozen.

Mrs. G. G. Bennett, Vaiden

ICE CREAM

8 eggs (not less than 6)	1 large can evaporated milk
1 cup sugar	2 teaspoons of vanilla
1 can sweetened condensed milk	additional milk

Mix sugar with eggs and beat well. Add condensed milk and beat well into egg mixture. Mix the evaporated milk and vanilla with above mixture. Pour mixture into a gallon ice cream container. Add plain milk until container is ¾ full and mix with long handled spoon. Freeze in freezer until firm using 8 to 1 portion of ice and salt. Serves 16.

Mary M. Jones, Lexington

APRICOT ICE CREAM

1 (16-ounce) can apricots	1 pint cream
1 banana	1 (14-ounce) can condensed milk
juice of 2 oranges	¼ teaspoon salt
1 cup sugar	
1 quart sweet milk	

Drain apricots reserving juice. Put apricots and banana through sieve. Add apricot juice, orange juice and sugar. Stir until sugar is dissolved. Chill thoroughly. Then add milk, cream and condensed milk and blend well. Stir in salt. Freeze in hand or electric freezer. Remove from freezer can and pack in containers and store in deep freeze until ready to serve.

Mrs. Sam Page, Summit

COFFEE ICE CREAM

1 large can evaporated milk
1 can condensed milk

4 heaping tablespoons instant
coffee powder (crystals are
not suitable)

Chill the cans of evaporated and condensed milk until very cold. Beat the evaporated milk until whipped cream consistency. Add the can of condensed milk. Beat. With a rubber or plastic spatula fold in the powdered coffee. Pour into refrigerator ice tray and freeze. Do not stir. *Do not use any liquid flavoring.* Serves 4 to 6.

Miss Ella Somerville, Oxford

STRAWBERRY ICE CREAM

1 quart strawberries
2 or 3 cups sugar, as
preferred

1 pint whipping cream
1 pint half and half cream

Mash berries through a colander, sweeten with sugar to taste, add cream and freeze.

Mrs. O. A. White, West Point

PEACH ICE CREAM

2½ cups sugar
3 tablespoons flour
5 eggs, beaten

2 quarts sweet milk
2 teaspoons vanilla
1 (no. 2½) can peaches

Mix sugar and flour, add eggs and mix well. Add milk and vanilla. Stir until sugar is melted. Mash peaches and add to mixture. Pour into freezer can. Pack with ice and salt and freeze. Serves 16.

Mrs. Myrtis Bass, Smithdale

ORANGE SHERBET

1 cup sugar
1½ cups milk
1 cup orange juice

4 tablespoons lemon juice
1 cup cream, whipped
2 egg whites, beaten

Dissolve sugar and milk. Stir constantly while adding the juices. Partly freeze, then fold in 1 cup cream whipped, and the 2 beaten egg whites. Complete freezing.

Mrs. Myrtle Patterson, Belmont

ORANGE CREAM SHERBET

1¼ cups sugar
1½ cups orange juice
few grains salt

1 cup cream
2 cups milk

Mix sugar, orange juice and salt. Stir in cream and milk slowly. Pour into trays and freeze. When mixture begins to freeze, remove and stir. Return to refrigerator.

Mrs. Martee B. Rayburn, Pontotoc

APRICOT SHERBET

1 large can peeled apricots
1 cup crushed pineapple
3 cups sugar
juice of 3 lemons

3 egg whites
1 pint whipping cream
sweet milk

Mash apricots; add pineapple, sugar and lemon juice. Mix well. Beat egg whites until stiff and add fruit to mixture. Add whipping cream (not whipped) and mix. Pour into a 1-gallon freezer can. Finish filling can with whole milk to within 2 inches of the top, or, if desired fill can with any leftover juice from apricots and pineapple instead of additional milk. Stir with long spoon. Freeze until hard.

Mrs. Victoria Dean, Iuka

SHERBET

1 (3-ounce) package orange
  gelatin
2 cups hot water
1 cup sugar

¼ cup lemon juice
1 (8-ounce) can crushed
  pineapple
2 cups sweet milk

Stir gelatin into hot water, add sugar and let cook for about 5 minutes at simmering stage. Then add lemon juice and pineapple. Remove from heat and let cool for 10 minutes. Chill and add milk last. Serves 5.

Mrs. Karl Shaw, Indianola

PINEAPPLE SHERBET

2/3 cup sugar
2 cups milk
½ cup pineapple juice

1 tablespoon lemon juice
1 tablespoon grated lemon rind

Stir together and set in refrigerator tray. Take out and whip occasionally for lightness. Serves 4.

Mrs. Virginia Nunn, Jackson

GRAPE SHERBET

6 cups grape juice
2 tablespoons plain gelatin
3 lemons (juice)

1½ cups sugar
1 pint whipping cream
1 quart milk

Soften gelatin in ¼ cup cold grape juice. Heat ¾ cup juice to boiling point and dissolve gelatin in it. Stir until well dissolved. Add five cups grape juice, stirring all the time. Add juice of three lemons and sugar. Put cream and milk in large container and slowly add grape mixture to it. Freeze in a gallon freezer. Serves 12.

Mrs. A. P. Mullins, Macon

LIME SHERBET

1 (3-ounce) package lime
  gelatin
1 cup pineapple juice
1 cup sugar
juice of 2 lemons and grated
  rind

1 quart sweet milk
1 cup crushed pineapple,
  drained

Bring pineapple juice to boil; dissolve gelatin in boiling juice. Add sugar, lemon juice and rind and set aside to cool. Add sweet milk; pour into trays and freeze. Remove from trays, beat with mixer and refreeze. Serves 8.

Miss Wilma Roberts, Carriere

MUSCADINE SHERBET

1 gallon fully ripe
  muscadines
½ gallon water

2 cups sugar
2 packages plain gelatin
2 egg whites

Wash muscadines well. Place in pan and cover with boiling water. Let set 10 minutes, then drain, saving water. Pop out pulp into separate container. Boil hulls in water that was reserved until wilted. Drain and save for jelly. Cover hulls with boling water and simmer until tender. Heat pulp until seeds are cleared; pour through colander to remove seed. Add

3 cups of pulp to hulls (after well tender) and add sugar to taste. Dissolve gelatin in ½ cup water and add to hot mixture. Whip egg whites until stiff but not dry; add cooled muscadine mixture. Freeze as for ice cream. Sherbet may be stored in small cartons in the freezer.

Mrs. J. A. Gardner, Walls

DATE PUDDING

1½ cups sugar
2½ tablespoons butter
½ teaspoon salt
2 eggs, beaten
1½ cups buttermilk
1 teaspoon soda
3½ cups graham cracker crumbs

1 cup chopped dates
1 cup sugar
1½ cups hot water
3 tablespoons flour
1 cup chopped pecans
½ teaspoon vanilla

Cream sugar, butter and salt. Add eggs. Add soda to buttermilk. Add to above mixture. Mix in cracker crumbs until smooth. Bake in 10 x 12-inch greased pan lined with waxed paper for 30 minutes in 300 degree oven. Meanwhile, combine remaining ingredients and cook, stirring constantly, until just thickened. When cake is done, pour on topping while it is still hot. Serve warm with whipped cream. Serves 12 to 15.

Mrs. William Bost, Sr., Starkville

DATE PUDDING

1 cup chopped dates
2 tablespoons sifted all-purpose flour
¼ teaspoon salt
1 teaspoon baking powder

2 eggs, separated
1 cup powdered sugar
1 cup chopped pecans
1 cup whipped cream

Add dates to sifted flour, salt and baking powder. Beat egg whites until stiff then beat in sugar and add well beaten yolks, nuts and floured dates. Mix lightly and turn into a well greased 9 x 13 inch pan. Bake 30 minutes in a 350 degree oven. Serve with whipped cream. Makes a delicious, chewy dessert. Serves 10.

Mrs. W. N. Jenkins, Port Gibson

[322]

BANANA PUDDING

½ cup sugar
3 tablespoons flour
2 eggs, separated
1 cup milk
3 tablespoons butter

1 teaspoon vanilla flavoring
vanilla wafers
2 large bananas
4 teaspoons sugar

Sift together sugar and flour. Add to beaten egg yolks. To this mixture add milk. Stir well. Cook over low heat or in double boiler until thickened. Add butter and flavoring. Line bottom of baking dish with wafers. On this put a layer of sliced bananas. On this put half of the cooked custard. Now another layer of wafers, another layer of sliced bananas and the remainder of custard. Top with egg whites which have been beaten stiff with 4 teaspoons sugar. Brown in 350 degree oven until a golden, toasty color. Serve cold. Serves 6.

Miss Wilma Roberts, Carriere

APPLE PUDDING

½ cup shortening
1 cup sugar
1 egg
1 cup all-purpose flour
½ cup buttermilk
½ teaspoon soda

½ teaspoon cinnamon
½ teaspoon allspice
1¼ cups pared and diced
    fine apples
½ cup nuts

Cream shortening and sugar, add egg and beat well. Sift dry ingredients together except soda, which is added to milk. Add flour mixture and milk alternately. Add apples and nuts. Bake in slow oven (300 degrees) until a custardy, firm consistency. Serves 8.

Mrs. Colleen Porter, Heidelberg

OZARK PUDDING

1 egg
¾ cup sugar
2 tablespoons flour
1¼ teaspoons baking powder

⅛ teaspoon salt
½ cup chopped pecans
½ cup chopped peeled apples
1 teaspoon vanilla

Beat eggs and sugar together. Combine flour, baking powder and salt; stir into egg mixture. Add nutmeats, apples and vanilla. Bake in greased pie pan in moderate oven (350 degrees) 35 minutes. If you like, add whipped cream or ice cream. Serves 4.

Mrs. S. B. Webb, Indianola

FRENCH PUDDING

2½ cups confectioners sugar
¾ cup butter
3 eggs
¾ to 1 pound vanilla wafers

1 pint whipping cream
1½ cups chopped pecans
2 small packages frozen
    strawberries

Cream butter and sugar, add well beaten eggs. Roll wafers and line greased pan or dish with crumbs. Layer crumbs, batter mix, fruits and nuts and whipped cream, alternately. Repeat layers of each and refrigerate 24 hours before serving. Cut in squares.

Mrs. E. Maurice King, Jr., Clinton

RAISIN CUSTARD PUDDING

5 slices white bread
¼ cup soft butter or
    margarine
½ cup raisins
1 teaspoon cinnamon

3 cups milk
2/3 cup sugar
4 eggs
1 teaspoon vanilla

Preheat oven to 350 degrees. Lightly butter 12 x 8 x 2-inch baking dish. Trim bread crusts and spread slices generously with butter. Cut each slice of bread into 4 squares. Sprinkle raisins over bottom of baking dish and arrange the bread squares buttered side up over the raisins. Sprinkle cinnamon over squares. In saucepan, heat milk until bubbles form around edge of pan. Remove from heat; add sugar to milk, and stir until sugar dissolves. Beat eggs in large bowl and gradually add hot milk. Stir in vanilla. Add this mixture over bread squares. Place dish in pan of hot water and bake 40 to 50 minutes. Remove pan from water and let pudding cool a little before serving. Serve warm or cold. Serves 8.

Mrs. Helen Gillis, Fayette

PERSIMMON PUDDING

2 cups ripe persimmon pulp
2 cups sugar
2 eggs, beaten
1¾ cups sifted all-purpose
   flour
2 teaspoons baking powder

1 cup half and half cream
   (undiluted evaporated
   milk may be used)
1 cup buttermilk
1 teaspoon soda
½ cup melted butter or
   margarine
dash of cinnamon

Mix ingredients in order given. Pour into 13 x 9 x 3-inch greased pan and bake for 1 hour at 325 degrees. Serves 8.

Mrs. Raymond Reinbold, Leland

FRUIT COCKTAIL PUDDING

1 cup sugar
1 cup flour
1 teaspoon soda
¼ teaspoon salt
1 egg

1 (no. 303) can fruit
   cocktail
½ cup nuts, chopped
½ cup brown sugar

Mix dry ingredients together. Stir in egg and fruit cocktail. Mix well. Pour into lightly greased 9 x 9-inch pan. Mix together the nuts and brown sugar and sprinkle over top of mixture. Bake in 325 degree oven 45 minutes. Serves 6 to 8.

Mrs. W. J. Voorhies, Greenville

SWEET POTATO PUDDING

½ cup butter
1½ cups sugar
4 eggs, well beaten
4 cups grated raw sweet
   potatoes

1 teaspoon cinnamon
1½ cups sweet milk
1 teaspoon nutmeg
½ teaspoon salt
2 cups marshmallows

Cream butter with sugar, add eggs, mix well. Add all other ingredients except marshmallows, mix well. Pour into buttered pan. Bake in 250 degree oven until potatoes are tender, about 2 hours. Cover with marshmallows. Soften in oven. Serves 6.

Mrs. C. R. Gullick, Bruce

LEMON SPONGE PUDDING

1 cup sugar
1½ tablespoons butter
2 eggs, separated
pinch of salt

2 rounded tablespoons flour
1 cup milk
juice of 1 lemon

Cream sugar and butter together. Add egg yolks beaten with a pinch of salt. Add flour, milk and lemon juice. Fold in stiffly beaten egg whites. Bake in buttered baking dish set in a pan of water for 45 minutes at 325 degree oven. Serves 6. *Mrs. K. B. Presley, West Point*

ENGLISH PLUM PUDDING

1 quart seeded raisins
1 pint currants
½ pint finely chopped
   citron
1 quart finely chopped apples
1 quart finely chopped beef
   suet
8 separated, well-beaten eggs
1 pint sugar
1 quart sweet milk
1 teaspoon salt

1 quart packed stale bread
   crumbs
1 teaspoon cinnamon
1 teaspoon allspice
1 quart unsifted all-purpose
   flour
½ pound butter
¾ pound brown sugar
1 egg yolk
1 (4-ounce) glass plum jelly

Flour fruit thoroughly, using part of flour. In a large bowl mix egg yolks, sugar, milk and salt. Stir in fruit, bread crumbs, egg whites, suet, one after the other until all are used. Add enough flour to make fruit stick together.

Fill pudding mold allowing room to swell, or fill a can and cover with cloth that has been dipped in water and dredged with flour. Tie with string. Drop in boiling water; boil slowly three hours.

Cream together butter, brown sugar and 1 egg yolk. Heat until boiling. Add jelly. Boil until thick. Pour over pudding. Serves 20.

Mrs. A. A. Batton, Port Gibson

DEEP SOUTH CHARLOTTE RUSSE

1 package of Knox gelatin
½ cup cold water
1 egg
¾ cup sugar
1 cup milk

½ cup whiskey or wine
1 pint whipped cream
chopped nuts, chopped
   cherries and cherry juice to
   taste (optional)

Dissolve gelatin in cold water. Beat egg and sugar until lemon color. Bring milk to boil; add to egg and sugar mixture. Return to heat and let come to boil. Remove and add to gelatin mixture. Let cool. Add spirits. When mixture thickens, fold in cream (if used, at this time add nuts and cherries). Dot with whipped cream when ready to serve. Serves 6.

Mrs. Charles Dean, Holly Springs

CREAM PUFFS

1 cup water	1 cup flour
½ cup shortening	4 unbeaten eggs
¼ teaspoon salt	any desired filling

Bring water, shortening and salt to boil. Stir in flour and cook until dough forms a smooth ball and leaves sides of saucepan clear. Remove from heat and cool slightly. Add eggs, one at a time, beating well after each addition. Drop by spoonfuls onto a greased cookie sheet and bake at 450 degrees for 10 minutes. Reduce heat to 400 degrees and bake 25 minutes more. Cool. Slit and fill with sweetened whipped cream, custard, chocolate or fruit filling. Yield: 12 large cream puffs.

Mrs. Virgil Burge, Poplarville

JELLY ROLL

3 eggs, beaten	1 teaspoon vanilla
1 cup sugar	confectioner's sugar
3 tablespoons water	jelly
1 cup self-rising flour	

Beat first five ingredients together and pour into a 12 x 14 jelly roll pan that has been thoroughly greased and lined with waxed paper. Bake at 350 degrees until done when touched. Turn out on waxed paper covered with confectioners sugar; peel off waxed paper from cake. Cover lavishly with jelly and roll quickly while hot. Wrap sugared paper around it and let set until cool, or eat while hot. This must be worked quickly after it is removed from oven. Serves 6 to 8.

Mrs. Hiram Kettle, West

MERINGUES

1 egg white	1 teaspoon vanilla
1 cup sifted brown sugar	2 cups chopped pecans

Beat egg white stiff. Add sugar and vanilla. Fold in, by hand, chopped pecans. Form small tart size meringues on ungreased baking sheet and bake at 225 degrees about 50 minutes.

Mrs. Martin Carroll, Newton

SUGARLESS MERINGUES

2 egg whites
⅛ teaspoon salt
¼ teaspoon cornstarch

¼ teaspoon vanilla flavoring
½ cup red label Karo

Beat egg whites till frothy, add salt and cornstarch and continue to beat until stiff peak is formed. Add vanilla. Add Karo, 1 tablespoon at the time, beating thoroughly after each addition. When all is added and meringue is stiff and glossy, place on ungreased baking sheet or brown paper by the large spoonful. Bake at 250 degrees for 1 hour or until dry. Cool 5 minutes, remove from sheet or paper. Serves 6.

Mrs. William J. Klaus, Cary

POLYNESIAN FRUIT

½ cup sugar
3 tablespoons cornstarch
3 tablespoons orange juice
1 tablespoon curry powder
1 pound green grapes

1 (16-ounce) can pineapple
    chunks
1 (16-ounce) can pears
1 (16-ounce) can coconut
1 small jar maraschino cherries

Combine sugar, cornstarch and orange juice with juice from pineapple and pears and cook until mixture thickens, stirring constantly. Let cool and add curry powder. Combine with grapes, pineapple, pears, coconut and cherries. Let chill 6 to 8 hours before serving. Serves 10.

Mrs. Emma Mackey, Batesville

HOT FRUIT CASSEROLE

1 (16-ounce) can pineapple
    chunks
1 (no. 2½) can sliced peaches
1 (no. 303) can cut pears
1 (no. 2½) can whole blue
    plums or pitted black
    cherries

2 cut bananas
1 (no. 2½) can applesauce
1 small bottle cherries
1/3 cup butter
¾ cup brown sugar

Drain fruit, with the exception of the cherries. Melt butter with brown sugar and applesauce, heating to boiling point. Place all fruit in a 9 x 14 baking dish and pour the hot sauce over the fruit. (Sprinkling with 3 tablespoons brown sugar and 1 cup chopped pecans is optional.) Bake 1 hour at 300 degrees. Serves 12.

Mrs. Rowland A. Doerr, Brookhaven

AMBROSIA

12 oranges
1 (20-ounce) can crushed
  pineapple
¼ cup sugar

1 grated coconut
1 (6-ounce) bottle red or
  green cherries

Peel and skin oranges. Chop, removing seeds. Place in large bowl and add pineapple, including juice. Add sugar and stir. Stir in half of grated coconut and place bowl in refrigerator. Serve in sherbet glasses and top with coconut and cherries. Serves 12.

Mrs. Gayle Ross, Fayette

BELGIAN DESSERT

½ pound crushed vanilla
  wafers
¾ cup butter or oleo
1 pound confectioners sugar
2 slightly beaten eggs.
4 tablespoons whiskey

½ pint whipping cream,
  whipped
1 (no. 2) can crushed
  pineapple
¾ cup chopped pecans

Line bottom of a buttered 8 x 12 x 2-inch pyrex pan with crushed vanilla wafers. Save ¼ cup of wafer crumbs for top. Cream butter and sugar well. Add eggs and continue to cream well. Add whiskey to the creamed mixture and pour over wafers. Over this spread the whipped cream. Dot with *well drained* pineapple. Sprinkle nuts over this. Top with crumbs. Cover and refrigerate. Keeps one week and is better if made at least 24 hours before serving. Serves 12.

Mrs. J. H. McCaleb, Clarksdale

SINFUL DESSERT

2 tablespoons chocolate
  syrup
1 large scoop vanilla ice
  cream

2 tablespoons fresh
  grated coconut
1½ tablespoons crème de
  menthe

Layer into a sherbet dish the syrup, ice cream and coconut, one on top of the other. Pour the crème de menthe over all and serve. Serves 1.

Hazel H. Bequette, Mayersville

ANGEL DESSERT

1 pound size angel food cake	1 pint semi-thawed
3 quarts softened vanilla	strawberries
ice cream	1 cup chopped pecans
1 (8¼-ounce) can crushed,	½ pint whipping cream
drained pineapple	

Break cake into small pieces. Mix ice cream with cake. Add crushed, drained pineapple, strawberries and pecans. Mix well. Whip the cream and fold into mixture. Pour mixture into a 17 x 11½ x 2½-inch pan. Cover and freeze. Remove from freezer shortly before serving so it will slice and serve easily. Serves 12 to 15.

Mrs. Dave Thomas, Clarksdale

COBBLER

1/3 cup oleo	1 cup flour
1 cup sugar	pinch salt
½ cup milk	1 (1-pound 13-ounce) can
2 teaspoons baking powder	peaches

Cream shortening and sugar together. Add other ingredients. Heat desired fruit (can of peaches and syrup). Pour batter in greased baking dish. Pour fruit and syrup over top. Bake at 375 degrees for 45 to 50 minutes. Serves 6.

Mrs. Marilyn J. Bailey, Prentiss

BUTTERED APPLES

1 cup sugar	butter
¼ teaspoon salt	jelly (any kind)
1 cup water	2 tablespoons sugar
6 medium tart apples	

Combine sugar, water and salt in a saucepan. Bring to boiling point. Peel and core apples. Leave whole and place in boiling syrup. Cover

[330]

and cook until half done (about 10 minutes). Transfer apples from syrup to a buttered baking dish. Fill the cavities with butter, spread with jelly and sprinkle with sugar. Bake at 375 degrees for 30 minutes or until tender. Serves 6.

Mrs. Daisy Burnett, Charleston

HONEY GLAZED BAKED APPLES

6 large tart apples
6 tablespoons honey
¼ cup orange juice

sugar
nutmeg

Core apples, being careful not to cut all the way through. Peel about 1/3 way down from stem end. Combine honey and orange juice and pour into center of apples. Set in baking dish. Pour a little hot water in bottom of pan. Bake at 400 degrees for 50 to 60 minutes, or until apples are tender. Remove from oven. Brush tops with additional honey, sprinkle with a little sugar and nutmeg. Run under broiler to glaze. Serve warm or cold with plain cream. Serves 6.

Mrs. C. E. Orr, Corinth

APPLE CRUNCH

1 (no. 303) can sliced apples
2/3 cup sugar
½ box cake mix (regular size),
    yellow, white or spice

1 stick oleo
½ cup chopped pecans

Empty apples into buttered 8 or 9-inch square baking dish. Sprinkle sugar over apples. Sprinkle cake mix evenly over apples. Melt oleo and pour evenly over cake mix. Sprinkle pecans over oleo. Bake at 350 degrees until done and a crust has formed on top, about 1 hour. Serves 9.

Mrs. Berlin Tindoll, Vaiden

APRICOT CAKE

2 sticks butter
2 cups sifted powdered sugar
4 whole eggs, well beaten
1 pound crushed vanilla wafers

2 cups chopped pecans
2 cups sweet whipped cream
1 (no. 2½) can peeled apricots,
    drained and mashed

[331]

Cream butter and sugar, add eggs and cook in double boiler until thick. Cool. Butter a 9 x 13 x 2-inch dish and spread 2/3 of crushed vanilla crumbs on bottom of dish. Pour custard mixture over the crumbs. Add 1 cup nuts, ½ cup whipped cream, all the mashed apricots, the remaining whipped cream, remainder of nuts and balance of crumbs. Refrigerate for 24 hours. Slice and serve. Serves 12.

Mrs. Charles Morganti, Friars Point

EGGNOG TORTONI

1 cup dairy eggnog
1 slightly beaten egg yolk
¼ teaspoon vanilla extract
¼ teaspoon almond extract
¼ teaspoon salt
1/3 cup vanilla wafer crumbs
¼ cup finely chopped toasted
   almonds or pecans
¼ cup finely grated toasted
   coconut
1 stiffly beaten egg white
2 tablespoons sugar
½ cup whipping cream,
   whipped

Combine eggnog and egg yolk. Cook and stir just until mixture starts to bubble. Cool. Add flavorings and salt. Stir in the vanilla wafer crumbs, nuts and coconut. Beat egg white with sugar till soft peaks form. Fold into eggnog mixture. Fold in whipped cream. Spoon into 8 paper baking cups set in a muffin pan. Freeze firm, 4 hours or overnight. Serves 8.

Ursula Morton, Brookhaven

EGG CUSTARD

¾ cup sugar (scant)
2 heaping tablespoons flour
¼ teaspoon salt
4 eggs
2 cups homogenized milk
2 teaspoons vanilla flavoring
1 teaspoon butter flavoring
1 (10-inch) unbaked pastry
   shell

Mix in order given. Pour into pastry shell, sprinkle top lightly with nutmeg and bake about 25 or 30 minutes at 350 degrees.

Mrs. M. T. Brooks, Wiggins

POTATO CUSTARD

2 cups sugar
3 teaspoons flour
2 eggs
1 stick oleo
1 teaspoon vanilla flavoring
1 teaspoon lemon flavoring
1 cup mashed sweet potatoes
1 (8-inch) unbaked pastry
   shell

Mix sugar and flour. Slightly beat eggs and stir in sugar and flour. Cut oleo into mixture; add vanilla and lemon flavorings. Add cup of potatoes and mix; pour into pastry shell. Cook 45 minutes at 350 degrees.

Mrs. S. V. Kelley, Quitman

SWEET POTATO CUSTARD

1½ cups sugar
1 stick margarine
1 (5 1/3-ounce) can evaporated
  milk
2 eggs, beaten
3 tablespoons plain all-purpose
  flour

1 cup cooked sweet potatoes
1 teaspoon lemon flavoring
1 teaspoon vanilla flavoring
1 (9-inch) unbaked pie shell
½ teaspoon nutmeg

Mash potatoes and sieve out any stringy parts. Mix all ingredients except nutmeg and put into unbaked pie shell. Sprinkle nutmeg over top. Bake at 350 degrees for about 35 minutes. Serves 6.

Mrs. Cora Stubbs, Magee

PINK DESSERT

1 cup flour
¼ cup brown sugar
½ cup finely chopped nuts
¼ cup melted butter
2 egg whites

2/3 cup sugar
2 teaspoons lemon juice
1 pound frozen strawberries
1 cup whipped cream or
  other whipped topping

Stir together flour, brown sugar, nuts and melted butter and spread in a shallow pan. Bake at 300 degrees for 20 minutes. Stir occasionally. Sprinkle 2/3 of this crumb mixture in a 9 x 13-inch pan. Reserve 1/3 of crumbs. Combine egg whites, sugar, lemon juice and strawberries in large bowl and beat at high speed until stiff peak forms (about 20 minutes). Fold in whipped cream and spread over crumbs. Top with remaining crumbs and put in freezer overnight. Serves 15.

Mrs. Curtis Riley, Duck Hill

BLUEBERRY DESSERT

½ cup melted butter
½ cup chopped pecans
1 1/3 cups graham cracker
  crumbs
½ cup milk

½ pound marshmallows (24)
½ pint cream, whipped
1 can prepared blueberry pie
  filling
1 tablespoon lemon juice

Combine milk and marshmallows in top of double boiler. Stir until melted. Cool but don't let thicken. Combine melted butter, pecans and cracker crumbs. Spread half of mixture in buttered 8-inch cake pan. Combine whipped cream and marshmallow-milk mixture. Spread half on top of crumbs. Mix blueberry filling and lemon juice and spread on top of whipped cream layer. Cover with remaining whipped cream mixture and top with remaining crumbs. Chill overnight. Serves 12.

Mrs. O. R. Diamond, McComb

BLUEBERRY DESSERT PIE

1 (8-ounce) package cream
   cheese
½ cup confectioners sugar

1 cup cream, whipped
1 can blueberry dessert
1 (9-inch) pie shell, baked

Mix cream cheese and sugar until smooth. Beat whipping cream until it holds soft peaks. Fold into cheese mixture. Pour into baked and cooled pie shell. Top with blueberry dessert. Chill in refrigerator at least 2 hours before serving. Serves 8.

Mrs. Robert K. McDonald, Biloxi

LEMON TARTS

3 cups sifted flour, plain
1½ teaspoons salt
1 cup shortening
6 tablespoons cold water
   (approximately)
grated rind of 2 medium
   lemons

½ cup lemon juice
2 cups sugar
1 cup butter
4 eggs, well beaten

Sift flour and salt, cut in shortening until size of large peas. Sprinkle water over mixture; mix thoroughly until a smooth dough is formed. Roll on floured surface to ⅛-inch thick; cut into rounds; fit in muffin tins. Prick. Bake at 450 degrees for 10 to 15 minutes until brown.

Combine rind, juice and sugar in top of double boiler. Add butter. Heat over boiling water, stirring until butter is melted. Stir in eggs. Continue cooking, stirring constantly, till mixture is thick enough to pile slightly. Cool thoroughly. Spoon into baked tart shells. Makes 4 dozen.

Mrs. C. S. Woodruff, Boyle

DESSERTS

CHERRY CHEESE TARTS

1¼ cups graham cracker
    crumbs
2 tablespoons sugar
2/3 stick butter
1 (8-ounce) package cream
    cheese

1 egg
1 teaspoon salt
4 tablespoons sugar
1 can of cherry pie filling

Combine first three ingredients for tart shells. Use cupcake papers set in muffin tins. Press crumb mixture onto bottom and sides. Then mix remaining ingredients except cherry pie filling with mixer until very smooth. Place 1 tablespoon of the mixture in each paper cup and bake in 325 degree oven for 10 minutes. After out of oven, put ½ teaspoon of cherry pie topping on each tart. Let stand in cupcake pan until completely cooled to prevent papers from spreading out. Put in refrigerator until serving time. Serves 8 to 10.

Mrs. Pat Stephens, Dennis

PECAN TASSIES

1 cup plain flour
3-ounces cream cheese
1 stick oleo
1 egg

2/3 cup chopped pecans
1 teaspoon vanilla
¾ cup brown sugar

Mix flour, cheese and oleo until well blended. Chill for about 1 hour. Make into small balls, (approximately 24) and press into small muffin tins. Combine remaining ingredients for filling and put into pastry lined tins, filling each about ¾ full. Bake for 30 minutes at 325 degrees. Can be frozen. Serves approximately 24.

Mrs. X. L. Carney, Crystal Springs

BLACKBERRY JAM TRIFLE

18 lady fingers
3 dozen almond macaroons
1 cup chopped nuts

1½ cups blackberry jam
¾ cup sherry
½ pint cream, whipped

Split the lady fingers. Cover the bottom of an ungreased 9 x 9 x 2-inch dish with half the split lady fingers. Crumble the macaroons and sprinkle half the crumbs over the lady fingers. Spread the chopped nuts over the crumbs. Spread the blackberry jam over the nuts, and sprinkle on remaining macaroon crumbs. On top, arrange remaining split lady fingers. Spoon the sherry evenly over the lady fingers. Refrigerate for several hours before cutting into squares. Whip the cream and serve on the squares. Serves 8 to 10.

Mrs. Carl H. Gerrard, Clarksdale

PINEAPPLE DELIGHT

2 dozen graham crackers
2 whole eggs, beaten
1 cup sugar
1 (no. 1½) can crushed pineapple
1 (3-ounce) box of lemon flavored gelatin

1 (14½-ounce) can of evaporated milk, chilled
½ pint of whipping cream
2 teaspoons sugar

Line an ungreased 8 x 12 x 2-inch pyrex dish with graham crackers. Beat eggs, add sugar and stir well. Place over low heat and stir while sugar melts and mixture starts to cook. Add whole can of crushed pineapple. While stirring, bring to a simmer and let bubble for 3 minutes. Stir in lemon flavored gelatin in powder form, and remove from heat to cool slightly. Whip well the pre-chilled evaporated milk in large bowl and fold cooled mixture into it. Pour into graham cracker crust. Whip whipping cream and sweeten with 2 teaspoons of sugar. Spread cream over top of dessert and let chill. Do not freeze. Cut into squares. Serves 12.

Mrs. W. B. White, Booneville

NO CHOCOLATE BROWNIES

4 eggs
1 pound light brown sugar
1½ cups flour (plain)

1½ teaspoons baking powder
1 teaspoon vanilla
1 cup chopped nuts

Beat eggs well in a bowl. Beat in the light brown sugar. Heat the mixture over a double boiler until sugar is melted. Remove from heat. Sift together flour and baking powder. Add this to egg-sugar mixture. Add the vanilla and chopped nuts. Pour into a 13 x 9 x 2-inch pan, bake at 350 degrees for 20 to 25 minutes. Let cool and cut into squares. Serves 12.

Miss Kathleen Butler, Summit

FROSTED PINEAPPLE SQUARES

½ cup sugar
3 tablespoons cornstarch
¼ teaspoon salt
1 egg yolk, lightly beaten
1 (1-pound 13½-ounce) can
  crushed pineapple, undrained
2/3 cup milk
1 teaspoon sugar
1 package active dry yeast
¼ cup warm water (105 to
  115 degrees)

½ teaspoon salt
4 egg yolks, lightly beaten
4 cups sifted flour
1 cup margarine
1½ cups sifted powdered
  sugar
1 to 2 tablespoons milk
½ teaspoon vanilla

Mix ½ cup sugar, cornstarch and salt in saucepan. Stir in egg yolk and crushed pineapple. Cook over medium heat, stirring constantly until thick and smooth, about 7 minutes. Cool to lukewarm while preparing dough. Scald milk, add 1 teaspoon sugar, cool to lukewarm. Dissolve yeast in warm water, add to milk mixture. Stir in beaten egg yolks. Measure flour into large bowl, cut margarine into flour, using pastry blender, until mixture resembles coarse meal. Stir in yeast and milk mixture. Blend thoroughly. Dough will be soft and moist. Divide in half. Roll half out on floured board to fit bottom of jelly roll pan and overlap edges, about 16 x 10 inches. Spread with cooled pineapple filling. Roll remaining dough large enough to cover filling. Seal edges. Snip surface of dough with scissors to let steam escape. Cover, let rise in warm place, free from draft, until doubled in bulk, about 1 hour. Bake at 375 degrees for 35 to 40 minutes. Frost with icing made of the powdered sugar, milk and vanilla. Serves 15.

Mrs. John Foster, Natchez

LEMON SQUARES

1½ cups sifted flour
½ teaspoon salt
¼ teaspoon double acting
  baking powder
3 eggs, separated
1 cup confectioners sugar
½ cup butter
1 cup sugar

1/3 cup lemon juice
2 tablespoons grated lemon
  rind
1 cup confectioners sugar
1 tablespoon cream
2 tablespoons butter
chopped nuts

Sift together flour, salt and baking powder. Beat egg whites until soft mounds begin to form. Add 1 cup confectioners sugar gradually, beating after each addition. Continue beating until stiff, straight peaks are formed. Cream butter; add 1 cup sugar creaming well. Add egg yolks, one at a time. Beat for 1 minute. Add lemon juice alternately with dry ingredients. Blend thoroughly. Add grated lemon rind. Fold in beaten egg whites gently but thoroughly. Pour into well greased and lightly floured 13 x 9 x 2-inch pan. Bake in 350 degree oven 25 to 30 minutes. Combine remaining ingredients, except nuts and frost cake in pan while warm. Sprinkle with chopped nuts. Serves 12.

Mrs. Virginia Jones, Tylertown

LEMON SQUARES

2 cups sifted flour (plain)
1 cup butter
½ cup powdered sugar
4 eggs, beaten well
¼ cup lemon juice
1 tablespoon powdered sugar
2 cups granulated sugar

Blend butter, ½ cup powdered sugar and flour with pastry blender until well mixed and press into ungreased glass pan, 12 x 8½-inch (or larger). Bake 20 minutes at 350 degrees. Beat eggs, lemon juice and sugars together well and pour over hot crust. Bake 15 minutes at 350 degrees. Serves 8 to 10.

Mrs. W. V. Price, Cleveland

GINGERBREAD

½ cup margarine
½ cup sugar
½ cup Brer Rabbit syrup
   (no substitute)
2 eggs, beaten
1 teaspoon soda
½ cup sour milk
1½ cups plain flour
1 teaspoon ginger
1 teaspoon allspice
1 heaping teaspoon plain flour
1 cup sugar
1 egg yolk
½ cup sweet milk
4 teaspoons margarine
2 tablespoons brandy or 2
   teaspoons rum flavoring

Cream margarine and sugar. Add syrup and beat in eggs. Then add soda to sour milk, mix and stir into creamed mixture alternately with flour and spices, which have been sifted together. Bake in heavy greased and floured pan (9-inch iron skillet is great for this) at 350 degrees until done when tested with straw. This makes a delicate, tender gingerbread and care should be taken not to overcook. Serve warm or cold with sauce made of the last six ingredients. To make sauce, mix flour and sugar. Beat egg yolk, add to sweet milk and stir into flour and sugar. Add butter. Pour into heavy saucepan and cook over low to moderate heat, stirring constantly, until slightly thicken (it thickens more as it cools). Add desired flavoring after removing from heat.

Mrs. Kate Woods, Starkville

GINGERBREAD

½ cup sugar
½ cup shortening
2 eggs
2½ cups sifted all-purpose
 flour
3 teaspoons ginger

1 teaspoon cinnamon
1 cup buttermilk
1 cup molasses (Louisiana
 cane)
2 teaspoons soda
¼ cup boiling water

Work sugar into shortening, add slightly beaten eggs. Stir in flour, spices and buttermilk. Beat in molasses. Dissolve soda in boiling water. While foaming stir into mixture. Beat 2 minutes. Pour into two greased 10-inch square pans. Bake 30 minutes at 350 degrees. Serves 10.

Evelyn D. Sullivan, Port Gibson

GINGERBREAD WITH WHISKEY SAUCE

¾ cup sugar
½ cup butter or shortening
1 egg, beaten well
1 cup dark molasses
2½ cups sifted all-purpose
 flour
1½ teaspoons soda
1 teaspoon cinnamon
1 teaspoon ginger

½ teaspoon cloves
¼ teaspoon salt
1 cup hot water
½ pound powdered sugar
1 egg
½ stick butter
whiskey to taste (about ¼
 cup)

Cream sugar and butter; add egg. Mix well. Add molasses to mix. Sift dry ingredients together then gradually add to mixture. Add hot water; mix well. Bake in greased 9 x 13-inch pan in 350 degree oven for 40 to 45 minutes.

Cream powdered sugar and butter, add egg and beat well. Add

whiskey slowly, beating all the time. Serve sauce on top of cake. Serves 12.

Mrs. Jim Alexander, Houston

EASY FRUIT COBBLER

1 stick butter or margarine	¾ cup milk
1 cup sugar	dash of salt
1 cup flour	1 can pie fruit
1 teaspoon baking powder	

Melt butter in 8 x 8 x 2-inch pan or pyrex dish. Mix all other ingredients except fruit in separate bowl. Pour this over butter. Add pie fruit last. Bake at 350 degrees 45 to 60 minutes or until crust is golden brown. Serves 8.

Mrs. Frank W. Skinner, Jr., Vicksburg

CHEESE CAKE

2 envelopes unflavored gelatin	1 cup heavy cream, whipped
1 cup sugar	2 tablespoons melted butter or margarine
¼ teaspoon salt	½ cup chocolate cookie crumbs
2 eggs, separated	
1 (6-ounce) can frozen concentrated orange juice, thawed	
3 cups (24-ounces) creamed cottage cheese sieved	

Mix gelatin, ¾ cup sugar and salt in top of double boiler. Beat egg yolks and orange juice; add to gelatin mixture. Cook over boiling water, stirring constantly, until gelatin dissolves and mixture thickens, about 10 minutes. Remove from heat; cool. Stir in cottage cheese. Chill, stirring occasionally, until mixture mounds slightly when dropped from a spoon. Beat egg whites until stiff but not dry; gradually add remaining ¼ cup sugar and beat until very stiff. Fold into mixture. Blend in whipped cream. Pour into an 8-inch spring form pan. Combine butter and cookie crumbs; sprinkle over top of cake; chill until firm. Serves 10 to 12.

Mrs. Charles Leon, Canton

GERMAN CHEESE CAKE

1 cup sifted all-purpose
   flour
2 tablespoons sugar
¼ teaspoon salt
¼ cup softened butter
1 egg, slightly beaten
2 (8-ounce) packages cream
   cheese

2 cups sour cream
2 egg yolks, well beaten
2 teaspoons vanilla
½ lemon rind, grated
1/3 cup cornstarch
1 cup sugar
3 egg whites, stiffly beaten

Sift flour, 2 tablespoons sugar and salt together. Make well in center of flour mixture and add softened butter and 1 slightly beaten egg. Quickly mix together with flour. Shape dough into ball, wrap in waxed paper, and store in refrigerator for 2 hours. Set out a 9-inch spring-form pan, grease and flour bottom. Remove dough from refrigerator and roll out as for pie crust, on lightly floured surface. Cover bottom of pan only with dough, bake at 450 degrees for 10 minutes. Cool. Combine softened cream cheese and sour cream; beat until creamy; add well beaten egg yolks, vanilla, lemon rind, cornstarch and sugar. Beat well, fold in stiffly beaten egg whites. Pour onto cooled crust in spring-form pan. Bake at 350 degrees for 40 minutes and 375 degrees for 20 minutes. Turn off oven and open door slightly. Let cake cool in oven for at least 30 minutes.

Mrs. L. C. Ryan, Booneville

ICE BOX CHEESE CAKE

1 small package lemon
   gelatin
1 cup hot water
1 large can chilled evaporated
   milk
1 tablespoon lemon juice,
   if desired

8 ounces cream cheese,
   softened
1 cup sugar
2 teaspoons vanilla
graham cracker crust

Pour hot water over gelatin, stir until dissolved, set aside to cool. Whip can of evaporated milk (cold) until stiff. Add lemon juice to taste. Cream softened cheese with sugar. When gelatin begins to thicken, mix into cheese mixture. Fold in whipped milk and vanilla. Pour into graham cracker crust. Let set several hours to firm and ripen.

Mrs. Everett Smith, Chunky

[341]

DATE CRISPIES

1 stick oleo
1 pound dates, chopped
2 egg yolks
¾ cup sugar

1 cup pecans
1 cup coconut
2 cups Rice Krispies

Melt oleo in pan. Add dates and cook until soft. Remove from heat. Beat egg yolks and sugar. Add to date mixture. Add pecans, coconut and Rice Krispies. Mix well and form into balls. Roll balls in coconut. These can be frozen.

Mrs. Jack Ross, Hazlehurst

⁚[Cakes and Icings]⁚

A cake is perhaps the universal dessert. There are almost as many different cake recipes as there are cooks. A young bride cherishes the recipe for Grandmother's pound cake and Auntie's Christmas fruit cake. A popular Southern custom is to take a freshly baked cake to a friend who is ill, to a new neighbor down the street, or to an acquaintance who has done a special favor.

There are two classes of cakes, butter and sponge. Butter cakes are made with shortening, margarine or butter. True sponge or foam-type cakes have no fat and no liquid or leavening except that furnished by the eggs.

Frostings or icings of various kinds are used for decorating cakes. They are used both between the layers and on the outside, whereas fillings are used only on the inside of cakes.

Frostings may be either cooked or uncooked. They should always be adapted to the cake or other food on which they are to be used. If the cake is rich, frostings should be plain, and vice versa. Sponge cakes and rich cakes are often served without icings.

GRANDMOTHER'S BLACKBERRY JAM CAKE

¾ cup butter	½ cup of sweet milk
1 cup sugar	1 cup blackberry jam
3 eggs	1 teaspoon each, soda,
2½ cups flour	cinnamon, all-spice, cloves
1 teaspoon cream of tartar	

ICING:

2 cups sugar	1 cup cream
¼ cup butter	½ teaspoon vanilla

Cream butter and sugar. Add beaten eggs and beat well. Then combine flour and cream of tartar and add alternately with milk. Add jam, mixing well. Then add soda, all-spice, cloves and cinnamon. Pour into two 9-inch layer pans which have been greased and lined with waxed paper. Bake at 350 degrees for 30 minutes. Cool.

To make the icing, cook 1½ cups sugar with cream. Melt remaining ½ cup sugar, then add to the cooked sugar and cream. Cook until soft ball forms when icing is dropped in water. Remove from heat. Add butter and beat. Stir in vanilla and spread on layers.

Felders Camp Ground, located eight miles east of Summit, Mississippi, is the site of an annual ten-day workshop and fellowship attended by members of the Felder family and their friends. One of the highlights of these annual occasions is the sharing of fine food. Grandmother's Blackberry Jam Cake has been a dessert favorite for many years.

Mrs. Charles W. Felder, Summit

APPLE BUTTER CAKE

1 (18-ounce) jar apple butter	3 teaspoons soda (dissolved
½ cup sugar	in 3 teaspoons water)
3 eggs	1 tablespoon nutmeg
1 cup butter	1 tablespoon cinnamon
1 cup pecans, chopped	1 tablespoon all-spice
1 cup raisins	3 cups sifted all-purpose
	flour

ICING:

4 egg yolks	2 cups raisins
1 cup sour milk	2 cups pecans
½ cup butter	2 cups fresh coconut
2 cups sugar	

Cream apple butter, sugar, eggs and butter. Stir in nuts and raisins. Mix well. Blend in soda. Sift spices and flour together. Stir into butter mixture. Pour into two 9-inch layer pans that have been greased and floured. Bake at 350 degrees for 30 minutes.

For icing, cook egg yolks, milk, butter and sugar until thick. Stir in raisins, pecans and coconut. Spread between layers. Cake will make 20 servings.

Mrs. Wade Parker, Perkinston

OLD FASHIONED JAM CAKE

1 cup butter	1 tablespoon nutmeg
2 cups sugar	1 tablespoon cinnamon
6 eggs	1 teaspoon cloves
4 cups cake flour	1½ cups buttermilk
1 teaspoon soda	2 cups blackberry jam

Cream butter and sugar together, add eggs one at a time. Sift flour, soda, and spices together, then add flour mixture alternately with the buttermilk. Add jam last. Bake in greased and floured 9-inch layer cake pans at 350 degrees for 35 minutes. Remove from pan, cool and frost with caramel frosting. Makes 4 layers.

Mrs. C. B. Perry, Sr., Walls

FIG PRESERVE CAKE

2 cups flour	1 teaspoon cinnamon
1 teaspoon salt	1 cup cooking oil
1 teaspoon soda	3 eggs
2 tablespoons cornstarch	1 cup buttermilk
1½ cups sugar	1 cup chopped fig preserves
1 teaspoon nutmeg	½ cup chopped pecans
½ teaspoon cloves	1 tablespoon vanilla

SAUCE:

1 cup sugar	1 tablespoon corn syrup
½ cup buttermilk	½ teaspoon soda
1 tablespoon butter or margarine	

Sift together flour, salt, soda, cornstarch, sugar and spices in large bowl, add oil and beat well. Add eggs one at a time, beat well. Add buttermilk and beat. Stir in fig preserves, nuts and vanilla. Mix well.

[345]

Pour into a 9 x 13 inch greased pan and bake 45 minutes at 325 degrees or until tested done.

Mix all of the last five ingredients together and boil 3 to 5 minutes. Pour over warm cake.

Mrs. Steve Frank, Egypt

STRAWBERRY PRESERVE CAKE

2 quarter-pound sticks
  of margarine
2 cups of sugar
4 eggs
1 cup buttermilk
1 teaspoon soda

1 cup strawberry preserves
1 teaspoon vanilla
½ teaspoon ground cloves
1 teaspoon cinnamon
3 cups all-purpose flour
1 cup chopped pecans

Cream margarine and sugar together. Add eggs one at a time, stirring well after each addition. Stir soda into buttermilk; add to mixture. Add strawberry preserves and vanilla. Mix well. Mix cloves, cinnamon and flour; add to mixture. Blend well and stir in nuts. Pour into greased and floured 10-inch tube pan. Bake 1 hour and 15 minutes in a 325 degree oven. Do not open oven for first hour. Makes 15 or more slices.

Mrs. E. G. Woodward, Hattiesburg

DELTA DELIGHT FRUIT CAKE

8 eggs
2 cups sugar
3 cups flour (plain)
2 teaspoons baking powder
1 teaspoon salt
3 tablespoons vanilla
  flavoring
1 tablespoon almond
  flavoring

2 pounds dates or 1 pound
  dates and 1 pound white
  raisins
1 pound candied pineapple
1 pound candied cherries
8 cups pecans

Beat eggs well, add sugar and cream well. Add flour, baking powder, salt, vanilla and almond flavoring. Mix well. Add chopped dates, raisins, pineapple (cut large), whole cherries, and whole pecans. Pack in 6 (7 x 3 x 2-inch) pans which have been lined with well greased and floured brown paper. Bake for 1½ hours in 250 degree oven which has pan of hot water on bottom rack. Remove water last 30 minutes. Wrap in foil while hot. *Mrs. Weyman Carty, Pheba*

KENTUCKY BOURBON CAKE

2 cups bourbon
½ pound golden raisins
1 pound red candied
  cherries, halved
3 sticks butter
1 pound granulated sugar
6 eggs, beaten separately
1 pound light brown sugar

2 teaspoons fresh grated
  nutmeg
1 teaspoon baking powder
5 cups flour, sifted before
  measuring
1 pound nut meats, finely
  chopped
½ cup white corn syrup,
  heated

Pour bourbon over raisins and cherries. Soak in covered bowl 48 hours, or longer if need be. Before mixing in cake, drain fruit well, and reserve bourbon. Soften butter at room temperature and cream until light. Add granulated sugar and continue creaming until fluffy. Beat egg yolks until very light, then add brown sugar and beat well to dissolve sugar. Combine the two sugar mixtures and blend thoroughly. (Do not hurry this process!) Mix nutmeg and baking powder with 4½ cups of the flour; combine remaining ½ cup flour with the nuts. Add flour mixture and bourbon alternately to butter-sugar-egg mixture, mixing thoroughly after each addition. Add soaked fruit to creamed mixture, fold and blend; then the flour-nut mixture, and mix again. Beat egg whites until stiff but not dry. Fold into batter until evenly and completely blended. Pour into greased 10-inch tube pan lined with greased brown paper. Place pan of water in bottom of oven, and bake cake 3½ to 4 hours at 250-275 degrees. Watch baking time, as some ovens vary. Remove from oven and let set a few minutes before turning out to cool. When partially cooled, sponge top and sides heavily with bourbon-saturated cheesecloth. Cover the cake with this cloth, then wrap in plastic and let set overnight, or until thoroughly cold. Remove the wrap; pour the hot corn syrup over top of cake. When this has lost its "stickiness", stuff the center hole with cheesecloth which has been soaked in bourbon. Cover cake all over and around with the first piece of saturated cheesecloth. Wrap well with plastic wrap, then in foil, and store in airtight tin to mellow, at least a month before using. This makes a large and truly delicious cake.

Mrs. Kate Woods, Starkville

PINEAPPLE–COCONUT FRUITCAKE

3 cups sugar
½ pound butter
6 eggs
3½ cups flour
1 cup whiskey
  (mixture of coconut milk
  and orange juice (1 cup)
  may be used instead of
  whiskey, if desired)
3 teaspoons baking powder
1 teaspoon lemon extract
1 teaspoon almond extract

2 teaspoons vanilla
1 whole grated fresh coconut
1 pound shelled pecans
1 pound shelled walnuts
3 pounds candied pineapple
  (1 pound white, 1 pound
  red, 1 pound green)
1 pound candied cherries
½ pound candied citron
⅛ pound candied lemon peel
⅛ pound candied orange peel

Mix sugar, butter and eggs, beat well. Combine 2½ cups flour with baking powder. Add to egg mixture, alternating with whiskey (or fruit juice) to which extracts have been added. Add grated coconut to batter. Chop nuts, dredge with ½ cup flour. Add to batter. Chop fruits and peels. Dredge cut-up candied fruit and peels with remaining flour. Add to batter. Cook in loaf pans in very low oven (275 degrees) for 1½ hours for small cakes, 2 hours for large cakes. (Recipe makes 12 pounds of fruitcake). Keep cakes in air-tight containers from two weeks to 1 month. Season with wine or fruit juice to ripen. Chill thoroughly before slicing to avoid crumbling.

Mrs. L. L. Monroe, Jackson

WHITE FRUIT CAKE

3½ cups flour
1 pound candied pineapple
1 (15-ounce) box white
  raisins
1 pound candied cherries
4 cups chopped pecans

½ pound or 2 sticks
  butter
2 cups sugar
6 eggs
½ cup whiskey
1 teaspoon baking powder

Add ½ cup flour to fruits and nuts and set aside. Cream butter and sugar, add eggs and beat well. Add whiskey, flour and baking powder and mix in fruits and nuts. Bake in well greased and floured 10-inch tube pan about 1 hour and 15 minutes, or until done, at 250 degrees. Let set 10 minutes and remove to serving plate.

Mrs. H. McInnis, Leakesville

LEMON PECAN FRUITCAKE

1 (1-pound) box brown sugar
1 pound margarine
6 beaten egg yolks
2 cups flour
1 teaspoon baking powder
1 (2-ounce) bottle lemon
   extract

1 quart chopped pecans
½ pound candied pineapple,
   chopped
½ pound candied cherries,
   chopped
2 cups flour
6 beaten egg whites

Cream together sugar and margarine until smooth; add beaten egg yolks and mix well. Combine 2 cups flour and baking powder and add to creamed mixture. Add lemon extract. Coat pecans, pineapple and cherries with 2 cups flour and add to creamed mixture. Fold in beaten egg whites. Cover and let stand overnight.

The next day, put mixture into a greased 10-inch tube pan and bake at 250 degrees for 1½ hours.

Mrs. Jeannette Pyron, Winona

PECAN CAKE

1 (4-ounce) jar each red and
   green maraschino cherries
1 quart shelled pecans
2 (15-ounce) boxes seedless
   raisins
3½ cups all-purpose flour
1 cup butter or oleo

2 cups sugar
6 eggs
2 tablespoons baking powder
1 grated nutmeg
1 cup whiskey (grape juice
   may be substituted)

Mix cut-up cherries, nuts and raisins in ½ cup of flour. Cream butter and sugar. Add eggs one at a time beating well. Sift flour with baking powder and nutmeg. Add to butter and sugar mixture, adding whiskey alternately. Pour batter mixture over fruit and nuts. Mix well. Pour in greased 10-inch tube pan. Bake in 350 degree oven for 2 hours. Set a pan of water underneath. Makes about a 5 pound cake. Freezes well and is better if allowed to set for a week to mellow while wrapped in a cloth soaked in wine. Delicious!

Mrs. Louise G. Davis, Jackson

[349]

BLACK WALNUT CAKE

½ cup butter
2 cups brown sugar
3 beaten egg yolks
1 cup finely chopped or
  ground black walnut meats
2 cups flour

3 teaspoons baking powder
½ teaspoon salt
2/3 cup milk
1 teaspoon vanilla
3 stiffly beaten egg whites

ICING:
2 tablespoons butter
2 tablespoons cream

2 cups powdered sugar
1 teaspoon vanilla

Cream butter and sugar; add egg yolks and nut meats. Sift flour baking powder and salt. Add to creamed mixture alternately with the milk. Add vanilla and fold in stiffly beaten egg whites. Pour into 13 x 9 x 2-inch loaf pan and bake 1 hour and 10 minutes in a moderate oven (350 to 375 degrees).

To make icing cream the butter, cream and sugar until smooth. Add vanilla. Smooth icing on the cake, wrap cake in waxed paper and store in cake box for one to four weeks before cutting. This recipe makes 15 to 20 slices, depending on their thickness.

Mrs. Jim Oden, Ovett
Mrs. E. R. Rickman, Artesia

HOLIDAY CAKE

¾ pound (3 sticks) butter
2 cups white sugar
2¼ cups light brown
  sugar, packed
6 eggs

5½ cups sifted all purpose
  flour
¼ teaspoon salt
1 teaspoon mace
2 cups bourbon whiskey
3½ cups pecans, chopped

Cream butter until soft in large bowl. Combine white and brown sugars thoroughly. Gradually work half the sugar mixture into butter, keeping it as smooth as possible. In a separate bowl, beat eggs until light and fluffy. Gradually beat in remaining sugar until you have a smooth, creamy mixture. Stir egg mixture into butter mixture thoroughly. Sift flour, salt and mace together. Add flour combination and whiskey alternately to batter, beginning and ending with flour. Break pecans into pieces and stir into batter. Pour into a well greased 10-inch tube pan. Batter should almost fill the pan. Bake in preheated 300 degree oven for 2½ hours or until cake shrinks slightly from pan. Allow to cool in the pan for 15 minutes, then turn out onto cake rack to cool completely. Cake improves with age. It should be well wrapped in foil and stored in refrigerator. Do not freeze.

Mrs. J. B. Graves, Gulfport

MOLASSES CAKE

½ cup butter or margarine
½ cup sugar
2 egg yolks
1 cup molasses
½ cup seedless raisins
¾ cup chopped nuts
2½ cups self-rising flour

½ teaspoon salt
¼ teaspoon all-spice
¼ teaspoon cloves
1 teaspoon cinnamon
½ cup milk
2 egg whites, stiffly beaten

ICING:

3 tablespoons molasses
3 tablespoons evaporated
  milk
3 tablespoons coffee (liquid)

4 tablespoons butter
1 teaspoon vanilla
powdered sugar

Cream butter and sugar together. Beat in egg yolks. Stir in molasses, nuts and raisins. Sift flour, salt and spices together. Fold in flour and milk alternately. Fold in beaten egg whites. Bake in three 9-inch cake pans for approximately 30 minutes in 350 degree oven. Make an icing by combining molasses, evaporated milk, coffee, butter and vanilla. Add enough powdered sugar to make spreading consistency. Spread between layers and on top. Sprinkle chopped nuts over top and between layers.

Mrs. E. L. Steele, Bruce

ORANGE SLICE CAKE

1 pound candy orange slices
1 (8-ounce) package dates
2 cups chopped nuts
3½-ounces coconut
3½ cups plain flour

1 cup butter or margarine
2 cups sugar
4 eggs
1 teaspoon baking soda
1 cup buttermilk

GLAZE:

1 small can frozen undiluted
  orange juice

2 cups powdered sugar

[351]

Chop candy orange slices and dates. Coat orange slices, dates, nuts and coconut with ½ cup flour and set aside. Cream margarine or butter and sugar. Add eggs, one at a time, mixing well after each addition. Dissolve soda in buttermilk. Alternately add remaining 3 cups flour and milk to creamed mixture. Fold nut-candy mixture into batter. Bake in greased 10-inch tube pan for 2 to 2½ hours at 275 degrees.

Mix the orange juice and powdered sugar well and pour over hot cake. Let stand until the glaze has soaked into cake.

Mrs. Charles Porter, Tupelo

PLUM CAKE

2 cups self-rising flour, sifted
2 cups sugar
3 eggs
2 small jars plum baby food
1 teaspoon cinnamon
1 teaspoon cloves
¾ cup cooking oil
1 cup chopped nuts

Combine all ingredients adding oil last and mix well. Pour into a greased and floured tube pan and cook at 350 degrees for one hour.

Cheri Simpson, Jackson

AMBROSIA CAKE

½ cup butter or shortening
2 cups sugar
3 eggs
3 cups sifted cake flour (sift three times)
1 cup buttermilk
2 scant teaspoons soda in buttermilk
½ teaspoon cloves
1 teaspoon cinnamon
1 teaspoon nutmeg
½ cup cocoa dissolved in ½ cup hot water

ICING:
3 cups sugar
1½ cups sweet milk
1 teaspoon baking powder
1 pinch soda
¼ cup butter
1 grated coconut
1 cup chopped nuts
1 cup seeded raisins
juice of 1 orange with grated rind

Cream butter and sugar. Add eggs, beating well. Add sifted flour and milk with soda alternately beating well after each addition. Add cloves, cinnamon and nutmeg. Add cocoa and hot water last. Bake in three 8-inch round layer cake pans at 350 degrees for 30 minutes or until done. Make an icing using remaining ingredients.

To make icing, boil first four ingredients until a soft ball forms. Remove from heat, then add butter and remaining ingredients. Spread on cake while slightly warm.

Mrs. Mildred M. Johnson, Morgan City

LANE CAKE

1 cup butter
2 cups sugar
3 cups sifted cake flour
⅛ teaspoon salt

3 teaspoons baking powder
1 cup milk
1 teaspoon vanilla extract
7 egg whites beaten very stiff

ICING:

7 egg yolks
1 cup sugar
½ cup butter or oleo
1 (15-ounce) box seedless
   raisins

1 cup chopped nuts
1 cup coconut (more may
   be used)
1 teaspoon vanilla
½ cup wine (if desired)

Cream butter and sugar until fluffy. Sift flour, salt and baking powder together. Add sifted dry ingredients alternately with milk. Stir in vanilla. Fold in beaten egg whites and pour into 2 well greased and floured 9-inch cake pans. Bake at 350 degrees about 25 minutes.

To make icing, cook egg yolks, sugar and butter until thick (over low heat or double boiler). Stir constantly. Add raisins, nuts, coconut, vanilla and wine. Spread thick between layers, on top and sides.

Mrs. Carrie E. Hinton, Wiggins

HOLIDAY CAKE

3½ cups sifted cake flour
3 teaspoons baking powder
½ teaspoon salt
1 cup butter or other
   shortening

2 cups sugar
1 cup milk
10 egg whites, stiffly beaten

[353]

ICING:

½ cup sugar
¼ cup butter
8 egg yolks
¼ to ½ cup fruit juice
(¼ cup sherry, brandy or rum may be used)

1 (29-ounce) can crushed pineapple with juice
1 cup nuts, chopped
1 fresh coconut, grated
1 cup dark raisins
½ cup maraschino cherries, cut in halves or fourths

Sift flour once, measure, add baking powder and salt and sift three times. Cream butter. Add sugar and cream until fluffy. Add flour alternately with milk. Mix thoroughly. After each addition fold in egg whites. Bake in three floured, greased 9-inch layer pans in 350 degree oven for about 25 to 30 minutes. Remove from pans, cool. Spread icing between layers and on top.

Make icing by cooking sugar, butter, egg yolks, and fruit juice in top of double boiler until thick, stirring constantly after it is heated. Remove from heat and add remaining ingredients.

Mrs. M. A. Rowzee, State College

ITALIAN CREAM CAKE

1 stick margarine
½ cup vegetable shortening
2 cups sugar
5 egg yolks
2 cups sifted flour
1 teaspoon soda

1 cup buttermilk
1 teaspoon vanilla
1 (3½-ounce) can flake coconut
1 cup chopped nuts
5 egg whites, stiffly beaten

ICING:

1 (8-ounce) package cream cheese, softened
½ stick margarine

1 pound box powdered sugar
1 teaspoon vanilla
1/3 cup chopped pecans

Cream margarine and shortening; add sugar and beat until mixture is smooth. Add egg yolks and beat well. Combine flour and soda and add to creamed mixture alternately with buttermilk. Stir in vanilla. Add coconut and nuts. Fold in egg whites. Pour batter into three greased and floured 8-inch cake pans. Bake at 325 degrees for 25 minutes or until cake tests done. Cool.

To make a cream cheese icing, beat cream cheese and margarine until smooth. Add sugar and mix well. Add vanilla and beat until smooth. Spread on cake. Sprinkle top with pecans.

Mrs. Berlin Tindell, Vaiden

FRESH APPLE CAKE

4 cups fresh-peeled diced
  apples
2 cups sugar
1 cup chopped nuts
  (pecans)
3 cups sifted all purpose
  flour

½ teaspoon nutmeg or
  cinnamon
½ teaspoon salt
2 teaspoons soda
1 cup vegetable oil
1 teaspoon vanilla
2 eggs, well beaten

Mix the apples, sugar and nuts in large mixing bowl and let stand for an hour. Stir often so that the mixture makes its own juice. Combine dry ingredients and add to apples. Then add oil, vanilla and eggs. Do not use a mixer. Stir ingredients together by hand. Pour batter into greased and floured 10-inch tube pan. Bake 1 hour and 15 minutes at 350 degrees.

Mrs. Janie W. Protho, Hazlehurst

FRESH APPLE LOAF

1 cup cooking oil
2 cups sugar
2 well beaten eggs
3 cups all-purpose flour
1 teaspoon soda

½ teaspoon salt
1 teaspoon cinnamon
2 teaspoons vanilla
3 cups chopped fresh apples

Combine cooking oil and sugar. Add well beaten eggs. Measure and sift together dry ingredients. Add dry ingredients to first mixture. Add vanilla and chopped apples. Bake in well greased 13 x 9 x 2-inch loaf pan for 55 minutes at 300 degrees.

This cake keeps moist and fresh for days and is very good served with coffee.

Mrs. Elizabeth Wages, Baldwyn

VERMONT APPLE CAKE

3 cups sifted all-purpose flour
1 teaspoon baking powder
1 teaspoon salt
1 teaspoon baking soda
1 teaspoon cinnamon
¾ cup butter
1 1/3 cups granulated sugar
1 cup maple syrup

2 eggs
1 teaspoon vanilla
1/3 cup milk
3 cups finely chopped
  cooking apples
1 cup chopped pecans
2 apples thinly sliced,
  dipped in lemon juice

ICING:

¾ cup brown sugar
½ cup maple syrup
1 stick butter
1 tablespoon flour

¼ cup evaporated milk
1 teaspoon vanilla
½ cup coconut

Sift together dry ingredients. Cream together butter and sugar. Blend in syrup. Beat in eggs and vanilla. Gradually add dry ingredients and milk. Beat until well blended. Stir in pecans and apples. Pour into 2 well greased and floured 9-inch layer pans or a 13 x 9 x 2-inch loaf pan. Spread thinly sliced apples over top. Bake in preheated 350 degree oven for 40 to 45 minutes. Remove from oven and cool for 5 minutes before removing from pan. Spread maple icing, made from remaining ingredients, between layers and on top.

To make icing combine all ingredients except vanilla extract and coconut. Bring to a boil and cook while stirring for about 8 minutes. Remove from heat and stir in vanilla and coconut. Beat 2 or 3 minutes. Spread on warm cake, letting drip down sides.

Mrs. C. E. Orr, Corinth

APPLE SAUCE CAKE

½ cup shortening
1½ cups sugar
2 beaten eggs
2 cups flour
¼ teaspoon salt
1 teaspoon baking powder
½ teaspoon soda

1 teaspoon cinnamon
½ teaspoon allspice
½ teaspoon cloves
1 cup thick apple sauce
1 cup raisins
1 cup nuts

Cream shortening and sugar. Add beaten eggs. Sift all flour, except 4 tablespoons, with salt, baking powder, soda and spices. Add flour mixture and apple sauce alternately to creamed mixture. Roll raisins and nuts in the remaining flour and stir into batter. Bake in 10-inch tube pan in 350 degree oven for 45 to 60 minutes. Let cool slightly before removing from pan.

Mrs. Virginia Hicks, Fayette

BANANA CAKE

1 cup butter
2 cups sugar
4 eggs
1½ cups nut meat
½ cup raisins
3 cups flour

2½ teaspoons cinnamon
1½ teaspoons cloves
2 teaspoons soda
½ teaspoon salt
6 ripe bananas, mashed to a
   pulp

Cream butter and sugar. Add whole eggs and beat. Add nuts and raisins that have been dredged in part of the flour. Mix dry ingredients and add to mixture. Add mashed bananas last. Bake in greased and floured 13 x 9 x 2-inch loaf pan. Bake in a 350 degree oven for 1 hour.

Ella D. Burke, Wesson

SOUR CREAM BANANA CAKE

¼ cup (½ stick) margarine
1 1/3 cups sugar
2 eggs
1 teaspoon vanilla
2 cups sifted all-purpose flour
1 teaspoon baking powder

1 teaspoon soda
¾ teaspoon salt
1 cup dairy sour cream
1 cup mashed ripe banana
   (2 medium)
½ cup chopped nuts

ICING:

1 (8-ounce) package cream
   cheese
½ stick margarine

1 pound box confectioners
   sugar
½ cup nuts

In a mixing bowl cream margarine; gradually add sugar and beat until high and fluffy. Beat in eggs one at a time. Add vanilla. Sift together flour, baking powder, soda and salt; add to creamed mixture alternately with sour cream, beginning and ending with dry ingredients. Add bananas and nuts, mixing until blended. Turn into buttered baking pan 13 x 7 x 2-inches. Bake in preheated 350 degree oven 40-45 minutes.

Use the remaining ingredients for icing. Cream cheese and margarine at room temperature with sugar until smooth; add nuts. Ice top and sides of cake.

Mrs. Harold Graham, Hickory

BANANA DELIGHT CAKE

2½ cups all-purpose flour
1 2/3 cups sugar
1¼ teaspoons baking powder
1¼ teaspoons soda
1 teaspoon salt

1 teaspoon ground cinnamon
2/3 cup vegetable shortening
2/3 cup buttermilk
1¼ cups mashed bananas
2 eggs

ICING:

1/3 cup margarine
2 pounds powdered sugar,
   sifted
¾ cup mashed bananas

1 teaspoon lemon juice,
   on bananas
1 cup toasted coconut
1 cup finely chopped nuts

Sift dry ingredients into large mixing bowl, add shortening, buttermilk
and bananas. Mix until ingredients are dampened. Then beat at low
speed for 2 minutes, add eggs, and beat 1 minute. Bake in three 8-inch
or two 9-inch greased and floured layer pans at 350 degrees for 25 to 30
minutes. Cool.

Combine remaining ingredients and mix well. A few drops of yellow
food coloring makes icing more attractive. Spread between layers and on
top. Serves 15-20.

Mrs. H. N. Finnie, Courtland

BANANA NUT CAKE

1 cup soft vegetable
   shortening
2½ cups sugar
3 cups sifted all-purpose
   flour
1½ teaspoons soda

4 beaten egg yolks
6 tablespoons buttermilk
2 teaspoons vanilla
2 cups mashed ripe bananas
1 cup chopped pecans
4 stiffly beaten egg whites

Cream shortening and sugar. Sift flour and soda together and add to
creamed mixture alternately with egg yolks and buttermilk. Add vanilla,
mashed bananas and pecans. Fold in stiffly beaten egg whites. Bake in
a 10 or 11-inch greased bundt cake pan at 325 degrees for about 1½
hours. This cake freezes well.

Mrs. R. B. Harris, Midnight

DATE AND NUT CAKE

1 cup shortening, butter
  or margarine
2 cups sugar
4 eggs
1 teaspoon soda dissolved in
  milk

1 cup buttermilk
3½ cups flour
1 pound package dates,
  chopped fine
2 cups nuts, chopped fine
juice of one large orange

Cream shortening and sugar. Add one egg at the time. Dissolve soda in milk. Sift flour and use ½ cup to flour dates. Mix remainder into other mixture. Add nuts, milk, dates and orange juice. Bake in greased and floured 10-inch tube pan at 300 degrees for 1½ hours. Yields 1 tube cake pan or about 15 servings.

Mrs. Lillie Maxwell, Durant

CRANBERRY CAKE

1 cup chopped dates
1 cup chopped nuts
1 cup chopped raw
  cranberries
½ cup flour
½ cup butter or shortening
1 cup sugar
2 eggs

2 cups all-purpose flour
1 teaspoon baking powder
1 teaspoon soda
¼ teaspoon salt
1 cup buttermilk
2 tablespoons fresh grated
  orange rind

ICING:
2/3 cup orange juice

2/3 cup sugar

Combine dates, nuts and cranberries in bowl and coat with ½ cup flour and set aside. Cream butter, gradually add sugar and beat until fluffy. Add eggs one at a time and beat well. Sift all dry ingredients together and add to creamed mixture alternately with milk. Add orange rind. Remove from mixer and fold fruit and nuts into batter. Turn into a greased 9-inch tube or bundt cake pan. Bake in preheated oven at 350 degrees for 1 hour or until cake tested comes out clean.

While cake is baking, make an icing by heating orange juice and sugar until sugar is dissolved. Pour over hot cake while still in pan. Let stand 15 minutes and remove to a rack to cool. Cover and let flavors blend for 12 to 24 hours before serving.

Mrs. Esther K. Gunn, Laurel

[359]

PRUNE NUT CAKE

2 cups sifted flour
1 teaspoon salt
1 teaspoon soda
1 teaspoon cinnamon
1 teaspoon all-spice
¾ cup sugar
¾ cup packed brown sugar
1 cup butter flavored
    vegetable oil

1 teaspoon vanilla
3 eggs
1 cup pitted, cooked prunes
1 cup chopped toasted pecans
    (toast pecans 8 minutes
    at 300 degrees for better
    flavor)

Sift flour, salt, soda and spices together; add sugars, oil, vanilla and eggs. Mix thoroughly with mixer. Add prunes and beat. Stir in nuts. Pour into lightly greased and floured 9 or 10-inch tube pan or bundt cake pan. Bake 1 to 1½ hours at 325 degrees. Cool in pan 10 minutes before removing to cake plate.

Mrs. Jack Johnson, Marks

FRESH STRAWBERRY CAKE

1 stick butter or oleo
1/3 cup shortening
1¾ cups granulated sugar
½ cup fresh crushed
    strawberries
1 (6-ounce) package
    strawberry gelatin

2 2/3 cups sifted all-purpose
    flour
3½ teaspoons baking powder
¾ teaspoon salt
1 1/3 cups sweet milk
1 teaspoon vanilla
4 egg whites, stiffly beaten

ICING:

1 pound box sifted
    confectioners sugar
¼ stick butter or oleo,
    softened

½ cup fresh crushed
    strawberries

Cream butter, shortening and sugar until fluffy. Add strawberries and gelatin; beat well. Sift together dry ingredients and add alternately with milk. Add vanilla and beat well. Fold in egg whites. Turn into 3 greased and floured 9-inch cake pans. Bake at 350 degrees for 30 to 35 minutes. When cake is cool, blend the confectioners sugar, softened butter, and strawberries. Beat thoroughly and spread between layers.

Mrs. Guy Vaughn, Mantee

ONE–PAN PINEAPPLE CAKE

1 (20½-ounce) can pineapple
   chunks
½ cup flaked coconut
½ cup sliced blanched
   almonds

1 (1-pound 2½-ounce)
   package yellow cake mix
1 cup butter or margarine

Spread pineapple and pineapple juice in a greased 13 x 9 x 2-inch baking pan. Sprinkle coconut, almonds, and dry cake mix over pineapple. Dot with butter. Bake in 350 degree oven 1 hour, or until golden brown. Serve warm with whipped cream or whipped cream cheese. Makes ten large servings. *Mrs. George Nolen, Macon*

PINEAPPLE–COCONUT CAKE

2 cups cake flour
1 1/3 cups sugar
2½ teaspoons baking powder
1 teaspoon salt
½ cup shortening

1 cup less 2 tablespoons milk
1½ teaspoons vanilla
1 teaspoon butter extract
2 eggs, unbeaten

FILLING:

1 (no. 303) can crushed
   pineapple, undrained

1/3 cup sugar
2 tablespoons cornstarch

ICING:

2 egg whites, unbeaten
1½ cups sugar
5 tablespoons cold water
1 teaspoon corn syrup,
   light (more in rainy weather)
⅛ teaspoon salt

½ teaspoon pineapple
   extract
½ teaspoon almond extract
1 (3½-ounce) can flaked
   coconut

Cake: Put all ingredients in bowl and beat on medium speed for 4 minutes. Pour batter into three 8-inch layer pans greased and lined with waxed paper. Bake in moderate (375 degrees) oven about 20 to 30 minutes.

Filling: Place undrained pineapple, sugar and cornstarch in saucepan. Cook over medium heat until thickened, stirring constantly (will scorch quickly). Cool and spread filling between cool layers

Icing: Combine remaining ingredients except coconut in top of double boiler. Beat with mixer while it cooks over boiling water for 7 minutes, or until sharp peaks form. Spread over top and sides of cake. Cover with coconut. *Mrs. J. Robert Wilson, Biloxi*

HAWAIIAN DELIGHT CAKE

1 cup shortening
3 cups sifted flour
½ teaspoon salt
2 cups sugar
3½ teaspoons baking powder

1 cup red Hawaiian punch
½ teaspoon vanilla
½ teaspoon almond extract
4 eggs

FILLING:

½ cup drained, crushed
  pineapple
½ cup flaked coconut
½ stick whipped margarine

¼ cup chopped maraschino
  cherries
2½ cups powdered sugar or
  more
½ cup chopped pecans

Cream shortening until light. Sift flour and measure. Sift flour with salt,
sugar and baking powder into shortening. Add punch and flavorings.
Beat at medium speed for 2 minutes. Add eggs, one at a time, beating
thoroughly after each addition. Bake in two 9-inch greased and floured
layer pans at 350 degrees for 25 minutes or until tests done. Make filling
of pineapple, coconut, margarine, and cherries. Add powdered sugar
for spreading consistency. Add pecans. Put cooled layers together with
filling. Ice with a 7-minute icing. Sprinkle generously with coconut.

Mrs. Maurice C. O'Keefe, Jr., Long Beach

FRUIT COCKTAIL CAKE

3 cups all-purpose flour
1½ cups sugar
2 teaspoons baking soda
dash of salt
2 eggs

1 (no. 303) can of fruit
  cocktail
¼ cup brown sugar
½ cup nuts

ICING:

1 stick butter
¾ cups of evaporated milk

½ cup sugar
1 can of coconut

Mix flour, sugar, soda and salt together, add eggs and cocktail. Beat 5
minutes. Pour into greased 13 x 9 x 2-inch floured pan. Sprinkle brown
sugar and nuts on top. Bake 40 minutes at 375 degrees.

Make an icing of the butter, evaporated milk, sugar and coconut. Mix
all together in saucepan. Cook slowly 5 minutes. Pour on cake while
hot. Let cool 2 hours before cutting.

Mrs. Vashtie Turner, Vicksburg

CARROT CAKE

2 cups sugar	1 teaspoon soda
1½ cups vegetable oil	1 teaspoon salt
2 cups flour	4 eggs, unbeaten
2 teaspoons baking powder	3 cups raw grated carrots
2 teaspoons cinnamon	½ cup nuts

ICING:

8-ounces cream cheese	2 teaspoons vanilla
½ stick oleo	1 pound confectioners sugar

Cream sugar and vegetable oil until light and fluffy. Sift dry ingredients together. Add alternately to cream mixture with eggs. Fold in carrots and chopped nuts. Bake at 300 degrees for 30 to 40 minutes in three greased 9-inch cake pans. Make icing of remaining ingredients, as follows: Soften cream cheese and oleo at room temperature. Mix cream cheese and oleo well. Add vanilla and gradually add confectioners sugar. Mix well. Ice layers and sides of cakes.

Mrs. Bettie J. Stepps, Hattiesburg

SWEET POTATO CAKE

1½ cups cooking oil	¼ teaspoon salt
2 cups sugar	1 teaspoon ground cinnamon
4 eggs, separated	1 teaspoon ground nutmeg
4 tablespoons hot water	1½ cups grated raw potatoes
2½ cups sifted cake flour	1 cup chopped nuts
3 teaspoons baking powder	1 teaspoon vanilla

ICING:

1 (13-ounce) can evaporated milk	3 egg yolks
	1 teaspoon vanilla
1 cup sugar	1 1/3 cups flaked coconut
1 stick margarine	

Combine cooking oil and sugar and beat until smooth. Add egg yolks and beat well. Add hot water. Then add dry ingredients which have been sifted together. Stir in potatoes, nuts and vanilla and beat well. Beat egg whites until stiff and fold into batter. Bake in three greased 8-inch layer cake pans at 350 degrees for 25 to 30 minutes.

Use remaining ingredients for icing. Combine milk, sugar, margarine, and egg yolks in sauce pan. Cook over medium heat about 12 minutes, stirring constantly until mixture thickens. Remove from heat, add vanilla and coconut. Beat until cool and spread.

Mrs. R. D. Daves, Black Hawk

PUMPKIN CAKE

2 cups sugar
1½ cups vegetable oil
4 eggs
2 cups flour (plain)
1 tablespoon salt

2 teaspoons cinnamon
¾ cup pecans, chopped fine
2¼ cups pumpkin or 1 #303
   can

ICING:

1 stick or ¼ pound butter
1 (6-ounce or 8-ounce)
   package Philadelphia cream
   cheese

1 pound box white powdered
   sugar
1 teaspoon vanilla
1 cup pecans, chopped fine

Mix sugar and oil. Beat in eggs one at a time. Add flour mixed with salt, spice and nuts. Fold in pumpkin. Bake in 10-inch tube pan at 325 degrees for approximately 1 hour or until done.

For icing, cream and soften butter and cheese, add sugar in small amount at a time. Then stir in vanilla and nuts. Spread on cake.

Pauline McNeil, Louin

PUMPKIN CAKE

2 cups sugar (granulated)
1½ cups cooking oil
1½ cups canned pumpkin
4 eggs, slightly beaten

2 cups cake flour
2 teaspoons soda
4 teaspoons cinnamon

ICING:

1 (8-ounce) package cream
   cheese (at room
   temperature)
1 stick oleo (at room
   temperature)

1 (16-ounce) package
   confectioners sugar
1 cup chopped pecans
2 teaspoons vanilla

Combine sugar, oil and pumpkin. Mix well, add eggs. Sift together cake flour, soda and cinnamon. Add to mixture gradually and continue beating with electric mixer on medium speed for 5 minutes. Place in three greased 9-inch layer pans and cook at 325 degrees for 25 to 30 minutes. Remove from pans and cool.

To make icing, cream cheese and oleo until smooth. Add sugar gradually. Stir until smooth. Add pecans and vanilla. Ice top and sides of cake.

Kathye Coker, Carthage

FRESH COCONUT CAKE

1 cup butter
2 cups sugar
3 cups cake flour
3 teaspoons baking powder

½ teaspoon salt
1 cup sweet milk
4 eggs, whole
1 teaspoon vanilla

FILLING:

3 tablespoons sugar
¾ cup sweet milk

¼ stick butter or margarine
¼ cup coconut

ICING:

2 cups sugar
1 cup water
¼ cup white corn syrup

2 egg whites, stiffly beaten
1 teaspoon vanilla
1 large coconut, grated

Cream butter and sugar for at least 10 minutes. Sift flour, baking powder and salt together. Alternately add milk and flour to creamed mixture. Beat in one egg at a time. Add vanilla. Pour in three greased and floured 8-inch layer pans. Bake 25 to 30 minutes at 350 degrees. For a moist cake, make a filling by combining sugar, milk, butter and coconut. Heat almost to a boiling point and put mixture over each layer of cake.

Make a divinity icing of last six ingredients. Boil sugar, water and corn syrup until mixture spins a thread. Slowly pour boiled mixture over stiffly beaten egg whites. Add 1 teaspoon vanilla. Continue beating until spreading consistency is reached. Heap icing and coconut between layers and on top and sides of cake.

Mrs. J. C. Craig, Louisville

COCONUT CAKE

3 cups sifted cake flour
2 teaspoons baking powder
¼ teaspoon salt
1 cup (½ pound) butter
1 pound powdered sugar
4 egg yolks, well beaten

1 cup milk
1 teaspoon vanilla
1 cup shredded coconut,
    packed lightly
4 egg whites, well beaten

ICING:

1 cup sugar
½ cup light corn syrup
3 tablespoons water
3 egg whites

¼ teaspoon cream of tartar
¼ teaspoon salt
1½ teaspoons vanilla
2 cups grated coconut

[365]

Sift flour, once, then measure. Add baking powder and salt. Sift three times. Cream butter thoroughly and add sugar gradually. Continue creaming until light and fluffy. Add egg yolks and beat well. Add flour mixture alternately with milk, beating after each addition. Stir in vanilla and coconut. Fold in egg whites carefully. Bake in 4 greased 8-inch pans at 350 degrees for about 30 minutes or until done. Cool thoroughly.

Make an icing by combining sugar, corn syrup, water, egg whites, cream of tartar and salt in top of double boiler. Cook over rapidly boiling water, beating with electric or rotary beater until mixture stands in peaks. Remove from heat and add vanilla. Continue beating until icing holds deep swirls. Ice cake. Sprinkle with grated coconut on top and sides.

Mrs. Charles Conlee, Senatobia

COCONUT POUND CAKE

2 sticks butter
3 cups sugar
5 separated eggs
3 cups all-purpose flour
¼ teaspoon soda
1 teaspoon hot water

1 cup buttermilk
1 teaspoon vanilla
½ teaspoon butter flavor
   extract
1 (8-ounce) can flake coconut

Cream butter and sugar well. Add egg yolks one at a time, beating well after each addition. Sift flour three times. Dissolve soda in one teaspoon hot water and add to buttermilk. Add flour and milk alternately, beginning and ending with flour. Add flavorings, then fold in beaten egg whites and coconut. Bake in 9-inch greased tube pan at 350 degrees for 30 minutes. Then bake at 325 degrees for 1 hour.

Mrs. Jim Alexander, Houston

COCONUT SOUR CREAM POUND CAKE

3 sticks butter or margarine
2 cups sugar
6 eggs
3 cups flour
¼ teaspoon soda
¼ teaspoon salt

1 (8-ounce) package sour
   cream
¼ teaspoon vanilla
1 (6-ounce) package frozen
   coconut or fresh grated
   coconut

Blend well margarine and sugar. Add eggs one at a time and blend in well. Sift flour, soda and salt together. Add alternately with sour cream. Be sure to start with dry ingredients and end with dry ingredients. Fold in vanilla and coconut. Grease and flour 10-inch tube pan or 3 small loaf pans. Bake in 300 degree oven for 1 hour or longer until done. Loaf pan requires less cooking time. This cake freezes well; in fact, it improves the flavor to freeze it.

Mrs. Harold Lott, Isola

SOUR CREAM CAKE

2 sticks butter
3 cups sugar
6 eggs, separated
3 cups cake flour

¼ teaspoon soda
1 (8-ounce) package sour cream
1 teaspoon vanilla

ICING:
1 stick oleo
1 cup sugar
½ cup milk

1 cup coconut
1 cup pecans

Cream butter and sugar. Add egg yolks one at a time, beating well after each addition. Sift cake flour and soda 3 times and stir into the above mixture. Add sour cream and vanilla. Fold in stiffly beaten egg whites. Bake in greased 10-inch tube pan for 1 hour in 350 degree oven. Make an icing of the last five ingredients to pour over cake when it is cool. Cook oleo, sugar and milk until thick. Stir in coconut and pecans. Cool and pour over cake.

Mrs. Luther Flanagan, Corinth

SOUR CREAM COFFEE CAKE

2 sticks softened margarine
2 cups sugar
2 eggs
1 cup sour cream
2 cups sifted all-purpose flour
¼ teaspoon salt

1 teaspoon baking powder
1 teaspoon vanilla
½ cup finely chopped nuts
1 tablespoon cinnamon
2 tablespoons powdered sugar

Preheat oven to 300 degrees. Mix together thoroughly the margarine, sugar and eggs. Add sour cream. Sift flour, salt and baking powder together and add to creamed mixture. Add vanilla. Mix nuts, cinnamon and powdered sugar together and set aside. Pour one half batter into lightly greased 10-inch bundt pan. Sprinkle half the nut mixture over this. Add remaining batter, then remaining nut mixture on top. Increase oven temperature to 350 degrees. Bake 1 hour and 20 minutes. Let cool slightly. Invert onto dish. Sprinkle top with powdered sugar.

Mrs. Annie Cage, Clarksdale

SOCK–IT–TO–ME CAKE

1 (1-pound 3-ounce) box
    butter cake mix
1 (8-ounce) carton sour
    cream
¾ cup butter flavor Wesson
    Oil (Do not substitute)

4 eggs
½ cup brown sugar
3 teaspoons cinnamon
½ cup chopped pecans

GLAZE:

1 cup confectioners sugar
3 tablespoons lightly
    browned butter

2 tablespoons milk

Combine cake mix, sour cream, and Wesson Oil. Beat well. Add eggs one at a time, beating well after each addition. Grease and flour a 10-inch bundt or 10-inch tube pan. Pour half of batter in pan. Sprinkle with mixture of brown sugar, cinnamon, and pecans. Pour remaining batter on top of mixture and bake at 350 degrees for 50 to 60 minutes. Do not underbake. Let cool 10 minutes before removing from pan. Glaze with the well blended mixture of confectioners sugar, browned butter and milk.

Mrs. Mary L. Erwin, Ackerman

CREAM CHEESE POUND CAKE

1 stick butter
2 sticks oleo
1 (8-ounce) package cream
    cheese

3 cups sugar
3 cups cake flour
6 eggs
2 teaspoons vanilla

Cream butter, oleo, cream cheese and sugar till smooth and creamy. Add other ingredients and beat well. Bake in 10-inch bundt cake pan at 325 degrees for 1 hour and 20 minutes.

Mrs. Leon Horn, Carthage

WHIPPED CREAM POUND CAKE

1 cup butter
3 cups sugar
6 eggs

1 cup whipped cream
2 teaspoons vanilla
3 cups sifted plain flour

Cream butter and sugar for 20 minutes. Add 6 eggs, beating well after each addition. Whip cream and vanilla in chilled bowl. Sift plain flour three times. Add flour and whipped cream alternately to other mixture. Pour mixture in a 10-inch tube pan that has been greased and floured. Bake at 300 degrees for 1½ hours. Place a pan of water in the oven in order to keep the cake moist.

Mrs. Marilyn Bailey, Prentiss

LINCOLN WHITE CAKE

1½ cups egg whites	1 cup shortening
3 cups sugar	1½ teaspoons salt
2 teaspoons warm water	4 cups flour
½ teaspoon soda	1½ teaspoons cream of tartar
1 cup buttermilk	2 teaspoons lemon flavoring

Beat egg whites until foamy. Add 1 cup of sugar and beat until soft peaks form. Dissolve soda in warm water and add to buttermilk. In another bowl, cream shortening with salt and 2 cups of sugar. Sift flour and cream of tartar together. Add to shortening, mix alternately with milk. Beat well. Add flavoring. Fold in beaten egg whites. Bake in 10-inch tube pan at 300 degrees for 1 hour and 30 minutes.

Mrs. E. Maurice King, Jr., Clinton

BUTTERMILK CAKE

1 cup butter	½ teaspoon soda
3 cups sugar	1 cup buttermilk
5 eggs, separated	3 cups plain flour
2 teaspoons vanilla	

Cream butter and sugar then add egg yolks, one at a time. Beat well. Stir in vanilla. Dissolve soda in one teaspoon of warm water. Add to milk. Add flour and milk alternately to sugar mixture, beginning and ending with flour. Fold in egg whites which have been beaten well. Pour in greased 10-inch tube pan. Bake at 350 degrees for 1 hour and 10 minutes. Cool in pan. Do not invert. Serve plain or with icing.

Mrs. W. M. Hughes, Collins

EXTRACT POUND CAKE

½ cup shortening
1 stick or ½ cup real butter
1 stick oleo
2¾ cups sugar
1 cup sweet milk
6 large eggs
3 cups sifted all-purpose
  flour

1 teaspoon vanilla extract
1 teaspoon almond extract
1 teaspoon brandy extract
1 teaspoon rum extract
1 teaspoon lemon or black
  walnut extract

Combine shortening, butter, oleo and sugar until fluffy. Alternately add milk, eggs, and flour, beating well after each addition. Add extracts. Bake for 2 hours in greased and floured 10-inch tube pan. Start in cold oven, then turn on 325 degrees. Yields: 12 to 16 servings.

Mrs. Bill Shirley, Rosedale

BROWN SUGAR POUND CAKE

1 cup butter
½ cup shortening
1 pound brown sugar
1 cup sugar
5 eggs
½ teaspoon salt

1 teaspoon baking powder
3 cups sifted cake flour
1 cup milk
1 teaspoon vanilla
1 cup chopped nuts

GLAZE:

1 cup sifted confectioners
  sugar
2 tablespoons butter
6 tablespoons cream

½ teaspoon vanilla
½ cup nuts (pecans or
  walnuts)

Beat butter and shortening together, gradually adding the sugars, and creaming until mixture is light and fluffy. Beat in eggs one at a time. Sift salt, baking powder and flour together and add alternately with milk and vanilla to the creamed mixture. Stir in nuts. Pour batter into greased and floured 10-inch tube pan. Bake in 350 degree oven for 1 hour and 15 minutes. Cool 10 minutes, then remove from pan. Make a glaze by creaming together the last five ingredients and pour over hot cake.

Mrs. Esther K. Gunn, Laurel

POUND CAKE

1 pound of butter	1 teaspoon vanilla extract
3 1/3 cups sifted sugar	1 teaspoon lemon extract
10 large eggs	1 teaspoon almond extract
4 cups sifted flour	

Have all ingredients at room temperature. Cream butter. Gradually add sugar. Add eggs one at a time, beating well after each addition. Gradually add flour and beat well. Add vanilla, lemon flavoring and almond flavoring. Continue beating 5 or 10 minutes, until smooth and creamy. Pour into a well greased and floured 10-inch tube pan. Bake at 325 degrees for 1 hour and 45 minutes. This makes a large, moist cake that will keep well and will freeze well.

Mrs. Ray Leeper, Pontotoc

FOOL PROOF POUND CAKE

1 pound oleo	6 eggs, beaten
1 pound box powdered sugar	1 powdered sugar box of plain flour

Cream oleo. Add powdered sugar, eggs and flour alternately. Mix well. Pour into a greased and floured 10-inch bundt pan and bake at 325 degrees for 1 hour and 15 minutes. If aluminum pans are used, bake at 350 degrees for 1 hour and in two 4 ½ x 8-inch loaf pans or for 1 hour and 15 minutes in a 10-inch tube pan.

Mrs. J. W. Smollen, Vicksburg

WHITE LAYER CAKE

2¼ cups sifted cake flour	¼ teaspoon lemon extract
2 teaspoons baking powder	1 teaspoon vanilla
½ teaspoon salt	½ cup egg whites
½ cup shortening	1 cup milk
1 1/3 cups sugar	

Sift flour. Measure, and resift 3 times, with baking powder and salt. Cream shortening until soft and smooth. Then add 1 cup sugar and blend thoroughly. Add flavorings. Add half the egg whites, unbeaten, and beat vigorously until mixture is light and fluffy. Add flour mixture

[371]

and milk alternately in 3 or 4 portions, beginning and ending with flour and beating well after each addition. Beat remaining egg whites until stiff, then gradually beat in remaining 1/3 cup sugar. Fold lightly, blending thoroughly, into batter. Turn into two 9-inch layer cake pans lined with wax paper in the bottom and buttered on the sides. Bake in moderate oven (350 degrees) 28 to 30 minutes or until cake springs back when lightly pressed with finger tips. Cool in pans and turn out on cake racks. Spread desired icing between layers and on top and side of cake. Yield: 16 slices.

Mrs. J. W. Upton, Kokomo

WHITE CAKE AND CARAMEL ICING

1 cup butter or shortening
2 cups sugar
5 egg whites
½ cup corn starch
3 cups sifted all-purpose
    flour

½ teaspoon salt
1 teaspoon baking powder
1½ cups sweet milk
1 teaspoon vanilla

ICING:

3 cups sugar
3 tablespoons corn syrup
1½ cups sweet milk

½ stick butter
1 teaspoon vanilla

Cream butter and sugar. Add egg whites. Cream well. Sift corn starch, flour, salt and baking powder three times. Add the milk and flour mixture, alternately. Beat well. Blend in vanilla. Bake in three 8-inch pans at 350 degrees about 30 minutes or until cake leaves sides of pan.

Make icing of remaining ingredients. Brown ½ cup of sugar in skillet. Cook melted sugar, sugar, syrup, and milk until it forms a soft ball in cold water. Add butter and vanilla. Remove from heat, cool. Beat to spreading consistency.

Mrs. H. L. Goodwin, Sr., Philipp

LEMON CAKE

1 cup butter
2 cups sugar
4 eggs
3 cups plain flour

1 teaspoon soda
2 teaspoons cream of tartar
1 cup sweet milk

FILLING:

4 lemons	2½ cups sugar
4 eggs	4 tablespoons butter

Cream butter and sugar. Add eggs one at a time. Sift flour and measure. Sift soda, cream of tartar and flour together. Add flour alternately with milk. Bake in five 8-inch cake pans at 350 degrees about 30 minutes or until done. Stack layers with lemon filling.

To make filling, grate rind of lemons, mix with juice. Beat eggs together. Mix together, eggs, sugar, butter, lemon juice and rind. Cook in double boiler until thick. Spread between layers and on top of cake.

Mrs. Henry Fletcher, Carthage

POUND CAKE WITH ORANGE GLAZE

3 sticks butter, softened	½ teaspoon salt
2 cups sugar	4 teaspoons baking powder
6 egg yolks, plus 2 whole eggs	1 1/3 cups sweet milk
4 cups cake flour	2 tablespoons lemon extract

GLAZE:

¾ cup orange juice	¾ cup sugar

Cream the pre-softened butter, add sugar and beat until creamy on high speed of electric mixer. Beat eggs and yolks together. Add to creamed sugar and butter, and beat. Sift flour, then add salt and baking powder. Sift twice. Add dry ingredients alternately with milk. Beat 3 minutes on medium speed of electric mixer. Add extract. Beat 2 minutes. Pour in tube pan 4 inches deep and 10-inch top diameter. Bake in 320 degree oven for 1 hour.

For glaze, mix the orange juice and sugar. Stir until sugar dissolves. Pour over cake top and sides.

Mrs. Lydia Thomas, Batesville

CHOCOLATE POUND CAKE

1 cup butter	½ teaspoon baking powder
½ cup shortening	½ teaspoon salt
3 cups sugar	4 tablespoons cocoa
5 eggs	1 teaspoon vanilla
3 cups sifted flour	1 cup milk

[373]

ICING:

1 stick oleo
6 tablespoons milk
4 tablespoons cocoa
1 pound box confectioners
  sugar

½ cup pecans
1 teaspoon vanilla

Cream butter, shortening and sugar together. Add eggs one at a time. Sift flour, baking powder, salt and cocoa together. Stir vanilla into milk. Add flour mixture alternately with milk. Bake in greased 10-inch tube pan at 325 degrees for 1 hour and 30 minutes. Remove from pan and ice while still warm.

To make the icing, melt oleo, add milk and cocoa, bring to a quick boil, and pour over 1 box confectioners sugar. Beat until smooth. Add ½ cup pecans and 1 teaspoon vanilla. Add hot water, if it gets too stiff. Spread over cake.

Mrs. Marteal Alexander, Kosciusko

GERMAN CHOCOLATE POUND CAKE

2 cups sugar
1 cup shortening
4 eggs
2 teaspoons vanilla
2 teaspoons butter flavor
1 cup buttermilk

3 cups sifted all-purpose
  flour
½ teaspoon soda
1 teaspoon salt
1 package German's
  sweet chocolate

Cream sugar and shortening. Add eggs one at a time. Stir in flavorings and buttermilk. Sift together flour, soda, and salt and add to mixture. Mix well. Add German's chocolate that has been softened in warm oven or in double boiler. Blend together well. Pour into 9-inch tube pan that has been well greased and dusted with flour. Bake about 1½ hours at 300 degrees. Test with a toothpick for doneness. Place cake under a tight fitting cake cover, while still hot, and leave to cool.

Mrs. H. B. McNeill, Wesson

CHOCOLATE DEVILS FOOD

3 eggs whites
¼ cup sugar
1 cup shortening
2 cups sugar
3 egg yolks
3 cups sifted, plain flour
½ teaspoon salt

1 cup cocoa
1½ teaspoons soda
1½ teaspoons cinnamon
1½ teaspoons cloves
1½ teaspoons all-spice
1½ cups sour milk
1 teaspoon vanilla

Beat egg whites, adding ¼ cup sugar as for a meringue. Set aside. Cream thoroughly, shortening, 2 cups sugar and egg yolks. Sift flour, salt, cocoa, soda and spices together. Add sifted flour mixture alternately with milk. Stir in vanilla. Then fold in beaten egg whites. Bake in 350 degree oven 30 to 40 minutes. Makes three 9-inch layers or sheet cake. May frost with seven minute icing or chocolate butter icing.

Mrs. D. M. Dowdell, Port Gibson

CHOCOLATE POTATO CAKE

½ cup shortening
¾ cup hot mashed Irish potatoes
2 cups sugar
3 eggs
¾ cup cocoa
3 cups plain flour

1¼ teaspoons soda
2 level teaspoons baking powder
½ teaspoon salt
1 cup buttermilk
2 teaspoons vanilla flavor

ICING:

1 (1-pound) box powdered sugar
¾ cup cocoa

1 stick butter, melted
¼ cup boiling water
2 teaspoons vanilla

Cream shortening and potatoes. Add sugar and beat until fluffy. Add eggs, one at a time, and beat after each addition. Sift dry ingredients together and add alternately with buttermilk to first mixture. Stir in vanilla. Pour into three greased 8-inch pans. Bake 25 minutes at 350 degrees.

To make icing, combine sugar and cocoa. Add melted butter. Add boiling water and vanilla. Beat well, spread on cool cake.

Mrs. J. O. Johnson, Mantee

GERMAN CHOCOLATE CAKE

1 cup butter or shortening
2 cups sugar
pinch of salt
4 egg yolks
2½ cups sifted cake flour
1 cup buttermilk

1 teaspoon soda
6 blocks of German chocolate
3 tablespoons hot water
4 egg whites, beaten stiff
1 teaspoon vanilla

ICING:

1 pound box powdered sugar
1½ tablespoons cocoa
¼ cup butter
1 teaspoon vanilla

6 to 8 tablespoons hot coffee
1 cup chopped nuts, if desired

Cream butter and sugar. Stir in salt. Beat in egg yolks. Sift flour. Combine buttermilk and soda. Fold flour and buttermilk alternately into creamed mixture. Melt chocolate in hot water. Fold in chocolate and vanilla. Fold in beaten egg whites. Bake at 325 degrees for 30 minutes or until done in two 8 x 8 x 2-inch layer cake pans.

Make icing of remaining ingredients. Sift the powdered sugar with the cocoa. Combine with remaining ingredients and spread on cake.

Mrs. Mildred M. Johnson, Morgan City

SCRUMPTIOUS CHOCOLATE CAKE

3 squares unsweetened chocolate	1 teaspoon salt
1 stick margarine	2 eggs
1 cup water	1 (8-ounce) carton sour cream (1 cup)
2 cups sifted cake flour	2 cups sugar
1¼ teaspoons baking powder	1½ teaspoons vanilla

ICING:

2 egg whites	dash salt
¾ cup sugar	2½ teaspoons cold water
½ teaspoon cream of tartar	1 teaspoon vanilla

TOPPING:

1 square of unsweetened chocolate	1 tablespoon margarine

Combine 3 chocolate squares, 1 stick margarine, and water in top of double boiler. Heat over simmering water until chocolate and margarine melt. Remove from heat. Cool. Sift the flour, baking powder, and salt into large bowl. In a separate, medium size bowl, beat eggs and sour cream until blended. Beat in sugar and vanilla, stir in cooled chocolate mixture. Beat this mixture into flour mixture, half at a time, just until smooth. Makes thin batter. Pour evenly into two 8-inch round layer cake pans. Bake at 350 degrees for 40 minutes, or until centers spring back when pressed with finger tips. Cool in pans on cake racks. Loosen edges with knife and turn onto racks.

Make icing by combining egg whites, sugar, cream of tartar, salt and cold water. Place in top of large double boiler. Beat until blended. Place top over pan of simmering water. Cook, beating constantly with mixer, about 7 minutes or until mixture stands in stiff peaks. Remove from heat and stir in vanilla. Ice top and sides of cake.

Make topping by heating last two ingredients, chocolate and margarine. Heat in a cup set in hot water. Stir until melted and smooth. Drizzle over cake.

Mrs. L. A. Gurley, Silver Creek

FEATHERY FUDGE CAKE

2/3 cup soft butter or
   margarine
1¾ cups sugar
2 eggs
1 teaspoon vanilla
2½ (1-ounce) squares
   unsweetened chocolate,
   melted and cooled

2½ cups sifted cake flour
1¼ teaspoons soda
½ teaspoon salt
1¼ cups ice water

ICING:

1 (6-ounce) package (1 cup)
   semi-sweet chocolate pieces
¼ cup butter or margarine
½ cup sour dairy cream

1 teaspoon vanilla
¼ teaspoon salt
2½ to 2¾ cups sifted
   confectioners sugar

Cream butter, sugar, eggs and vanilla together till fluffy (beat 5 minutes at high speed on mixer, scraping bowl occasionally to guide batter into beaters, or beat 5 minutes by hand). Blend in chocolate. Sift flour with soda, and salt, then add to creamed mixture alternately with ice water. Beat after each addition. Bake in 2 wax paper-lined 9 x 1½-inch round pans in moderate oven (350 degrees) 30 to 35 minutes or till done.

Make an icing of the remaining ingredients. Melt chocolate pieces and butter over hot (not boiling) water. Remove from hot water and blend in sour cream, vanilla and salt. Gradually beat in enough confectioners sugar to make a frosting of spreading consistency. Makes enough icing for top and sides of two 9-inch layers or a 10-inch tube cake. Serves: 12 to 16.

Mrs. George Morley, Skene

CRAZY CAKE

1½ cups flour
1 cup sugar
½ teaspoon salt
1 teaspoon soda
3 tablespoons cocoa

6 tablespoons vegetable oil
1 cup cold water
1 tablespoon vinegar
1 teaspoon vanilla

Use fork to mix all ingredients together thoroughly. Bake in layer cake pan 8 x 8 x 2-inches. Bake 25 minutes at 350 degrees, or until done. Serve with your favorite icing.

Mrs. Ruth Jones, Lake

RED VELVET CAKE

1 cup shortening	2 cups all-purpose flour
1½ cups sugar	1 heaping tablespoon cocoa
1 (1-ounce) bottle red food color	½ teaspoon salt
	1 cup buttermilk
1 teaspoon vanilla	1 teaspoon vinegar
2 eggs	1 teaspoon soda

ICING:

¼ cup flour	1 cup sugar
¼ teaspoon salt	1 teaspoon vanilla
1 cup milk	1 cup coconut
1 cup shortening	

Cream shortening and sugar. Add (one at a time) food coloring, vanilla, and eggs, mixing well. Sift flour, cocoa and salt together 3 times. Add flour mixture and milk to creamed mixture. Blend in vinegar and soda. Makes 3 (8-inch) layers. Grease and flour pans. Bake at 350 degrees for 30 minutes. Let cool.

For the icing, cook flour, salt and milk together until thick, stirring as it is cooking. Let cool. Cream shortening, sugar and vanilla and add to cooked mixture. Beat well. Spread on cake and sprinkle with coconut.

Mrs. Ray Graves, Steens

HEAVENLY HASH CAKE

4 eggs	1½ cups self-rising flour
2 stick butter (melted)	2 teaspoon vanilla
2 cup sugar	2 cup chopped pecans
¼ cup cocoa	4 cups marshmallows

ICING:

¼ cup cocoa	6 tablespoons evaporated milk
¼ cup butter	
1-pound box powdered sugar	

Mix eggs, butter, sugar, cocoa, flour, vanilla and pecans and pour into greased, floured 13 x 9 x 2-inch pan. Bake at 300 degrees for 30 to 40 minutes. Cut marshmallows in half and put on top of hot cake while cake is still in pan.

To make icing, mix the cocoa, butter, powdered sugar and evaporated milk in saucepan over low heat and pour while hot over hot cake.

Mrs. Leroy Smith, Woodville

CHOCOLATE MALT DELIGHT

4 eggs
2 cups sugar
¼ teaspoon salt
1½ cups self-rising flour
1 teaspoon vanilla

2 sticks margarine
1/3 cup chocolate malt
1½ cups chopped pecans
1 (16-ounce) bag halved
  marshmallows

ICING:

½ stick margarine
1/3 cup chocolate malt
1 (16-ounce) box
  confectioner's sugar

¼ teaspoon salt
1½ teaspoons vanilla
1/3 cup milk

Grease and flour 12¾ x 9 x 2-inch cake pan. Combine eggs, sugar, salt, flour and vanilla and mix well. Melt margarine, add chocolate malt, and simmer 1 minute. Add to egg mixture and beat until well mixed. Add nuts. Pour into large cake pan. Bake at 350 degrees for 30 minutes. Place marshmallow halves close together on top of cake. Return cake to oven just long enough to melt marshmallows. Cool. Let stand overnight before cutting.

Ice top with icing made of remaining ingredients in following manner, melt margarine, add chocolate malt, sift in sugar and salt, add vanilla and milk, and mix well. Yield: 10 servings.

Mrs. Anne Stafford, Columbus

CHOCOLATE SHEET CAKE

2 cups sugar
2 cups all-purpose flour
2 sticks oleo
4 tablespoons cocoa
1 cup water

½ cup buttermilk
2 eggs, well beaten
1 teaspoon soda
1 teaspoon cinnamon
1 teaspoon vanilla

ICING:

1 stick of oleo
4 tablespoons of cocoa
6 tablespoons of sweetmilk

1 box of powdered sugar
1 teaspoon vanilla
1 cup of chopped nuts

Sift 2 cups sugar and 2 cups of all-purpose flour together in a large bowl. Mix 2 sticks of oleo, 4 tablespoons of cocoa and 1 cup of water in a saucepan and bring to rapid boil. Pour over the sugar and flour mixture. Stir until well blended. Add buttermilk, well beaten eggs, baking soda, cinnamon, and vanilla. Mix well and pour in a long baking pan or 2 square pans, 8 x 8 x 2-inches, well greased on the bottom. Bake 20 minutes or a little longer at 400 degrees. Five minutes before the cake is to come out of the oven start preparation of the icing, using the remaining ingredients.

To make icing, mix stick of oleo, cocoa, sweetmilk. Bring to a boil. Remove from heat and stir in powdered sugar, vanilla and chopped nuts. Pour over the hot cake.

Mrs. Iona Wainwright, Bay St. Louis

FUDGE UPSIDE–DOWN CAKE

1 tablespoon butter
¾ cup sugar
½ cup milk
1 cup flour

½ teaspoon salt
1 teaspoon baking powder
1½ tablespoons cocoa

SYRUP:
½ cup white sugar
½ cup nuts
½ cup brown sugar

¼ cup cocoa
1¼ cups boiling water

Cream butter and sugar; add milk. Sift together flour, salt, baking powder and cocoa and add to creamed mixture. Stir well and put in 9-inch buttered pan. Mix ½ cup white sugar, ½ cup nuts, ½ cup brown sugar, ¼ cup cocoa and spread over top. Pour 1¼ cups boiling water over the top of all. This makes a delicious rich chocolate syrup in bottom of pan to be spooned over the cake when served. Bake at 350 degrees for 30 minutes.

Mrs. John Haley, Canton

COCA COLA CAKE

2 cups sugar
2 cups flour (plain)
1½ cups miniature
  marshmallows
1 stick oleo
½ cup oil

1 tablespoon cocoa
1 cup Coca Cola
2 eggs
½ cup buttermilk
1 teaspoon soda

ICING:
6 tablespoons Coke
1 stick oleo
1 pound box confectioners
  sugar

2 tablespoons cocoa
1 cup chopped nuts,
  if desired

Mix sugar, flour and marshmallows in a large mixing bowl and set aside. Melt and bring to boil oleo, oil, cocoa and cola. Pour over flour mixture. Mix well. In a separate bowl, beat eggs, buttermilk and soda. Add to mixture. The batter will be thin. Bake in greased 13 x 9 x 2-inch pan at 350 degrees for 30 to 35 minutes.

To make icing, heat Coke and oleo to boiling. Remove from heat and add confectioner's sugar and cocoa. Mix well. Add nuts, if desired. Spread on cake while hot and still in pan.

Mrs. P. D. Houston, Raleigh

MAYONNAISE CAKE AND ICING

2 cups all-purpose flour
1 cup sugar
4 tablespoons cocoa
1½ teaspoons soda

1½ teaspoons baking powder
1 cup mayonnaise
1 cup cold water
1 tablespoon vanilla

ICING:
2 cups sugar
½ cup cocoa
½ cup milk

¼ pound margarine
1 tablespoon vanilla

Sift flour, sugar, cocoa, soda and baking powder into a large bowl and mix. Then add mayonnaise, water and vanilla. Pour into 2 well-greased and floured cake pans. Bake in 350 degree oven for 25 minutes or until cake pulls away from pan. Makes two 8-inch layers.

Using remaining ingredients to make an icing. Mix sugar, cocoa, milk and margarine in saucepan. Bring to boil. Cook for 2 minutes. Remove from heat; add vanilla. Beat and spread on cake.

Mrs. Troy Moore, Booneville

HUNDRED DOLLAR CAKE

2 cups sugar
1 stick margarine
1 egg
1 (5¾-ounce) package
  chocolate chips

2 cups flour
1½ teaspoons baking powder
1½ cups milk
1 teaspoon vanilla
1 cup chopped pecans

ICING:
1 1/3 cups powdered sugar
1 stick margarine or butter
2 squares semi-sweet
  chocolate

1 egg
1 teaspoon lemon juice
1/16 teaspoon salt
1 cup pecans

Cream sugar and margarine. Add egg and melted chocolate chips. Sift
flour and baking powder together. Add flour alternately with milk and
vanilla. Fold in nuts. Bake in 10-inch tube pan in 350 degree oven for
1 hour. Cool. Make the icing by creaming powdered sugar and margarine
or butter; add melted semi-sweet chocolate, beaten egg, lemon juice,
salt and pecans. Ice cake, cover and refrigerate.

Mrs. C. L. Marron, Fayette

CHEESE CAKE

2 envelopes (2 tablespoons)
  unflavored gelatin
1 cup sugar
¼ teaspoon salt
2 eggs, separated
1 (6-ounce) can frozen
  concentrated orange juice,
  thawed

3 cups cream cottage cheese,
  sieved
1 cup heavy cream,
  whipped
2 tablespoons melted butter
  or oleo
½ cup chocolate or
  plain cookie crumbs

Mix gelatin, ¾ cup of the sugar, and salt in top of double boiler.
Beat together egg yolks and concentrated orange juice; add to gelatin
mixture. Cook over boiling water, stirring constantly until gelatin dissolves and mixture thickens (about 10 minutes). Remove from heat
and cool. Stir in cottage cheese. Chill, stirring occasionally, until mixture
mounds slightly. Beat egg whites until stiff but not dry. Gradually add
remaining ¼ cup sugar and beat until very stiff. Fold beaten egg whites
and whipped cream into gelatin-cheese mixture. Turn into 9-inch spring
form pan or a gelatin dessert mold. Combine butter and cookie crumbs;
sprinkle over top and chill until firm. Serves 10 to 12.

Mrs. W. T. Grantham, Greenville

STUFFED ANGEL FOOD CAKE

1 angel or orange sponge
  cake
1 cup drained crushed
  pineapple
1 package gelatin, plain
½ cup cold water
1 cup cream, whipped
1 cup chopped pecans

1 cup marshmallows, salad
  or cut-up large ones
1 cup chopped maraschino
  cherries
1 cup cream
1 tablespoon confectioner's
  sugar

Slice ½-inch off top of cake. Set aside to be put back on cake later. Cut about ½-inch around sides of cake so crumbs can be removed, leaving a cake shell ½-inch thick on sides and bottom. Drain pineapple. Heat juice. Soften gelatin in ½ cup cold water. Add to hot pineapple juice and stir to dissolve. Cool. Pour over cake crumbs. Whip 1 cup cream, fold in cake crumbs, pineapple, pecans, marshmallows and cherries. Spoon the mixture into the cake shell and replace top of cake. Whip remaining 1 cup of cream until stiff. Fold in confectioner's sugar. Ice with sweetened whipped cream. Decorate with cherry halves.

Mrs. Jim Best, Yazoo City

OATMEAL CAKE

1½ cups boiling water	2 eggs
1 cup oatmeal	1½ cups flour
1 cup sugar	1 teaspoon soda
1 cup brown sugar	½ teaspoon cinnamon
½ cup shortening	½ teaspoon salt

ICING:

¾ stick butter	1 cup chopped nuts
½ cup brown sugar	1 cup shredded coconut
¼ cup cream	

Pour 1½ cups boiling water over 1 cup oatmeal. Let stand approximately 20 minutes. In a separate bowl, cream 1 cup sugar, 1 cup brown sugar, ½ cup shortening. Add 2 eggs and beat. Sift flour, soda, cinnamon, and salt. Mix dry ingredients into creamed mixture adding oatmeal last. Bake 30 minutes at 350 degrees in 7 x 13-inch pan. Melt ¾ stick butter. Mix in brown sugar, cream, nuts and coconut. Spread over cake and brown lightly under broiler 2 to 3 minutes.

Mrs. Frank Skinner, Vicksburg

MISS B'S PINEAPPLE TEA CAKE

½ cup butter or margarine	1¾ cups sifted cake flour
1 cup sugar	½ teaspoon soda
2 eggs	1 teaspoon baking powder
1 cup crushed pineapple with juice	½ teaspoon lemon extract

Cream butter. Add sugar, blending well. Add eggs one at a time, beating well after each addition. Add the pineapple. Sift the dry ingredients together and add to the first mixture, blending well. Add the lemon

[383]

extract. Put in paper cup lined muffin tins. Bake at 375 degrees for 10 minutes. Makes 24 small tea cakes.

Mrs. William Giles, State College

TINY ORANGE MUFFINS

½ cup butter	2 cups all-purpose flour
1 cup sugar	2 eggs, slightly beaten
1 cup buttermilk	1 cup ground raisins
1 teaspoon soda, dissolved in milk	2 orange rinds, grated

Mix ingredients together in order given. Put dough in well greased muffin pans. Small muffin cups are best. Cook for 15 minutes in a 400 degree oven. Remove from pans and, while still hot, dunk in a syrup made of 1 cup brown sugar and 1 cup orange juice. Yields approximately 2 dozen, depending on size pan used.

Mrs. John E. Sherrod, Sr., Jackson

CUPCAKES

¾ cup shortening	½ cup raisins
1 cup white sugar	2 cups unsifted self-rising flour
½ cup dark brown sugar	1 tablespoon vanilla flavoring
2 eggs, slightly beaten	1 cup chopped pecans
½ cup mashed ripe bananas	
¼ teaspoon baking soda	

ICING:

1½ cups sifted confectioner's sugar	1 teaspoon corn syrup
1 teaspoon softened margarine	4 tablespoons dark brown sugar
2 tablespoons lemon juice	

Blend shortening and sugars, add eggs, bananas, soda, raisins, flour, flavoring and pecans. Mix well. Drop small portions into greased and floured small muffin cups. Bake at 325 degrees 15 to 18 minutes, or until a rich brown color. Yield: 24 cupcakes. Leave 8 cupcakes uniced, ice 8 with white icing, and 8 with brown sugar icing.

In mixing bowl, blend confectioner's sugar and margarine; add lemon juice and corn syrup. Beat until smooth. If necessary, add warm water drop by drop to make a creamy spread. Ice 8 cupcakes. To remaining icing add the dark brown sugar for the 8 brown iced cupcakes.

Mrs. Jean M. Griffin, Purvis

CHOCOLATE ICING

2 cups sugar
2 or 3 tablespoons cocoa
2 eggs
½ cup evaporated milk or
    cream

½ stick margarine
1 teaspoon vanilla

Mix ingredients together well. Bring to a rolling boil. Remove from heat and beat until cool. Spread on cake. Makes icing for two 9-inch cake layers.

Mrs. J. T. Darnell, DeKalb

THE "BEST" CHOCOLATE ICING

1 tablespoon flour
3 cups sugar
1 cup milk
2 squares chocolate

2 egg yolks
¼ pound butter
1 teaspoon vanilla

Mix flour, sugar, milk and chocolate. Beat eggs well and add to mixture. Bring to boil and stir until soft ball stage or 236 degrees. Take off heat, add butter and vanilla. When cool, beat and spread. Makes icing for three 8-inch cake layers.

Mrs. Tillman Wilson, Indianola

NEVER FAIL CREAMY CARAMEL ICING

2½ cups sugar
1 slightly beaten egg
1 stick of butter

¾ cup milk
1 teaspoon vanilla

Melt ½ cup sugar in iron skillet slowly, until brown and liquid. Mix egg, butter, remaining sugar, and milk in a saucepan and cook over low heat until butter melts. Turn the heat up to medium and add the browned sugar. Cook until it reaches the soft ball stage. or until mixture leaves sides of pan. This takes about 10 minutes. Remove from heat, let cool slightly, and add vanilla. Beat until right consistency to spread. Add a little cream, if it gets too thick. Will ice two 9-inch cake layers.

Mrs. Mary B. Smith, Midnight

CARAMEL ICING

1 cup milk
3 cups sugar

3 tablespoons butter
1 teaspoon vanilla

Mix milk and 2 cups sugar and cook slowly. Caramelize 1 cup sugar in separate saucepan large enough to hold entire mixture. When this turns to an amber color, slowly add first mixture, stirring constantly. Cook to a soft ball stage. Remove from heat and add butter and vanilla. Let stand 5 minutes without stirring and then beat to spreading consistency. Makes icing for three 9-inch or 10-inch cake layers.

Mrs. N. A. Walker, Wiggins

CARAMEL ICING

1 pound light brown sugar	1½ cups evaporated milk,
2 cups white sugar	undiluted
¼ pound butter	1 teaspoon vanilla flavoring

Combine all ingredients and stir thoroughly. Cook over medium heat using candy thermometer until it reaches 238 degrees. Remove from heat and cool to lukewarm. Beat. Makes icing for three 9-inch cake layers. This is a good icing for German chocolate cake.

Mrs. Marvin A. Law, Jr., Pass Christian

AMALGAMATION CAKE FILLING

8 very lightly beaten egg yolks	1 pound chopped pecans
2 cups sugar	1 pound chopped English
1 cup butter	walnuts
1 pound chopped seeded raisins	1 grated fresh coconut

Place beaten eggs, sugar and butter in double boiler and cook until thick. Mix in a large bowl the raisins, pecans, walnuts and coconut. When filling is done, pour over fruit mixture and mix well. Spread between three 9-inch cake layers. Cover cake with any white icing.

Mrs. Harry G. Carpenter, Rolling Fork

MARSHMALLOW ICING

½ cup water	10 large marshmallows
1 1/3 cups sugar	(cut up)
2 egg whites	

Boil water and sugar, stirring until sugar melts. Continue cooking at low heat until mixture spins a thread. Beat egg whites until stiff. Pour mixture into egg whites slowly, beating constantly. Add marshmallows and keep beating until all are melted. Spread on cake. Makes icing for two 9-inch cake layers.

Mrs. Winfred Cox, Vaiden

DIVINITY ICING

2½ cups sugar
½ cup water
½ cup white corn syrup
2 egg whites
1 teaspoon vanilla

Boil sugar, water and corn syrup 1 minute. Add 4 tablespoons of this to stiffly beaten egg whites, beating constantly. Continue beating and cook remainder of sugar mixture until it spins a thread or to soft ball stage. Gradually pour over egg whites. Add vanilla and beat until thick enough to spread on cake. A few drops of hot water may be added to make it spread better. Makes icing for two 9-inch cake layers. This may be stored in a covered jar in refrigerator and used later. This also makes delicious divinity candy. Add chopped nuts, a few drops of almond flavoring and food coloring, if desired. Drop by spoonfuls onto waxed paper.

Mrs. Ray Leeper, Pontotoc

WHITE ICING

1 2/3 cups sugar
1/3 cup white corn syrup
dash of salt
½ cup water
2 egg whites
1 teaspoon vanilla

Mix all ingredients. Cook in top of double boiler over boiling water, beating with an electric beater at high speed, until it stands in peaks. Spread between layers and on top of cake. This will ice two or three 8-inch cake layers.

Mrs. Henry Ashford, Clarksdale

COCONUT CAKE FILLING

2 cups sugar
2 cups milk
1 grated fresh coconut
1 egg white, beaten with pinch of salt
1 teaspoon vanilla flavoring
1 teaspoon butter flavoring

Cook sugar, milk and coconut together on low heat until it thickens. Add to egg white, beating as mixed. Add vanilla flavoring and butter flavoring. Pour over cake while hot. Makes filling for three 9-inch cake layers.

Mrs. Whit Stewart, Sallis

ORANGE DELIGHT TOPPING

½ cup firmly packed brown
  sugar
¼ cup butter or margarine
1 tablespoon grated orange peel

1 tablespoon orange juice
1 cup flake coconut
½ cup chopped walnuts

Combine sugar, butter, grated peel, and orange juice in small saucepan. Bring to a boil and cook 1 minute stirring constantly. Add coconut and walnuts. Stir until blended. Will cover top of two 8-inch cake layers.

Georgia L. Williams, Hazlehurst

ᵒ₀[Candies]ᵒ₀

Candy-making is an art that can be easily mastered with a little time and effort. The homemaker who has acquired this skill will be appreciated by her family and friends, especially at Christmas and other festive occasions.

There are a few fundamental rules that need to be remembered to make candy at home that will equal or surpass that made in the finest professional shops.

First, use only the highest quality ingredients. Cane and beet sugar are equally good. When brown sugar is used, a light brown is preferable because the flavor is more delicate. The flavor of butter is pleasing in candies. When oiling pans, use butter or margarine.

Next, choose correct utensils. Pans chosen for candy making should be large enough to allow space for boiling. A pan made of heavy guage metal is best. Wooden spoons are preferable for stirring candy, because they do not scratch the pan and do not get hot when stirring. Use a thermometer to insure accurate cooking. A baking sheet, large platter or other smooth surface may be used for working candy.

Most candy should be stirred gently while cooking. Stirring or beating candy after cooking, before the syrup is cooled, may result in grainy, coarse textured candy.

DIVINITY

2½ cups sugar
½ cup corn syrup
⅛ teaspoon salt
2/3 cup water

2 egg whites, well beaten
1½ cups chopped nuts
1 tablespoon vanilla

Cook sugar, syrup, salt and water in a saucepan until a small amount forms a soft ball when tested in cold water. Take out ½ cup of this mixture and cook the remainder until it forms a hard ball when tested in cold water. Pour the ½ cup mixture slowly over the beaten egg whites. Beat constantly. Continue beating and add the remainder of the syrup when ready. Stir in nuts and vanilla. Continue beating until mass thickens and becomes heavy. Drop with a teaspoon onto waxed paper or pour into a buttered pan and cut when cold. Yields 48 servings.

Mrs. Virginia Harrison, Silver Creek

LUCY'S DIVINITY FUDGE

2 cups boiling water
½ cup white corn syrup
3½ cups sugar

3 egg whites
¼ teaspoon baking powder
1 teaspoon vanilla

Combine water and syrup in saucepan. Bring to a boil and add sugar. Boil until it threads from a spoon. Pour 1/3 cup of syrup slowly over well beaten egg whites to which the baking powder has been added. Beat with electric mixer at high speed until only a small grain can be tasted. Add vanilla and mix well, then drop by spoonfuls on well greased pan. One quart of pecans or candied fruit may be added, if desired. Yields 1½ to 2 pounds divinity.

Mrs. L. S. McKnight, Jackson

RAINBOW DIVINITY

3 cups sugar
¾ cup light corn syrup
¼ teaspoon salt
¾ cup hot water
2 egg whites
½ (3-ounce) package
  raspberry gelatin or lime,
  if preferred

1 teaspoon vanilla
1 cup finely chopped nuts
  for raspberry gelatin
  or ¾ cup fine flaked
  coconut for lime

Butter sides of heavy 2-quart saucepan. Combine sugar, corn syrup, salt and hot water. Cook and stir until sugar dissolves and mixture reaches boiling point. Reduce heat and cook, covered, stirring only occasionally, to hard ball stage (252 degrees). Remove from heat. Meanwhile, have ready egg whites beaten to soft peaks; gradually add gelatin to beaten egg whites and beat to stiff peaks. Add vanilla. Pour hot syrup slowly over egg whites, beating constantly with electric mixer at high speed, until soft peaks form and mixture begins to lose its gloss. Remove beaters. Fold in nuts or coconut and drop from teaspoon onto waxed paper. Work swiftly, as the candy firms rather quickly at this stage. If it becomes too stiff a few drops of hot water will keep mixture at dropping stage. Yields about 4½ dozen medium-sized candies.

Mrs. Kate Woods, Starkville

AFTER DINNER MINTS

2 cups sugar
½ teaspoon salt
½ stick butter
¾ cup cold water

½ teaspoon vinegar
few drops oil of peppermint
or wintergreen

Put all ingredients except flavoring into 2-quart saucepan. Boil without stirring to hard ball stage or 260 degrees. Pour into buttered pan. Add few drops oil of peppermint or wintergreen. When cool enough to hold, pull like taffy. When hard, twist into ropes and cut. Keep in an airtight container. Yields about 1 pound.

Mrs. John A. Evans, Jackson

BUTTERMILK CANDY

2 cups sugar
1 cup buttermilk
2 tablespoons white corn
syrup

2 tablespoons butter
1 teaspoon vanilla
1 cup pecans

In a saucepan add sugar, milk and corn syrup. Cook over medium heat, stirring constantly. Cook until small amount forms a soft ball in cold water when tested. Remove from heat; add butter and vanilla. Beat until it begins to cool and get thick. Then add pecans. Continue to beat until it is very thick or no longer glossy. Quickly spread on a greased pan or platter. When firm, cut into small squares. A dash of food coloring may be added to make different colors of candy. Yields 12 servings.

Mrs. Joe E. Askew, Starkville

WRAPPED CARAMEL CANDY

2 cups sugar
2 cups pure cream
3 cups chopped pecans
1¾ cups white corn syrup

1 stick oleo or butter
pinch of salt
1 teaspoon vanilla

Put first 5 ingredients in saucepan. Stir well and cook until mixture forms a firm ball in cold water. Add salt and vanilla. Pour into a well greased cookie sheet 15 x 10 x ¾-inch pan. When cool cut in squares and wrap in waxed paper. This wrapped candy cannot be made with evaporated milk. Only pure cream can be used. Yields about 1½ pounds.

Mrs. Clyde Smith, Pattison

CARAMEL CANDY

3 cups sugar
1 cup cream
⅛ teaspoon soda

¼ cup butter
½ teaspoon vanilla
1 pound broken pecans

Melt 1 cup of the sugar in heavy skillet over low heat, stirring constantly until melted and light caramel colored. Pour slowly into saucepan containing remaining sugar and cream. Cook to firm stage (246 degrees), stirring constantly. Remove from heat. Add soda and stir vigorously. Add butter. Cool 10 minutes and add vanilla. Beat until mixture is thick and loses gloss. Blend in nuts. Spread in 9 x 12-inch pan or drop by spoonfuls onto waxed paper. Yields 3 dozen pieces.

Mrs. Grady Marter, Duck Hill

OKLAHOMA BROWN CANDY

6 cups sugar
2 cups milk or light cream
¼ teaspoon soda

¼ pound butter
1 teaspoon vanilla
4 cups nuts

Put 2 cups of sugar in heavy skillet and place over low heat. Stir sugar in skillet with wooden spoon constantly until melted and light brown in color. Do not scorch. The remaining 4 cups of sugar and milk should be simmering in large heavy kettle during this time. Pour melted sugar into hot sugar and milk in very fine stream, stirring constantly. Cook to 244 degrees or 248 degrees. To test without a thermometer, drop a small amount in cold water until mixture forms firm ball. Remove from heat and add soda. Beat until it foams. Add butter. Set aside for 20 minutes. Add vanilla and beat until candy is thick and turns dull. Fold in nuts. Turn into buttered pans. Yields 6 pounds.

Mrs. Mildred Darsey, Roxie

BUTTERSCOTCH YULE LOG

1 (6-ounce) package
  (1 cup) butterscotch
  flavored morsels
1/3 cup sweetened
  condensed milk

½ teaspoon vanilla
1/3 cup chopped pecans
egg white, slightly beaten
pecan halves

Melt butterscotch morsels over hot (not boiling) water. Stir in condensed milk and vanilla. Add chopped pecans; mix well. Chill until firm enough to handle. Form into 12-inch roll on waxed paper. Roll tightly in waxed paper to shape evenly. Unroll and mark surface lengthwise with tines of fork; brush with egg white. Press pecan halves into roll to completely cover surface. Wrap in waxed paper. Chill. Cut in ½-inch slices with sharp knife. Yields about 2 dozen slices.

Mrs. Garrett W. Taylor, Brooksville

MILLIONAIRE CANDY

60 light caramels
2 tablespoons water
2 cups nuts

15 to 18 Hershey chocolate
  bars
½ block (2-ounces)
  paraffin

Melt caramels in 2 tablespoons water in a double boiler. Add nuts and mix well. Drop by teaspoonfuls on buttered wax paper. (Work fast while candy is soft and easy to work with.) Chill one to two hours. Melt Hershey bars and parraffin in double boiler over low heat. With toothpick dip and spin each piece of chilled candy in melted chocolate bars and place on wax paper. Let stand 30 minutes to 1 hour. Yields 5 dozen pieces.

Mrs. B. F. Howington, Petal

CHOCOLATE FUDGE

4 cups sugar
½ pound butter
1 (13-ounce) can evaporated
milk
1 (12-ounce) package
chocolate chips

1 (8-ounce) jar marshmallow
creme
2 cups chopped pecans
1 teaspoon vanilla

Combine sugar, butter and milk in a saucepan. Cook to soft ball stage. Remove from heat and add chocolate chips, marshmallow creme, pecans and vanilla. Mix well. Pour in a buttered flat pan. Cut in squares when cool. Yields about 4 pounds.

Mrs. Bill Brent, Raymond

CHOCOLATE FUDGE

¾ cup cocoa
3 cups sugar
3 tablespoons white
corn syrup
¼ teaspoon salt

1½ cups half & half
cream
2 teaspoons vanilla
3 cups nut meats

Mix cocoa, sugar, corn syrup, salt and cream in heavy saucepan. Heat over medium heat, stirring until sugar dissolves and mixture comes to a boil. Cook to soft ball stage (234 degrees), stirring when necessary. Cool slightly. Add vanilla and nuts. Beat until fudge becomes very thick and starts to lose its gloss. Pour into buttered 9 x 9 x 2-inch pan. When cool cut into squares. Yields 3 dozen small squares.

Mrs. J. A. Glasgow, Tupelo

MOCHA FUDGE

2 tablespoons butter
2/3 cup undiluted evaporated
milk
1 2/3 cups sugar
½ teaspoon salt
2 cups miniature marshmallows
1 cup semi-sweet chocolate
pieces

½ cup butterscotch
pieces
1 tablespoon instant coffee
1 teaspoon vanilla
½ cup chopped nuts

Combine butter, evaporated milk, sugar and salt in saucepan. Place over medium heat and bring to boil. Cook 4 to 5 minutes, stirring constantly.

Start timing when mixture begins to bubble around edge of pan. Remove from heat. Stir in marshmallows, chocolate pieces, butterscotch pieces, instant coffee, vanilla and nuts. Stir vigorously 1 minute until marshmallows melt and blend. Pour into 8-inch square pan. Cool and cut in squares. Yields 3 dozen small squares.

Mrs. C. L. Paschal, Newton

NO–COOK CHOCOLATE CANDY

1 stick butter
2 pounds powdered sugar
1 (14-ounce) can condensed
  milk
1 (14-ounce) can angel
  flake coconut
2 cups finely chopped pecans

1 tablespoon orange juice
grated rind of 2 oranges
1 (8-ounce) package
  unsweetend chocolate
¼ (1-ounce) package
  paraffin wax

Melt butter. Cool and add all other ingredients except chocolate and paraffin. Form into balls. Stick toothpick into each ball and refrigerate overnight. Melt chocolate and paraffin together. Dip each ball in melted mixture—hold a few seconds before placing on waxed paper to cool. Yields about 3 dozen balls.

Mrs. Richard Davis, Wayside

MARTHA WASHINGTON CANDY

2 pounds powdered sugar
1 stick butter or oleo,
  room temperature
1 (14-ounce) can condensed
  milk

1 quart cut-up pecans
2 (8-ounce) packages
  semi-sweet chocolate
½ (4-ounce) block parraffin

Pour all ingredients except last two into a large bowl or small dish pan. Mix together by hand. It is too stiff to mix with a spoon. Mix until all of the sugar is dissolved in the milk. Roll in small balls about the size of a marble. Place balls on a cookie sheet to harden. Balls may be placed in freezer overnight or longer. Cover well to keep from drying out. Take out a few at a time and dip in mixture of chocolate and paraffin which have been melted together. A medium-sized tin can set in hot water makes a good container for this purpose. Dip balls in this melted mixture one at a time. Set aside to dry. Yields about 4 dozen balls.

Mrs. L. C. Brown, Sr., Brookhaven

APRICOT BALLS

7/8 cup orange juice
  (about 2 oranges)
grated rind of 2 oranges
2 cups granulated sugar

1 (1-pound) package
  apricots, ground
powdered sugar
pecan halves

Cook orange juice, orange rind, granulated sugar and apricots 10 minutes in a saucepan. Stir constantly while cooking. Drop from spoon. When cool, shape into balls. Roll in powdered sugar. Put a pecan half on top of each ball. Yields approximately 4 dozen balls.

Dr. Louise Burnette, University

APRICOT COCONUT BALLS

1½ cups dried apricots,
  ground
2 cups moist shredded
  coconut

½ cup ground pecans
1 cup sweetened condensed
  milk
powdered sugar

In a large mixing bowl, blend apricots, coconut and pecans. Stir in condensed milk, shape into small balls, roll in powdered sugar or coconut and let stand in air until firm.

These apricot balls are nice to serve on a party luncheon plate or at a holiday open house. The number served will depend on size of balls. Yields approximately 3 dozen balls.

Mrs. E. B. Jarratt, Duck Hill

COCONUT CANDY

2 cups sugar
2 tablespoons butter
½ cup milk

1 cup grated coconut
1 teaspoon vanilla

Stir sugar, butter and milk over quick heat until sugar is dissolved. Continue stirring while cooking slowly to soft ball stage, 238 degrees. Remove from heat. Stir in coconut and vanilla. Beat until creamy. Place in buttered dish and cut into squares at once. Yields approximately 20 servings.

Mrs. O. A. White, West Point

PINEAPPLE CREAM CANDY

2 teaspoons butter
3 cups sugar
1 cup crushed pineapple
2 tablespoons white corn syrup

24 marshmallows
3 cups pecans
1 teaspoon vanilla

Cook butter, sugar, pineapple and corn syrup in a saucepan until mixture forms a hard ball when dropped in water. Remove from heat. Add remaining ingredients. Beat until creamy and pour on a buttered platter. Cut in squares. Yields approximately 4 dozen small squares.

Mrs. Beulah Hendrix, Vicksburg

PINEAPPLE FUDGE

2 cups sugar
1 packed cup brown sugar
½ cup light cream
1 (no. 2) can crushed pine-
    apple, drained

2 tablespoons butter or
    margarine
2 teaspoons ginger
2 teaspoons vanilla
1 cup broken walnuts

Combine sugars, cream and pineapple. Cook, stirring occasionally, to soft ball stage, 236 degrees. Remove from heat. Add butter, ginger and vanilla. Cool at room temperature without stirring until lukewarm. Beat until mixture loses its gloss. Add nuts. Pour into a buttered 8 x 8 x 2-inch pan. Score candy in squares. Press walnut half on each. Finish cutting when firm. Yields 16 to 20 pieces.

Mrs. John L. Webb, Clarksdale

MEXICAN ORANGE CANDY

1 cup granulated sugar
1½ cups whole milk
2 cups granulated sugar
pinch of salt

¼ cup butter or margarine
grated rind of 2 oranges
1 cup broken pecans

Melt 1 cup of sugar in a large kettle (4 of 6-quart capacity) while the milk is scalding in a double boiler. When the sugar is melted and a light golden color, add the hot milk—all at once. This will boil quickly so stir vigorously. Add the 2 cups of sugar and stir until dissolved. Continue cooking to 246 degrees (or until a little dropped in cold water forms firm ball). Remove from heat, add salt, butter, grated orange rind and nuts. Beat until creamy and cool enough to hold its shape when dropped from a teaspoon. Drop by teaspoon onto buttered plates. Top each piece with a pecan half, if desired. Yields 36 pieces.

Mrs. J. H. Burt, Wayside

MAMA'S DATE LOAF

3 cups sugar (full measure)
1 stick margarine or butter
1 (13-ounce) can evaporated
  milk
1 cup chopped dates,
  packed firmly

⅛ teaspoon salt
1 teaspoon pure vanilla
  extract
2 cups pecan halves

Note: A heavy, deep cast iron container will probably produce best cooking results.

Mix sugar, margarine (or butter) and milk together. Place over medium heat until dissolved, stirring constantly. When mixture has reached a rolling boil, add chopped dates. Cook on medium to high heat, stirring constantly to avoid scorching. Cook until soft ball is formed when small amount of mixture is dropped into cold water. Remove from heat and beat until mixture begins to pile. Add salt, vanilla and pecan halves. Shape candy with hands into a roll 2½ to 3 inches in diameter. Roll up in a cup towel which has been wrung out of cold water. Allow to stand until cool and cut in ¼-inch thick slices to serve. Do not refrigerate. Roll in waxed paper, aluminum foil and a cloth to preserve moisture and freshness. Cut from roll as needed. Yields approximately 3 dozen slices.

Mrs. Harold Stubblefield, Oxford

CANDIED PINEAPPLE AND/OR CHERRIES

2 (1-pound 4-ounce) cans
  sliced pineapple
2 cups sugar
½ cup light corn syrup

1 2/3 cups pineapple syrup
3 (8-ounce) jars maraschino
  cherries, drained

Drain cans of sliced pineapple and reserve syrup. Combine sugar, light corn syrup and 1 2/3 cups pineapple syrup in a heavy 10-inch skillet. Cook over medium heat, stirring constantly, until mixture boils. Cook until temperature reaches 234 degrees. Add 1/3 of pineapple slices; bring to a boil. Reduce heat; simmer 25 minutes or until pineapple is transparent around edges. Remove, drain on wire rack. Repeat with remaining pineapple. Then add drained maraschino cherries. Simmer for 25 minutes. Let dry 24 hours at room temperature. Yields 10 slices pineapple and cherries.

Mrs. Robert Stuart, Macon

STRAWBERRIES

4 (3-ounce) packages strawberry gelatin
2 (3½-ounce) cans angel flake coconut
2 cups ground nuts

1 (14-ounce) can sweetened condensed milk
granulated sugar, tinted red

Mix well all ingredients except sugar in bowl. Shape, roll in red granulated sugar, put green leaves on top with purchased cake and cookie decoration or with an icing decorator. Makes about 90 strawberries.

Lucille DeLap, Charleston

OLD FASHIONED VINEGAR TAFFY

2 cups sugar
⅛ teaspoon cream of tartar
2 tablespoons butter

½ cup vinegar
dash of salt

Combine all ingredients and boil to a hard ball stage. Cool in buttered pan until cool enough to handle. Pull until white and porous. Break into pieces when cold. Yields approximately 5 dozen pieces.

Eleanor Weaver, Wiggins

PECAN LOGS

1 teaspoon vanilla
1 (8-ounce) jar marshmallow cream
1 (1-pound) box confectioners sugar

1 pound caramels
1 pound pecans, finely chopped

Mix vanilla into marshmallow cream. Work in confectioners sugar, small amount at a time. Roll into logs. Melt caramels in saucepan over low heat. If needed, add a small amount of milk to thin. Roll logs in caramel and then roll in chopped pecans. Chill in refrigerator before cutting. Yields approximately 4 dozen small slices.

Deborah Weaver, Wiggins

PEANUT BRITTLE

1½ cups sugar
¾ cup white corn syrup
¼ cup hot water

1 pint raw, shelled peanuts
1½ teaspoons soda

Cook sugar, syrup, and hot water in a saucepan at high temperature until mixture just begins to spin a thread from spoon. Add peanuts. Cook at medium high temperature until peanuts stop popping or until syrup turns amber color. Add soda, stirring constantly. When entire mixture foams, pour onto greased cookie sheet to cool. When cool, break into pieces. Yields approximately 5 dozen small pieces.

Mrs. Roy Duncan, Pontotoc

EASY PRALINES

1½ (3-ounce) packages non-instant butterscotch pudding
1½ cups sugar
¾ cup brown sugar

¾ cup evaporated milk
1½ tablespoons butter or margarine
2¼ cups pecan halves

Mix all ingredients except pecans in a heavy 2-quart saucepan. Cook and stir the mixture over low heat until sugar dissolves. Add pecans. Continue cooking and stirring to a full all-over boil. Then boil slowly about 3 to 5 minutes, stirring often until candy reaches soft ball stage (234 degrees). Remove from heat and beat until candy thickens, but still looks shiny. Drop quickly by tablespoonfuls onto waxed paper, spreading each with the spoon as it is dropped, to form patties about 2 inches across. Let stand until firm. Yields 32 pralines.

Mrs. Anthony Garst, Clarksdale

NEW ORLEANS PRALINES

1 pound light brown sugar
1 (6-ounce) can evaporated milk
2 tablespoons light corn syrup

¼ cup butter or margarine
1 teaspoon vanilla
1½ cups pecan halves

Mix sugar, evaporated milk and corn syrup in a two-quart saucepan. Cook over medium heat, stirring constantly, until the mixture comes to a boil. Continue cooking, stirring occasionally, until the temperature reaches 238 degrees on a candy thermometer, or until a small amount of the mixture forms a soft ball when tested in very cold water. Remove from heat. Add butter but do not stir. Cool to lukewarm (110 degrees on a candy thermometer). Add vanilla and beat until creamy. Stir in pecans. Drop by teaspoons onto waxed paper. Shape with a spoon into 2½-inch circles, spreading pecans. Allow to remain undisturbed until the pralines are firm and sugared. Makes 1½ pounds of candy.

Trudy Landrum, Poplarville

COFFEE COATED PARTY PECANS

1 cup sugar
½ cup water
1 tablespoon instant coffee
1 cup pecans

Combine sugar, water and instant coffee in saucepan. Cook over low heat, stirring constantly, until mixture comes to a boil. Continue cooking until a drop forms a ball when dropped in cold water. Pour the hot syrup slowly over 1 cup of pecans and stir until nuts are coated evenly. Place on rack to dry. Yields approximately 20 servings.

Mrs. George Massey, Columbia

ORANGE PECANS

2 cups sugar
½ cup water
juice and grated rind of
1 orange
3 tablespoons white corn
syrup
2 cups pecans

Mix sugar, water, orange juice, orange rind, and corn syrup. Boil to 230 degrees or until soft ball stage. Stir until it begins to sugar. Add pecans and pour into a buttered 9 x 13 x 2-inch pan. Break apart when thoroughly cold and hardened. Yields 1½ pounds.

Mrs. Annie Cage, Clarksdale

CANDIED WALNUTS

1½ cups sugar
½ cup orange juice
1½ teaspoons finely grated
orange rind
6 drops red coloring
2½ cups walnuts
1 teaspoon white corn syrup
¼ teaspoon salt

In a two-quart saucepan, mix all ingredients except walnuts. Cook to a soft ball stage (238 degrees). Add walnuts and stir until creamy. Quickly turn out on waxed paper and separate with fork. For flavor variation, another fruit juice may be substituted for the orange juice. Yields approximately 1½ pounds.

Mrs. Ida Whitney, Bay St. Louis

WALNUT BOURBON BALLS

2½ cups finely crushed
   vanilla wafers
1 cup powdered sugar
1 tablespoon cocoa
1 cup finely chopped nuts

1 cup coconut (if desired)
3 tablespoons corn syrup
¼ cup bourbon or wine
powdered sugar (to roll
   balls in)

Mix well the first 4 ingredients and if desired, coconut. Add corn syrup and bourbon. Mix well. Roll into 1 inch balls. Roll in powdered sugar. Yields approximately 6 dozen balls.

Mrs. Martha Rutherford, Bay St. Louis

PECAN DAINTIES

1 egg white
1 cup light brown sugar

1½ cups pecan halves

Beat egg white until stiff. Add brown sugar gradually, beating constantly. Add pecan halves. Drop by spoonfuls onto a greased cooky tin, and bake at 250 degrees for 30 minutes. Remove from tin and cool. Yields 2 dozen.

Mrs. R. L. Agnew, Macon

PEANUT BUTTER ROLL

2 cups white sugar
1 cup brown sugar
½ cup white corn syrup
1 cup undiluted evaporated
   milk

1 teaspoon white vinegar
½ cup peanut butter
1 cup sifted confectioners
   sugar
½ cup chopped pecans

Combine sugars, corn syrup, milk and vinegar in a saucepan. Cook to the soft ball stage. Stir and continue cooking until sugar is dissolved. Cool, without stirring, to lukewarm. Beat until creamy. Stir in peanut butter. Turn onto a surface dusted with confectioners sugar. Knead in the sugar to make firm. Shape into a 2-inch roll 12 inches long. Roll in chopped pecans pressing the nuts firmly into the roll. Wrap in waxed paper and chill. Cut into slices. Yields approximately 4 dozen slices.

Mrs. Juanita Ormon, Ashland

POP CORN BALLS

1 cup dark corn syrup	⅛ teaspoon soda
1 cup sugar	1 teaspoon vanilla
1 teaspoon vinegar	4 quarts popped corn
2 tablespoons butter	

Combine syrup, sugar and vinegar in a saucepan over medium heat. Boil until it reaches hard boil stage, 248 degrees. Remove from heat. Add butter, soda and vanilla. Stir. Pour syrup over popcorn, a small amount at a time and stir until well-coated. Shape into balls with lightly buttered hands. Place on a buttered baking sheet to cool. Yields 12 popcorn balls.

Mrs. B. F. Hendricks, Wesson

·⟦Cookies⟧·

Cookies are a universal favorite. They have a national character and are popular the world round.

Every country has its own collection of favorites. England has its scones and shortbread so popular with tea. The Scandinavian countries have their recipes for rich, buttery cookies, and France is known for her elegant chocolate peaks and petits fours. And of course there's the gingerbread of Germany. American cooks can collect a rich and varied repertoire of cookie recipes from throughout the world.

Pecans are plentiful in Mississippi and show up often in delicious cookie recipes. Magnolia State cooks can contribute their share of recipes for rich brownies, an American favorite, and for old-fashioned sugar cookies. There are drop cookies, rolled cookies, refrigerator cookies, molded cookies and bar cookies—all easy to make and easy to keep.

Crisp and soft cookies should be stored in separate containers. Empty coffee or shortening cans are good for this. Soft cookies should be stored in a container with a tight-fitting lid. A slice of apple or bread in the container helps to keep the cookies moist. Replace fruit or bread often to prevent mold. Store crisp cookies in a container with a loose-fitting lid. If the cookies lose their crispness, heat at 300 degrees about five minutes before serving. Bar cookies should be stored right in the baking pan and covered tightly with foil or freezer wrap. Cookies may be frozen either baked or unbaked and kept about one month at 0 degrees F.

COCOONS

¾ cup butter
¼ cup whipping cream or
evaporated milk
1 teaspoon vanilla

1¾ cups plain flour
6 tablespoons powdered sugar
1 cup finely chopped nuts

Cream butter, add whipping cream and vanilla. Sift together flour and powdered sugar. Add to the creamed mixture. Add chopped nuts. Chill. Pinch off dough and roll into balls the size of big marbles. Bake in 360 degree oven for 20 minutes. Roll in powdered sugar. Yield: 3 dozen.

Mrs. R. B. Nance, Louisville

BUTTER FINGERS

2 sticks butter (½ pound)
5 tablespoons powdered sugar
3 cups sifted flour, plain

1 teaspoon vanilla
2 cups chopped pecans

Cream butter and sugar; add sifted flour, vanilla and nuts. Mix well to a smooth texture. Pinch off small pieces and roll into balls or cocoon shaped fingers. Bake at 375 degrees until lightly browned, about 10 minutes. Roll in additional powdered sugar when cool. Yield: About 12 dozen.

Hazel H. Bequette, Mayersville

SUGAR BALLS

1 cup margarine
½ cup granulated sugar
2 cups flour
½ teaspoon salt

2 teaspoons vanilla
1 to 2 cups chopped pecans
½ cup powdered sugar

Cream margarine and sugar. Add flour and salt sifted together. Add vanilla and stir in pecans. Roll in balls and bake in 350 degree oven for 15 to 20 minutes. Roll in powdered sugar. Yield: 3 dozen.

Mrs. Mary Geoghegan, Fayette

SWEDISH COOKIES

1 cup butter or margarine
1 tablespoon vanilla
1 cup confectioners sugar

½ teaspoon salt
1¼ cups ground pecans
2 cups instant flour

Cream butter, vanilla, sugar and salt. Add pecans. Blend in flour. Shape dough into balls using a rounded teaspoonful for each. Flatten with hand. Bake on ungreased cookie sheet at 325 degrees for 15 to 18 minutes. Cookies do not brown on top. Yield: About 4½ dozen.

Mrs. W. D. Andrews, Jr., Biloxi

CHRISTMAS COOKIES

1 cup shortening	1 teaspoon soda
2 cups packed brown sugar	1 teaspoon salt
2 whole eggs	1½ cups chopped pecans
½ cup buttermilk	2 cups candied diced cherries
3½ cups sifted all-purpose flour	2 cups chopped dates

Cream stortening and sugar; add eggs and beat well. Add buttermilk and mix. Sift dry ingredients together and add gradually to creamed mixture, mixing until thoroughly blended. Add chopped pecans, diced cherries and dates. Mix well. Drop by teaspoonfuls on greased cookie sheet. Bake at 375 degrees for 10 to 12 minutes, or until browned. Yield: 5 dozen medium-sized cookies.

Mrs. George Rone, Clarksdale

CHRISTMAS COOKIES

1½ cups light brown sugar	1 pound white raisins
1 cup oleo	1 pound chopped candied cherries
4 large eggs	
3 cups sifted plain flour	1 pound chopped candied pineapple
3 teaspoons soda	
1 teaspoon salt	1 pound pitted, chopped dates
1 teaspoon cinnamon	6 cups chopped fine pecans
1 teaspoon nutmeg	½ cup fresh orange juice
3 tablespoons milk	

Cream sugar and oleo lightly. Beat eggs, add to sugar mixture. Sift 2 cups flour with soda, salt, cinnamon and nutmeg. Add to creamed mixture. Add milk. Sift 1 cup flour over chopped fruit, raisins and pecans; mix well; add this mixture to other ingredients, and then add orange juice. Mix well. Drop from teaspoon by small amounts onto greased cookie sheet. Bake 12 to 15 minutes in slow (325 degree) oven. Watch closely while cooking as cookies burn easily. These cookies may be frozen and kept for months. Yield: About 300 cookies.

Mrs. Joe Priddy, Rolling Fork

WHITE CHRISTMAS COOKIES

1½ cups soft butter
3 cups powdered sugar
4 eggs, well beaten
3 cups sifted plain flour

½ teaspoon salt
3 tablespoons sherry
½ tablespoon nutmeg

Cream butter and sugar. Add eggs. Beat together. Sift flour and salt together several times. Add to other ingredients with wine and nutmeg. Stir well but do not beat. Place in refrigerator overnight. Next morning, roll out on floured board, very thin. Cut in shapes, (hearts, stars, diamonds, etc.) and bake in 350 degree oven. Yield: About 80 cookies.

Mrs. Marguerite Shelton, Fayette

CHRISTMAS FRUIT CAKE COOKIES

1 stick of butter
1 cup brown sugar
4 eggs, well beaten
3 cups all-purpose flour
1 teaspoon soda
½ teaspoon salt
3 tablespoons sour milk

½ cup whisky, wine or
    orange juice
½ teaspoon nutmeg
1 pound cherries
1 pound pineapple
1½ pounds whole pecans
1 pound white raisins

Cream butter and sugar then add eggs, dry ingredients and liquids. Last, add chopped fruit and whole pecans. Drop by spoonfuls onto greased cookie sheet. Bake at 350 degrees about 15 minutes. Yield: 4 pounds.

Mrs. Louise Hammons, Glen Allen

SUGAR COOKIES

2 cups sifted all-purpose
    flour
1½ teaspoons baking powder
½ teaspoon salt
½ cup butter

1 cup sugar
1 egg
1 teaspoon vanilla
1 tablespoon cream or milk

Sift together 1½ cups flour, baking powder and salt. Cream butter until soft. Beat in sugar, egg, vanilla and cream. Stir in the flour mixture. Gradually add the remaining flour until dough is stiff enough to roll. Chill thoroughly. Place on lightly floured board and roll ⅛ inch thick. Cut with floured cutter as desired. Place on greased baking sheet. Sprinkle with sugar. Bake in moderate to hot oven (375 degrees to 400 degrees) 8 to 10 minutes. Store in closely covered cookie jar. Yield: 4 to 5 dozen.

Mrs. Cherry Renfro, Columbia

OLD FASHION TEA CAKES

1 cup butter	1 teaspoon nutmeg
2 cups sugar	1 teaspoon vanilla
4 eggs	4 cups flour, sifted 3 times
1 tablespoon milk	3 tablespoons baking powder

Cream butter and sugar. Add eggs, one at a time, mixing well after each addition. Add milk, nutmeg and vanilla. Sift flour and baking powder together and combine with other mixture. Add enough additional flour to roll out, then cut. Bake on ungreased cookie sheet in oven at 325 degrees for 15 minutes. Yield: approximately 4 dozen.

Mrs. Phayes Carter, Woodville

AMBER COOKIES

1 pound candy orange slices, cut fine	2 (14-ounce) cans sweetened condensed milk
2 (3½-ounce) cans flaked coconut	1 teaspoon orange flavoring
1 cup finely chopped pecans	1 teaspoon vanilla
	1½ cups powdered sugar

Combine all ingredients except powdered sugar, and mix well. Spread mixture in slightly oiled cookie sheet or jelly roll pan and bake at 275 degrees for 30 minutes. Remove from oven and while still warm, make into balls the size of small walnuts. Roll in powdered sugar and place on cake racks to cool. Yield: About 6 dozen.

Mrs. Carolyn Ellard, Kosciusko

PECAN MACAROON COOKIES

2 large egg whites	½ teaspoon vanilla
¾ cup sugar	20-22 Ritz crackers, crushed
½ cup flake coconut	1 cup pecans, chopped

Beat egg whites until stiff, fold in sugar, add coconut and vanilla and fold into cracker crumbs and pecans. Mix well. Drop with spoon onto slightly greased cookie sheet. Bake at 300 degrees until light brown, about 5 minutes. Let cool in pan before lifting out. Yield: 24 to 28 cookies.

Mrs. Hilda Boyd, Madison

ALMOND MACAROON CRESCENTS

1 (8-ounce) can of almond
    paste
1 cup sugar

2 stiffly beaten egg whites
1 (3 or 4-ounce) package
    sliced almonds

Cut up almond paste in small pieces and add sugar and egg whites. Mix until smooth, no lumps remaining. Roll rounded teaspoons of this mixture into sliced almonds and shape into crescents. Place on a greased baking sheet and bake in a 350 degree oven for 20 minutes. Yield: About 2 dozen.

Mrs. T. H. Brooks, Jackson

PEANUT BUTTER SURPRISES

1¾ cups sugar
½ cup evaporated milk,
    undiluted
½ stick butter or oleo

½ cup peanut butter
⅜ pound saltines, coarsely
    broken
1 teaspoon vanilla

Mix sugar, milk and oleo and bring to a boil. Boil 1 minute. Stir in peanut butter. Blend well. Then add broken crackers and vanilla. Drop by spoonfuls onto wax paper and let cool. No additional cooking is necessary. Yield: 2 to 3 dozen.

Mrs. Robert C. Morris, Leland

CRISP OAT COOKIES

2 cups sifted all-purpose
    flour
½ teaspoon salt
½ teaspoon baking powder
½ teaspoon baking soda
1 teaspoon cinnamon
½ teaspoon allspice

1 cup shortening
1 cup brown sugar
½ cup granulated sugar
2 eggs, beaten
2/3 cup sour milk
1½ cups rolled oats
1 cup chopped nuts

Sift flour, salt, soda, baking powder and spices together. Cream shortening with both sugars until fluffy. Add beaten eggs and mix well. Add sifted ingredients alternately with sour milk. Add rolled oats and nuts. Drop from teaspoon onto greased baking sheet and bake in moderate oven (350 degrees) about 10 to 12 minutes or until browned. Yield: About 5 dozen.

Mrs. Curtis Friday, Jr., West Point

COCOA OATMEAL COOKIES

1¼ cups all-purpose flour
½ teaspoon baking powder
½ teaspoon salt
1/3 cup cocoa
1¼ cups sugar
1 egg, well beaten

½ cup milk
1½ teaspoons vanilla
1/3 cup shortening, melted
1/3 cup butter, melted
2 cups rolled oats

Sift flour, measure and resift twice with baking powder, salt, cocoa and sugar. Combine beaten eggs, milk and vanilla. Add melted butter and shortening. Mix thoroughly with the sifted dry ingredients. Then stir in the rolled oats and drop by teaspoonfuls onto a buttered cookie sheet. Bake in a moderate oven (350 degrees) 15 to 20 minutes. Remove to cake racks to cool. Yield: 5 dozen.

Mrs. B. J. Crevitt, Jr., Vicksburg

BUTTERFUDGE FINGERS

2 squares unsweetened
   chocolate (2 ounces)
1/3 cup butter
1 cup sugar
2 eggs

¾ cup sifted all-purpose
   flour
½ teaspoon baking powder
½ teaspoon salt
½ cup broken nuts

TOPPING:
¼ cup butter, softened
2 cups powdered sugar,
   sifted
2 tablespoons cream

1 teaspoon vanilla
1 square unsweetened
   chocolate
1 tablespoon butter

Heat oven to 350 degrees. Melt chocolate and butter over hot water. Beat in sugar and eggs. Sift dry ingredients together and stir in. Add nuts. Spread in greased 8-inch square pan. Bake 30 to 35 minutes, until top has dull crust. Cool slightly. Brown ¼ cup soft butter over medium heat. Blend with powdered sugar, cream and vanilla. Spread on brownies. Melt 1 square (1 ounce) unsweetened chocolate and 1 tablespoon butter. When cooled, spread very thin coating over icing. When set, cut in 2 x 1-inch fingers. Yield: 32 fingers.

Mrs. John Mixon, Hattiesburg

BLOND BROWNIES

2/3 cup melted margarine	½ teaspoon soda
2 cups packed brown sugar	1 teaspoon vanilla
2 whole eggs	1 cup chopped pecans
2 cups sifted all-purpose flour	1 (6-ounce) package
1 teaspoon baking powder	semi-sweet chocolate chips

Mix margarine, sugar and eggs well. Add flour, baking powder and soda. Add vanilla and chopped pecans. Pour into a greased 9 x 12-inch pan and sprinkle chocolate chips on top. Bake at 350 degrees for 25 minutes. Yield: 2½ dozen.

Mrs. Henry Ashford, Clarksdale

BACHELOR BUTTONS

1 cup shortening	2 cups plain flour
1 cup light brown sugar	1 teaspoon soda
1 egg	1 cup chopped nuts
1 teaspoon salt	1 cup coconut

Mix as listed. Roll into balls about 1-inch in diameter. Press centers with fingers. Bake at 400 degrees for 10 minutes. Yield: About 5 dozen.

Mrs. C. L. Cahoon, Chunky

GINGER SNAPS

2½ cups all-purpose flour	¼ teaspoon cinnamon
½ cup shortening	¼ teaspoon nutmeg
½ cup sugar	⅛ teaspoon cloves
½ cup molasses	½ teaspoon soda
1 egg, beaten	1 tablespoon hot water
1 teaspoon ginger	1 teaspoon vinegar

Sift flour, measure and resift. Cream shortening, blend in sugar and add molasses and beaten egg. Beat until smooth. Mix spices thoroughly with soda and blend until smooth with hot water and vinegar. Stir into creamed mixture. Add flour, mixing thoroughly until smooth. Drop from teaspoon onto buttered baking sheet, at least two inches apart. Bake 10 minutes in a moderate oven (375 degrees). Remove to cake racks to cool. Yield: 4 to 5 dozen, depending on size.

Mrs. Norma W. Smith, Summit

GRANDMA CORINE'S GINGER CAKES

½ cup butter or 1 stick
    margarine
1 teaspoon ginger
½ teaspoon cloves

dash of black pepper
1 cup molasses syrup
1 teaspoon soda
3 cups sifted flour

Cream margarine and spices. Mix soda in the syrup and add to margarine. Stir well. Mix in flour until all is one mass. Roll on floured board and cut cookies in any shape or ginger men. Place on greased cookie sheet. Place raisins or candied fruit on top if desired and bake at 400 degrees for about 10 minutes. Yield: About 3 dozen medium round cookies.

Mrs. T. A. Baines, Jackson

MOLASSES CRINKLES

2¼ cups sifted all-purpose
    flour
2 teaspoons soda
¼ teaspoon salt
½ teaspoon cloves
1 teaspoon cinnamon

1 teaspoon ginger
¾ cup shortening
1 cup packed brown sugar
1 egg
¼ cup molasses

Mix dry ingredients. Stir in the creamed shortening, sugar, egg and molasses. Chill dough. Heat oven to 375 degrees. Roll dough into balls the size of large walnuts. Dip tops in sugar. Place, sugared side up, 3 inches apart on greased baking sheet. Bake 10 to 12 minutes. For crackled surface sprinkle each cookie with 2 or 3 drops of water. Yield: 4 dozen.

Mrs. Hilman Wedgeworth, Laurel

[413]

MOLASSES-ORANGE COOKIES

1 (6-ounce) can frozen
 orange concentrate
½ cup rolled oats
1 cup raisins
½ cup shortening
½ cup sugar

½ cup molasses
2 cups all-purpose flour
2 teaspoons soda
1 teaspoon ginger
1 teaspoon cinnamon
¼ teaspoon salt

Combine orange concentrate, oats and raisins, and set aside. Cream sugar and shortening, add molasses. Sift together flour, soda, spices and salt. Add to molasses mixture. Blend well. Drop by teaspoonfuls onto greased cookie sheet and bake in 325 degree oven for 25 minutes.

Mrs. Edith Clark, Utica

CHERRY TEA DAINTIES

½ cup margarine
¼ cup sugar
1 egg yolk
1 teaspoon vanilla
¼ teaspoon salt

1¼ cups sifted cake flour
1 egg white
1 cup chopped nuts
21 candied cherries

Mix until creamy, margarine, sugar, egg yolk, vanilla and salt. Add flour, mix well. Refrigerate until easy to handle. Form into 1 inch balls. Dip balls in unbeaten egg white. Roll in nuts, place on greased cookie sheet. Press cherry half into top of each cookie. Bake in 350 degree oven for 20 to 25 minutes. Yield: About 40.

Mrs. John Foster, Natchez

BUTTER–CRISPS

1 pound soft butter or
 margarine
2 cups flour
1 cup confectioners sugar

1 cup cornstarch
1 teaspoon vanilla or
 almond flavoring

Cream butter adding dry ingredients slowly. Add flavoring. Divide into four portions. Wrap each portion in foil. Chill thoroughly.

Shape into 1 inch balls, working quickly with one portion of dough at a time, keeping other portions in the refrigerator. Place balls 2 inches apart on ungreased cookie sheet. Flatten with floured tines of fork. Bake at 325 degrees for 18 to 20 minutes until lightly browned. Very delicate—melts in your mouth. Yield: About 7 dozen.

Mrs. H. T. Matthews, Raymond

DATE BALLS

½ stick butter
1 cup sugar
1 egg
½ cup chopped dates

1 teaspoon vanilla
2 cups Rice Krispies
1 cup pecans
flaked coconut

Mix butter, sugar, egg and dates together and cook until thick. This doesn't take too long, less than 10 minutes. Add vanilla, Rice Krispies and pecans. Make into 1 inch balls and roll in flaked coconut. This makes a good cookie to serve with coffee. Yield: 24 cookies.

Mrs. Florine Wallace, Fayette

MUDHENS

½ cup butter or margarine
1 cup white sugar
2 eggs
1½ cups plain flour
1 teaspoon baking powder

½ teaspoon salt
½ teaspoon vanilla
1 cup chopped nuts
1 cup brown sugar

Cream butter and sugar. Add 1 egg and 1 yolk, one at a time. Mix in dry ingredients and vanilla. Spread into a greased 9 x 13 inch pan. Sprinkle with nuts. Beat remaining egg white. Add brown sugar gradually. Beat until stiff. Spread over nuts. Bake at 350 degrees for 30 minutes or until done. Yield: About 24.

Mrs. Tressie Bonds, Iuka
Mrs. M. L. Dilworth, Booneville

STRAWBERRY COOKIES

½ pound butter
1 cup sugar
2 eggs yolks
2 cups plain flour

½ teaspoon salt
1 cup broken nuts
½ cup strawberry jam

Cream butter and sugar together. Add egg yolks. Then add flour, salt and nuts. Mix well together. Put ½ of mixture into 8-inch square greased pan. Spread jam over mixture, then add other half on top of this. Bake in 325 degree oven for 1 hour. Yield: 24 cookies..

Mrs. Jack Gomillion, Union

RUM COOKIES

2 cups applesauce
2 teaspoons soda
¾ cup butter
2 cups sugar
4 cups plain flour
1 teaspoon cinnamon
1 teaspoon nutmeg
1 teaspoon cloves

¼ teaspoon salt
1 (15-ounce) package raisins
2 cups pecans
1 pound box powdered sugar
½ cup butter, melted
¼ cup rum flavoring
6 tablespoons hot water

Cream first four ingredients. Add mixture of flour, cinnamon, nutmeg, cloves and salt. Then add 1 package raisins and 2 cups pecans (Put through food chopper). (Mixed fruit may be substituted for raisins and nuts.) Bake at 375 degrees about 20 minutes in small cup cake pans.

Mix powdered sugar and melted butter, rum flavoring and hot water. Blend well and frost the cakes.

Mrs. Rosa Lee Benigno, Bay St. Louis

SHORT BREAD

1 cup butter
½ cup sugar

2 1/3 cups sifted plain flour
¼ teaspoon salt

Cream butter and sugar gradually until light and fluffy. Work in the flour and salt, using finger tips. Press evenly into greased 9 x 9 x 2-inch pan and prick with fork. Bake for 50 minutes in a 300 degree oven. Cool slightly, then cut into oblong bars. Keeps well in tight containers for weeks. Better if stored a week before eating. Yield: About 40 bars 1¾ by 1 inch.

Mrs. Nellie Moore, Woodville

CRUNCHY TOP BAR COOKIES

¾ cup soft oleo or butter
½ cup brown sugar
½ cup granulated sugar
3 eggs, separated
1 teaspoon vanilla
2 cups sifted all-purpose
   flour
1 teaspoon baking powder

¼ teaspoon soda
¼ teaspoon salt
1 (6-ounce) package
   chocolate chips
¾ cup chopped nuts
1 cup coconut
1 cup brown sugar

Mix butter or oleo, brown sugar, granulated sugar, egg yolks and vanilla.

Sift flour, baking powder, soda, salt together and add to butter mixture. Mix well. Press into a 13 x 9 inch greased pan. Over this spread chocolate chips, nuts and coconut. Beat egg whites until frothy but not stiff, add brown sugar, mix. Put this over the top of mixture in pan. Bake at 350 degrees for 40 minutes. Yield: About 24.

Mrs. Steve Frank, Egypt

RUM BARS

3 cups pecans or walnuts, chopped
2¼ cups packed light brown sugar
1 cup butter
4 eggs
2¼ cups sifted all-purpose flour
2 tablespoons vanilla
½ pound candied pineapple, chopped

¼ pound candied citron, chopped
1 pound candied cherries, chopped
1 cup dried figs, chopped (optional)
1½ cups pecans, chopped
rum

Place 3 cups chopped pecans or walnuts in bottom of a 9 x 13 inch greased pan. Cream sugar and butter. Add eggs, one at a time beating well after each addition. Add flour and vanilla. Mix well. Spread dough over walnuts in the greased pan being careful not to displace walnuts. Mix candied and dried fruit and pecans and sprinkle over batter pressing it into the batter. Bake at 200 degrees for 3½ hours. Remove from oven and cool slightly. Cut into bars and pour a small amount of rum on each bar. Store two to three weeks to mellow. Yield: 4 to 5 dozen bars, depending on size of each bar.

Mrs. M. A. Rowzee, State College

CALIFORNIA DREAM BAR

1 cup flour
1 stick melted margarine
1½ cups brown sugar
2 eggs

1 cup chopped pecans
1 cup grated coconut
2 tablespoons flour
½ teaspoon baking powder

Combine and thoroughly blend the flour, margarine and ½ cup brown sugar. Pat crust in 10-inch square pan. Bake 15 minutes in 350 degree oven. Mix remaining ingredients and spread over crust. Bake 15 more minutes. Cool and cut in squares. Yield: About 24.

Mrs. Lenora Beatus, Belzoni

PEANUT BUTTER BARS

1/3 cup shortening
½ cup peanut butter
¼ cup brown sugar
1 cup granulated sugar
1 teaspoon vanilla

2 eggs
1 cup plain flour
1 teaspoon baking powder
¼ teaspoon salt
1 cup cookie coconut

Cream together shortening, peanut butter and sugars until light and fluffy. Add vanilla and eggs; beat well. Mix in flour, baking powder and salt, stirring only until blended. Stir in coconut. Spread evenly in greased 13 x 9 x 2 inch pan. Bake in 350 degree oven about 25 minutes or until golden brown. Cut into bars. Yield: About 32.

Mrs. Charles Patterson, Kosciusko

SPICY NUT SQUARES

1 cup soft butter
1 cup sugar
1 egg, separated
2 cups sifted plain flour

1 teaspoon cinnamon
1 cup walnuts or pecans, finely
  chopped
½ cup chocolate chips

Cream together butter and sugar. Add egg yolk, beat well. Sift flour and cinnamon, and gradually add to creamed mixture. Stir well. Mix in nuts. Spread dough evenly in well greased 15 x 10 inch jelly roll pan. Beat egg white slightly, brush over top smooth surface with finger tips. Sprinkle with chocolate chips and press on top of dough. Bake in low oven (275 degrees) for one hour. While warm cut in 1½ inch squares. Yield: About 20.

Miss Bea Waldrup, Courtland

TOFFEE SQUARES

1 cup butter
1 cup brown sugar, packed
1 egg yolk
1 teaspoon vanilla
2 cups sifted plain flour

¼ teaspoon salt
3 to 4 milk chocolate bars
  (7/8 ounces each)
½ cup finely chopped
  nuts

Preheat oven to 350 degrees. Mix butter, sugar, egg yolk and vanilla. Sift flour and salt. Stir in flour and salt until well blended. Bake in greased 13 x 9 x 2 inch pan for 25 minutes. Crust will still be soft. Remove from oven. Immediately place separated squares of chocolate on top. Let stand until soft; spread evenly over entire surface. Sprinkle with nuts. Cut in small squares while warm. Yield: 5 dozen squares.

Mrs. Jack Fletcher, Cleveland

QUICK DATE NUT SQUARES

¾ cup margarine or
  butter
2¼ cups firmly packed
  brown sugar
1 teaspoon vanilla
3 eggs
1 cup pecans

2¾ cups sifted plain flour
½ teaspoon salt
2½ teaspoons baking
  powder
1½ teaspoons instant coffee
1 (8-ounce) package dates
  (cut into small pieces)

Cream margarine and sugar. Add vanilla and eggs. Beat thoroughly. Add sifted dry ingredients slowly. Add remaining ingredients. Mix well. Bake in a large greased cookie pan at 350 degrees for 25-35 minutes. Cut into squares. Yield: 24 to 30.

Mrs. Lee Carter, Woodville

OVER LAYER CANDY CAKE

1 stick of butter or oleo
1 cup graham cracker crumbs
1 cup flaked coconut

1 cup chopped pecans
1 cup chocolate chips
1 can condensed milk

Melt butter first in a 9 x 9 x 2 inch pan. Add crumbs, spreading them evenly over bottom of pan; add coconut and pecans and spread each ingredient evenly as you add it. Add chocolate chips in like manner. Pour the can of condensed milk, be sure it is spread evenly. Bake in oven 350 degrees for 30 minutes. Let cool then cut in squares. This freezes real well. Yield: 36 squares.

Mrs. A. M. Aust, Macon

BROWN SUGAR COOKIES

½ cup shortening
1 well beaten egg
½ teaspoon soda
1 cup nuts

1 cup light brown sugar
1¾ cups plain flour
⅛ teaspoon salt
1 teaspoon vanilla

Cream shortening, sugar and egg. Add all remaining ingredients. Form into rolls 1½ to 2 inches in diameter. Wrap in waxed paper. Refrigerate several hours. Slice and place on greased cookie sheet. Bake at 350 degrees 12 to 15 minutes.

Mrs. Lewis Tabb, Belzoni
Mrs. Joy Frizell, Lexington

DELICATE LEMON SQUARES

½ cup melted butter or margarine
¼ cup powdered sugar
1 cup sifted all-purpose flour
2 beaten eggs

1 cup sugar
2 tablespoons lemon juice
2 tablespoons sifted all-purpose flour
½ teaspoon baking powder
3 tablespoons powdered sugar

Combine first 3 ingredients; mix well and pat into a greased 9-inch square pan. Bake 15 minutes at 350 degrees. Combine remaining ingredients except powdered sugar and pour over the cooked layer and bake at 350 degrees for 25 minutes. While cake is still warm sprinkle with 3 tablespoons powdered sugar. Yield: 1½ dozen.

Mrs. Fred Carroll, Lyon
Janie L. Washington, Vicksburg

DATE NUT PINWHEEL COOKIES

2 (8-ounce) packages dates
2 cups sugar
2 cups chopped nuts
2 cups water
4 cups brown sugar
2 cups shortening

6 eggs, well beaten
8 cups flour
1 teaspoon soda
2 teaspoons vanilla
pinch of salt

In double boiler mix dates, sugar, nuts, water and cook over medium heat until thick, but not too thick to spread. Set aside to cool. Meanwhile, cream brown sugar and shortening. Add well beaten eggs. Add flour to which soda and salt has been added. Then add vanilla (makes a stiff dough). Chill. Divide chilled dough into 8 balls. Roll each ball in a large square. Spread thin with date-nut mixture. Roll into a long roll, 1½ to 2 inches in diameter, and wrap in foil or waxed paper and put in freezing unit of refrigerator overnight. Take out as needed. Slice ¼ inch thick. Bake on greased cookie sheet at 350 degrees. Cook 12 to 15 minutes. Yield: 4 dozen.

Mary M. Jones, Lexington

CHOCOLATE NUT CRUNCH

2 cups finely crushed
   vanilla wafers
1 cup chopped walnuts or
   pecans
½ cup butter or margarine
1 cup sugar

3 well beaten egg yolks
1½ squares unsweetened
   chocolate, melted
½ teaspoon vanilla
3 stiffly beaten egg whites

Combine crumbs and nuts. Line bottom of 9-inch square pan with half of crumb mixture. Cream butter and sugar; add egg yolks, chocolate and vanilla. Mix well. Fold in egg whites. Spread over crumb mixture. Top with remainder of crumbs. Chill in refrigerator overnight. Cut in squares. Serves 8.

Mrs. Ray Solomon, Greenville

BANANA SPICE COOKIES

½ cup soft shortening
1 cup packed brown sugar
2 eggs
1 cup mashed bananas (2)
2 cups sifted flour
¼ teaspoon soda

¼ teaspoon salt
¼ teaspoon cloves
½ teaspoon cinnamon
2 teaspoons baking powder
½ cup chopped nuts

Mix well, shortening, sugar and eggs. Stir in bananas. Sift dry ingredients; stir in. Blend in nuts. Chill about 1 hour. Heat oven to 375 degrees. Drop, two inches apart, onto greased cookie sheet. Bake 10 minutes. Cool and frost with a preferred thin confectioner's sugar icing. Yield: About 2½ dozen.

Mrs. Virginia Nunn, Jackson

EASY LEMON COOKIES

½ cup oleo
1 cup sugar
¾ teaspoon lemon extract

1 egg
1 cup self-rising flour

Cream oleo, sugar and extract together. Add egg and mix well. Stir in flour. Drop by teaspoon onto lightly greased cookie sheet. Bake at 375 degrees for 10 to 12 minutes. Yield: Approximately 2 dozen 2-inch cookies.

Mrs. Wesley Wilson, Vicksburg

RUTH'S CRISP SUGAR DROP COOKIES

2½ cups all-purpose flour
½ teaspoon soda
1 teaspoon salt
1 egg, slightly beaten
2 tablespoons white vinegar
1½ teaspoons grated lemon
   rind
1 teaspoon vanilla
½ cup butter
½ cup shortening
1 cup sugar

Sift flour, soda and salt together. Combine egg with vinegar, lemon rind and vanilla. Cream butter and shortening until fluffy and smooth. Add sugar gradually, creaming well after each addition. Add dry ingredients and egg mixture alternately, blending well after each addition.

Drop by teaspoonfuls onto ungreased cookie sheet and flatten with lightly floured fork. Sprinkle with sugar. Bake at 400 degrees for 10 to 12 minutes. Yield: About 36.

Mrs. Ruth Wallace, McCall Creek

RANGLER CHOCOLATE CHIPS

1 cup butter (do not
   substitute)
¾ cup brown sugar
¾ cup granulated sugar
2 beaten eggs
1 teaspoon soda
1 teaspoon hot water
2¼ cups flour
1 teaspoon salt
1 cup chopped nuts
1 (6-ounce) package chocolate
   chips
1 teaspoon vanilla

Cream butter, brown sugar, granulated sugar and 2 beaten eggs together until well mixed. Dissolve soda in water. Sift flour and salt together. Add liquid and dry ingredients alternately to creamed mixture. Stir in chopped nuts and chocolate chips. Add vanilla and mix well. Drop by half-teaspoonfuls onto a slightly greased cookie sheet and bake at 375 degrees for 10 minutes. Yield: 5 dozen.

Mrs. Walter McKellar, Senatobia

LADY BALTIMORE COOKIES

1 cup shortening
1½ cups sugar
3 eggs
½ teaspoon soda
2 teaspoons water
3 cups flour

1½ teaspoons salt
1 teaspoon cinnamon
1 teaspoon allspice
1 teaspoon nutmeg
1½ cups raisins
½ cup broken nut meats

Cream shortening, sugar and eggs together. Dissolve soda in water and add to creamed mixture. Mix and sift flour, salt and spices and add to the first mixture. Add raisins and nuts and mix thoroughly. Drop by teaspoons onto greased baking sheet. Bake in 350 degree oven for 15 to 20 minutes. Yield: About 70 cookies.

Julia Nevels, Brookhaven

⁙Pies and Pastry⁙

"As American as apple pie" is a favorite and true expression. Pies, as served today, are typically American. Pie-making did not originate in this country but came to us through our English ancestors. Most of the early pies were made primarily of meat. We still serve main dish pies which are filled with meat and tender, flavorful vegetables, or smooth cheese and egg combinations.

The beginning of a good pie is a good crust—one that is flaky, rough and blistered rather than smooth and firm. It is golden brown around the edge and lighter brown on the bottom. The crust should be crisp even though it contains a filling.

For the best pastry, use a pastry blender for cutting shortening into the flour. The particles formed will flatten during rolling and provide tenderness and flakiness, characteristic of good pastry. A fork or spoon should not be used because it creams or blends instead of cutting. Use cold water to keep the shortening from melting. Add just enough to moisten the flour. Adding too much flour during rolling toughens the pastry. Handle as little as possible. Rerolling and overhandling also toughens pastry.

When we think of pies, most of us think of rich, smooth cream pies; tart, mouth-watering fruit pies; airy, light chiffon pies; or tender, velvety custard pies. Popular recipes for these types plus other Mississippi favorites such as pecan, chess, Southern molasses, egg custard, sweet potato and pumpkin are to be found in this section.

[425]

PECAN PIE

3 slightly beaten eggs
3 tablespoons unmelted butter
1 cup white corn syrup
½ cup sugar
1 tablespoon meal
1 teaspoon vanilla

1 teaspoon vinegar
dash of salt
1 cup coarsely chopped
pecans
8-inch pastry shell, unbaked

Beat eggs slightly. Add unmelted butter. Heat syrup, sugar and meal till fairly hot but not boiling. Pour over eggs and butter, beating constantly while pouring. Add vanilla, vinegar and salt, then the nuts. Pour into unbaked 8-inch pastry shell. Bake at 300 degrees 1 hour and 45 minutes or until filling is set and crust is golden brown.

Miss Judy Lynn Bethay, Booneville

PECAN PIE

¾ cup granulated sugar
1 cup dark corn syrup
3 eggs, slightly beaten
4 tablespoons butter or
margarine

1 teaspoon vanilla
1 cup pecans (coarsely
broken)
9-inch unbaked pie shell

Preheat oven to 350 degrees. Boil sugar and syrup together for about 2 minutes. Pour over slightly beaten eggs, stirring vigorously. Add butter or margarine, vanilla and pecans. Pour into unbaked pastry lined pie plate. Bake at 350 degrees for 50-60 minutes. Serves 6 to 8.

Mrs. W. W. Bishop, Hazlehurst

PECAN PIE

2 tablespoons butter
½ cup sugar
3 eggs, beaten
1 tablespoon cornstarch
¼ teaspoon salt

1 teaspoon vanilla extract
1 cup white corn syrup
1 cup chopped pecans
9-inch unbaked pastry shell

Preheat oven to 300 degrees. Cream butter and sugar. Add beaten eggs, cornstarch, salt, vanilla extract and syrup. Stir well. Add chopped pecans and pour into a 9-inch crust. Bake 45 minutes to 1 hour in a 300 degree oven.

Mrs. J. D. Mann, Fayette

MISSISSIPPI PECAN PIE

1 cup white corn syrup
1 cup pecans
½ cup sugar
3 eggs

1 teaspoon vanilla
½ teaspoon salt
9-inch unbaked pastry shell

Place syrup, pecans, sugar, slightly beaten eggs, vanilla and salt in bowl and stir to combine ingredients. Pour into unbaked 9-inch pastry shell and bake 50 minutes at 325 degrees. Pecans will float to top forming a crust that will brown nicely, if baked slowly.

Mrs. Webster Meredith, Clarksdale

INDIVIDUAL PECAN PIES

2 sticks oleo
2 (3-ounce) packages cream
  cheese
2 cups flour
2 eggs

1½ cups brown sugar
2 tablespoons oleo
½ teaspoon salt
1 teaspoon vanilla
2 cups finely chopped pecans

Cream oleo, cream cheese and flour. Make balls about the size of a walnut. Press them in small muffin pans. Mix together well the remaining ingredients and fill each pastry nearly full. Bake at 350 degrees for 15 to 17 minutes. Reduce heat to 300 degrees for 10 minutes.

Joy Durr, Brookhaven

BROWNIE PECAN PIE

½ cup grapenut cereal
½ cup warm water
¾ cup sugar
1 cup light corn syrup
2 squares unsweetened
  chocolate

3 tablespoons butter
3 slightly beaten eggs
1 teaspoon vanilla
½ cup chopped nuts
8-inch unbaked pie shell

Combine cereal and water and let stand until water is absorbed. Combine sugar and syrup in saucepan and bring to boil stirring until sugar is dissolved. Boil 2 minutes. Remove from heat, add chocolate and butter. Stir until blended. Slowly pour over eggs and stir constantly. Add cereal mixture, nuts and vanilla and pour into pie shell. Bake at 350 degrees about 45 minutes. When done it will be puffed and browned on top.

Mrs. B. F. Mott, Newton

CHESS PIE

3 eggs
1¼ cups sugar
2 teaspoons cornmeal
½ stick margarine

2 tablespoons lemon juice
1 teaspoon vanilla
8-inch unbaked pie shell

Beat eggs, then add sugar and cornmeal. Melt margarine and pour in, then add lemon juice and vanilla. Pour into an unbaked 8-inch pie shell and bake at 350 degrees until softly firm and brown.

Mrs. Johnnie Lee Williams, Pachuta

PECAN CHESS PIE

½ cup butter or margarine
1 cup sugar
¼ cup flour
⅛ teaspoon salt
3 eggs yolks

½ cup evaporated milk
1 teaspoon vanilla extract
2/3 cup coarsely chopped
   pecans
9-inch unbaked pastry shell

Cream the butter. Add sugar gradually and continue creaming until light and fluffy. Add flour, salt and egg yolks; mix well. Stir in evaporated milk and vanilla. Pour into prepared pastry shell and sprinkle pecans over top. Bake in preheated oven (425 degrees) for 10 minutes. Then reduce heat to 300 degrees and continue baking until set, at least 40 minutes longer. Serves 6 to 8. Serve hot or cold.

Mrs. Everette Bruce, Vaiden

LEMON CHESS PIE

2 cups sugar
1 tablespoon all-purpose
   flour
1 tablespoon cornmeal
4 eggs
½ stick butter or margarine,
   melted

¼ cup lemon juice
1 tablespoon grated lemon
   rind
¼ cup milk
9-inch unbaked pie crust

Sift flour and meal into sugar. Beat eggs slightly and add sugar mixture. Mix well. Add butter, lemon juice, lemon rind and milk. Pour into a 9-inch unbaked pie crust. Bake at 350 degrees for 45 minutes.

Mrs. Hazel M. Copeland, Baldwyn
Mrs. Lillie Maxwell, Durant

OLD FASHION MOLASSES PIE

4 eggs
½ cup sugar
2 tablespoons plain flour
⅛ teaspoon salt
2 cups molasses
1 teaspoon vanilla flavoring

1 tablespoon grated orange
  rind
¾ stick butter or
  margarine, melted
9-inch pie shell, unbaked

Beat eggs until light and fluffy. Combine sugar, flour and salt, and add to beaten eggs. Mix well. Add remaining ingredients and continue beating until well blended. Pour into unbaked pie shell and bake in a preheated oven at 400 degrees for 10 minutes; then reduce oven temperature to 350 degrees and continue baking until firm in the center.

Clara B. Jordan, Purvis

EGG PIE

1 cup sugar
5 eggs
1½ cups sweet milk

1 teaspoon lemon flavoring
½ stick margarine
9-inch unbaked pie crust

Beat sugar and eggs until well blended; then add milk and beat for about 2 minutes. Add flavoring and beat 1 minute. Line a 9-inch pie plate with unbaked pie crust. Dot the bottom with the margarine; then pour filling into plate and bake at 300 degrees for 45 minutes, or until well done. Serves 6.

Mrs. A. J. Gregory, Bay Springs

OLD FASHION EGG CUSTARD

3 eggs
2½ cups sweet milk
½ cup sugar
2 tablespoons all-purpose
  flour

2 tablespoons butter
½ teaspoon nutmeg
9-inch unbaked pie shell

Beat eggs all together, then add milk, sugar, flour, butter and nutmeg. Beat well, pour into an unbaked 9-inch pie shell, and bake in a 350 degree oven 45 minutes.

Mrs. W. B. Jackson, Purvis

GRANDMOTHER'S BASIC CUSTARD PIE

3 eggs, slightly beaten
2 cups sugar
3 tablespoons all-purpose flour
½ cup melted oleo or
  butter

1 cup diluted evaporated
  milk (¾ cup milk and
  ¼ cup water)
1 teaspoon vanilla
2 9-inch unbaked pie shells

Beat eggs slightly. Mix sugar and flour. Add melted butter to sugar mixture and eggs. Add diluted milk and vanilla or lemon juice. Beat until mixed well and pour into two 9-inch unbaked pastry shells. Bake in 400 degree oven 10 minutes and then 325 degrees approximately 25 minutes until done and slightly firm to touch.

Use this basic custard recipe and make the following variations: SWEET POTATO-CUSTARD: 1½ cups mashed sweet potatoes, 1 teaspoon cinnamon; COCONUT: 1 cup flaked coconut, 1 teaspoon lemon juice; CHOCOLATE: ¼—1/3 cup cocoa added to sugar mixture.

Mrs. Jeanette S. Norment, State College

SWEET POTATO PIE

2 cups mashed sweet potatoes
1¼ cups granulated sugar
3 tablespoons butter
3 whole eggs
½ tablespoon salt
1¼ cups scalded milk

½ teaspoon cinnamon
½ teaspoon allspice
½ teaspoon nutmeg
½ teaspoon vanilla
9-inch unbaked pie shell

Combine all the above ingredients and pour into a 9-inch unbaked pie shell. Bake in a 350 degree oven about 1 hour or until done.

Mrs. Willard Smith, Brookhaven

SWEET POTATO CUSTARD PIE

3 cups mashed sweet potatoes
1 stick oleo (or more)
1 to 1½ cups sugar
2 eggs, well beaten

¼ cup hot milk
1 teaspoon vanilla
10-inch unbaked pie shell

Cook enough potatoes to make about 3 cups. Drain and mash well. Add oleo and sugar (to taste) and beat well. Add well beaten eggs, hot milk and vanilla and again beat well. Pour into unbaked 10-inch pie shell. Bake at 450 degrees for 10 minutes; reduce heat to 350 degrese for 40 to 45 minutes longer. Add spices, if desired. This makes a thick, light pie.

Mrs. Ray Leeper, Pontotoc

NO–BAKE SWEET POTATO PIE

1 (2-ounce) package Dream
    Whip
½ cup milk
½ teaspoon vanilla
1 (3¾-ounce) package instant
    vanilla pudding

2/3 cup milk
1 cup cooked sweet potatoes
¾ teaspoon apple pie spice
1 baked 8 or 9 inch pie shell

Prepare Dream Whip with ½ cup milk and vanilla. Combine 1 cup of the prepared Dream Whip with the instant pudding, 2/3 cup milk, sweet potatoes and spice. Beat slowly until well mixed, about 1 minute. Pour into pie shell, chill in refrigerator, top with remaining Dream Whip.

Mrs. John Foster, Natchez

SWEET POTATO PUDDING

2½ cups grated raw potatoes
3 cups sugar
2 eggs

2 tablespoons vanilla
1 stick margarine
3½ or 4 cups milk

Grate potatoes, add sugar and mix thoroughly. In a separate bowl, beat eggs, vanilla and margarine together, then stir in milk. Add potato mixture to milk mixture and stir until blended well. Pour into a round aluminum pan 3 inches deep by 10 inches wide. Bake in a 400 degree oven for 1 hour, or until pie is golden brown on top. Serves 8.

Note: Recipe is best made with new sweet potatoes.

Mrs. Brewer Golden, Senatobia

AUNT CARRIE'S SWEET POTATO OR
PUMPKIN PIE

1 cup sweet potatoes or
    pumpkin
2 cups sugar
1 stick butter or margarine
1 teaspoon lemon extract
1 lemon rind, grated

2 eggs, slightly beaten
¾ cup evaporated milk
2 tablespoons all-purpose flour
1 teaspoon vanilla
9-inch pie shell, unbaked

Cook potatoes and remove any stringy or fibrous portion. Place all ingredients in mixer bowl. Beat, using rotary or electric mixer, until smooth. Pour into the unbaked pie shell. Bake in oven at 425 degrees for 10 minutes, then reduce temperature to 325 degrees and bake until done, about 1 hour.

Mrs. Jep Cole, Hattiesburg

PUMPKIN PIE

½ pound margarine
2 cups sugar
1 heaping tablespoon plain
  flour
3 eggs (unbeaten)
1 cup pumpkin
  (cooked and mashed)

1 teaspoon lemon flavoring
¼ cup evaporated milk
½ teaspoon nutmeg (or more)
¼ teaspoon salt
10-inch unbaked pastry shell

Melt margarine. Mix sugar and flour. Add the margarine and mix well. Add eggs, one at a time, and beat well. Then add cooked pumpkin, lemon flavoring, evaporated milk, nutmeg and salt. Mix well and pour into a 10-inch unbaked pastry shell. Bake at 300 degrees for 1 hour.

Mrs. Ples Barrett, Carthage

PUMPKIN PIE

1 cup fresh cooked or
  canned pumpkin
1 cup sugar
1 cup scalded milk with piece
  of butter the size of a walnut
3 egg yolks
½ teaspoon ginger

¼ teaspoon cloves
¼ teaspoon cinnamon
¼ teaspoon allspice
pinch of salt
3 egg whites
9 or 10-inch unbaked pie shell

Mix well all ingredients, except egg whites. Fold in egg whites which have been beaten to stiff points. Pour into 9 or 10-inch unbaked pie shell and bake for 10 minutes in 400 degree oven. Lower temperature to 350 degrees and bake 35 to 40 minutes.

Mrs. Phillip Seburn, Hattiesburg

PUMPKIN PIE

½ stick butter
1 cup granulated sugar
½ cup dark brown sugar
3 whole eggs
1 cup cooked pumpkin
1/3 cup coffee cream
½ teaspoon salt

1 teaspoon vanilla extract
½ teaspoon cinnamon
¼ teaspoon ginger
¼ teaspoon nutmeg
⅛ teaspoon cloves
9-inch unbaked pastry shell

Cream butter and sugar together until light. Add eggs, one at a time, beating after each addition. Add pumpkin, cream, salt, vanilla and spices.

Pour into chilled unbaked 9-inch pastry shell. Bake at 350 degrees for 50 minutes. Pie should be well browned. Inserted knife should come out clean. Pie will be "shaky" in center. Let cool 1½ to 2 hours.

Mrs. J. D. Thompson, Carrollton

DUTCH APPLE PIE

2/3 cup sifted all-purpose
    flour
1/3 cup firmly packed
    light brown sugar
1/3 cup butter or margarine
2 pounds tart cooking apples

1 tablespoon lemon juice
2 tablespoons flour
¾ cup granulated sugar
dash of salt
1 teaspoon cinnamon
9-inch unbaked pie shell

Prepare pie shell using preferred recipe; refrigerate until ready to use. Combine flour and sugar in medium bowl. Cut in butter with pastry blender or two knives, until mixture is consistency of coarse cornmeal. Refrigerate until ready to use as a topping for the pie.

Preheat oven to 400 degrees. Core apples and pare, slice thinly, into large bowl. Sprinkle with lemon juice. Combine flour, sugar, salt and cinnamon, mixing well. Toss lightly with apples. Turn filling into unbaked pie shell, spreading evenly. Cover with the prepared topping. Bake 40 to 45 minutes, or until apples are tender. Serves 6 to 8. May be served hot or cold.

Frances Smith, Carthage

SOUR CREAM APPLE PIE

¾ cup sugar
2 tablespoons flour
1 cup sour cream
1 egg, well beaten
½ teaspoon vanilla flavoring
⅛ teaspoon salt

2 cups finely chopped tart
    apples
9-10 inch unbaked pie shell
1/3 cup light brown sugar
1/3 cup flour
1/3 cup oleomargarine

Combine sugar and flour. Add sour cream, egg, flavoring and salt. Beat until smooth. Add apples and mix thoroughly. Pour into pastry lined pan. Bake in hot oven (450 degrees) 15 minutes. Reduce heat to 350 degrees and bake 30 minutes more or until top is firm to touch. Remove from oven and cover with the topping made by combining light brown sugar, flour and margarine, mixed thoroughly before being sprinkled over the pie.

Mrs. A. P. Mullins, Macon

BLUEBERRY PIE

1 (no. 2) can blueberries
¼ cup sugar
2 tablespoons flour
1 tablespoon lemon juice
¼ teaspoon cinnamon
1 (3-ounce) package cream
cheese

½ cup confectioners sugar
1 teaspoon vanilla
½ pint whipping cream
9-inch pie shell, baked

Combine blueberries, sugar, flour, lemon juice and cinnamon in saucepan and cook until thickens. Cool. Blend cream cheese, confectioners sugar and vanilla until creamy. Whip cream until stiff and fold into cream cheese mixture. Pour into baked pie shell and top with blueberry mixture. Store in refrigerator until ready to serve.

Mrs. Glen McCullough, Tupelo

CHERRY PIE

2 unbaked 8-inch pie shells
½ cup finely chopped pecans
2 cups powdered sugar
1 (8-ounce) package cream
cheese, softened

1 (4-ounce) package Dream
Whip
1 (22-ounce) can cherry pie
filling

Line two unbaked 8-inch pie shells with the finely chopped pecans and bake in 300 degree oven until golden brown. Cream the powdered sugar and the cream cheese. Put half of mixture in each baked, cooled pie shell for first layer.

Mix one large package of Dream Whip as directed on package. Divide in half, and spread on top of first layers of cream cheese and sugar. Top the two layers with the cherry pie filling and let set in refrigerator 3 to 4 hours before serving. May be made up a day ahead of time.

Mrs. Ruth Martin, Cary

EASY CHERRY PIE

1 (22-ounce) can cherry pie
filling
1 teaspoon lemon juice
1 (1-pound 1¼-ounce or 1
pound 2½-ounce) package
white cake mix

½ cup melted oleo
½ cup nuts

Place pie filling in a 9-inch pie pan. Sprinkle with lemon juice. Combine cake mix, melted oleo and nuts and sprinkle this over pie filling. Bake at 350 degrees until top is lightly browned and when tested with toothpick, there is no raw dough; about 35-45 minutes.

Mrs. Richard Cooper, Carrollton

BING CHERRY PIE

Pastry for 9-inch double
   crust pie
2 cups pitted Bing cherries
Bing cherry juice

¾ cup sugar
3 tablespoons flour
2 tablespoons butter

Line pie pan with half of the pastry. Put cherries into pie shell, with enough juice to barely cover. Mix sugar and flour and sprinkle over cherries. Dot with butter. Cover top with lattice strips cut from remaining pastry. Bake at 350 degrees for 30 to 40 minutes.

Mrs. Georgia H. Dodds, Hazelhurst

QUICK PEACH TARTS

1 (no. 2½) can sliced
   peaches
2 tablespoons cornstarch
1 tablespoon lemon juice

1 teaspoon cinnamon
5 tablespoons shortening
16 canned biscuits

Blend first 3 ingredients and boil 1 minute. Add cinnamon, let cool. Roll biscuits into 5-inch circles. Spoon on 2 tablespoons of filling, fold, moisten edges and press to seal. Preheat shortening in electric skillet to 350 degrees. Fry tarts until golden brown on both sides. Carefully lift tarts into and out of fat with pancake turner. Yield: 16 tarts.

Mrs. Elnora Breland, Leakesville

EASY PEACH PIE

½ stick oleo
½ cup flour (self-rising)
1 cup sugar

½ cup milk
1 quart fresh peaches

Melt oleo in baking dish. Make batter of flour, ½ cup sugar and milk. Pour over melted oleo. Sweeten peaches with remaining ½ cup sugar and pour over batter. Do not stir!! Bake in a 9 x 9 x 2½ pan in a 350 degree oven until brown around edges (about 30 minutes). If plain flour is used, add ¼ teaspoon baking powder and pinch of salt to flour. Frozen peaches may be used.

Mrs. Alden McNair, Learned

STRAWBERRY PIE

1½ cups sugar
1½ cups water
¼ cup cornstarch
⅛ teaspoon salt
⅛ teaspoon red food coloring
1 (3-ounce) package strawberry
   gelatin

1 cup fresh unsweetened
   strawberries
9-inch baked pie shell
½ pint whipped cream

Combine sugar, water, cornstarch and salt; cook until glazed and thickened. Remove from heat and add red food coloring. Add gelatin; stir well. Let cool. Arrange strawberries in baked pie shell. Pour sauce over them. Chill. Top with whipped cream before serving.

This recipe may be used with frozen sweetened berries, if sugar is reduced to ¾ cup.

Mrs. Clare Keys Alexander, Batesville

STRAWBERRY PIE

1 quart fresh strawberries
½ cup sugar
5 tablespoons cornstarch
1 tablespoon lemon juice

3 drops red food coloring
½ pint cream, whipped
9-inch pastry shell

Crush 1 cup strawberries, add sugar and cornstarch to berries and juice. Cook until thick, add lemon juice and food coloring. Let cool. Add the remaining sliced strawberries. Pour into baked 9-inch pastry shell. Top with whipped cream. Keep in refrigerator until ready to serve. Serves 6 to 8.

Mrs. Sathelle McMinn, Batesville

FRESH STRAWBERRY PIE

¼ cup cornstarch
¼ cup strawberry gelatin
1 cup sugar

1½ cups hot water
1 quart fresh strawberries
9-inch baked pie shell, cooled

Mix the cornstarch, gelatin and sugar well. Add hot water slowly and cook over high heat until thick. Set off and cool. Sprinkle 1 tablespoon sugar in pie shell. Place berries in pie shell, and pour sauce over them. Place pie in refrigerator until ready to serve. Serve with whipped topping or ice cream. Serves 8.

Mrs. Beatrice Beard, Fayette

STRAWBERRY SOUR CREAM PIE

1 cup water
½ cup sugar
1 (3-ounce) package strawberry gelatin
½ cup white grape juice
½ teaspoon grated lemon peel
1 cup dairy sour cream

1½ cups sliced fresh
  strawberries
9-inch vanilla wafer crumb
  crust
½ pint whipping cream
whole fresh strawberries
  with hulls

Combine water and sugar in a saucepan. Heat to boiling, stirring until sugar is dissolved. Remove from heat, pour over gelatin in a bowl, and stir until completely dissolved. Cool slightly. Mix in white grape juice and lemon peel. Chill until partly set, then whip until light in color. Whip sour cream (about 5 minutes at high speed of electric beater). Fold into whipped gelatin and gently mix in the sliced strawberries. Turn into cooled crust and chill until set. When ready to serve, garnish pie with the whipped cream and whole berries.

Evelyn H. Grant, Mayersville

STRAWBERRY ANGEL PIE

3 egg whites
1 teaspoon vanilla
¼ teaspoon cream of tartar
dash of salt
1 cup sugar
1 (3-ounce) package strawberry
  gelatin

1¼ cups boiling water
1 cup sliced fresh strawberries,
  OR 1 (10-ounce) package
  frozen sliced strawberries,
  thawed and drained
1 cup whipping cream,
  whipped

Prepare meringue shell. Have egg whites at room temperature. Add vanilla, cream of tartar and dash of salt. Beat till frothy, gradually adding sugar, a little at a time, beating till very stiff peaks form and sugar is dissolved. Spoon into lightly greased 9-inch pie plate and shape into shell,

[437]

swirling sides high. Bake at 275 degrees for 1 hour. Turn off heat and let dry in oven (door closed) at least 2 hours.

Dissolve gelatin in boiling water. Chill until consistency of unbeaten egg whites. Fold in strawberries and whipped cream, reserving a bit to garnish top. Chill until mixture mounds slightly when spooned. Pile into meringue shell. Chill 4 to 6 hours or overnight. Garnish with whipped cream and strawberry halves. Serves 6 to 7.

Mrs. Hilman Wedgeworth, Laurel

STRAWBERRY PIE

9-inch baked pie shell
1 (3-ounce) package cream
    cheese
1 quart fresh strawberries

¾ cup sugar
2 tablespoons cornstarch
1/3 cup water
½ pint cream, whipped

Make 9-inch pie crust and bake. Cool. When cool, soften cream cheese and spread over bottom of crust. Wash, hull and drain berries and cut in halves. Put half of berries in pie crust over cream cheese. Put other half (reserving 8) in boiler with ¾ cup sugar, 2 tablespoons cornstarch and 1/3 cup water which has been mixed together. Let cook until thick. Then cool. Pour over other strawberries. When well cooled, spread with whipped cream and decorate with 8 whole strawberries. Chill, and its heavenly.

Mrs. J. V. Gage, Port Gibson

NO–BAKE MINCE PIE

1 (3¾-ounce) package
    Whip and Chill, vanilla
    dessert mix
½ cup cold milk
1/3 cup cold water

½ cup sour cream
1 cup moist mincemeat
    with brandy flavor
9-inch baked pastry shell
2 cups whipped cream

Combine dessert mix and milk. Blend thoroughly. Whip at highest speed of electric mixer for 1 minute. Mixture will be very thick. Blend in water and sour cream. Whip at high speed about 2 minutes. If necessary, chill until mixture will mound. Fold in mincemeat and spoon into pie crust. Chill 2 hours or more. Top with whipped cream. This is good without the whipped cream.

Mrs. G. R. Jones, Rich

JEFF DAVIS PIE

2 tablespoons flour
2 cups sugar
3 large eggs, beaten
2 cups sweet milk

¼ cup real butter
1 cup plum preserves
9-inch pie shell

Mix flour and sugar together. Add eggs and beat well. Add milk and butter to mixture and blend. Have 9-inch pie shell ready and line the bottom with plum preserves. Cover with the liquid mixture and bake in a 350 degree oven 30 minutes, or until mixture is softly firm in center.

This recipe was given to Mrs. Hilliard about 25 years ago by Mrs. Allie Swann, Sr. who said it had been in the family over a hundred years.

Mrs. J. R. Hilliard, Macon

TEXAS PIE

1 stick oleo (melted)
2 cups sugar
4 eggs (slightly beaten)
1 tablespoon cornmeal
1 tablespoon flour
1 teaspoon vanilla

1 (3½-ounce) can flaked
coconut
1 (no. 1) can crushed
pineapple
9-inch unbaked pie shell

Mix first 8 ingredients well. Pour into pie shell. Bake at 350 degrees for 45 minutes to 1 hour.

Mrs. W. R. Neely, Hattiesburg

PINEAPPLE COCONUT PIE

4 egg yolks
1/3 cup butter
1 cup sugar
1 cup milk
1 tablespoon flour

1 cup coconut
1 cup crushed pineapple
1 teaspoon vanilla
9-inch unbaked pie shell

Beat eggs well, then add butter, sugar, flour and milk. Mix well. Add coconut, pineapple and vanilla. After combining all mixture, pour into a 9-inch pastry lined pie plate. Cook at 350 degrees for 45 minutes. Serves 6.

Miss Arilla Kerney, Como

PINEAPPLE PIE

3 eggs
¼ cup melted butter
1½ cups sugar
3 tablespoons plain flour

1 (8½-ounce) can crushed
 pineapple
1 teaspoon vanilla extract
8-inch unbaked pie shell

Beat eggs slightly. Add melted butter, sugar and flour and beat until smooth. Add pineapple and vanilla. Bake in unbaked 8-inch pie shell in slow oven (325 degrees) until edge of crust is brown. Reduce heat to 300 degrees and cook about 45 minutes or until done in center.

Mrs. C. L. Cahoon, Chunky

PEAR PIE

2 tablespoons flour
1½ cups sugar
9-inch unbaked pie shell

½ stick butter
4 eggs, beaten
3 medium pears

Scatter a mixture of 2 tablespoons flour and ½ cup sugar over bottom of unbaked 9-inch pie shell. Cream 1 cup sugar and ½ stick butter. Add 4 beaten eggs. Grate 3 peeled pears, drain and put pears into bottom of pie shell. Cover with sugar mixture. Bake at 300 degrees about 45 minutes to 1 hour or until firm.

(Thawed frozen, grated pears may be used instead of fresh pears.)

Mrs. Monette Gunby, Centreville

HAWAIIAN DELIGHT PIE

juice of 1 lemon
1 (14-ounce) can sweetened
 condensed milk
1 (8-ounce) package cream
 cheese
1 (3½-ounce) can angel flake
 coconut

1 (11-ounce) can mandarin
 oranges, drained
1 (20-ounce) can crushed
 pineapple, drained
1 cup chopped pecans
2 8 or 9-inch baked pie shells

Combine the lemon juice, condensed milk and cream cheese. Add the coconut, mandarin oranges, crushed pineapple and pecans. Mix well. Pour mixture into the 2 baked pie shells and chill. Before serving, top with whipped cream or other whipped topping, if desired.

Mrs. Jerry Martin, Raleigh

ONE HUNDRED DOLLAR PIE

1 (14-ounce) can sweetened
   condensed milk
1/3 cup lemon juice
½ cup crushed pineapple,
   drained
½ cup maraschino cherries,
   drained and chopped

½ cup pecans, chopped
9-inch baked pie shell
½ cup whipping cream
2 tablespoons sugar

Blend together milk and lemon juice. Then fold in other ingredients, pineapple, cherries and pecans. Pour into a 9-inch pie shell that has been baked and cooled. Refrigerate. Whip the cream and add sugar. Just before serving, top pie with whipped cream. A few cherries, cut in halves and placed on top of whipped cream, adds appetizing color.

Mrs. Guyton McGee, Kosciusko

MILLIONAIRE PIE

1¼ cups sugar
1 stick oleo
3 eggs, beaten
2 tablespoons water
2 tablespoons vinegar
dash of salt

1 teaspoon vanilla
1 cup coconut
1 cup raisins
1 cup nuts
9 or 10-inch unbaked pie shell

Cream butter and sugar, add beaten eggs, water, vinegar, salt and vanilla and beat well. Then add coconut, raisins and nuts. Place in 9 or 10-inch unbaked pie shell and bake 45 minutes at 350 degrees.

Mrs. H. O. George, Pontotoc

BLACKBOTTOM PIE

20 gingersnaps
5 tablespoons melted butter
4 egg yolks
½ cup sugar
1 tablespoon cornstarch
2 cups milk
1 tablespoon plain gelatin
¼ cup water
1½ squares of unsweetened
   chocolate

1 teaspoon vanilla
3 tablespoons of rum flavor or
   whiskey
4 egg whites
¼ teaspoon cream of tartar
3 tablespoons of confectioners
   sugar
½ pint whipping cream

Make a 10-inch pie crust with crushed gingersnaps and melted butter. Bake in 275° oven for 10 minutes and cool. Mix egg yolks, sugar and cornstarch. Pour over this 2 cups of hot milk and cook until the custard begins to thicken. To this add 1 tablespoon gelatin which has been dissolved in ¼ cup water. In a small bowl chop the 1½ squares of unsweetened chocolate and pour 1 cup of the hot custard over this. Add 1 teaspoon of vanilla. When the chocolate mixture begins to set, pour it into the pie crust. Let the rest of the plain custard cool, then add the rum flavor or whiskey. Let this begin to set. When this begins to set, fold into this 4 well beaten egg whites to which have been added ¼ teaspoon cream of tartar and 3 tablespoons of confectioners sugar. Pour this over the chocolate layer of the pie and refrigerate until firm. When ready to serve, top the pie with whipped cream and sprinkle with a little grated unsweetened chocolate.

When this recipe is doubled, it will make 3 pies and will serve 18 persons.

Mrs. John Clark Boswell, Jackson

CHOCOLATE ALMOND ICE BOX PIE

20 vanilla wafers, rolled fine
½ cup melted butter
6 small size Hershey
  chocolate almond bars
1 square Baker's bitter
  chocolate

20 marshmallows cut up
¾ cup milk
½ teaspoon salt
½ teaspoon almond extract
½ pint cream, whipped

Stir butter into crumbs and press into greased 8 or 9-inch pie pan. Bake about 7 minutes at 350 degrees. Cool. Melt candy bars, chocolate, marshmallows and milk over low heat. Cool. Fold in salt, flavoring and cream. Pour in chilled crust and refrigerate over night or at least 4 hours.

Mrs. J. C. Totten, Holly Springs

CHOCOLATE PIE

3 eggs, separated
1½ cups sugar
2 tablespoons flour
2 tablespoons butter
1 teaspoon vanilla

2 squares of chocolate, grated
1 cup sweet milk
8-inch pie shell, unbaked
¼ teaspoon cream of tartar
4 tablespoons sugar

Beat egg yolks (to which flour has been added), sugar and butter well. Add vanilla, chocolate and milk and mix well. Pour into 8-inch unbaked pie shell and bake at 375 degrees until firm.

Beat 2 egg whites stiff with ¼ teaspoon cream of tartar; slowly add 4 tablespoons sugar. Spread on pie and bake slowly (325-350 degrees) until brown.

Mrs. W. B. Maxwell, Belzoni

FUDGE PIE

½ cup butter
3 squares unsweetened
   chocolate
4 eggs
3 tablespoons white corn syrup

1½ cups sugar
¼ teaspoon salt
1 teaspoon vanilla
9-inch pie shell, unbaked

Melt butter and baking chocolate over low heat. Meanwhile, place 4 eggs in mixing bowl and beat until light. Beat the corn syrup, sugar, salt and vanilla into eggs. Add chocolate mixture and blend thoroughly. Pour into 9-inch pastry lined pie plate. Bake at 350 degrees for 25-30 minutes or until top is crusty and filling is set but still soft. Serve with topping of vanilla ice cream.

Mrs. O. W. Scott, Duck Hill

CHOCOLATE MERINGUE PIE

3 egg yolks
1 cup sugar
3 tablespoons cocoa
4 tablespoons plain flour
½ teaspoon salt
2 cups milk

1 teaspoon vanilla
3 egg whites
6 tablespoons sugar
pinch of salt
9-inch baked pie shell

Mix three egg yolks with 1 cup sugar. Stir until creamy. Sift cocoa, flour and salt together and add to egg mixture. Thin this mixture with ¼ cup milk. Put remainder in 1 quart size copper bottomed boiler, stirring constantly over direct medium heat. Let milk warm slightly, then add sugar mixture. Continue stirring till creamy. Add vanilla. Place in 9-inch baked pie shell. Make meringue with 3 egg whites, 6 tablespoons sugar and pinch of salt beaten together until sugar is dissolved and soft, but firm, peaks form. Bake at 350 degrees till brown.

Mrs. Charles E. Estess, Jackson

[443]

GERMAN CHOCOLATE PIE

1 (4-ounce) package German
    sweet chocolate
¼ cup butter
1 2/3 cups (14½ ounce can)
    evaporated milk
1½ cups sugar
3 tablespoons cornstarch

⅛ teaspoon salt
2 eggs
1 teaspoon vanilla
10-inch pie shell, unbaked
1 1/3 cups angel flake coconut
½ cup chopped pecans

Melt chocolate with butter over low heat. Cool. Gradually blend milk, sugar (mixed with cornstarch) and salt. Beat in eggs and vanilla. Mix in chocolate and butter and stir until there is a thorough blend. Pour into 10-inch unbaked pie shell. Mix coconut and pecans and sprinkle over top. Bake 45 minutes at 375 degrees.

Mrs. Cara Frederick, Iuka

CARAMEL PIE

1½ cups sugar
5 tablespoons flour
2 cups milk
4 eggs, separated
4 tablespoons butter
¼ teaspoon salt

1 teaspoon vanilla
9-inch baked pie shell
2 egg whites, stiffly beaten
4 tablespoons sugar
½ teaspoon vanilla

Mix 1 cup sugar with the flour. Add a little milk, then add egg yolks. Add rest of milk and butter. Cook in double boiler until thick. Melt until brown ½ cup sugar and add to other mixture, stirring constantly. Add salt and vanilla. Pour into baked pie shell. Top with meringue made of beaten egg whites, to which sugar and vanilla has been beaten in gradually. Brown in a 350 degree oven until golden brown.

Mrs. S. E. Ormon, Hickory Flat

LEMON RUB PIE

1½ cups sugar
2 tablespoons all-purpose
    flour
¾ stick of butter
3 eggs, beaten

¼ cup lemon juice
1 lemon rind, grated
¼ teaspoon salt
9-inch unbaked pie shell

Mix sugar and flour. Cream softened butter with sugar-flour combination. Add beaten eggs, lemon juice, grated rind and salt. Mix, Pour into pie shell. Bake at 350 degrees for 45 minutes. Remove from oven while pie will "tremble" in center.

Mrs. Harold H. Robertson, Booneville
Mrs. Terry H. Walters, Midnight

BUTTERMILK LEMON PIE

½ cup sugar
3 tablespoons cornstarch
1 cup buttermilk
3 egg yolks
1 lemon (juice and grated rind)

1 tablespoon butter
8-inch baked pie crust
3 egg whites
6 tablespoons sugar

Mix sugar and cornstarch. Stir in buttermilk gradually. Cook in double boiler, until mixture thickens, stirring constantly. Add beaten egg yolks, lemon juice and grated lemon rind and butter. Pour into 8-inch baked crust. Make meringue of 3 egg whites beating until stiff. Then gradually add 6 tablespoons sugar, beating as added. Spread over the filling and brown in 325-350 degree oven. Serves 6.

Mrs. Effie Busby, Laurel

LEMON PIE

6 tablespoons cornstarch
2 cups sugar
2 lemons, grated rind and juice
3 egg yolks, beaten

2 cups boiling water
9-inch pie shell, baked
3 egg whites
6 tablespoons sugar

Mix cornstarch with sugar and cover wtih grated rind and juice of lemons. Add to the mixture the beaten yolks of 3 eggs and 2 cups boiling water. Cook until thick. Pour into baked pie shell. Cover with the whites of 3 eggs beaten with 6 tablespoons sugar until stiff but not dry. Spread carefully over entire surface of pie. Brown in 350 degree oven. Serves 6.

Mrs. Jim Oden, Ovett

TENDER LEMON PIE

1 cup sugar
5 tablespoons cornstarch
¼ teaspoon salt
2 cups milk
1 tablespoon butter
3 egg yolks, slightly beaten

6 tablespoons lemon juice
1 teaspoon grated rind
9-inch baked pastry shell
3 egg whites
6 tablespoons sugar

[445]

Mix thoroughly the sugar, cornstarch and salt in top of double boiler. Add milk slowly and blend thoroughly. Stir over low heat until thickened and continue cooking. Let mixture bubble about 2 minutes, stirring constantly. Remove from heat and add separately, mixing well each time, butter, egg yolks, fresh lemon juice and grated rind. Place over hot water in double boiler and cook for 2 minutes. Cool. Pour into 9-inch baked pastry shell. Beat egg whites until frothy, gradually add sugar until soft peaks will stand. Cover pie with meringue and bake at 350 degrees until golden brown.

Mrs. Elton Castlebury, Steens

LEMON SOUR CREAM PIE

1 cup sugar
3 tablespoons cornstarch
¼ cup oleo
1 tablespoon lemon rind
¼ cup lemon juice
3 unbeaten egg yolks

1 cup milk
1 cup sour cream
9-inch pie shell, baked
1 (4½-ounce) carton
  whipped topping

Combine sugar and cornstarch. Add remaining ingredients except sour cream and whipped topping. Cook until thick. Cool. Fold in sour cream. Pour into shell. Chill. Spread chilled pie with whipped topping.

Mrs. Joe McGinty, Magee

EASY COCONUT PIE

1 stick soft oleo
1½ cups sugar
3 eggs, slightly beaten
1 tablespoon vinegar

1 teaspoon vanilla
1 cup coconut
8-inch unbaked pie shell

Mix all ingredients in order listed. Mix well, adding coconut last. Pour into unbaked 8-inch pie shell and bake in oven for 1 hour at 325 degrees.

Mrs. Paul Adams, Aberdeen

TOASTED COCONUT PIE

3 beaten eggs
1½ cups sugar
½ cup butter or 1 stick oleo
4 teaspoons lemon juice

1 teaspoon vanilla
1 (3½-ounce) can flaked
  coconut
9-inch unbaked pastry shell

Thoroughly combine eggs, sugar, butter, lemon juice and vanilla. Stir in coconut. Pour filling into unbaked 9-inch pastry shell. Bake in moderate oven (350 degrees) for 40 to 50 minutes or until knife comes out clean when inserted in middle of pie. Garnish with whipped cream.

Mrs. J. T. Kerr, Rolling Fork

CRUSTY COCONUT PIE

½ cup milk
1¼ cups coconut
1 cup sugar
¼ cup butter

3 eggs
1 teaspoon vanilla or
  lemon extract
9-inch unbaked pie shell

Pour milk over coconut and let set while creaming butter and sugar. After creaming butter and sugar until light and fluffy, add eggs one at a time and mix well. Add milk, coconut and flavoring and mix well. Pour into 9-inch unbaked pie shell. Bake in 350 degree oven about 30 minutes or until pie is firm and golden brown.

Pearl B. Burkett, Hattiesburg

COCONUT PIE

3 whole eggs, beaten
2/3 cup white corn syrup
1 cup sugar
pinch of salt
1 teaspoon vanilla

1 stick oleo, melted
¼ cup sweet milk
1 (14-ounce) package
  coconut
9-inch unbaked pie shell

Mix all ingredients together. Pour into 9-inch pastry lined pie pan. Bake in 375 degree oven 40 to 50 minutes, or until set.

Mrs. Frank Burch, Kosciusko

COCONUT CHIFFON PIE

20 chocolate creme-filled
  cookies
¼ cup melted oleo
½ cup sugar
1 cup milk
4 egg yolks

1 tablespoon gelatin
1 teaspoon vanilla
½ cup shredded coconut
4 egg whites
½ cup sugar

[447]

Crush chocolate creme cookies. Add ¼ cup melted oleo. Mix. Press into 9-inch pie plate and chill.

Mix sugar, milk, egg yolks and gelatin and cook until thick. Add vanilla and coconut. Chill.

Whip egg whites, add ½ cup sugar and whip until very stiff. Fold into gelatin mixture. Pour into pie shell, chill and serve with whipped cream.

Mrs. R. A. Baggett, Tupelo

COCONUT CREAM PIE

1 cup sugar
5 tablespoons all-purpose flour
3 egg yolks, well beaten
2 cups milk
1 tablespoon butter or oleo
1 teaspoon vanilla
1 cup coconut
9-inch baked pie shell
3 egg whites
6 tablespoons sugar
¼ teaspoon cream of tartar
1 teaspoon vanilla

Combine first 3 ingredients, then add milk and butter. Cook over low heat, stirring until thickened. Remove from heat and add vanilla and coconut. (Reserve 2 tablespoons of coconut for meringue.) Pour into baked 9-inch pie shell.

Add cream of tartar to egg whites and beat, gradually adding sugar to egg whites while beating. Add vanilla, and beat until meringue holds peaks. Spread on pie sealing to crust. Sprinkle reserved coconut on top of meringue. Brown in 350 degree oven.

Mrs. J. C. Rainey, Sr., Hattiesburg

PEANUT BUTTER PIE

9-inch baked pie shell
1 cup powdered sugar
½ cup peanut butter
¼ cup cornstarch
2/3 cup sugar
¼ teaspoon salt
2 cups milk, scalded
3 egg yolks, beaten
2 tablespoons butter
¼ teaspoon vanilla extract
3 egg whites

Combine powdered sugar and peanut butter. Blend until the appearance of biscuit mix. Spread half of this mixture on 9-inch pie shell. Combine cornstarch, sugar and salt. Add scalded milk and mix well. Pour small amount over beaten egg yolks, mix well, then return to milk mixture. Cook in top of double boiler until mixture thickens. Add butter and vanilla; then pour into prepared pie shell. Top with meringue made from 3 beaten egg whites. Sprinkle remainder of peanut butter mixture over meringue. Bake at 325 degrees until meringue is brown.

Mrs. John S. Grimes, Sr., Neshoba
Mrs. John G. Holder, Hattiesburg

O–SO–GOOD PIE

1 cup sugar	½ teaspoon cinnamon
1 tablespoon melted butter	½ cup raisins
2 tablespoons vinegar	¼ cup chopped nuts
1 tablespoon water	2 eggs, well beaten
¼ teaspoon cloves	9 or 10-inch unbaked pie shell

Mix all ingredients together, adding eggs last. Pour into unbaked pie shell. Bake in hot oven (400 degrees) for 5 minutes, then in moderate oven (350 degrees) for 30 minutes, or until crisp golden brown crust is formed.

Mrs. N. C. Jensen, Macon

BUTTERMILK PIE

3 eggs	1 cup buttermilk
2 cups sugar	½ lemon (juice)
3 tablespoons flour	nutmeg to flavor
½ cup butter, melted	8-inch unbaked pie shell

Beat the 3 eggs. Add sugar and flour. Beat well, add melted butter. Add buttermilk, flavoring and spice. Pour into unbaked pie shell. Bake at 450 degrees for 10 minutes; reduce heat to 300 degrees and bake for 35 or 40 minutes.

Mrs. A. E. Wilson, West Point

SALTINE CRACKER PIE

3 egg whites	1 cup pecans (chopped)
¼ teaspoon cream of tartar	½ pint whipping cream
1 cup sugar	2 tablespoons pineapple
1 teaspoon vanilla	preserves
16 saltine crackers (single)	2 tablespoons coconut

Beat egg whites until foamy, add cream of tartar and beat stiff. Add sugar and vanilla gradually as beating proceeds. Crumble crackers and mix with pecans. Fold into beaten egg whites and mix gently. Bake in 9-inch

[449]

greased pie pan at 350 degrees for 30 minutes. Let cool. Whip cream and fold in preserves. Spread on top of pie and sprinkle with grated coconut.

Mrs. McArthur Williams, Perkinston

PECAN DELIGHT

20 Ritz crackers
1 teaspoon baking powder
1 teaspoon vanilla
½ to 1 cup pecans,
    chopped

3 egg whites, beaten
1 cup sugar
½ pint cream, whipped

Roll the crackers (crush) and add baking powder, vanilla and pecans. Beat egg whites as if for meringue. Gradually add sugar, a small amount at a time; beat until very stiff. Fold into cracker mixture. Bake in a greased 9-inch pie pan for 30 minutes at 350 degrees. Cool, serve with whipped cream.

Genevieve Harris, Hazlehurst

RITZ CRACKER PIE

3 egg whites, stiffly beaten
1 cup sugar
1 (2-ounce) box Ritz
    crackers, crushed

1 cup chopped pecans
1 teaspoon vanilla
1 Hershey bar, grated
1 cup whipping cream

Whip egg whites. Add sugar, little at a time. Add crushed Ritz crackers and chopped pecans. Add vanilla. Place in a 8-inch greased pie plate. Bake approximately 45 minutes at 300 degrees. Mix grated chocolate bar into whipped cream for topping and spread over pie. Place in refrigerator and chill. Serves 6.

Mrs. O. T. Lovorn, Louisville

HOLIDAY WALNUT PIE

4 tablespoons butter or
    margarine, melted
½ cup granulated sugar
½ cup brown sugar
¼ teaspoon salt
3 eggs, beaten

½ cup evaporated milk
¼ cup light corn syrup
½ teaspoon vanilla
1 cup coarsely chopped
    California walnuts
9-inch pastry shell, unbaked

Combine butter or margarine, granulated sugar, brown sugar and salt. Add eggs and mix well. Stir in evaporated milk, corn syrup, vanilla and nuts. Turn into pastry shell. Bake at 400 degrees for 25 to 30 minutes or till knife inserted off center comes out clean. Cool.

Mrs. LaVerne Y. Lindsey, Lexington

LIME FROST PIE

4 fresh eggs, separated
1 (14-ounce) can condensed
    milk
½ cup fresh lime juice
1 egg white, beaten
9-inch baked pie shell

3 egg whites, stiffly beaten
6 tablespoons sugar
½ teaspoon cream of tartar
1 teaspoon vanilla extract
    (optional)
dash of salt

Beat egg yolks thoroughly in mixing bowl. Add condensed milk and stir in. Gradually stir in lime juice. Mix well. Beat 1 egg white in small mixing bowl until it forms stiff peaks. Fold in milk mixture. Spoon into baked pie shell.

Beat the 3 egg whites and gradually add the sugar, cream of tartar and salt. Fold in vanilla. Pile meringue on top of pie filling and spread to edges of crust, being sure to seal meirngue to edges of crust. Bake at 345 degrees until golden brown. Serve cooled and chilled.

Mrs. Mary S. Parkman, Monticello

EGG PASTRY

3 cups sifted plain flour
1½ teaspoons salt
1 cup shortening or lard

1 teaspoon vinegar
1 egg
½ cup ice water

Sift flour and salt together and cut in shortening. Beat egg slightly. Add water and vinegar to egg. Add egg mixture gradually to dry ingredients. Mix just enough to hold dough together. Makes 4 9-inch pie shells.

Mrs. Jeffie Temple, Bude, Mrs. Elsie Saucier, Wiggins, Mrs. Kathleen Bullen, Fayette, Mrs. Lewis Tabb, Belzoni, Mrs. Earl Sharp, Pontotoc

NEVER FAIL PIE CRUST

3 cups plain flour
1 teaspoon salt
1¼ cups shortening or
    lard (room temperature)

1 egg
5 tablespoons water
1 tablespoon vinegar

[451]

Sift flour and salt together. Place flour and salt mixture in a bowl and make a well in the center. Combine shortening, egg, water and vinegar. Pour this mixture into well made in flour. Mix until it is a moist mixture. Makes 6 single pie crusts, or 3 double crusts. This dough keeps well in the refrigerator several days.

Mrs. George Hill, Edwards
Mrs. Henry Pike, Oakland

BROWN SUGAR PASTRY

1 stick margarine
1 cup plain flour

¼ cup brown sugar packed
½ cup chopped pecans

Place all ingredients in pie pan, do not mix. Bake in 400 degree oven for 15 minutes. Remove from oven and stir well with fork at once. Pat out into 9-inch pie plate.

This is good for any cream filling or chiffon pie.

Mrs. Robert Agnew, Baldwyn, Mrs. O. T. Ray, Pontotoc, Nancy Loague, Dorsey

---

FOR YOUR INFORMATION

SUBSTITUTIONS AND EQUIVALENTS, MEASURING INGREDIENTS
DEFINITIONS, TIME AND TEMPERATURE GUIDES,
AND SERVINGS OF FOOD

SUBSTITUTIONS AND EQUIVALENTS

EQUIVALENTS FOR ONE UNIT AND FRACTIONS OF A UNIT

TABLESPOON	CUP	PINT
1 Tbsp = 3 tsp	1 c = 16 Tbsp	1 pt = 2 c
7/8 Tbsp = 2-1/2 tsp	7/8 c = 14 Tbsp	7/8 pt = 1-3/4 c
3/4 Tbsp = 2-1/4 tsp	3/4 c = 12 Tbsp	3/4 pt = 1-1/2 c
2/3 Tbsp = 2 tsp	2/3 c = 10-2/3 Tbsp	2/3 pt = 1-1/3 c
5/8 Tbsp = 1-7/8 tsp	1/2 c = 8 Tbsp	5/8 pt = 1-1/4 c
1/2 Tbsp = 1-1/2 tsp	3/8 c = 6 Tbsp	1/2 pt = 1 c
3/8 Tbsp = 1-1/8 tsp	1/3 c = 5-1/3 Tbsp	3/8 pt = 3/4 c
1/3 Tbsp = 1 tsp	1/4 c = 4 Tbsp	1/3 pt = 2/3 c
1/4 Tbsp = 3/4 tsp	1/8 c = 2 Tbsp	1/4 pt = 1/2 c
	1/16 c = 1 Tbsp	1/8 pt = 1/4 c
		1/16 pt = 2 Tbsp

QUART	GALLON	POUND
1 qt = 2 pt	1 gal = 4 qt	1 lb = 16 oz
7/8 qt = 3-1/2 c	7/8 gal = 3-1/2 qt	7/8 lb = 14 oz
3/4 qt = 3 c	3/4 gal = 3 qt	3/4 lb = 12 oz
2/3 qt = 2-2/3 c	2/3 gal = 10-2/3 c	2/3 lb = 10-2/3 oz
5/8 qt = 2-1/2 c	5/8 gal = 5 pt	5/8 lb = 10 oz
1/2 qt = 1 pt	1/2 gal = 2 qt	1/2 lb = 8 oz
3/8 qt = 1-1/2 c	3/8 gal = 3 pt	3/8 lb = 6 oz
1/3 qt = 1-1/3 c	1/3 gal = 5-1/3 c	1/3 lb = 5-1/3 oz
1/4 qt = 1 c	1/4 gal = 1 qt	1/4 lb = 4 oz
1/8 qt = 1/2 c	1/8 gal = 1 pt	1/8 lb = 2 oz
1/16 qt = 1/4 c	1/16 gal = 1 c	1/16 lb = 1 oz

SUBSTITUTION OF INGREDIENTS

For:	Substitute:
1 tablespoon flour (used as thickener)	1/2 tablespoon cornstarch, potato starch, rice starch, or arrowroot starch, *or* 1 tablespoon quick-cooking tapioca
1 cup sifted all-purpose flour	1 cup unsifted all-purpose flour minus 2 table-spoons
1 cup sifted cake flour	7/8 cup sifted all-purpose flour, *or* 1 cup minus 2 tablespoons sifted all-purpose flour
1 cup corn syrup	1 cup sugar plus 1/4 cup liquid*
1 cup honey	1-1/4 cups sugar plus 1/4 cup liquid*
1 ounce chocolate	3 tablespoons cocoa plus 1 tablespoon fat
1 cup butter	1 cup margarine, *or* 7/8 to 1 cup hydrogenated fat plus 1/2 teaspoon salt, *or* 7/8 cup lard plus 1/2 teaspoon salt
1 cup coffee cream (20 percent)	3 tablespoons butter plus about 7/8 cup milk
1 cup heavy cream (40 percent)	1/3 cup butter plus about 3/4 cup milk
1 cup whole milk	1 cup reconstituted nonfat dry milk plus 2-1/2 teaspoons butter or margarine, *or* 1/2 cup evaporated milk plus 1/2 cup water, or 1/4 cup sifted dry whole milk powder plus 7/8 cup water
1 cup milk	3 tablespoons sifted regular nonfat dry milk plus 1 cup minus 1 tablespoon water, or 1/3 cup instant nonfat dry milk plus 1 cup minus 1 tablespoon water
1 cup buttermilk or sour milk	1 tablespoon vinegar or lemon juice plus enough sweet milk to make 1 cup (let stand 5 minutes), *or* 1-¾ teaspoons cream of tartar plus 1 cup sweet milk
1 teaspoon baking powder	1/4 teaspoon baking soda plus 5/8 teaspoon cream of tartar, *or* 1/4 teaspoon baking soda plus 1/2 cup fully soured milk or buttermilk, *or* 1/4 teaspoon baking soda plus 1/2 table-spoon vinegar or lemon juice used with sweet milk to make 1/2 cup, *or* 1/4 teaspoon baking soda plus 1/4 to 1/2 cup molasses
1 tablespoon active dry yeast	1 package active dry yeast, *or* 1 compressed yeast cake

APPENDIX

SUBSTITUTION OF INGREDIENTS

For:	Substitute:
1 whole egg	.2 egg yolks, *or* 3 tablespoons plus 1 teaspoon thawed frozen egg, *or* 2 tablespoons and 2 teaspoons dry whole egg powder plus an equal amount of water
1 egg yolk	.3-1/2 teaspoons thawed frozen egg yolk, *or* 2 tablespoons dry egg yolk plus 2 teaspoons water
1 egg white	.2 tablespoons thawed frozen egg white, *or* 2 teaspoons dry egg white plus 2 tablespoons water

* Use whatever liquid is called for in the recipe.

MEASURING INGREDIENTS

Accurate measuring of ingredients is essential for success in most food preparation. Varied procedures are required for different ingredients.

Baking powder, salt, spices and small amounts of dry ingredients. Measure in standard measuring spoons. Pile ingredients high in spoon. Then level off with a spatula.

Flour. Unless recipe specifies otherwise, sift flour before measuring. Pile lightly into standard dry measuring cup. Level off the top with a spatula.

Liquids. Use a standard liquid measuring cup. Place it on a table. Fill cup to desired level. Check measurement at eye-level for accuracy.

Shortening, butter and other *fats.* Use standard dry measuring cup or spoon of correct size for desired measurement. Pack ingredients into cup or spoon so no air spaces remain. Level top with metal spatula.

Sugar. If lumpy, sift or stir to remove lumps. Use measuring procedure for flour.

Brown sugar. Pack firmly into standard dry measuring cup. Level with spatula.

DEFINITIONS

Bake. Cook in oven. Food is heated from all sides.
Barbecue. Cook with direct heat and baste during cooking with a highly seasoned sauce.
Beat. Mix rapidly with a spoon in an over-and-under motion.
Boil. Cook over high heat. Liquid bubbles hard and steams.
Braise. Pan-fry to brown, then cook in meat juices or add liquid. Cover and simmer slowly.
Broil. Cook under direct heat from broiler in oven or separate broiling unit.
Chill. Make food cold all the way through by refrigerating it.
Chop. Reduce solid food to small pieces by using sharp knife or other sharp tool and chopping board.

Caramelize. Heat sugar or foods containing sugar until a brown color and characteristic flavor develops.

Cream. Press the ingredients against the side of the bowl with the spoon or other instrument until it is soft and fluffy.

Dice. Cut food into small cubes using sharp knife and chopping board. Kitchen shears may be used.

Dredge. Coat food with flour, fine cereal or crumbs before frying.

Fold. Combine two mixtures (1 or 2 ingredients such as beaten egg whites and sugar) by gently cutting down through mixture, turning over, and repeating until well mixed.

Grease. Rub a thin film of cooking fat or oil over surface of pan before using.

Knead. Press, stretch, and fold dough or other mixture to make it elastic or smooth.

Marinate. Let foods stand in a liquid (usually mixture of oil with vinegar or lemon juice) to add flavor or to make more tender.

Mince. Cut food in tiny pieces, finer than chopping.

Parboil. Boil until partly cooked.

Peel. Remove thin layer of skin from fruit or vegetable with sharp paring knife.

Poach. Cook food covered by liquid at or below simmering.

Pot roast. Cook large cuts of meat by braising.

Reconstitute. Restore concentrated food, such as frozen orange juice or dry milk, to its original state, usually by adding water.

Rehydrate. Soak or cook dried foods to restore the water lost in drying.

Roast. Cook in heated air, usually in an oven, without water, uncovered.

Sauté. Brown or heat quickly in small amount of fat, with frequent stirring or turning.

Score. Cut shallow slits or gashes in food. Used to decorate, release melting fat or to tenderize.

Shred. Cut or tear food into long narrow pieces.

Sift. Put dry ingredients through sifter or fine sieve to separate particles; to fluff those ingredients that pack; to mix several kinds of ingredients evenly.

Simmer. Heat liquids to almost boiling. Tiny bubbles will appear at edge.

Skewer. Fasten or hold food in place with wooden picks or metal pins while it cooks.

Sliver. Cut or split into long, thin strips with a knife on a cutting board.

Steam. Cook by steam in a closed container. Food may be steamed faster under pressure in a pressure cooker.

Steep. Let food stand in hot liquid, below boiling, to extract flavor, color or both.

Stew. Simmer or cook food slowly in a lot of liquid in a covered pan.

Stir. Mix by using round and round motion of spoon.

Strain. Separate a liquid from solid pieces of food through a coarse sieve or colander.

Toss. Tumble ingredients lightly with a lifting motion. Used to coat salads with dressing.

Truss. To tie meat or fowl with a string or to skewer it so it keeps shape during cooking.

APPENDIX

TIME AND TEMPERATURE GUIDES

OVEN TEMPERATURES AND TERMS

Term	Temperature Degrees Fahrenheit (F)
Extremely hot	500 to 525
Very hot	450 to 475
Hot	400 to 425
Moderate	350 to 375
Slow	300 to 325
Very slow	250 to 275

TIMETABLE FOR BROILING MEATS

Kind and cut of meat	Approximate thickness	Degree of doneness	Approximate total cooking time[1]
	Inches		Minutes
Beef steaks	1	Rare	10 to 15
(Club, porterhouse, rib, sir-	1	Medium	15 to 20
loin, T-bone, tenderloin)	1	Well done	20 to 30
	1½	Rare	15 to 20
	1½	Medium	20 to 25
	1½	Well done	25 to 40
	2	Rare	25 to 35
	2	Medium	35 to 45
	2	Well done	45 to 55
Hamburgers	¾	Rare	8
	¾	Medium	12
	¾	Well done	14
Lamb chops	1	Medium	12
(Loin, rib, shoulder)	1	Well done	14
	1½	Medium	18
	1½	Well done	22
Cured ham slices	¾	Well done	13 to 14
(Cook-before-eating)	1	Well done	18 to 20

[1] Meat at refrigerator temperature at start of broiling.

[457]

APPENDIX

TIMETABLE FOR BRAISING MEATS

Kind and cut of meat	Approximate ready-to-cook weight or thickness	Approximate total cooking time
BEEF		*Hours*
Pot roast, such as chuck or round	3 to 5 pounds	3 to 4
Steak, such as chuck or round	1 to 1½ inches	2 to 2½
Short ribs	2 to 2½ pounds	2 to 2½
VEAL		
Chops	½ to ¾ inch	¾
Shoulder, rolled	3 to 5 pounds	2 to 2½
LAMB		
Chops	½ to ¾ inch	½ to ¾
Shanks	1 pound each	1½ to 2
Shoulder, rolled	3 to 5 pounds	2 to 2½
PORK		
Chops	½ to 1 inch	¾ to 1
Spareribs	2 to 3 pounds	1½ to 2½

TIMETABLE FOR ROASTING MEATS

Kind and cut of meat	Ready-to cook weight	Approximate roasting time at 325° F.	Internal temperature of meat when done
BEEF			
Standing ribs:	*Pounds*	*Hours*	*°F.*
Rare	6 to 8	2½ to 3	140
Medium	6 to 8	3 to 3½	160
Well done	6 to 8	3 2/3 to 5	170
Rolled rump:			
Rare	5	2¼	140
Medium	5	3	160
Well done	5	3¼	170
Sirloin tip:			
Rare	3	1½	140
Medium	3	2	160
Well done	3	2¼	170
VEAL			
Leg	5 to 8	2½ to 3½	170
Loin	5	3	170
Shoulder	6	3½	170
LAMB			
Leg (whole)	6 to 7	3¼ to 4	180
Shoulder	3 to 6	2¼ to 3¼	180
Rolled shoulder	3 to 5	2½ to 3	180

PORK, FRESH			
Loin	3 to 5	1½ to 3	170
Shoulder	5 to 8	2½ to 4½	170
Ham, whole	10 to 14	4 to 6½	170
Ham, half	6	3½ to 4	170
Spareribs	3	1½ to 2½	170
PORK, CURED			
Cook-before-eating:			
Ham, whole	12 to 16	3½ to 5¼	160
Ham, half	6	2¼ to 2½	160
Picnic shoulder	6	3 to 3½	170
Fully cooked:[1]			
Ham, whole	12 to 16	3 to 4¾	140
Ham, half	6	1¾ to 2	140

[1] Can also be served without heating, if desired.

ROASTING GUIDE FOR POULTRY

Kind of poultry	Ready-to-cook weight[1]	Approximate roasting time at 325° F. for stuffed poultry[2]	Internal temperature of poultry when done
	Pounds	*Hours*	° F.
Chickens . . . . .1½ to 2½		. .1 to 2 . . .	
(Broilers, fryers, or roasters) 2½ to 4½		. .2 to 3½ . .	
Ducks . . . . .4 to 6		. .2 to 3 . . .	
Geese . . . . .6 to 8		. .3 to 3½ . .	
8 to 12		. .3½ to 4½ . .	
Turkeys . . . . .6 to 8		. .3 to 3½ . .	180 to 185 in center of inner thigh muscle
8 to 12		. .3½ to 4½ . .	
12 to 16		. .4½ to 5½ . .	
16 to 20		. .5½ to 6½ . .	
20 to 24		. .6½ to 7 . . .	
Boneless turkey roast . . . . . .3 to 10		. .3 to 4 . . .	170 to 175 in center

[1] Weight of giblets and neck included.
[2] Unstuffed poultry may take slightly less time than stuffed poultry. Cooking time is based on chilled poultry or poultry that has just been thawed—temperature not above 40° F. Frozen unstuffed poultry will take longer. Do not use this roasting guide for frozen commercially stuffed poultry; follow package directions.

[459]

APPENDIX

TIMETABLE FOR COOKING FISH

Cooking method and market form	Approximate ready-to-cook weight or thickness	Cooking temperature	Approximate cooking time in minutes
BAKING			
Dressed	3 pounds	350° F.	45 to 60
Pan-dressed	3 pounds	350° F.	25 to 30
Fillets or steaks	2 pounds	350° F.	20 to 25
Portions	2 pounds	400° F.	15 to 20
Sticks	2¼ pounds	400° F.	15 to 20
BROILING			
Pan-dressed	3 pounds		10 to 16[1]
Fillets or steaks	½ to 1 inch		10 to 15
Portions	⅜ to ½ inch		10 to 15
Sticks	⅜ to ½ inch		10 to 15
CHARCOAL BROILING			
Pan-dressed	3 pounds	Moderate	10 to 16[1]
Fillets or steaks	½ to 1 inch	Moderate	10 to 16[1]
Portions	⅜ to ½ inch	Moderate	8 to 10[1]
Sticks	⅜ to ½ inch	Moderate	8 to 10[1]
DEEP-FAT FRYING			
Pan-dressed	3 pounds	350° F.	3 to 5
Fillets or steaks	½ to 1 inch	350° F.	3 to 5
Portions	⅜ to ½ inch	350° F.	3 to 5
Sticks	⅜ to ½ inch	350° F.	3 to 5
OVEN-FRYING			
Pan-dressed	3 pounds	500° F.	15 to 20
Fillets or steaks	½ to 1 inch	500° F.	10 to 15
PAN-FRYING			
Pan-dressed	3 pounds	Moderate	8 to 10[1]
Fillets or steaks	½ to 1 inch	Moderate	8 to 10[1]
Portions	⅜ to ½ inch	Moderate	8 to 10[1]
Sticks	⅜ to ½ inch	Moderate	8 to 10[1]
POACHING			
Fillets or steaks	2 pounds	Simmer	5 to 10
STEAMING			
Fillets or steaks	2 pounds	Boil	5 to 10

[1] Turn once.

BOILING GUIDE FOR FRESH VEGETABLES

Vegetable	Boiling time (minutes)	Vegetable	Boiling time (minutes)
Asparagus:		Collards	10 to 20
Whole	10 to 20	Corn, on cob	5 to 15
Tips	5 to 15	Kale	10 to 15
Beans:		Okra	10 to 15
Lima	25 to 30	Onions	15 to 30
Snap, 1-inch pieces	12 to 16	Parsnips:	
Beets:		Whole	20 to 40
Young, whole	30 to 45	Quartered	8 to 15
Older, whole	45 to 90	Peas	12 to 16
Sliced or diced	15 to 25	Potatoes:	
Beet greens, young	5 to 15	Whole, medium size	25 to 40
Broccoli, heavy stalks,		Quartered	20 to 25
split	10 to 15	Diced	10 to 15
Brussels sprouts	15 to 20	Rutabagas, pared, cut up	20 to 30
Cabbage:		Spinach	3 to 10
Shredded	3 to 10	Squash:	
Quartered	10 to 15	Summer, sliced	8 to 15
Carrots:		Winter, cut up	15 to 20
Young, whole	15 to 20	Sweetpotatoes, whole	35 to 55
Older, whole	20 to 30	Tomatoes, cut up	7 to 15
Sliced or diced	10 to 20	Turnips:	
Cauliflower:		Cut up	10 to 20
Separated	8 to 15	Whole	20 to 30
Whole	15 to 25	Turnip greens	10 to 30
Celery, cut up	15 to 18		
Chard	10 to 20		

TEMPERATURES AND TESTS FOR SYRUP AND CANDIES

Product	Final Temperature of Syrup at Sea Level*		Test of Doneness	Description of Test
Syrup	230°F to 234°F	110°C to 112°C	Thread	Syrup spins a 2-inch thread when dropped from fork or spoon.
Fondant Fudge . . . . . . Panocha	234°F to 240°F	112°C to 115°C	Soft ball	Syrup, when dropped into very cold water, forms a soft ball which flattens on removal from water.
Caramels	244°F to 248°F	118°C to 120°C	Firm ball	Syrup, when dropped into very cold water, forms a firm ball which does not flatten on removal from water.
Divinity Marshmallows . . Popcorn balls	250°F to 266°F	121°C to 130°C	Hard ball	Syrup, when dropped into very cold water, forms a ball which is hard enough to hold its shape, yet plastic.
Butterscotch Taffies	270°F to 290°F	132°C to 143°C	Soft crack	Syrup, when dropped into very cold water, separates into threads which are hard but not brittle.
Brittle Glacé	300°F to 310°F	149°C to 154°C	Hard crack	Syrup, when dropped into very cold water, separates into threads which are hard and brittle.
Barley sugar . . .	320°F	160°C	Clear liquid	The sugar liquefies.
Caramel	338°F	170°C	Brown liquid	The liquid becomes brown.

* For each increase of 500 feet in elevation, cook the syrup to a temperature 1° F *lower* than temperature called for at sea level. If readings are taken in Centigrade, for each 900 feet of elevation, cook the syrup to a temperature 1° C *lower* than called for at sea level.

APPENDIX

SERVINGS OF FOOD

MEAT, POULTRY, AND FISH

The amount of meat, poultry, and fish to buy varies with the amount of bone, fat, and breading.

Servings per pound[1]

MEAT

Much bone or gristle	1 or 2
Medium amounts of bone .	2 or 3
Little or no bone	3 or 4

POULTRY (READY-TO-COOK)

Chicken	2 or 3
Turkey	2 or 3
Duck and goose	2

FISH

Whole	1 or 2
Dressed or pan-dressed . .	2 or 3
Portions or steaks	3
Fillets	3 or 4

[1] Three ounces of cooked lean meat, poultry, or fish per serving.

VEGETABLES AND FRUITS

For this table, a serving of vegetable is ½ cup cooked vegetable unless otherwise noted. A serving of fruit is ½ cup fruit; 1 medium apple, banana, peach, or pear; or 2 apricots or plums. A serving of cooked fresh or dried fruit is ½ cup fruit and liquid.

Servings per pound[1]

FRESH VEGETABLES

Asparagus	3 or 4
Beans, lima[2]	2
Beans, snap	5 or 6
Beets, diced[3]	3 or 4
Broccoli	3 or 4
Brussels sprouts	4 or 5
Cabbage:	
Raw, shredded	9 or 10
Cooked	4 or 5

Carrots:	
Raw, diced or shredded[3]	5 or 6
Cooked[3]	4
Cauliflower	3
Celery:	
Raw, chopped or diced .	5 or 6
Cooked	4
Kale[4]	5 or 6
Okra	4 or 5
Onions, cooked	3 or 4
Parsnips[3]	4
Peas[2]	2
Potatoes	4
Spinach[5]	4
Squash, summer	3 or 4
Squash, winter	2 or 3
Sweetpotatoes	3 or 4
Tomatoes, raw, diced or sliced	4

[1] As purchased.
[2] Bought in pod.
[3] Bought without tops.
[4] Bought untrimmed.
[5] Bought prepackaged.

Servings per package (9 or 10 oz.)

FROZEN VEGETABLES

Asparagus	2 or 3
Beans, lima	3 or 4
Beans, snap	3 or 4
Broccoli	3
Brussels sprouts	3
Cauliflower	3
Corn, whole kernel	3
Kale	2 or 3
Peas	3
Spinach	2 or 3

Servings per can (1 lb.)

CANNED VEGETABLES

Most vegetables	3 or 4
Greens, such as kale or spinach	2 or 3

APPENDIX

DRY VEGETABLES

Servings per pound

Dry beans 11
Dry peas, lentils . . . . . . 10 or 11

Servings per market unit[1]

FRESH FRUIT

Apples ⎫
Bananas ⎪
Peaches ⎬ . . . . . 3 or 4 per pound
Pears ⎪
Plums ⎭

Apricots ⎫
Cherries, sweet ⎬ . 5 or 6 per pound
Grapes, seedless ⎭

Blueberries ⎫
Raspberries ⎬ . . . . 4 or 5 per pint

Strawberries . . . 8 or 9 per quart

[1] As purchased.

Servings per package (10 or 12 oz.)

FROZEN FRUIT

Blueberries . . . . 3 or 4
Peaches . . . . 2 or 3
Raspberries . . . . 2 or 3
Strawberries . . . . 2 or 3

Servings per can (1 lb.)

CANNED FRUIT

Served with liquid 4
Drained . . . . 2 or 3

Servings per package (8 oz.)

DRIED FRUIT

Apples 8
Apricots 6
Mixed fruits 6
Peaches 7
Pears 4
Prunes . . . . 4 or 5

Dairy Products	*Cups per pound*	*Servings*	
		No.	Size
Butter	2	48	Small squares
Cheese, American	4, grated	Varies with use	
Cheese, cottage	2	Varies with use	
	Cups per ½ pint		
Cream, whipping	1	12 rounded tablespoons	

Breads and Cereals	*Cups per pound*	*No. 2/3 cup Servings*
Hominy grits	2½	15
Rice	2¼	12
Macaroni	4 - 5	18
Noodles	6 - 8	18
Rolled oats	5	12
Spaghetti	4 - 5	15
	Slices per pound	
Bread	12 - 16	

INDEX

[465]

INDEX

INDEX

INDEX